THE ENDLESS WAR

Our Party and our people shall forever treasure the memory of their best sons and daughters who have fallen in the fight for the cause of national liberation and the ideal of Communism. . . . The South has proved worthy of its glorious title, "Brass Wall of the Fatherland."

HO CHI MINH, September 5, 1960

Let every nation know, whether it wishes us well or ill, that we shall pay any price, bear any burden, meet any hardship, support any friend, oppose any foe to assure the survival and the success of liberty.

JOHN F. KENNEDY, January 20, 1961

The enemy is like fire and we like water. Water will certainly get the better of fire. . . . In the long war of resistance, each citizen is a combatant, each village a fortress.

HO CHI MINH, June 19, 1947

THE ENDLESS WAR
Fifty Years of Struggle in Vietnam

James Pinckney Harrison

THE FREE PRESS
A Division of Macmillan Publishing Co., Inc.
NEW YORK
Collier Macmillan Publishers
LONDON

THE FREE PRESS
A Division of Macmillan Publishing Co., Inc.
866 Third Avenue, New York, N.Y. 10022

Collier Macmillan Canada, Ltd.

Library of Congress Catalog Card Number: 81-67160

Printed in the United States of America

printing number

1 2 3 4 5 6 7 8 9 10

Library of Congress Cataloging in Publication Data

Harrison, James P.
The endless war.

Bibliography: p.
1. Vietnam—History—20th century. I. Title.
DS556.8.H37 959.704 81-67160
ISBN 0-02-914040-4 AACR2

The map of Vietnam before 1975 and the accompanying key on pages 16–17 are reprinted from Vo Nguyen Giap, *The Military Art of People's War*, edited by Russell Stetler (New York: Monthly Review Press, 1970), by permission of the publisher.

For

Chantal and Olivia

CONTENTS

LIST OF MAPS

PREFACE

THE ORIGINS OF THIS BOOK go back to the increasing perplexity I shared with most people who tried to understand the events unfolding in Vietnam in recent decades, especially given the usual interpretations of those events. When, even after the Communist conquest of the south in 1975, there still existed no adequate and up-to-date explanation of what had taken place in that far-off land so important to recent world history, I decided to try my hand at a brief history and analysis.

That was no doubt overambitious, given the complexity of the topic and the difficulties for historical perspective posed by such recent and controversial events. But the importance of the subject spurred me, and the timing coincided with my completion of a history of the Chinese Communists, *The Long March to Power*. It also coincided, happily as it turned out, with the fiscal crisis of the City University of New York. For that crisis enabled me to secure necessary released time for research and writing, in Paris as well as New York, with frequent leaves of absence.

This book, primarily a history of the Vietnamese Revolution, concentrates on the Vietnamese side of the events that have shaken that land for over thirty years. In the introduction I address some questions about American intervention in that far-off land, but then shift to the Vietnamese perspective, which alone can supply keys to the understanding of these extraordinary events. The outside actors, France, Japan, China, Russia, and the United States are always in the background, but my principal goal is to give some historical understanding of how the Communists took command of the Vietnamese Revolution and went on to defeat enemies so many times more powerful than they. To feature the drama of that achievement, I begin Part One with the final Communist victory of 1975 and then move backward, giving data on the lives of the exceptional men and women who led the Vietnamese Revolution. I then discuss the historical circumstances that bred the Revolution, and finally move forward once more to cover in Part Three the terrible thirty-year war of 1945–1975.

Such a work draws on many sources. For help beyond their writings, I want to thank especially Georges Boudarel, Pierre Brocheux, Wilfred Burchett, William Duiker, Gloria Emerson, Frances FitzGerald, Daniel Hemery, Don Luce, Ngo Vinh Long, and Jayne Werner. In addition, the following have given generously of their time and knowledge: Malcolm Browne, Joseph Buttinger, King Chen, Philippe Devillers, Jean and Simon Lacouture, Le Thanh Khoi, Marjorie Norman, and Troung Nhu Tang, as have Peter Arnett, Ben Cherry, Alexander Casella, Arlette Laduguie, Do Hau Nhu, Pierre-Richard Feray, Roger Jellinek, Diana Johnstone, Maria Jolas, Father Nguyen Binh Thi, Nguyen Van Trung, Christine Rageau, Sarah Rosner, Jay Scarborough, Thai Quang Trung, Abe Weisburd, Christine White, and John K. Whitmore.

It goes without saying that numerous librarians, especially in Paris and New York, have given indispensable aid. Thanks go also to Hunter College History Department, which allowed me much released time for the preparation of this book, and to the numerous students of my course on the Vietnamese Revolution and wars whose queries have helped to form my analysis. Alison Wilson and Debbie Bell have ably typed earlier versions of the manuscript, and Ellen Stern McCrate and Claude Conyers at the Free Press have greatly helped with its final presentation. Remaining discrepancies are of course my own.

NOTE ON VIETNAMESE NAMES

WHEN VIETNAMESE NAMES are given in full, the surname or family name is traditionally put first and the given name last. When shortened names are used, Vietnamese are normally called by their given names. Thus Vo Nguyen Giap is universally referred to as Giap or General Giap, and Pham Van Dong as Dong or Premier Dong, although their surnames are respectively Vo and Pham. Certain historical figures, however, like Ho Chi Minh, are addressed by their surnames, as Ho or Uncle Ho. The bibliography and index are organized by surname, so that the writings of Giap, for example, are listed under *Vo* Nguyen Giap.

The Latin transcription for Vietnamese (Quoc Ngu or national language) gives a reasonably intelligible pronunciation of most names for speakers of Western languages. But one common problem of pronunciation may be mentioned. That is, that some names transcribed with the letter *d* sound more like *z*. Thus, for example, Ngo Dinh *D*iem and Le *D*uan, among important figures discussed in this book, are pronounced more like Ngo Dinh Ziem and Le Zuan. The common surname Nguyen is pronounced something like Noo-Yen.

LIST OF ABBREVIATIONS

ARVN	Army of South Vietnam
ASEAN	Association of Southeast Asian Nations
COMECON	Council for Mutual Economic Assistance (USSR)
COSVN	Central Office for South Vietnam
DMZ	Demilitarized Zone along the seventeenth parallel
DRV	Democratic Republic of Vietnam (to 1976)
FULRO	Front Unifié de Lutte des Races Opprimées (Front for Liberation of Oppressed Races)
MACV	Military Assistance Command, Vietnam
MAAG	Military Assistance Advisory Group
NLF	National Liberation Front
PLAF	People's Liberation Armed Forces (South)
PAVN	People's Army of Vietnam (North)
PRG	People's Revolutionary Government
PRP	People's Revolutionary Party
SEATO	Southeast Asia Treaty Organization
SRV	Socialist Republic of Vietnam (after 1976)
VCP	Vietnamese Communist Party
VNQDD	Vietnam Quoc Dan Dang (Vietnamese National Party)

INTRODUCTION

The United States and the Vietnam War

THE TRIUMPH OF THE COMMUNISTS in Vietnam in 1975 and its implications for the United States almost immediately came to be treated as ancient history—"it's like talking about Carthage" according to one journalist.[1] But if many, understandably, wanted to forget the Vietnam War, many others, equally understandably, will long remember it.

What after all did it mean that a people whose per capita income in 1975 was estimated at $160 per year defeated the allies of a people five times more numerous, then with a per capita income of over $6,000? And why was it that a half million American soldiers and their million South Vietnamese allies, using over three times the tonnage of bombs dropped in all of World War II on an area smaller than California,* could not stop the Communists, where until 1940 some 11,000 French troops and police had largely kept order?

Such questions, of course, lead to others, and we may begin with some about the U.S. escalation of the mid-1960s.

*Vietnam (about 128,000 square miles) is slightly larger than New Mexico or Italy, but smaller than California. Also, Vietnam is larger than neighboring Cambodia (69,900 square miles) and Laos (91,400 square miles). Vietnam is close to 80 percent mountainous and stretches some 1,000 miles from north to south on latitudes corresponding roughly to those between Havana and Panama City. Its population increased from an estimated ten million is 1878 to twenty million in 1936 to close to fifty-three million in 1980.

ON FEBRUARY 7, 1965, the United States began its bombing raids on North Vietnam, just after a Viet Cong* attack on an American installation at Plei Ku in the Central Highlands of South Vietnam, and just after the arrival in Hanoi of Alexei Kosygin, premier of arch-enemy and Vietnamese ally, the Soviet Union.

Why was the United States bombing a small, poor country halfway around the world?

Because the Communists in Vietnam were on the verge of winning again what they had largely won in 1945, and again in 1954, and would finally win in 1975. And in 1965, Washington refused to tolerate the idea of the Communists taking another inch of territory—provided the country, like Vietnam, was not strong enough to strike back dangerously.

Therefore, to establish the U.S. prohibition against the spread of communism, not only for Vietnam but worldwide, President Lyndon Johnson decided to proceed with the bombing of the North even if, by seemingly dangerous accident, a leader of the Soviet Union, which indeed was strong enough to strike back, happened to be on the scene. Perhaps Kosygin's visit even seemed fortuitous. How better to demonstrate U.S. resolve?

Then on October 10, 1972, a bomb intended for military targets hit the chief of the French diplomatic mission in Hanoi, Delegate-General Pierre Susini, who died a few days later.

The beginning of the bombing in 1965, precisely on the occasion of the state visit of the prime minister of the rival superpower, and the killing of the ranking diplomat of a key allied country toward the end of the war, are only two in a series of astonishing episodes dating back a half century to the beginning of the Communist Revolution in Vietnam. They are mentioned first because of their international implications.

During the First or French Indochina War, 1945–1954, there had been enough extraordinary events to keep statesmen and writers preoccupied for many years. Yet the French never had more than 140,000 of their troops backed by some 300,000 "loyal" Indochinese in all five "countries" of French Indochina—that is, Cam-

*Abbreviation of Viet Nam Cong San (Vietnamese Communist). Coined about 1956, the term Viet Cong (or simply VC) was used to designate all who fought the government, whether Communist or not. Before 1954, the French had used Viet Minh, short for the Vietnam Independence League founded in 1941 by Ho Chi Minh, in the same way.

bodia and Laos as well as Tonkin (North Vietnam), Annam (Central Vietnam) and Cochin China (South Vietnam).

Fiscal anomalies also demonstrate bizarre discrepancies of the war. Prior to 1975, the United States spent well over $150 billion* there to suppress an insurrection by largely peasant soldiers, who in 1964 were reportedly paid the equivalent of $1 per month. The Communists received increasing aid from Russia and China, but prior to the 1970s nothing on remotely the same scale as their enemies, and there was a similar disparity in weaponry at least prior to the final campaigns. A bitter joke reportedly had it that many Viet Cong soldiers, who averaged 5′2″ and 110 pounds, must have "died laughing" at the misery of hulking Americans, who averaged 5′10″ and 180 pounds but could barely move through the tropical heat, swamps, and jungles further weighted down as they were by equipment and firearms, like some Gulliver in Lilliput.

Most fantastic of all are the statistics on the bombing. For eight years after the 1965 escalation, the United States sent countless waves of aircraft to bomb the countries of Indochina. It dropped over 7½ million tons of bombs, more than half on South Vietnam, and detonated an approximately equal amount of explosives on the ground, almost all on the South. Over 1 million tons of bombs fell on North Vietnam, about 1½ million tons on Laos, and over ½ million tons on Cambodia.[3] Incredibly, this equaled the explosive force of over 700 Hiroshima-type atomic bombs, and included up to 400,000 tons of napalm. For South Vietnam, the averages came to over 1,000 pounds of explosive for each man, woman, and child, and to several tons for every soldier. Despite the relative smallness and isolation of the country, this was many times the destructive force ever used in warfare. It might be recalled that typical explosive devices used by terrorists in Western countries in recent years have often been on the order of about 10 pounds of TNT but, nonetheless, have caused deaths and considerable damage, not to speak of banner headlines. Therefore, as will be seen in more detail beginning with Chapter Seven, it is hardly surprising that such an overwhelming use of American arms in Indochina was heavily responsible for over 10 million refugees and up to 2 million deaths between

*The U.S. Department of Defense put expenses of the war at $159.42 billion, while the American Friends Service Committee in 1979 estimated its true cost at $274.7 billion, without considering veterans' benefits and the like. The figures have to be more than doubled because of inflation.[2]

1960 and 1975, mostly in the south, whose population in 1973 was estimated at twenty million.

THE OFFICIAL REASONS for U.S. intervention on such a scale often seemed as difficult to comprehend as the military means that were employed. According to President Johnson in February 1965, the United States moved to stop an attack on South Vietnam "that is controlled . . . and directed from outside the country," as he added a little later, "an attack of one country upon another." Yet, virtually throughout the 1960s, there were fewer North Vietnamese than American troops in the South, and in any case few Vietnamese would have argued that the North was "outside their country." No doubt, Johnson's reasons lay beyond Vietnam. As he explained on April 7, 1965, "Over this war—and all Asia—is another reality: the deepening shadow of Communist China. The rulers in Hanoi are urged on by Peking." Above all, therefore, it was the example of a victorious, Maoist-style revolutionary war that had to be stopped. As Johnson had put it on February 28, 1964 "Our strength imposes on us an obligation to assure that this type of aggression does not succeed," thereby reemphasizing the 1961 warning of adviser Walt Rostow that in Indochina, we must "demonstrate that the Communist technique of guerilla warfare can be dealt with."

Secretary of State Dean Rusk repeatedly advanced the other most important argument, namely, that American credibility was tied to Vietnam to the extent that "our guarantees to Berlin" and around the world would be hopelessly undermined if the Communists won in Vietnam. Similarly, on March 24, 1965, Assistant Secretary for Defense John T. McNaughton stated that whereas in effect only 10 percent of U.S. efforts aimed to help the South Vietnamese people, 20 percent aimed "to keep South Vietnam [and adjacent] territory from Chinese hands," and the greatest part, or 70 percent, aimed "to avoid a humiliating U.S. defeat [to our reputation as a guarantor]."[4]

The memory of "the Munich syndrome" (the failure to stop Hitler in the 1930s), vague ideas of defending "freedom," and the current fear of communism as the "new fascism," therefore, all seemed to Washington to dictate its fateful involvement in Vietnam.

Yet, as became embarrassingly clear, the situation was vastly different from that portrayed by Washington. The American intervention of 1965 to stop the spread of communism, for example,

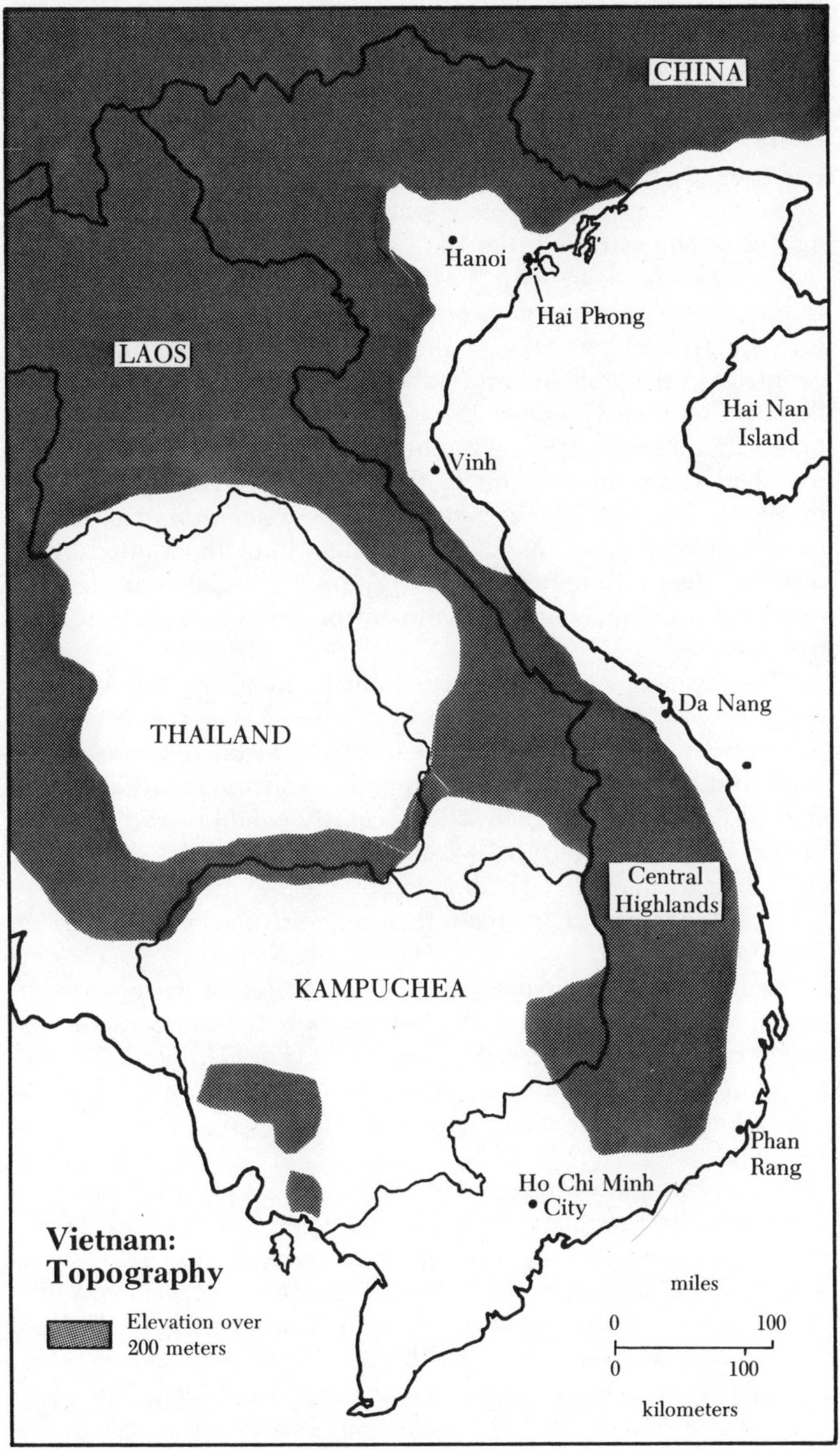
CHINA
Hanoi
Hai Phong
LAOS
Hai Nan
Island
Vinh
Da Nang
THAILAND
Central
Highlands
KAMPUCHEA
Phan
Rang
Ho Chi Minh
City
Vietnam:
Topography
Elevation over
200 meters
miles
0
100
0
100
kilometers

came exactly fifteen years before the brief Chinese invasion of Vietnam in February 1979, albeit fifteen years after Mao's triumph in China. Even if some responsible U.S. officials knew that Vietnam had fought China on many occasions over the centuries, most decision makers continued to place priority on "keeping our promises" and on "demonstrating that the Communist technique of guerilla warfare can be dealt with." Above all, willfully ignoring the nationalist content of Vietnamese communism, they went back to the idea that, if the Communists gained power in South Vietnam, other countries in the area and around the world might also go Communist, as President Eisenhower had predicted in April 1954, like so many "falling dominoes." Truman's secretary of state, Dean Acheson, had stated in reaction to the Communist victory in China in 1949: "You will please take it as your assumption that it is a fundamental decision of American policy that the United States does not intend to permit further expansion of Communist domination [after China] on the continent of Asia or in the Southeast Asia area. . . ."[5]

In September 1956, Senator John F. Kennedy stated: "Vietnam represents the cornerstone of the Free World in Southeast Asia, the keystone to the arch, the finger in the dike. Burma, Thailand, India, Japan and the Philippines, and obviously Laos and Cambodia are among those whose security would be threatened if the red tide of Communism overflowed into Vietnam. . . ."[6] In August 1964, Richard Nixon elaborated that if the Communists won in Vietnam, they would "increase their aggressive action, not only in Asia, but in Africa, Latin America and the Near East." Such logic led Senator Strom Thurmond to state in 1968 that if we were unable to win in Vietnam, "before you know it [the Communists] would be up the beaches of Hawaii." As late as October 1967, Secretary of State Rusk still alluded to the necessity to stop "Chinese aggression" as a principal reason for the U.S. commitment in Vietnam.[7]

It was logically more convincing but in fact just as difficult for the United States to claim it was defending "freedom and democracy" in Vietnam as it was to claim it was trying to stop Chinese aggression. Not only were most South Vietnamese government officials largely representatives of the very forces that had been defeated in 1954, but there had been at least a half dozen coups d'état between the overthrow and murder of President Ngo Dinh Diem in November 1963 and mid-1965. Thereafter for ten years, the dictatorship of Nguyen Van Thieu proceeded to incarcerate many additional tens of thousands of its citizens as Diem had done in the 1950s, and perpetuated an all too obvious, if also obviously inefficient, police state in the South. President Kennedy's January 1961 inaugural declaration that "we shall pay any price . . . to assure the survival and the success of liberty" was a noble ideal, but one that proved impossible to apply in Vietnam.

Also inexplicable, this time from the cherished legal point of view, was the fact that, in 1956, with U.S. backing, Diem had refused to hold the elections specified by the Geneva treaty of 1954. Diem refused to sign precisely because most observers expected these elections would lead to a unified Vietnam under Ho Chi Minh and, therefore, Diem and the United States in effect did in Vietnam something similar to what the Soviet Union did in Eastern Europe, namely, refused to hold elections that would have led to the establishment of regimes that had grown out of the nations' past but that were unacceptable to the great powers involved.

These troubling facts are mentioned at the outset, because the American escalation of the 1960s, even more than that of the French in the 1940s, made of the Vietnamese Revolution, not only a problem of Asian history, but of world history.

PART ONE

History Read Backward

The Final, First, and Second Victories of the Vietnamese Communists

CHAPTER ONE

The Fall of Saigon

THE MARCH OF COMMUNIST ARMIES into Saigon on April 30, 1975, stunned the world. It marked the end of over thirty years of one of history's most brutal wars and the fiftieth anniversary of the founding of the first Vietnamese Marxist group. Coming only two years after the withdrawal of American forces in 1973, it also made glaringly apparent the extent to which the United States, and earlier France, had prolonged a war in which the Communists had already taken predominant power thirty years before.

What happened and why during the final offensive in 1975, as in earlier years and decades, will long be debated. Enemies of the Communists argue, as they did a generation earlier about similar events in China, that if the United States had continued or increased its aid to the existing anti-Communist government, or earlier had placed less restraint on the operations of U.S. forces in South Vietnam, the Communists could not have won.

Such arguments ignore the fact that the Communists had already won power twice in North Vietnam, in 1945 and 1954, and were close to power in South Vietnam also in 1945 and 1954, and again in 1964. Massive United States intervention in 1965, like that of the French in 1945, attempted at terrible cost, to stop the Communists. But the whole concept of considering Communist "aggression" in such a situation as an external threat that could be stopped by military force short of genocide obscures rather than clarifies the significance of the over thirty years of warfare in Vietnam that preceded the final Communist offensive. Throughout both wars Vietnamese fought Vietnamese, and even though the Communists used a "foreign" ideology, it was equally evident that the greater direct foreign presence by far, especially until 1973, was on the side of the anti-Communists.

The Communists used a foreign ideology for the purposes of Vietnamese nationalism. The anti-Communists used, or were used by, France and then the United States, to try to stop Vietnamese who had become Communists.

As crucial as questions of external forces at work, and a principal concern of this book, is the question of how the Communists managed to survive at all against such incredible odds for over a generation. They did this far less by relying on external aid than by learning to organize what they later called "brass walls" and "steel fortresses" of fighters drawn from radical peasants, workers, and intellectuals. And this they worked out in principle at more or less the same time that their then Chinese comrades were developing what came to be called the "mass line" in the difficult years after 1927 in China. Because of French repression, the Vietamese successes came later, as will be described in greater detail in succeeding chapters, but they were not simply the result of "learning from China." Rather they were a parallel development. Conditions were different, but the problems involved and principles devised to meet them were similar.

FOLLOWING THE WITHDRAWAL of direct U.S. military intervention as arranged by the January 1973 "peace accords" and following continued intransigence by the Nguyen Van Thieu government, North Vietnamese divisions in conjunction with southern forces struck to achieve what turned out to be their final, and greatest, victory in the spring of 1975. As often before, the Communists were the first to apply major force, but they did so in response to innumerable hostile, if smaller, actions on the part of their adversaries. And they did so as the heirs to over a generation of leadership of the Vietnamese Revolution. What the United States had intervened to prevent a decade earlier—a northern invasion of the south—became a reality in 1975, and a classic case of self-fulfilling prophecy.

As early as October, 1973, as will be seen later in greater detail in Chapter Ten, the Twenty-first Plenum of the Communist Party's Central Committee called for new initiatives on the part of Communists to counter Saigon's actions in the South; and in March 1974 the Party's Military Committee decided to move toward the final offensive.* Crucial Political Bureau meetings in October and December 1974 confirmed these decisions to push more aggressively in the South, but only following intense debates between advocates of further patience and proponents of a new military strike. In the end, Communist troops were instructed to move, but with extreme caution, lest the United States reintervene, and only as military progress allowed, with the expectation either of new negotiations, or of a final military victory at best the following year, in 1976. But initial victories precipitated others in a manner that even the most optimistic Communist decision makers could not have foreseen.

The first push was a preliminary test of Saigon's defenses and the U.S. response. It began in December and on January 6, 1975, Communist forces were able to capture and hold their first provincial capital,† that of the province of Phuoc Long, some eighty miles north of Saigon, following three weeks of combat. On the next day they seized the strategic "black virgin" mountain just north of the key western city of Tay Ninh. These victories, together with reports of information on Saigon's expectations obtained from a spy high in Thieu's entourage, moved the Party's Political Bureau, in urgent session from December 18 to January 8, to order an acceleration in the planned offensive.[1]

Then after regrouping and final preparations, Communist armies began the great spring offensive of 1975, almost exactly twenty-one years after the defeat of the French at Dien Bien Phu, which by curious concidence also had followed close to fifty-five days of battle, from March 13 to May 7, 1954. On March 10, 1975, following diversions toward the strategic cities of Plei Ku and Kon Tum, the Communists struck a hundred miles farther south at Ban Me Thuot, a town of 70,000 and capital of Dar Lac province. According to one apparently apocryphal story, some sixty-five years be-

---

*This book will speak simply of the Communist Party or the Party, although the official name has changed several times. From October 1930 to November 1945, the Party was called the Communist Party of Indochina (Dong Duong Cong San Dang). In February 1951, after five years of fictional abolition, it was called the Vietnam Workers' Party (Vietnam Dang Lao Dong), and in January 1976 the Fourth National Congress renamed it the Vietnamese Communist Party (Vietnam Cong San Dang), returning to the name at the time of its founding in February 1930.

†Phuoc Binh, then a town of 26,000 residents, also called Song Be or Phuoc Long Town after 1975, was located in newly organized Song Be Province. The town had been captured for several hours by the Viet Cong in May 1965.

fore, Ban Me Thuot had been the site of a tiger hunt by American President Teddy Roosevelt.

But now it was the Communists who carried the big stick, and even though the estimated one or more million troops in all regions of the South under Saigon's command considerably exceeded the total number of Communist troops north and south, at Ban Me Thuot the Communists enjoyed a five to one superiority in troops. They also enjoyed almost complete surprise, helped by a Communist agent working at Saigon's Central Intelligence headquarters, where he prepared fake maps to show the greatest concentration of Communist troops around Plei Ku and Kon Tum rather than at Ban Me Thuot. Moreover, thanks to careful preparations and an increased flow of supplies over new roads buttressing the "Ho Chi Minh trail" linking North and South Vietnam, the Communists even enjoyed superior armament in this battle. That was exceptional and offset the Communist lack of airpower in stunning contrast to their space-age-equipped enemies.* Because of these detailed preparations, the general handicap of having no air power was minimized; with surprising ease, Liberation Army troops captured Ban Me Thuot after thirty-two hours of fighting. So serious was the news of this Communist victory that at first Saigon not only denied the loss of the city, but failed to stop the killing by local police of a French newsman, Paul Leandri, who had reported, not only the capture of Ban Me Thuot, but the part in it played by a few minority tribesmen apparently organized by the Communists as in other key battles during both wars.[2]

Following the fall of Ban Me Thuot came the blunder that accelerated beyond control the collapse of Thieu's forces. General Nguyen Van Thieu, the leader of South Vietnam for a decade, knew better than to minimize the loss of Ban Me Thuot, the key to the Central Highlands; and on March 14, after consultation with only two of his field commanders, he decided to withdraw entirely from the Highlands and to concentrate on the defense of coastal areas. This decision led to a devastating panic, first in the Highlands and soon all along the densely populated coastal plains, as hundreds of thousands of refugees joined retreating government

*In a sad characterization of his dependency on American airpower, President Thieu resigned the presidency on April 22, 1975, a week before the fall of Saigon, with the statement, "I would challenge the United States army to do better than the South Vietnamese army without B-52s."[3] He did not thus challenge the Viet Cong.

troops in scenes of confusion seen on television sets around the world.

It was this panic as much as, or even more than, Communist military victories that sealed the fate of South Vietnam. In scenes of mad futility, soldiers and refugees sought to claw their way onto overloaded ships, aircraft, and helicopters, only to be stampeded, even crushed to death in the wheelwells, or shaken from departing aircraft like so much chaff in the wind. Within weeks, long columns of desperate people, dubbed "convoys of tears," added another million to the previous millions of refugees, one-half million streaming into the single city of Da Nang. The journalist T. D. Allman bitterly wrote of such scenes:

> The South Vietnamese soldiers fleeing an enemy which has not yet attacked and trying to push their motor bikes onto U.S. ships, sum up the product of American "nation building'—a militarist society with nothing worth fighting for; a consumer society that produces nothing; a nation of abandoned women conditioned to flee to the next handout of U.S. surplus rice; of dispossessed gangs hitching rides on U.S. planes to the next jerry built urban slum. . . .[4]

The refugees, of course, were seeking to escape the horrors of war and their fears of the Communists, but certainly also their fears of retaliatory anti-Communist bombing. In their anguish, hardly obscured by the clouds of dust marking the end of the dry season, they seemed to supply final proof of the changing of the Mandate of Heaven, the ancient Chinese idea that Heaven's favor was a precondition of rule. For no matter the motives of the refugees, the loss of authority of the Saigon government was all too evident.

The panic continued to spread as the entire Central Highlands, long considered absolutely essential to the sovereignty, as well as the military security, of South Vietnam, were abandoned almost overnight. Plei Ku and Kon Tum, 90 and 115 miles to the north of Ban Me Thuot, were abandoned March 16 and An Loc to the south on March 18. Saigon had bitterly defended all three strategic towns against earlier Communist offensives, and the news of their fall shocked the country and the world. Moreover, local Viet Cong rather than North Vietnamese troops were the first to enter Plei Ku.[5]

There followed one by one the surrender of important coastal towns, proceeding more or less from north to south. Quang Tri, which changed hands in bitter fighting at the time of the spring 1972 Communist offensive, fell on March 19, then farther south,

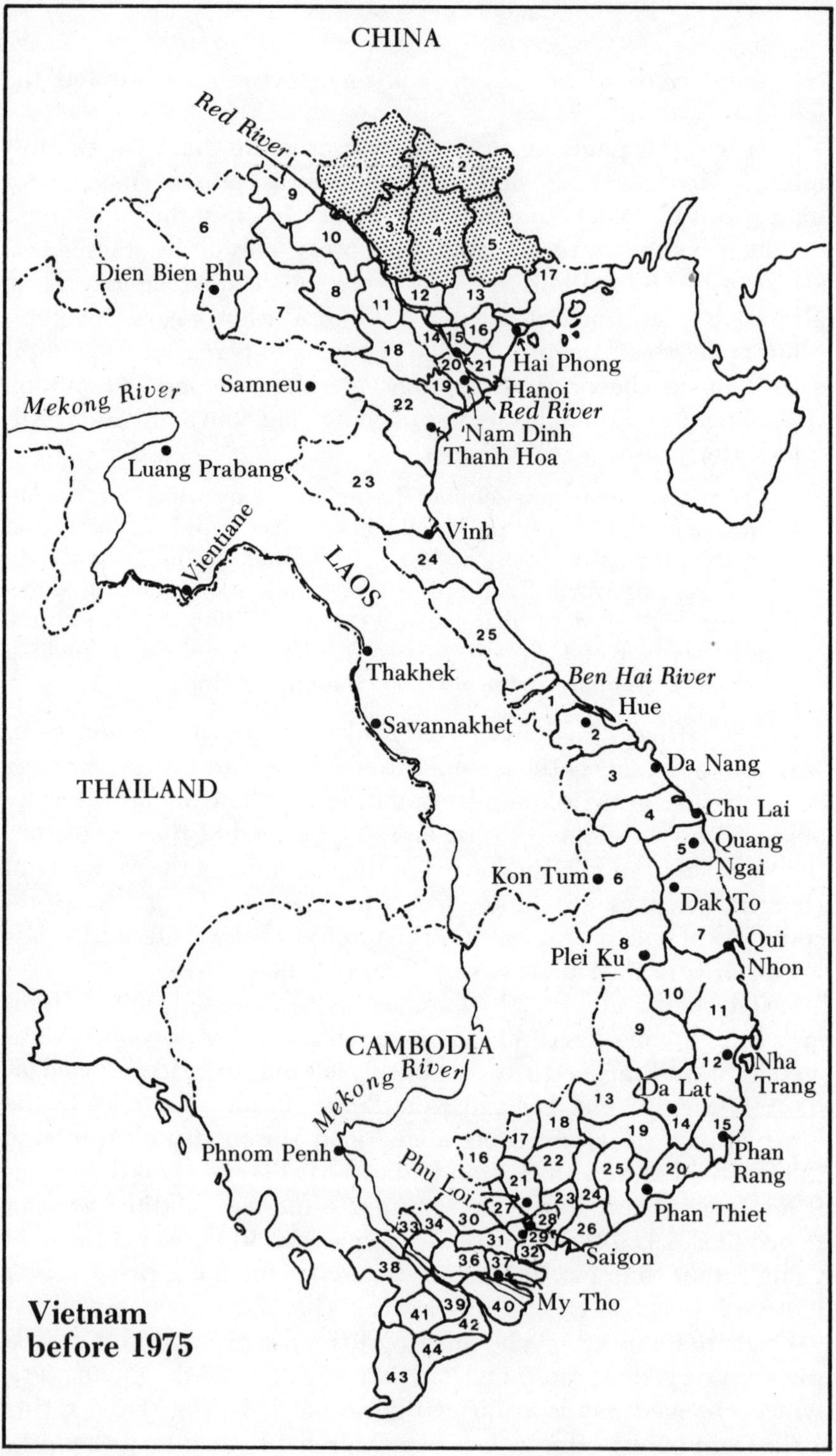

Vietnam before 1975

Provinces in the North

Bac Thai	4	Lai Chau	6	Quang Ninh	17
Cao Bang	2	Lang Son	5	Son La	7
Ha Bac	13	Lao Cai	9	Thai Binh	21
Ha Giang	1	Nam Ha	20	Thanh Hoa	22
Hai Duong	16	Nghe An	23	Tuyen Quang	3
Ha Tai	14	Nghia Lo	8	Vinh Phuc	12
Ha Tinh	24	Ninh Binh	19	Yen Bai	10
Hoa Binh	18	Phu Tho	11		
Hung Yen	15	Quang Binh	25		

Provinces in the South

An Giang	35	Go Cong	32	Phuoc Thanh	22
An Xuyen	43	Hau Nghia	27	Phuoc Tuy	26
Ba Xuyen	42	Khanh Hoa	12	Phu Yen	11
Bac Lieu	44	Kien Giang	38	Plei Ku	8
Bien Hoa	23	Kien Hoa	37	Quang Duc	13
Binh Dinh	7	Kien Phong	34	Quang Nam	3
Binh Duong	21	Kien Tuong	30	Quang Ngai	5
Binh Long	17	Kontum	6	Quang Tin	4
Binh Thuan	20	Lam Dong	19	Quang Tri	1
Binh Tuy	25	Long An	29	Tai Ninh	16
Chau Doc	33	Long Khanh	24	Thua Thien	2
Chuong Thien	41	Ninh Thuan	15	Tuyen Duc	14
Dar Lac	9	Phong Dinh	39	Vinh Binh	40
Dinh Tuong	31	Phu Bon	10	Vinh Long	36
Gia Dinh	28	Phuoc Long	18		

Tam Ky on March 24. On March 25, local sympathizers declared Quang Ngai "liberated" even before the entry of Communist forces.

The most damaging losses yet ensued, those of the nineteenth-century imperial capital of Hue on March 26, and on March 29 that of the country's second city, Da Nang. Hue had long represented the sentimental capital of the entire country as it was from there that the last independent government before the French, the Nguyen dynasty, had ruled. After its capture by the Communists for several weeks during the Tet offensive of 1968, Hue had been virtually "destroyed in order to save it,"* so important was its value judged by Saigon. Da Nang was, after Saigon, the South's second largest city and a principal American base area.

By the end of March, therefore, the northern half of South Vietnam, including two of its three principal cities, had come under Communist control. The south was much more than cut in half, a great fear of earlier years. Moreover, an estimated one-half of Sai-

*As reportedly stated by an American officer after the Communist capture in February 1968 of the town of Ben Tre in the Mekong Delta. See Chapter Ten.

gon's troops had been lost. The overwhelming majority of them simply disappeared, as the Mandate of Heaven worked its logic, with Vietnamese of all ranks, military as well as civilian, deciding the Communists had, indeed, won. The essential calculation immediately became to establish peace and come to terms with the victors, as another Chinese adage, long accepted by Vietnamese, telling applied; "He who wins is king, he who loses is a bandit."

Nonetheless, publicly, Saigon and Washington claimed the collapse could be stopped, and that the Saigon area and agriculturally rich southern delta could be held against the Communists. Still, Washington began the evacuation of nonessential personnel on March 31. On the same day, in Hanoi, the Political Bureau confirmed its March 25 decision to advance target dates and "liberate Saigon before the rainy season," that is, before the end of May.[6]

The relentless advance continued. Qui Nhon and Nha Trang fell on April 1, and on the fourth, the mountain resort of Da Lat. On the same day occurred the crash of an American airlift plane attempting to carry some 300 orphans out of the country, one of the most traumatic of the final horrors of the war.

Then, amid talk of a coup d'état against Thieu, on April 8, a South Vietnamese pilot, apparently a clandestine Party member, bombarded the Presidential Palace in Saigon. Ironically, this was only the second time during the long years of war that Saigon had witnessed directly a few of the millions of tons of bombs dropped on the country, and on both occasions the bombs came from Saigon's own planes.*

After a slight pause, on April 16, Phan Rang, less than 200 miles from Saigon, fell to the Communists, as did Phnom Penh, the next day; then Phan Thiet on the nineteenth, and on the twenty-first, the last strategic post, 40 miles east of Saigon, Xuan Loc. Saigon sought to make an effective stand there, and for almost two weeks seemed to be succeeding. Its troops held out for twelve days, supported by heavy air strikes, including the only use in the war of the dreaded CBU-55 bomb,† and a three to one superiority in heavy guns. But in the end, not even this most stubborn government stand

*The first bomb was dropped by an anti-Diem pilot in February 1962 and, given the panic on both occasions, one cannot but wonder if the war would not have ended many years earlier had the Communist possessed an effective air force.

†Cluster Bomb Unit, which sprayed asphyxiating gases and thousands of small, metal fragments across an area up to a half mile wide. Smaller versions of the fearsome bomb had been used since 1967.

of the final offensive could endure, as instructed, "to the last man." In early April also, there was heavy fighting to the south of Saigon at Thu Thua, only 12 miles away, and for control of the "rice road," Highway 4.

With the fall of Xuan Loc, the game was up, and the belated resignation of Nguyen Van Thieu followed the next day. For a week, his successor, Tran Van Huong, who had been prime minister twice before, in 1965 and 1968–1969, tried to patch together a government capable of negotiation with the Communists. It was much too little and much too late, as was the still briefer presidency of Duong Van ("Big") Minh, who replaced Huong on April 27. Minh had been one of the principal architects of the ouster and murder of Diem on November 1, 1963, and had emerged as one of the leaders of the so-called Third Force following his ouster by another general, Nguyen Khanh, in January 1964.

The Communists would accept nothing short of total victory now, and the advance proceeded with relentless finality. With the fall of the port of Vung Tao on April 28, exit by sea was cut off, and on the next day the United States ordered final evacuation of remaining Americans by helicopter. An accelerated evacuation from Than Son Nhut airport had begun on the twenty-first, but had been slowed and then halted by increased Communist shelling. The Communist delegates stationed there to observe the cease-fire of the January 1973 accords directed their comrades' fire to the air base and then took cover in underground shelters they had built for just such an eventuality.

On April 30, 1975, jubilant Communist troops entered Saigon. In a final extraordinary irony, the man who transmitted Big Minh's final cease-fire order, a one-star general named Nguyen Huu Hanh, was none other than a longtime Communist agent who fed information to Communist units from Saigon's Joint General Staff. Fittingly, and with feelings one can imagine as described by journalist Alan Dawson, he embraced the Viet Cong captain who liberated his unit's headquarters. At 11:30 A.M., other Communist troops raised their flag above the Presidential Palace signaling the triumph of the Provisional Revolutionary Government. By May 3, the Mekong Delta to the south and remaining areas were declared "liberated," and Saigon became Ho Chi Minh City, thirty years after revolutionaries first so named it.[7]

Such are the bare facts of one of the most spectacular military victories in history. To appreciate its significance, much more history and analysis is required.

To begin with, it was much more than a military victory and, indeed, in the perspective of the thirty-year war, was more political than military. For it was made possible by the organization of activists who replaced fallen comrades literally by the hundreds of thousands, thereby enabling the Communists to maintain effective leadership of Vietnamese nationalism. And to understand why this Communist leadership of Vietnamese nationalism was not a contradiction in terms, and to understand how the Communists so outclassed their enemies in motivation and resilience despite the enormous odds facing them, it is necessary to look at earlier developments.

Most of the leaders of the final victory of 1975 had not only survived ten years of bitter warfare against the United States and its Vietnamese allies, but were also veterans of nine years of full-scale warfare against the French from 1945–1954. Before that, many of them had faced decades of dangerous underground struggle against the French, Chinese, and Japanese, with frequent imprisonment and death, and then another nine years of underground war against Diem, followed in turn by the American escalation. In 1951 Ho Chi Minh had stated that of the Party's Central Committee (there were then forty-two full members), fourteen had been killed by the French since 1930, and the survivors had spent 222 years in prison, an average of perhaps seven years each! Surely no other leadership in history endured more hardships on its path to victory, and prison terms for the Vietnamese revolutionaries played somewhat the same role as did the famous "Long March" for the Chinese Communists.

The 1954 settlement of the First Indochina War, signed at Geneva on July 20, had ceded control of areas north of the seventeenth parallel to Ho Chi Minh's Communists, and specified that elections be held in 1956 to determine the fate of South Vietnam. This had been a compromise to induce the Communists to stop their advance temporarily and await a relatively easy, final victory, expected by most observors after the completion of French withdrawal. Contrary to expectations, however, anti-Communists in the South, under the leadership of Ngo Dinh Diem backed by decisive U.S. support, proceeded to consolidate power, and refused to hold the elections of 1956, thereby instituting a new division of the country into hostile northern and southern halves. Cambodia and Laos, the other parts of the old French colonial empire of Indochina, maintained a shaky independence, ostensibly as neutralist kingdoms.

The result of these developments for Communist activists remaining in the South was a continuation of the harsh struggles of previous decades. Indeed, following his destruction in 1955 of the non-Communist but still anti-Diem religious sects (the Cao Dai and Hoa Hao), and the French-backed secret society (the Binh Xuyen), Diem came quite close to annihilating the Communist underground in the south. A Communist cadre admitted that in the late 1950s "the enemy [came to] control the Plains almost entirely" below the seventeenth parallel, and a Saigon statement declared in 1957 the "Viet Minh have disintegrated." A year later American adviser Wesley Fishel declared that Vietnam "can be classed as about the most stable and peaceful country in all of Asia today." In mid-1961, there was talk that the Communists "would be finished in eighteen months," and on October 31, 1963, General Paul D. Harkins stated in a Tokyo interview that "the end of the war is in sight." They should have recalled the overoptimism of the French commanding general, Jean Leclerc, who declared in October 1945 that the pacification of the Communists would be "completed in ten weeks," or for that matter Chiang Kai-shek's boast of 1930, nineteen years before the Communist victory in China, that the "country should be rid of all Communist bandits within three or six months at the most."[8]

Still, unquestionably in the late 1950s, as will be seen in Chapter Eight, the Communists were on the ropes in South Vietnam. After the travails of the first war and the suppression by Diem, party members numbered no more than about 5,000 in mid-1957, and were further reduced by 1959. But it was a miracle that any survived at all, and those that did certainly remembered that approximately the same number of an earlier generation had carried out the "first Communist revolution" in Vietnam, which in August 1945 had set up the 1954 victory over the French. Moreover, the 5,000 of 1957* would grow rapidly after 1959 to an estimated 10,000 in 1960, 20,000 in 1961, and then spectacularly to 265,000 by the end of 1967, before being reduced again by an enormous American counterforce.

Those Communists who endured in the south did so literally underground. In one town of 35,575 persons, in the delta in 1975, as reported by Wilfred Burchett, the sole survivor out of seventy-five Communists who had been active in 1963–1964 lived for years

*Similarly, the 5,000 of 1945 had grown to 60,000 or 70,000 by the start of the war against the French in late 1946.

at a time underground in a complex system of trenches where children brought food and where it was possible to emerge only at night. There were similar stories of the survival in equally impossible conditions in the 1950s, as in the 1930s and 1940s. One militant described having lived underground for five years as of 1964, and another spent his life from 1955–1958 in a tunnel a French writer found difficult to stay in for only several hours. Still others spoke of the use of dense jungles in a similar manner as their shelters, "friend and fortress." Despite the jungle, life underground, and all manner of other precautions, as will be seen in greater detail in Parts Two and Three, in some areas 90 percent or more of the activists were arrested or killed in the late 1950s and 1960s. For example, of thirty-two members of the executive committee of Saigon-Gia Dinh, district only one survived into 1968, as did only one of twenty-three members of the provincial committee of Phu Yen.[9]

By the early 1970s there was reportedly a government policeman or military man for every four inhabitants of certain areas, and every resident was required to have his photograph and basic biographical data on file at the local government office. Any person without the requisite papers was subject to immediate arrest, and rewards were offered for information on the whereabouts of known revolutionaries. It was understandable in such conditions that only a small minority of Communist activists could survive in many localities. By the early 1970s, the life expectancy of an underground cell leader in Saigon was said to be only four months. One woman told Wilfred Burchett of twenty-one and another of fourteen members of their families being killed by the continuous government repressions and military sweeps. Of the military unit of several hundred troops guarding Cu Chi district northwest of Saigon, which frequently, as during the last offensive, served as a forward Communist headquarters, only four survived according to another report. Similar stories of survival of incredible odds dated from twenty and thirty and forty years before. In 1933, a Communist journal had argued the necessity of such sacrifices: "Everyone wants to live and fears to die . . . [but]revolutionary work is difficult and dangerous, and to carry it out we must be firm and brave the dangers. If it is necessary to die in order to save the lives of our brothers, we will die content."[10]

Yet survive the Communist leaders did, and their endurance of such appalling conditions for over a half century gave the survivors a formidable sense of discipline and destiny.

BIOGRAPHIES OF SOME of the "faceless Viet Cong"* who did survive to take part in the final offensive of 1975 may help to bring alive these aspects of the Vietnamese Revolution. They include Nguyen Thi Dinh, the leading woman among the southern revolutionaries; Pham Hung, first secretary of the Party in the south and hence political head of the Central Office for South Vietnam (COSVN); Le Duc Tho, the negotiator with Henry Kissinger of the January 1973 Paris "peace" accords; North Vietnamese Chief of Staff Van Tien Dung and his southern counterpart Tran Van Tra; Ho Chi Minh's successor as head of the Vietnamese Communist Party, Le Duan; and finally in this chapter, the two most prominent leaders of the National Liberation Front (NLF), Nguyen Huu Tho and Huynh Tan Phat. In the next two chapters similar sketches of Party founder Ho Chi Minh, of Ho's foremost political lieutenant Pham Van Dong, of the military genius behind key Communist victories, Vo Nguyen Giap, and of other early South Vietnamese Communist leaders will accompany a brief history of the Party's first years.

First of all, here are some details from the life of the extraordinary woman revolutionary Nguyen Thi Dinh, now a ranking member of the Central Committee.

The title of Nguyen Thi Dinh's 1968 memoirs, *No Other Road to Take*, aptly describes her conviction that for most Vietnamese there was no choice but to side with the revolutionaries. It recalls Andre Malraux's statement, "It is difficult to conceive of a courageous Annamite being other than a revolutionary," which had caused such a sensation in his native France in 1933.[11] Indeed, the revolutionary choice required extreme courage, and it was obviously infinitely easier to come to terms with "the system," first of the French, then of Diem and the Americans, than to undertake the difficult and dangerous road of revolution.

Nguyen Thi Dinh did not accept the system. Born in the Mekong Delta province of Ben Tre† about fifty miles south of Saigon in

*Term popularized in an article of that title by CIA officer George Carver in *Foreign Affairs*, April 1966.

†As was Nguyen Thi Binh, the foreign minister of the Provisional Revolutionary Government established in 1969, who represented the South Vietnam Communists at the Paris peace talks in the early 1970s. In fact, a grand niece of early Nationalist leader Phan Chu Trinh, Madame Binh's maiden name was Nguyen Thi Chau San, and she grew up in Cambodia. The colorful French Vietnamese colonel, Jean Leroy, who became an arch-enemy of the Communists in the French war, as will be discussed in Chapter Seven, was another native of Ben Tre province.

1920, of a peasant family, she was already an activist in her teens in the struggle against France. At the urging of her brother, who had been arrested and tortured for his part in the uprisings of 1930–1931, she undertook a variety of tasks for the revolutionaries, at first cooking, selling revolutionary newspapers, and propagandizing. In 1938 a handsome young woman, she determined to marry a fellow revolutionary despite warnings that "he might be jailed," a prediction that came true three days after the birth of her child in the winter of 1939.

She herself was arrested in July, not long before the November 1940 Mekong Delta uprising, and on her release in 1943 learned of the death of her husband in the notorious Poulo Condore Island prison. Her parents had also died violently, and echoing the words of a popular song, "the dead march with the living," she resolved, "I must live to bring up my son and to avenge my husband and comrades." Again active in the Revolution, in 1946 she left Ben Tre for the first time to accompany a shipment of arms from Hanoi to revolutionaries in the south. Surviving the trials of that adventure, she and her comrades in Ben Tre underwent innumerable bitter experiences in the ensuing war against the French. In the midst of numerous stories about being forced to move from home to swamp to cave to field, she reported laconically, "I myself came close to being killed many times." She claimed the Communists were near victory in the south as in the north, when the Geneva accords of July 1954 forced her side to lay down their arms.

Then, remaining in the south after the regroupment of many of her comrades to the Communist north, Nguyen Thi Dinh struggled to survive Diem's repressions against surviving Communists in the south. A reward of 10,000 piasters (more than an average annual income) having been offered for her arrest, she narrowly escaped apprehension on countless occasions. Too plump to pass as a man as frequently done by her comrades, she once disguised herself as a Buddhist nun, continuously hid in secret caches, and devised countless tactics to escape notice, or if noticed, to convince authorities of her innocence. Always in the populous Mekong Delta, this required the help of sympathizers who repeatedly risked and often lost their lives. As much as in China, the Vietnamese revolutionaries could only survive "as fish among the sea of the people," to use the phrase popularized by Mao Zedong.

Contact with Party committees was difficult to maintain because of arrests, deaths, and simple dispersal of key cadres. From

1930 and before, all the way to 1975, stories of suffering and heroism were legion. It frequently took days of wandering and questioning even to locate the whereabouts of comrades, and communications from one region to another or from abroad took months. Among many tales of woe, Mrs. Dinh relates one about a woman who refused to reveal the whereabouts of her husband and sons, all Communist activists. As she was being tortured to death, she screamed at her prosecutors, "My husband and my children are lodged deep in my heart. If you wretches want to find them, you'll have to cut out my heart and look inside." Government soldiers reportedly sometimes did just that, using the ear, or gall bladder, or whatever, to prove eligibility for the rewards given for the killing of Communists. Another lady reportedly masked her sympathy for the Revolution behind the ravings of a mad woman, feigning insanity as the only salvation in such a world.

Reflecting on such experiences, Mrs. Dinh stated: "During the darkest years of the revolution in the south, it was people like [these] . . . who taught me a very profound lesson about patriotism and the indominable spirit of a revolutionary. It was this which kept us from faltering and enabled us to stay by the side of the people, cling to the land, and resolutely maintain the movement without being deterred by hardships, dangers and death."[12] To say the least, forty years as in the case of Mrs. Dinh is a long time to endure such trials, and as we will analyze in Part Two, there must have been much truth in Mrs. Dinh's conclusion that "the main thing is for us to have confidence in the masses and to stay close to them to carry out the struggle. If we do this, we'll achieve success."

In 1959 came authorization from Hanoi and higher Party committees in the south for lower-level units to strike back against the aggressions of the Diem government. Nguyen Thi Dinh helped lead one of these actions that many historians take as the real beginning of the Second Indochina War, the January 17–18, 1960, uprising in Ben Tre province. In the action, Mrs. Dinh and her comrades captured their first relatively large supply of about one hundred weapons, which reportedly gave them about one to three weapons for each village in her region. They organized village trials of local tyrants, and in effect set up a "liberated area" completely on their own—far from any route of support from Communist North Vietnam.

Soon, forced to yield control of the larger villages and towns to government troops, Mrs. Dinh and other activists organized a new tactic of sending thousands of "old women, young girls and children," first to Mo Cay District Town to block roads and stage sit-ins and demonstrations, demanding an end to government sweeps of the area and compensation for losses incurred. On December 20, 1963, some 45,000 convened in Ben Tre for such a demonstration. Known, after the women's hair styles, as the "longhaired troops," such contingents of female, youthful, and aged supporters of the Revolution became a feature of Viet Cong warfare, partially offsetting the greatly superior forces of the anti-Communist troops. Not all government soldiers would fire on aged ladies and children who might have been their own grandmothers and grandchildren although, as later massacres dramatized, there also were some who would.

Such tactics, the first military victories, and renewed efforts to forge a wider united front led to the formation of the National Liberation Front (NLF) in December 1960. Mrs. Dinh went on to become a member of the presidium of the Front in 1964 and the following year became chairman of the South Vietnam Liberation Association and a deputy chairman of the Liberation armed forces of the south.

Following final victory in 1975, Nugyen Thi Dinh was elevated to the Party's Central Committee in Hanoi in December 1976. Concluding her memoirs with the events of 1960 signaling the beginning of the Second Indochina War, she wrote:

> There was no other road to take. In the face of this enormous and imposing force of the people, I felt very small, but I was full of self-confidence, like a small tree standing in a vast and ancient forest. . . . As I thought about the protection and support of the people, about the enormous efforts that the revolution had expended. . . . I felt more intimately bound, more so than ever before, to the road I had taken and had pledged to follow until my last days. This was the road for which I would sacrifice everything for the future of the revolution and for the interests of the masses. For me there was no other road to take.[13]

Acknowledging the propaganda content of Nguyen Thi Dinh's statements, it is nonetheless evident that such beliefs offer a principal explanation for the courage and extraordinary perseverance of the Vietnamese revolutionaries, a courage that made history. But few of the Vietnamese revolutionaries have left accounts of their formative experiences as has Nguyen Thi Dinh.

Pham Hung, for example, the superior of Mrs. Dinh and all Communists in South Vietnam after 1967, as head of the Party's Control Office for South Vietnam (COSVN), was almost unknown prior to the victory of 1975, although he would even be ranked ahead of General Giap at the Party Congress of 1976. Even though a member of the Political Bureau since 1957, prior to 1975 even Hung's closest associates admitted "he's an enigma for us too." For many years he had refused to be photographed, and when he appeared in Saigon two weeks after the final victory, he went virtually unrecognized.

A veteran revolutionary who joined Ho Chi Minh's Youth League (Thanh Nien) in the 1920s, Pham Hung was born in 1912 in Vinh Long on the lower Mekong. He was a founding member of the Party in 1930, and participated in the insurrections of that year. After his arrest on May Day 1931 in My Tho, following the killing there of a French officer, his death sentence was commuted to life imprisonment on Poulo Condore (Con Son Island), the infamous jail that became "a veritable school of revolutionary nationalism" for nearly all of the top Communist leaders. Not released until September 1945, Pham Hung went on to participate in the war against the French, becoming head of the Viet Minh liaison mission in Saigon, and a deputy of Le Duan before going to Hanoi in 1955. Returning south in the 1960s, he replaced General Nguyen Chi Thanh, who died in July 1967, as senior political leader in South Vietnam.

Joining Pham Hung in early April 1975, and carrying the most recent orders of the Political Bureau for the final offensive, was another veteran of Poulo Condor and of decades of struggle in the south, Le Duc Tho. As Hanoi's senior negotiator of the January 1973 accords, Le Duc Tho, unlike Pham Hung, was well known at least to readers of the Western press. But other details of his life are sparse. Born in Nam Ha province near Hanoi in 1911, he too was jailed in the 1930s, before becoming a principal political commander for the South and another deputy to Le Duan, in the later stages of the French war. After 1954, when his forces regrouped to the North, he made inspection trips for Hanoi to war zones of the south in 1967 and again in 1971–1972. Hence Tho was a logical, though in view of his role in the January 1973 accords, ironic choice to carry out politburo supervision of the final offensive, together with COSVN director Pham Hung and military commander Van Tien Dung. According to a recent account by a former National

Liberation Front leader, Tho in fact played a decisive role in persuading the Political Bureau in late 1974 to go ahead with the final offensive.

As throughout the Vietnamese wars, there was constant interaction between military and political leaders. This is well illustrated by the planning of the final offensive and by its commander, Van Tien Dung, who arrived in the south in February 1975. A former political commissar who was selected to lead the final military preparations, Dung was born in 1907 of a poor peasant family, just northwest of Hanoi. He became foreman of a French-owned textile factory there in the 1930s, and a Communist Party member in 1937. Jailed twice after 1939, he managed to escape twice and became secretary of the North Vietnam Party Committee in 1944 and a leading political commissar in the struggle against the French. A member of the Central Committee since 1951 and a representative of the International Control Commission in Saigon in the 1950s, in 1972 he became the youngest member of the Political Bureau. As commander of the final campaign, Van Tien Dung wrote its most authentic account, titled *Our Great Spring Victory*.

Dung of course worked with the South Vietnam revolutionaries. One of the most illustrative of these "faceless Viet Cong," and the ranking military leader in the South from 1967 until Dung's arrival, was Tran Van Tra. After the capture of Saigon, he became its ostensible leader as the head of the military management committee, though subordinate to COSVN and to the Party's Central Committee in Hanoi. No stranger to the region, Tra was born January 15, 1918, in the Mekong Delta province of My Tho, of a mason "too poor to send me to school." "My father was a patriot," he told French journalist Jean Lacouture. "I became a revolutionary."[14] Tra became involved in anti-French activity as a worker on railroads in the Saigon area and was twice arrested after 1939. After the war, he joined the fighting against the French in areas east and west of Saigon, at one point receiving weapons from Madame Nguyen Thi Dinh. He became Communist military commander of the Saigon area, and another French journalist, Lucien Bodard, flamboyantly labeled Tra's headquarters "a true ministry of death."

Following the 1954 truce, Tra spent some years in the north, and possibly also in China and Russia before returning to the south in 1964. Throughout, he maintained what another journalist, Italian Titziano Terzani, who saw him in Saigon after the military victory of 1975, called "more the look of a high school teacher than a guerrilla." Posing the dilemma over means and ends, classic for Vietnamese revolutionaries as for their predecessors, Terzani understandably found it impossible to reconcile his reactions of admiration and fear of Tra. Describing his interviews with Tra and other Vietnamese Communists, he wrote:

> I found in these people who were emerging from prison and the jungle a strength and a number of qualities that struck me as difficult to find now in the world from which I came. People here had an inner fire that made their lives an extraordinarily complete experience rather than an accidental one. And yet these same qualities, this capacity to overcome the natural and acceptable inclinations of man, seemed to me to lead the Revolution itself to the borders of inhumanity. . . . These people made me think of the saints I had seen in church paintings as a boy [in Italy], with their suffering and smiling faces, halos around their heads, and an almost mad light in their eyes. To me they had always seemed unbelievable, so remote from the world. Sometimes in Vietnam, I had the impression of finding them in front of me once again in a modern version, as revolutionaries with the same features, the same qualities: faith, abnegation, purity. . . . There was a . . . natural sublimation of everything in struggle, in revolutionary tension. . . . And yet in the pit of my stomach I could not help finding all this simultaneously extraordinary and disturbing.[15]

Yet Tran Van Tra maintained a sense of history. Asked by Lacouture to compare the French and American wars, he explained:

> The second was much more painful, more cruel. The means of annihilation of the Americans were formidable. But technology comes from man. [Therefore] in the last analysis, how can man not triumph over technology. In both wars, it was a war of the people. [And in this respect] in the second war, we had still better chances of victory. We had deepened our contacts with the masses and our revolutionary strategy. To increased means, we opposed increased skill.[16]

Thus, Tra maintained, the superior armament of the final offensive of 1975 was not so much a proof of the importance of armament as of the superiority of people's war. It was literally carried on the backs of the people who "opened the roads, dismantled [the weapons], carried them and reassembled them. Those tanks were the crowning of the people's war."

THE CAREER OF LE DUAN, one of the most important of all the Vietnamese Communists and from 1959 first secretary of the Party, well illustrates the intimate links between the revolutionaries in the south and the Vietnamese Communist movement. To begin with, Le Duan was born just south of the seventeenth parallel in Quang Tri in 1907, and is therefore another example of the oversimplification of American charges of "northern" aggression. In fact, about as many leaders of the Saigon regime came from the north and the center (the Bac Bo and Truong Bo regions), as among the Hanoi leadership there were people of the south and center (Nam Bo and Truong Bo). To be sure, the president of South Vietnam from 1965 to 1975, Nguyen Van Thieu, was a native of Phan Rang on the central southern coast not far north of Saigon, but his sometime vice-president Nguyen Cao Ky, was born in Son Tay, just northwest of Hanoi. And the ancestral home of Ngo Dinh Diem was just north of the seventeenth parallel, although Diem himself was probably born at Hue.

What of the other northerners besides Le Duan? In fact, the same even division between northerners and southerners by birth, as between the Saigon president and vice-president, existed for the top half dozen rulers of Hanoi during the Second Indochina War: including Le Duan, half were born south of the seventeenth parallel. Where Ho Chi Minh was born in Nghe Anh on the central northern coast, his successor as president, Ton Duc Thang, was born in Long Xuyen, in the Mekong Delta well south of Saigon. And where Hanoi's minister of defense, Vo Nguyen Giap, and leading theorist, Troung Chinh, were born respectively in Quang Binh just north of the parallel and at Nam Dinh, just south of Hanoi, Premier Pham Van Dong was born in Quang Ngai over two hundred miles south of the 1954 border. While a disproportionate number of Diem's officials and about half of some twenty-three leading Saigon generals in 1968 were northerners, all forty top *non*-Communist leaders of the National Liberation Front were southerners or centrists, that is, from southern parts of the former Annam.[17]

Hence, in terms of the birthplaces of opposing leaders, it is evident that the Second Indochina War was more of a civil war than was America's war of 1860–1865, which also saw a more substantial "Yankee invasion" from the north of a divided country than was the case in Vietnam.

But Le Duan's claims to the south were greater than his place of birth, or simply the nationalism shared by all Vietnamese of his generation. Most of his revolutionary career was in the south. The son of a carpenter, he entered the Youth League at the age of twenty in 1928, and the Party in 1930. He was arrested the following year for his political activities in the north at the time of the uprisings of 1930–1931, and received a sentence of twenty years. Freed as a result of the victory of the Popular Front in France in 1936, he opened a bookstore in Hue and resumed revolutionary activity. In 1937, he was named secretary of the Party Regional Committee for Trung Bo (Central Vietnam) and became a member of the Central Committee in 1939. The following year he was arrested again after the Japanese moved into Indochina. He later reported that only fifteen out of one hundred prisoners in his section survived the next five years in prison.

Released in August 1945, he became a political commissar in the war against the French and was named secretary of the Party's Nam Bo (South Vietnam) Regional Committee in 1951. With the death of Nguyen Binh in an ambush in 1951, Le Duan emerged as the principal leader of the war against the French in the south with Le Duc Tho and Pham Hung as deputies. And at this time Duan helped transform temporarily the Nam Bo Regional Committee, then located at Ca Mau in the far south (later Tay Ninh, near Saigon) into the Central Office for South Vietnam, or COSVN—in effect, into the southern or forward office of the Central Committee for the war zone.

Remaining in the south after 1954, Le Duan reportedly helped to build and maintain the Communist base in the U Minh Forest of the far south before returning to the north in late 1956. There in 1959, he took over the office of secretary-general of the Party, three years after Ho Chi Minh had replaced Troung Chinh in the post. Given Le Duan's long commitment to the Revolution in the south, this change undoubtedly signaled a rededication of the Hanoi leadership to the reunification, by force if necessary, of the two Vietnams. In his "Political Report" to the Party's Third National Congress of September 5–12, 1960, Le Duan strongly restated the need "to pay the greatest attention to the situation in the South" as well as to complete "the socialist revolution in the North, (which at present) is the most decisive task." His call for a broad national front directed against the United States and Diem, together with the upsurge of revolutionary actions after the Ben Tre uprising of January 1960, signaled the official founding of the National Liberation Front for South Vietnam (NLF) "somewhere in the South" on December 20 of that year.[18]

One of the principal names associated with the founding of the National Liberation Front in December 1960 was its president,

Nguyen Huu Tho. Tho was probably the figure most frequently mentioned in subsequent American stories about the "faceless Viet Cong," which was ironic since he was in jail at the time of the founding of the Front, and was not a ranking Communist. Even after the 1975 victory, Tho was not included as a member of the Party Central Committee, but rather became a non-Party vice-president, and then in 1980, acting president of the united Socialist Republic of Vietnam. Although definitely secondary in decision making for the Revolution to the Party leaders, non-Communist progressive leaders like Tho were nonetheless very important, above all for the utilization of the United Front, which procured the cooperation of non-Party forces and, together with the Party and the Army, formed one of the "three weapons of the Revolution" in Vietnam, as in China. Tho was precisely the kind of "progressive bourgeois" the Party hoped to recruit, and his life illustrates the diverse and compelling nature of the Vietnamese Revolution.

Born in Vinh Long on the Mekong about 1910, Nguyen Huu Tho was the son of a middle-class government worker who had become a French citizen and who had sent his son for middle and higher studies in France. Returning to South Vietnam in 1933 Tho became a well-known lawyer in Vinh Long and later Saigon. Though a moderate nationalist, he avoided activist politics and instead gained a reputation as something of a bon vivant, "the perfect representative of the progressive wing of the Southern French-educated bourgeoisie," and even "the caricature of a bourgeois liberal." This detachment disappeared, however, after he was stopped at a Viet Minh check point in 1948 and given a tour of a clandestine base. Apparently won over by Communist arguments and what he had seen, Tho became increasingly active in leftist circles. On March 19, 1950, he was among those leading some 100,000 demonstrators in Saigon against a visit by a U.S. naval squadron in support of the French war effort. Arrested the next day, he spent two years under surveillance on the northwest frontier, near Lai Chau. Then after the cease-fire of July 20, 1954, Tho helped organize the "Movement for the Defense of Peace and the Geneva Accords" and the "Saigon-Cholon Committee for Peace," which organized a large demonstration in Saigon on August 1, 1954.

Arrested a second time on November 7, 1954, he was held in various prisons of South Vietnam, then put under surveillance in Central Vietnam. In early 1961, a partisan group liberated Tho expressly for the purpose of assuming the presidency of the NLF, a rescue that required several attempts, as at first the partisans erroneously seized two look-alikes before returning to free Tho.[19]

About 1967, another southern radical, Huynh Tan Phat, appeared to supersede Nguyen Huu Tho in the activities of the Front. Although Tho remained president, his "intellectual" style yielded influence to the activist Phat, who was the Front's secretary-general, and who became president of the governmental structure set up for the South by the Communists in June, 1969, the Provisional Revolutionary Government. Although, so far as is known, he was not a Communist until at least late in the war, Phat's biography also reveals the deep southern roots of many and the hardships faced by all Vietnamese revolutionaries. Born in 1913 in My Tho on a branch of the lower Mekong, Phat obtained from Hanoi a degree in architecture, which he subsequently practiced off and on in Saigon along with activities in the moderately nationalist Democratic Party and among youth. A supporter of the Communist "August Revolution" of 1945, he was twice arrested and released by the French, and joined the anti-Diem forces about 1958.[20] After 1975, he became a vice-premier of the unified country and in February 1979 was named president of the State Commission for Construction.

From among the strands of such lives and events as these grew the Second Indochina War, more distant origins of which will now be explored.

CHAPTER TWO

The First Revolutionary Upsurge

THE VIETNAMESE REVOLUTION in its larger sense began over a century ago with the inevitable reaction to the establishment of the French presence there in the years after 1856. The early development of this Vietnamese version of anticolonialism and anti-imperialism was classic and strong, and with still earlier history, forms essential background for our subject. Accordingly, in this and the next two chapters, we will move back from the end of the Second Indochina War, to touch very briefly on earlier history, then move forward again to discuss the founding of Vietnamese communism in the 1920s and 1930s, the early years of the Viet Minh Front, founded in 1941, and the First Indochina War, 1945–1954. Following treatment of some highlights of the final Communist victory of 1975 and some of its leaders, the next three chapters give an overview of earlier developments and of earlier leaders of the Party that led that victory.

First of all, several paragraphs on the earlier history of Vietnam are necessary to understand the development of the nationalism that generated the Vietnamese Revolution.[1] Leaving aside more distant origins of the Vietnamese people, which recent archaeological discoveries are pushing ever farther back in time, it is now clear that an independent Vietnamese culture (the "Dong Son civilization") and states (Van Lang and then Au Lac) had come into existence in the centuries before the first Chinese invasions after 221 B.C. and 111 B.C. There followed the so-called Chinese millenium of Vietnamese history, during which the northern part of the country was ruled more or less directly by China. Few details exist for the period, although Vietnamese nationalists understandably make much of numerous revolts against the Chinese occupation, most importantly those of A.D. 40, 248, and 544. Then, with the collapse of the great Chinese Tang dynasty in the early tenth century, a Vietnamese revolt in 905 and a victory over another invading army in 939 set the stage for the development of the first important Vietnamese dynastic houses, the Ly (1009–1225) and Tran (1225–1400). Having expelled the Chinese, the Ly and Tran could more freely develop strengths of the traditional Chinese state system. The first state-organized exams to recruit bureaucrats were given in 1075, for example, and a hierarchy of officials elaborated shortly thereafter. The study of Confucianism supplemented traditional animist and Taoist-style beliefs, and complemented the contemporary importation of Buddhism both from China and from the Indianized states to the west. Thus strengthened, and perfecting further their already impressive record of resistance to China, the Tran resoundingly defeated imposing Mongol invasions on four occasions between 1257 and 1288.

The greatest of the traditional Vietnamese dynasties, the Le (1427–1778) was itself founded in the aftermath of a new war against China, whose Ming dynasty had occupied the country after 1407. The heroes of that long resistance war, Le Loi and Nguyen Trai, became the most famous of all Vietnamese patriots prior to Ho Chi Minh. However, despite further improvements in the state and economy and a notable fifteenth-century law code, the Le dynasty was unable to deal with the complexities caused by the Vietnamese expansion to the south.

After about A.D. 1000, the Vietnamese of the northern Red River Delta had begun to push southward along the coastal plains, against the important early states of the Cham and Khmer (Cambodian) peoples, and against Thai, Lao, and other peoples who mostly moved into the Highlands to become what the French called the "montagnard minorities." Reaching Central Vietnam by the 1400s and the extreme south by the 1700s, the greatly elongated community temporarily split apart, even as its population increased from an estimated five million about 1400 to some ten million in 1878. Civil wars broke out in the sixteenth and seventeenth centuries mostly between the northern Trinh and southern Nguyen families. Then in the 1770s and 1780s, the greatest popular rebellion prior to the Communists, the Tay Son, put an end to the Le dynasty. Yet, despite the divisions and rebellions of the sixteenth, seventeenth, and eighteenth centuries, the memory of a greater Vietnam and of its patriotic struggles against foreign enemies persisted. The last of the great dynasties, the Nguyen, was founded in 1802 after the defeat of the Tay Son, and survived in name until ended by Ngo Dinh Diem in 1955.

THE FRENCH, meanwhile, had entered the scene. A century following the first Portuguese explorations of the area in the early 1500s, French missionaries arrived, the most famous of whom was Alexandre de Rhodes, who after 1627 invented the system of transcription of Vietnamese into a Latin alphabet that became the national language (Quoc Ngu). Another French cleric, Pigneau de Behaine, won a promise of active French support for the founder of the Nguyen dynasty in 1787, but the outbreak of the great French Revolution two years later delayed direct action.

Then, after 1856, anxious to match English gains in China and elsewhere in the developing age of imperialism, Napoleon III authorized the beginnings of the French conquest of Indochina.* Early successes won most of South Vietnam (Cochin China) and Cambodia by 1862. Further fighting in the 1870s and 1880s, and the defeat of Vietnam's supposed protector, China, in 1884–1885, confirmed the French takeover of Central (Annam) and North Vietnam (Tonkin).

France founded the Indochina Union in 1887, added Laos in 1893, and by the turn of the century had established a colonial administration for the five countries of Cochin China, Annam, Tonkin, Laos, and Cambodia. At the same time, it allowed approved Nguyen emperors to continue ceremonial functions in Hue. Real power belonged to the French bureaucracy, headed by successive governor-generals in Hanoi, and his *résidents supérieurs* in the five capitals of French Indochina. As of 1931, these men headed a staff of 4,500 functionaries, backed by 10,500 soldiers, 500 police, and

*The United States also became indirectly involved in Indochina with the call of a trading vessel at Saigon in 1819, and the first reported "armed intervention" by a Western ship against Vietnam, in 1845. In that year, a U.S. ship seized some hostages and fired rounds off Tourane (Da Nang) in an attempt to force the release of an imprisoned French bishop. The ship soon withdrew, its self-appointed mission unfulfilled. But the French duplicated the action in 1847 and went on to an outright invasion of the country a decade later.

5,500 colons and their families. About that time, there were some 42,300 French citizens in the region, mostly in Saigon and Hanoi. The French administration in turn worked mostly with about 23,600 "native functionaries," recruited from an estimated 9,000 rich and 920,000 middle-class Vietnamese to rule the country. By contrast the British ruled India, ten or twelve times as populous, with approximately the same number of civil servants. On the other hand, by the latter part of the nineteenth century there were some 60,000–70,000 British troops in India backed by an Indian army of some 110,000, as against the 11,000 French troops and police in Indochina a generation later.

By the early twentieth century, therefore, as in the first millenium, Vietnam was under the domination of a foreign power. But even less to the French than to the Chinese did the Vietnamese prove docile subjects. From 1885 to 1896, a "scholar's movement to support the emperor" (the Can Vuong movement) bitterly fought the French, and there were almost continuous smaller revolts and terrorist actions thereafter. The dying words of a patriot executed in 1868 seemed justified: "As long as grass grows on our soil, there will be men to resist the invaders." Then after the Japanese defeat of Russia in 1905 and Sun Yat-sen's revolution against the Manchu dynasty in China in 1911, men like Phan Boi Chau and Phan Chu Trinh led the transformation of older style Vietnamese patriotism into a more modern, though still relatively moderate, nationalism.[2]

That brings us to the 1920s, the creation of a revolutionary nationalism, and the transition to the increasingly violent stage of the Vietnamese Revolution.

THE FIFTY-YEAR-LONG VIETNAMESE REVOLUTION, 1925–1975, was the work of many people, but of one man more than any other, the legendary Ho Chi Minh. Through the early life of Ho, can be traced the next stages, the founding of the Revolutionary Youth League in 1925, of the Communist Party in 1930, the difficult years leading to the revolutionary seizure of power in 1945, and the thirty-year war that followed.

In late 1924, when Ho Chi Minh made his way to Canton, not far from the country he had left a dozen years before, he was a revolutionary with an impressive background. Born May 19, 1890, in Nghe An province on the central northern coast, Ho was the son and grandson of rural, sometime destitute, but well-respected mandarin participants in the earlier struggles against France. After schooling briefly at the famous National Academy (Quoc Hoc) in Hue, and first jobs in various parts of Annam, he left his native land in the winter of 1911–1912,[3] not to return for thirty years. In his first two years abroad, as a cook's helper on the French liner *Latouche-Treville*, he visited many ports of the world from Asia to Africa to New York and London. Leaving the sea about the time of the outbreak of World War I, Ho continued his studies and explored Vietnam's situation with all who would listen, working meanwhile as laundry boy and gardener in France, and then in London as an assistant to the celebrated French chef Escoffier at the old Carlton Hotel.

Late in 1917, Ho settled in Paris, as he later said, to study "what lay behind the words, 'liberté, égalité, fraternité.' " He made his living at such diverse jobs as selling rum, painting "Chinese antiquities made in France," and then primarily as a retoucher of photographs. Taking the name by which he first became famous, Nguyen Ai Quoc (Nguyen who loves his country),* Ho made wide contacts among the French left wing, as well as among groups of close to 100,000 Vietnamese, a similar number of Chinese, and other overseas groups then in France. Many of these immigrant laborers had come to France for work-study programs organized for wartime labor needs, but continued in residence there after the war as well.

For many Vietnamese and Chinese Paris, as much as Moscow or Tokyo, was their overseas "home of the revolution." One-quarter of the 1956 Central Committee of the Chinese Communist party, for example, had been in France at the time of the founding of their

*In all, Ho used some twenty pseudonyms. King Chen compiled the following list: Nguyen Sinh Cung (1890–1900), Vietnam; Nguyen Tat Thanh (1900–1912), Vietnam; Ba (1912–1917), on ships and in Europe; Nguyen Ai Quoc (1917–1924), France and Russia; Nguyen O Phap (1923–1924), France and Russia; Ly Thuy (Li Jui, 1924–1927), China; Vuong Son Nhi (Mr. Vuong, or Old Vuong, 1924–1927), China; Wang Ta-jen (Vuong Dat Nhan, 1926), China; Tong Van So (Sung Wen-ch'u; Song Mancho in Cantonese, Sung Meng-tsu, 1924–1927), China; Thau Chin (1928–1929), Thailand; Nguyen Ai Quoc (1930–1933), Hong Kong, Amoy, and Shanghai; Linov (1933–1938), Moscow; Lin (1934–1938), Moscow; P. C. Lin (1938–1940), China; Ho Quang (Hu Kuang, 1938–1940), China; Comrade Vuong (1939–1941), China; Mr. Tran (Old Chen, 1930–1940), China; Ho Chi Minh (1940–1941), China; Thu (Old Thu, 1941–1942), Vietnam; Vuong Quoc Tuan (Hoang Quoc Tuan, 1941–1942), Vietnam; Ho Chi Minh (1942–1945), China; Mr. Tran (Old Chen, 1944), China; and Ho Chi Minh (after 1944), Vietnam.[4]

Party in 1921, and about then Ho Chi Minh may have met two of the most famous members of that group, Zhou Enlai and Deng Xiaoping.

Patriotism always remained at the core of Ho Chi Minh's work, and he first became famous among overseas Vietnamese for a nationalistic act. He tried to present to the Versailles conference of 1919 an eight-point program calling for greater equality and justice for his country. He was naive. In spite of the fact that he did not even propose independence for Vietnam, and in spite of the fact that the conference was paying lip service to President Wilson's fourteen points advocating "self-determination" of nations, Ho was completely ignored. Even the spiffy suit he had rented for the occasion failed to impress delegates of the august assembly.

Spurned by Western liberalism, Ho Chi Minh soon turned to communism as the means to "save his country." Impressed by arguments of the Communist Third International (Comintern),* he stated forty years later (April 1960), that Lenin's 1920 *Theses on the National and Colonial Questions* (written for the Second Congress of the Comintern) had convinced him that Marxism-Leninism "is what we need . . . is the path to our liberation." He elaborated: "At first patriotism, not yet Communism, led me to have confidence in Lenin, in the Third International. Step by step, along the struggle, by studying Marxism-Leninism parallel with participation in practical activities, I gradually came up with the fact that only Socialism and Communism can liberate the oppressed nations and the working people throughout the world from slavery."[5]

Joining the left wing of the French Socialist Party, he became a founding member of the Communist Party of France at the famous Eighteenth National Congress of the French United Socialist Party at Tours, December 25–30, 1920. In a speech to that congress Ho made clear his patriotic objectives: "I come here with deep sadness to speak as a member of the Socialist Party against the imperialists who have committed abhorrent crimes on my native land. . . . On behalf of the whole of mankind, on behalf of all the Socialist Party's members . . . we call upon you! Comrades, save us!"[6]

In the early 1920s in Paris, Ho went on to found and edit *Le Paria* (The Outcast, April 1922–April 1926), the journal of the Intercolonial Union created by diverse groups of refugees from colonial France. A continuing stream of anti-French pamphlets in a

*Founded in Moscow, March 1919.

variety of Socialist and Communist, Vietnamese and French publications—and even a satirical play (*Le Dragon de bamboo*) produced in 1922 on the occasion of the visit to France of Emperor Khai Dinh—made Ho a well-known figure in leftist circles. In late 1922, the Communist Party of France assigned him as a specialist for colonial affairs to attend the Fourth Comintern Congress in Moscow, and then in 1923, a Congress of the Peasant International (Krestintern), which in October elected him one of its ten executive members. Winding up his affairs in Paris, Ho spent most of 1924 in Moscow, the new "home of the revolution," studying at the University of the Toilers of the East and addressing the Fifth Comintern Congress, June–July 1924. There significantly, the scholar's son spoke of the "revolt of the colonial peasants," a point to which we will return.

Then in December 1924, Ho arrived in Canton to begin the twenty-year-long Chinese phase of his career. Officially, he was assistant and translator for Mikhail Borodin, the canny "permanent and responsible representative" of the Soviet Union to "revolutionary China." But in reality, as a member of the Comintern's Asian Bureau, Ho was almost entirely concerned with the formation and organization of what would become the Vietnamese Communist movement.

A number of other young Vietnamese revolutionaries had already come to Canton, which had become a leading center of revolutionary activity in the wake of Sun Yat-sen's abortive revolution of 1911. Sun had reestablished his base there after 1922, and soon "turned towards Russia" to seek aid for his intended reunification of China. Some hundreds of Soviet advisers and substantial military aid soon arrived in South China, and by the mid-1920s, therefore, Canton was a natural site for the implantation of Vietnamese communism. It was close to the homeland but protected from French repression, and provided access to the aid of Russian and Chinese revolutionaries.

The already agitated state of Vietnamese refugees there had been revealed a few months before Ho's arrival, when a young terrorist, Pham Hong Thai, allegedly inspired by early radical writings of Ho and others, threw a bomb at the car of Martial-Henri Merlin, the governor-general of Indochina, then on an official visit to Canton. The attempt failed, but made an unprecedented impression on Vietnamese exiles and within Vietnam itself, where the news soon spread. Revolutionary activists in Canton swore an oath to fulfill Thai's goal of a "free, independent Vietnam."

In a sense, the incident marked the passing of a stage, from intellectual to revolutionary activist nationalism. Mature Communists, however, realized that isolated acts of terrorism were not enough. As Ho's journal, *Thanh Nien*, stated in November, 1926: "Terrorism is not a means of revolution. On the contrary, it is an obstacle to the progress of revolution, since our enemies are numerous, and if one falls to our blows, he is replaced immediately by another."[7] Neither would individual efforts of a more diverse sort help, such as had been carried out in Canton and elsewhere by Ho's predecessor as the "grand old man" of Vietnamese nationalism, Phan Boi Chau. Rather, as Ho would write in his 1926 *Road to Revolution*, "the revolution is a task for the broad working class and peasant masses, not for a handful of men."[8]

The only effective way to "organize the masses" would have to be propaganda and organization. Ho accomplished both through the creation of the Revolutinary Youth League of Vietnam (Vietnam Thanh Nien Cach Mang Dong Chi Hoi, commonly called simply Thanh Nien or Youth.) An initial group existed by February 1925, and in June, the journal *Thanh Nien* (Youth) appeared. As will be seen at greater length later, *Thanh Nien* became required reading for Vietnamese revolutionaries, expounding a revolutionary nationalism and other basic ideas of Vietnamese communism in somewhat the same way as had Ch'en Du-xiu's *New Youth (Xin Ching Nien)* a few years earlier for Chinese communism.

WHO WERE THE EARLY RECRUITS to Vietnamese communism? Many had been followers, or sons of followers, of Phan Boi Chau, whose nearly defunct Restoration Society collapsed after his arrest in Shanghai in June 1925 and subsequent detention in Vietnam.* Phan Boi Chau in turn had been the most prominent successor to the "scholar rebels" against France of the generations of Ho Chi

*There have been accusations that Ho Chi Minh himself tipped off the French as to the whereabouts of Phan Boi Chau as a means of removing a rival, and simultaneously acquiring the reward, but recent refutations by George Boudarel, David Marr, and others are far more plausible. They argue that such a tip may have been passed on to the French by a certain Lam Duc Thu, a double agent in the entourage of Ho. Ho himself, as an agent of the Comintern then promoting an alliance between Communists and nationalists similar to Chau in China, would almost certainly have opposed such action.[9]

After a few months in prison, the French released Chau to house arrest in Hue, where he died in 1940, suffering as did Chen Du-xiu in China the ignominy of forced retirement from the revolutions they had done so much to launch.

Minh's father and grandfather. But organizationally, Chau's efforts to establish a constitutional monarchy on the Japanese model had remained relatively isolated, as did those of the other most famous modern Vietnamese nationalist before Ho Chi Minh, Phan Chu Trinh. Both men played important roles in the development of the ideas of revolutionary nationalism, and demonstrations, especially in Saigon after the arrest of Chau, and following the death of Trinh in March 1926, showed that Vietnamese revolutionaries were ready to move to a stage of still greater militancy, and especially toward greater organization for the Revolution.

Ho Chi Minh was the most famous, but far from the only Vietnamese of the next generation to take the lead in this transition. In Canton, two slightly younger men would also play large roles in the Vietnamese Revolution. The first was Le Hong Phong, who had helped found the Association of Like Minds (Tam Tam Xa), in Canton, to which had belonged the would-be assassin of the French governor-general in June 1924. In the 1930s, Phong would become briefly almost as famous as Ho himself, and a secretary-general of the Party prior to his arrest in 1938 and death in prison at the age of forty in 1942. Together with Ho and others, he was a founder of the Revolutionary Youth League in early 1925 in Canton. There they were soon joined by, among others, a second later famous Communist, the premier of Vietnam for over a quarter century after 1954, Pham Van Dong. Then just twenty years old, Dong probably came to have the closest ties of all with Ho Chi Minh during the turbulent decades that followed.

Other early participants in the developing Communist phase of the Revolution, like Ho himself, first learned their Marxism in France. The French Communist Party had been charged by the Comintern with fostering revolution among the overseas colonies in the 1920s, and there was particularly intense propaganda activity in the port cities of Marseilles and Bordeaux. A Cochin Chinese who early converted to Marxism, and who became famous as a leading participant* in the 1918 uprising in support of the Bolshevik Revolution by French sailors in the Black Sea, was Ton Duc Thang, Ho Chi Minh's first successor as president of the country from 1969 until his death in 1980. Returning to Vietnam, Thang established the first modern labor union in Saigon in 1920. In 1926 he joined the Revolutionary Youth League, but was arrested in 1929 and spent sixteen years in prison on Poulo Condor.

*Chosen to raise a red flag on the ship *Paris*.

Similarly, in North Vietnam in 1925, a union was established in the anthracite mines north of the Red River Delta by another Vietnamese old Bolshevik, Hoang Quoc Viet. After participation in strikes and radical activities and a year in France, Viet spent six years in prison and emerged to become a principal Communist labor leader.

Active in South Vietnam in the 1920s were several other radicals of great importance to the development of the Vietnamese Revolution, but activists who refused to go along completely with Ho Chi Minh's orthodox Communists. The first, Nguyen An Ninh, who was born in Cholon in 1900, has been called the "first western trained intellectual to undertake the road of revolution and commence to fill the gap separating the new intelligentsia from the people."[10] This he commenced through the founding in 1923 of a French-language journal in Saigon, *La Cloche fêlée* (The Cracked Bell), which reputedly played somewhat the same role for Westernized intellectuals in Vietnam as Ho Chi Minh's *Le Paria* played for Vietnamese in France, and it was *La Cloche fêlée* that first published in Vietnam a translation of the *Communist Manifesto* in the spring of 1926. Although Ninh had helped Ho Chi Minh with the publication of *Le Paria* in Paris after 1918, back in Saigon he refused to join the Thanh Nien, but instead in 1928 founded the Party of Idealistic Youth (Vietnam Thanh Nien Cao Vong Dang). Described as a secret society or simply as the Nguyen An Ninh Society, the organization was highly personal, but its founder nonetheless did make a start at preaching to the masses, and hence has been called a "pioneer of peasant communism." Many of Ninh's estimated 700 followers finally joined the Revolutionary Youth League after his arrest in 1929. Released in 1931, Ninh helped found two years later, *La Lutte*, the remarkable journal, edited not only by radical nationalists like himself, but as well by Stalinists and even more astoundingly by Trotskyists. The journal was suppressed in 1937, and its editors once again arrested. Nguyen An Ninh died in prison shortly afterwards.

One of the principal leaders of the Trotskyite movement and another of the most important unorthodox leaders was Ta Thu Thao. Born in the southern delta town of Long Xu Yen in 1906, he also contributed to *La Cloche fêlée* and other journals in the mid-1920s and, in December 1926, attempted to found a journal that would stress mass work, as shown by its title *Nha Que* (Peasant). The journal was immediately suppressed, however, and Thao then spent several years in France. Back in Saigon in April 1933, he helped found *La Lutte* and became the major leader of the Trotskyite group in Cochin China prior to his execution, apparently on Communist orders, in late 1945. We shall elaborate shortly on the activities of the Trotskyists and other mostly French-educated radicals who played such a large role in the 1930s, especially in the South.

Yet the revolutionary activists who would remake Vietnam were those who affiliated with Ho Chi Minh's Revolutionary Youth League. In 1926 there were said to be at least 200 members of that organization, 300 in 1928, and when the first fully organized Communist cell was formed in Hanoi in March 1929, there were an estimated 1,000 members of the Youth League in all areas of Vietnam and abroad. But the French banned all radical propaganda and even discussions of Marxism in Vietnam. And because of the efficiency of the French police network (La Sûreté), leadership of the Youth League remained in Canton until about 1928, a year after Chiang Kai-shek's attempt to destroy the Chinese Communists. In all, some 300 members of the Youth League went there for training, 100 of them studying at the famous Whampoa Military Academy. Some 200 returned to Vietnam, the rest going on to Russia as did Le Hong Phong, or remained in China as did Phung Chi Kien, who joined the Chinese Communist Party in 1927.

BEFORE WE PROCEED FURTHER with the organization of these thousand-odd activists into the Vietnamese Communist Party in 1930, attention must be given to some of the theoretical problems that formed the starting point for Marxist theorists. First of all, up to 90 percent of the first 1,000 activists were students and intellectuals, or in the Marxist vocabulary, small property owners and "petty bourgeois," as were the peasant masses. As of 1918, there were no more than an estimated 100,000 proletarians in Vietnam, but Marxist-Leninists of the time believed that the Socialist Revolution had to be a "proletarian revolution." As had been the case in part in Russia as interpreted by Lenin, and as was even more the case in China as guided by Mao Zedong, the Vietnamese solution to this seeming contradiction was to recruit all activists friendly to the Revolution, but to try to reeducate them in "proletarian ideology" and to make special efforts to recruit as many genuine workers and peasants as possible into the revolutionary organizations. Overall, the Vietnamese Communists apparently did recruit more proletarians into their movement than was the case in China after 1927.

Thus by 1929 the Revolutionary Youth League of Vietnam had adopted the slogan "proletarianize to mobilize the proletariat," and claimed to have organized some 10,000 proletarians as well as 70,000 peasants under its leadership. This had to be done in a society where the great majority of the population remained peasant, and where indeed it was estimated that only about 4 percent of the north was urban as against 14 percent of the south. At the most, the 220,000 "true proletarians" among the estimated 18 million people of Vietnam as of about 1930 included some 93,000 miners, mostly in the North, 55,000 workers on rubber plantations mostly in the south, and 53,000 actual factory workers. By the late 1930s, the number of proletarians had supposedly grown to 361,200, or about 1.5 percent of the total population, as against an estimated 0.5 percent in China. In addition there were an additional 250,000 artisans, while the poor peasants, especially the two-thirds who were landless, could be considered a vast "semiproletariat." Moreover, as in China, Vietnamese proletarians were but one step removed from the countryside where most had been born, and most continued to keep in constant contact with their peasant relatives. Then with accelerating urbanization, by 1965, Vo Nguyen Giap spoke of a "South Vietnamese working class of about 1.5 million."

In this situation, Party leaders early recognized the problem of the necessity to go beyond the largely intellectual elite first recruited to Marxism. Thus the program of the Revolutionary Youth League called, in good Leninist style, first for the destruction of French imperialism in Vietnam, and then for the creation of a "Dictatorship of the proletariat with the direct election of representatives of workers, peasants and soldiers." By 1929, the program required all members to find jobs in factory, mine, or plantation or, if that was impossible, jobs requiring close contact with such proletarians. From the mid-1920s, radicals began the organization of militant labor unions and peasant associations as well as other popular groups, such as youth, women's, mutual assistance associations and sports clubs, wherever possible in order to recruit activists from all levels of society.

As early as 1925, the journal *Thanh Nien* said in the introduction to its first issue, that to lead the revolution "it is necessary to have a directing force. And that is not the work of a few people, but must come from the union of thousands and thousands of individuals. . . ." Ho Chi Minh's *Road to Revolution*, which on its publication in 1926 became the bible of Vietnamese revolutionaries in Canton, added "workers and peasants are the principal forces of the revolution" and must be organized through a "revolutionary party"; that in turn could only be done effectively with a revolutionary doctrine such as Leninism.

Then, from 1926, the Youth League urged its activists to form Red Peasant and Worker Associations, with some resulting proletarianization by the time of the founding of the Party in 1930. Not surprisingly, as elsewhere, Vietnamese Communist leaders remained mostly intellectual in background. Nonetheless, as will be discussed later, they were proletarian to the extent that they gave their primary attention to working with the masses and for a Communist society. And most importantly, as will be analyzed in Chapter Six, the Vietnamese Marxists had already established a journal, *Youth* (*Thanh Nien*), albeit in exile, for the propagation of their proletarian ideas.

Another theoretical problem of the time, critical especially for working out such problems as those of the United Front, or with whom to ally, was the theory of the two-stage revolution. That in turn is part of the larger Marxist theory of history, which holds that all societies pass from primitive to slave to feudal to capitalist to Socialist societies according to the development of successive modes of production as forced by economic change and class struggle.

The two-stage revolution therefore holds that Communist revolutionaries must somehow work with the capitalist revolution against feudalism as well as for the Socialist revolution against capitalism. This was especially relevant for societies like China and Vietnam, where a "National Democratic Revolution," as the process was called, could combine the struggle against the medieval feudalism of their own countries with the struggle against foreign imperialism, the "highest stage of capitalism."

Therefore, in early stages of the Revolution the Communists should first work with native leaders of the capitalist revolution against feudalism, that is, with the "progressive" or "nationalist" bourgeoisie, and "petty bourgeois" intellectuals, as well as with the workers and peasants; in short, with all who would support the revolutions against imperialism and feudalism. The national and social revolutions would go hand in hand. Yet the theory of the two-stage revolution has operated a bit differently in Vietnam than in China, largely because of the greater role of imperialism in Vietnam. Given the victories over imperialist France, and later over neoimperialist America by "colonial and semi-feudal" Vietnam, Communist leaders there have spoken of the possibility to "advance to socialism without going through the period of capitalist development," and hence with minimal cooperation with bourgeois leaders. In "semi-colonial, semi-feudal China," on the other hand, according to the Communist International as well as to later Maoist historians, the longer development of capitalism under a bourgeoisie that was indigenous, even though to varying degrees dominated by Japanese, English, and other foreign capitalists, dictated a somewhat different strategy. That called for the Communists to work with progressive leaders like Sun Yat-sen, especially before 1927, as well as for a greater struggle against surviving capitalist ideology after 1949, as in the Great Proletarian Cultural Revolution of the 1960s.

The ultimate skipping of the stage of native capitalism in Vietnam, thanks to the defeats of foreign imperialism, however, could not mean an immediate Socialist revolution there in the 1920s and 1930s, and the country still "necessarily had to go through two stages, the national democratic and socialist revolutions." This in turn raised the "United Front" question of how to ally with indigenous Vietnamese bourgeois groups. In later decades this question ranked with the Party and the Military as one of the three "magic weapons" of the Revolution.

But in Vietnam in the 1920s, Communists correctly feared that the progressives among the expanding bourgeoisie were too weak and too hostile to social revolution to enable the kind of alliance the Chinese Communists felt forced to make with Sun Yat-sen's Kuomintang. There was even a Comintern proposal for the Youth League to form its own "mass nationalist Party" to meet the needs of Communist theory for the two-stage revolution.[11] But this was clearly beyond the capacity of Ho Chi Minh and his colleagues. Rather, instead of forming an alliance with a Vietnamese bourgeois group or groups, the Youth League absorbed where it could and influenced where it could and, in contrast to the situation in which the Chinese Communists found themselves, the Vietnamese Communists almost always kept a dominant position among revolutionary groups, accentuating their disunity and ineffectiveness while often absorbing the best activists of the other groups.

This was the case with many of the revolutionary groups that proliferated about this time, including the Vietnam Workers Party, the Vietnamese Revolutionary Party (the Tan Viet) and the Association of Like Minds (Tam Tam Xa). After the Association of Like Minds, which was especially active in Canton just before the founding of the Revolutionary Youth League, and most of whose members, like Le Hong Phong soon joined the Youth League, the ideas of the Revolutionary Party were closest to the revolutionary ideology of the Thanh Nien. Many of its members were sympathetic to Marxism, including the future military genious of the Party, Vo Nguyen Giap, and as of 1927 the Revolutionary Party was in fact the strongest revolutionary organization operating within Vietnam itself. Significantly, in view of later preoccupations with the almost exclusive role of Ho Chi Minh and the orthodox wing of the Communist Party, one of the first extant histories of the Party, published in 1938, gave equal credit to the Revolutionary Party and to the Revolutionary Youth League as "two predecessors" of the Communist Party before 1930, and stated that they shared "the same political program and principles of organization." Nonetheless, the two revolutionary groups were unable to unite, and no meaningful cooperation developed. There were instead organizational and ideological disputes, while many Tan Viet activists, such as Giap, joined the Communists.

Another group seemingly promising cooperation between bourgeois and Communists was the Vietnamese Nationalist Party (VNQDD), founded on Christmas Day, 1927. Although more radical at the time than its Chinese namesake, the Kuomintang, as events of 1930 would show, the 1,500 members of the VNQDD became almost as anti-Communist as anti-French in the late 1920s. However, while in their first year, they outdistanced the Revolutionary Youth League in numbers of adherents, VNQDD membership was located almost entirely in Tonkin or at Haiphong, and in significant contrast to the Marxists, the nationalists generally ignored the problems of the peasantry and even excluded them from membership in the Party.

Still other groups of Vietnamese nationalists were more reformist than revolutionary and would have little to do with the smaller group of Communists, whom they considered agents of the Comintern and dangerous exponents of class warfare and of a social revolution which could only compromise the national revolution. The strongest of these more conservative nationalist groups in the 1920s, especially in the south, was the Constitutionalist Party, founded by Bui Quang Chieu and others after 1917. Although relatively cooperative with the French, and seeking to force reforms in, rather than overthrow of, the system, the Constitutionalists continued to play an important role in the allegiances of more moderate nationalists. They had close ties with earlier figures, such as Phan Boi Chau and Phan Chu Trinh and their followers but, perhaps understandably, given the growing polarization of attitudes, were increasingly torn by dissension themselves, and were in any case rendered ineffective by the failure of the French to make meaningful compromises with Vietnamese nationalism.

In addition to such burgeoning nationalist groups, which remained mostly elite and bourgeois, the Communists would have to take account of new mass religious movements, which emerged in Vietnam, as elsewhere, during such times of troubles. Up to 10 percent of the country had long been converted to Catholicism (20 percent in some areas of the North), and except briefly in the late 1940s most Vietnamese Catholics were predictably anti-Communist. Attitudes toward the Revolution were more complicated for the great majority of the population, however, which practiced Buddhism even as it eclectically continued Confucian ancestor worship, Taoist mysticism, and other popular religious practices. Then in the second quarter of the twentieth century, there emerged two reformist religious groups that came to influence more of the South than did the Communists until at least the mid-1950s. The first of these, the Cao Dai ("high palace" or altar) was a remarkable syncretic religion, claiming inspiration from all the great religious and philosophical thinkers from Buddha and Confucius to Jesus Christ and Muhammad to Victor Hugo, and even Charlie Chaplin. Founded in 1919 and organized after 1926, it established a "Holy See" under its "Grand Master" at Tay Ninh, northwest of Saigon, and by the late 1930s claimed 300,000 adherents. The second new religion was the Hoa Hao, named after the village where Huynh Phu So in 1939 founded a "millenarian, anticolonial and egalitarian" reformist Buddhist movement.[12]

On numerous occasions to follow, we will explore the relations between the Communists and these groups, but here we may return to the situation as of the later 1920s, and remark that, in terms of national organization, none proved able to compete effectively with the Communists. In general, other groups proved unable to deal with problems of disunity, and even less with problems of mass organization and government repression. Therefore, a vacuum existed for the leadership of Vietnamese nationalism, and the Communists would fill that vacuum. But the road was scarcely easy, and difficulties abounded both at home and abroad.

IN CHINA, Chiang Kai-shek and conservative nationalists had broken violently with the Communists in the spring and summer of

1927, with the Chinese Communist Party reduced from 57,000 to under 10,000 members. Nonetheless, the Revolutionary Youth League, in return for promising to agitate exclusively against the French, for the moment was allowed to continue its work in China. Having organized more tightly with an inner core called the Communist Youth Group (which may have been attached to the Chinese Communist Party), the League was able to carry on despite the departure of Ho Chi Minh with Borodin for Russia in July 1927. However, following the arrest of Ho Tung Mau, Ho's first successor as leader of the Thanh Nien, and of other leading activists such as Le Hong Son about December 1928, the Youth League moved its headquarters briefly to Guang Xi province, and then to Hong Kong. It was here that the next stage in the formation of the Communist Party would be carried out.

Developments in Vietnam and abroad had proceeded by then to the point that various activists began to demand the establishment of a full-fledged Communist Party with all that that implied in terms of commitment to the Revolution and to the Communist International. In May 1929, delegates from all three regions of Vietnam, as well as from the Vietnamese community in Thailand, arrived in Hong King for a plenary session of the Revolutionary Youth League. The Thai group had been organized in part by Ho Chi Minh, who made his way to Bangkok about August 1928 and carried out revolutionary agitation there, at times disguised as a Buddhist monk. Thanks to the continuing formation of Marxist groups in such diverse places, the Revolutionary Youth League delegation from Tonkin, led by Tran Van Cung, who had just helped create the first authentic Party cell in Vietnam itself, proposed that the time had come for the immediate formation of a Communist Party. Others, however, balked on the grounds that such action might be premature.

Such division of opinion led to serious splits that almost doomed Vietnamese communism before it could be properly consolidated. In 1928, at a conference near Vinh about June, there had been unsuccessful efforts to deal with growing dissension. Now, on its return from Hong Kong in June 1929, the North Vietnamese delegation proceeded to act on its own to form the Indochina Communist Party. They were supported by most members of the Revolutionary Party in Annam and by followers of Nguyen An Ninh in the south. But other sections refused to follow what they considered the high-handed leadership of the Tonkin group, and there may also have been resentment of what were considered excessive efforts at proletarianization. Instead, other activists in the south, together with the Revolutionary Youth League leadership in Hong Kong, declared the establishment of a rival Annamese Communist Party. This in turn moved other activists in Central Vietnam and members of the Revolutionary Party to form a third Communist Party, the Indochinese Communist Federation. By late 1929 all three groups were in competition with each other.

The Comintern, on learning of these developments, reacted strongly. In October 1929, it scathingly denounced the factionalism of the Vietnamese revolutionary movement, and in December sent Le Hong Phong, who had been studying in the Soviet Union since 1926 (among other things, as the first Vietnamese to serve as a pilot in the Soviet air force), to Hong Kong to try to unite the rival groups. He failed, but at least he got the groups to talking, and at a new conference across the bay in Kowloon, on February 3–5, 1930, Ho Chi Minh had better luck. Twenty years Le Hong Phong's senior and enjoying far more Comintern authority, Ho proposed the founding of an entirely new Party that would unite equitably all groups of Vietnamese revolutionaries. Thus the Communist Party of Vietnam came into being, an early example of Ho Chi Minh's diplomatic genius.

The First Plenum of the Central Committee of the new Party met in October 1930 to change the organization's name to the Indochina Communist Party (Dang Cong San Dong Duong). This was done at the insistence of the Comintern, which felt that the economic ties and political needs of the larger region dictated a peninsula-wide name and approach. And until the 1950s, the few cells that came into being in Cambodia and Laos had to be organized almost exclusively among Vietnamese groups in the two countries, or among overseas Chinese groups. Nor did the Chinese leftists in Indochina cooperate much with their Vietnamese comrades. Only in the early 1930s was there a member of the Central Committee of Chinese origin, and he reportedly spoke little Vietnamese. Several important early Vietnamese Communists, however, such as Ho Tung Mau, Phung Chi Kien, and Hoang Van Hoan, became members of the Chinese Communist Party during their years in China.

Nor were there many Communists in Vietnam itself. One source speaks of 211 members at the time of the founding, another of 300, and still another of 1,500 later in 1930. By April 1931, the Party claimed variously about 2,000 or 3,000 members, or about two or three times the number of Youth League activists as of late 1929. But as we will see, intensifying French arrests and other problems soon cut the number of Party members to an estimated 300, with perhaps ten times that number of sympathizers out of a population of some 18 or 20 million. Nonetheless, in 1930 a newly formed Central Committee of nine, headed by Tran Phu, was able to begin operations, first briefly in Haiphong, and then, by the time of the First Plenum in October, in Saigon, where French surveillance was relatively less harsh, and where it was judged there could be easier contacts with overseas.

Most importantly in 1930, the Party adopted at its February Congress and elaborated at the October Plenum and subsequently a program that formed the basic guidelines for the "national democratic revolution." Primarily the work of Ho Chi Minh, the program shrewdly wed anti-French nationalism with an appeal for support for the world proletarian revolution and for greater economic and political justice for the Vietnamese masses. Although sometimes criticized by the Comintern and others for its excessive nationalism, the program in fact established a wide-ranging ten-point statement of the "essential tasks of the bourgeois democratic revolution," which was to be "directed by the worker class." This called for the "overthrow of French imperialism and Vietnamese feudalism and reactionary bourgeoisie" (point one) and for the "complete independence" of the country (point two). A "worker-peasant-soldier government" was to be established (point three), which would confiscate banks, redistribute land, implement an eight-hour working day, end unjust taxes, and realize freedom, education, and equality of sexes (points four to ten). The document even predicted the outbreak of a second imperialist world war. But above all it set the direction of the Party to concentration on two essential tasks, the struggle against imperialism for "national independence" from France, and the struggle against feudalism, with "land to those who worked for it," in short for both the national and social revolutions.[13] No other group had such a coherent and hard-hitting statement of principles, and with changes of emphasis, notably toward still greater nationalist content after the mid-1930s, it remained the Party's basic guide to action throughout the struggle against France.

THE YEAR 1930 was a watershed for the development of Vietnamese communism. That year saw not only the founding of the Party, but the two greatest anti-French insurrections up to that time, that led by some rebel soldiers under the leadership of the Nationalist Party (VNQDD) at Yen Bay in North Vietnam in February, and a more significant one by Communist-led peasants of Nghe An and Ha Tinh provinces in northern Annam after May 1930. There were also many other more scattered uprisings against the Vietnamese rich and their French backers in 1930–1931, especially in Cochin China and southern Annam. In addition, there was the example of the late 1929–1930 Communist-led uprisings among the Zhuang people just across the border in the Chinese province of Gwangxi, led briefly by the later famous Chinese leader Deng Xiaoping, and others. It is not known if there were direct contacts between Chinese and Vietnamese Communists in the area, but the French greatly feared the possibility of such cooperation.

The Yen Bay revolt was a desperate and as it turned out fatal attempt by the Nationalist Party (VNQDD) to take advantage of rising anti-French sentiment among troops of the colonial French army, and to stop the hemorrhaging of the organization in the wake of intensifying French repressions.* On the night of February 9–10, 1930, militants of the VNQDD infiltrated the upper Red River French military post of Yen Bay, killing a few of the 600 French soldiers there, before being quickly suppressed, as were other attempted Nationalist revolts. Hence, as it turned out, the principal result of the Yen Bay revolt was the virtual removal through subsequent arrests of the Communist Party's principal competition for the leadership of the revolution, and simultaneously, a further embitterment of most Vietnamese nationalists, already disillusioned by the gap between colonial practices and the reformist rhetoric of French Governor-Generals Varenne and Pasquier after 1925. Nonetheless, even though the VNQDD virtually disappeared from Vietnamese politics, the Yen Bay revolt spurred the imagination of nationalists, who remembered the words of one of its leaders who declared that he would "die for the purpose of letting the people of the world know that the Vietnamese people continued to live," and, of course, to fight.

The establishment of the Nghe Tinh soviets (in the provinces of Nghe An and Ha Tinh on the north central coast) later in 1930 and 1931 played equally into the hands of the Communists. Although

*Particularly after the February 1929 assassination of a certain Frenchman Bazin, a hated supervisor of labor recruitment for the rubber and tea plantations, by a dissident member of a VNQDD group.

the Party's newly organized central leadership was not prepared for such an uprising, the revolts were nonetheless the first involvement of the peasant and worker masses in armed action, and therefore later Communist historians described them as playing a role for their country, comparable to that of the Russian Revoluton of 1905, in preparing the way for later events.

As in peasant rebellions of traditional times, which were particularly significant in Vietnam as in China, the rebellions of 1930 were caused by a combination of difficult local conditions and increased agitation by radicals against intensifying government oppression, especially onerous taxation (on persons, land, salt, alcohol, wood, and so forth), in the face of low and falling peasant incomes caused by severe natural disasters and falling prices related to the world depression after 1929. This combustible mixture of abysmal conditions and increasing agitation led to an unprecedented series of rebellious actions. For example, in thirteen of twenty-one provinces of Cochin China in the south, there were some 125 largely peasant demonstrations against local authorities in the year after May 1930, and in Quang Ngai province on the central southern coast there were mass uprisings in October 1930 and January 1931.

Yet the most dramatic explosion by far, the Nghe Tinh soviet movement, came in traditionally rebellious Nghe An province, the home of both Phan Boi Chau and Ho Chi Minh (both born in the same district of Nam Dan), and in neighboring Ha Tinh province to its south. There, peasant poverty was rooted in overpopulation, in contrast to the south, where the problem was tenancy and landlordism. Not only was the average landholding in northern Annam very small (about half an acre), but many peasants (up to 90 percent in some localities) had no land at all. Moreover, the provinces were especially vulnerable to the combination of falling rice prices and natural and manmade disasters that hit after 1929, with disastrous floods in early 1930, followed by drought. Besides these economic problems, the area became the center of Communist organization for all of Vietnam early in 1930, as the Party sent strong reinforcements to assist its 300 Party members already there.

Thus, Nghe An and surrounding areas in 1930 were ripe for revolt, with a particularly severe combination of problems and accompanying radical agitation. Communist historians have claimed also that the rebellions of 1930–1931 first demonstrated what would be a feature of the Vietnamese Revolution, a particularly close link between the urban and rural revolutions.

Conditions were abysmal in both town and village. According to one study of conditions across the country in the early 1930s, the average Vietnamese worker earned less than one-tenth the average salary of the French worker and less than one-twentieth that of his American counterpart, while peasants probably earned at most one-third what their urban counterparts did. Moreover, the Vietnamese poor were taxed extremely, at 20 to 35 percent of their meager incomes. In these increasingly desperate conditions, strikes by factory workers throughout the country rose from seven in 1927, involving 350 workers, to ninety-eight in 1930, involving some 31,680 workers, including the "first strike under Communist direction" among plantation workers, who took over the Phu Rieng rubber plantation near Saigon for several days in February 1930. In the Nghe-Tinh area, a strike of some 400 out of the 1,700 workers in a match factory in Ben Thuy, a suburb of Vinh, the provincial capital, on April 19, 1930, and Communist-led activity at a nearby textile factory were particularly important in the development of the 1930 rebellion.

Yet, it was the action of peasants, frequently led by local and regional Communist activists, that dominated the Nghe Tinh soviet movement, as well as the other uprisings of 1930–1931. Where in the entire country there were some 129 workers' strikes from April 1930 to November 1931, there were 535 peasant demonstrations in the same period, while among activists arrested by the French in the south between December 9, 1929, and April 30, 1931, for "political" reasons, some 2,791 were peasants and 374 were workers, a ratio of seven to one. Similarly, peasants made up the great majority of Communists in Nghe An, as elsewhere.

In the Nghe An area, the organization of the peasants had begun by 1926, and by 1929 a provincewide Federation of Peasant Associations had come into existence. The appalling economic, social, and political conditions created a revolutionary situation in the area for both peasants and workers, and increasing numbers of Youth League and Communist activists played crucial roles in organizing them. About half of the alleged 3,000 Communists in the entire country were reported active there at the peak of the uprisings, working with perhaps another 1,500–2,000 cadre of the various Nghe-Tinh soviets. In February 1930, the newly founded Party established a regional committee for Annam, and there already existed provincial, prefecture, canton (district) and branch (cell) committees. In the wake of the Yen Bay revolt and its suppression, on March 28, 1930, activists called for the "preparation without delay of a second insurrection" that would link with the peasant and worker masses and hence avoid the errors of the Yen Bay soldiers who "had not organized . . . the assistance of the peasants and workers." Agitation escalated in scope and intensity throughout the spring.

On May Day, some 10,000 peasants and 1,200 workers from surrounding areas marched on the office of the French *resident* in the city of Vinh, capital of Nghe An province. It was suppressed, with some seven demonstrators killed, but new and bigger demonstrations followed, and extended into neighboring Ha Tinh. In all, French records speak of some 149 demonstrations in the two provinces, 54 of them especially large, during the year after May 1, 1930. They involved from several hundred to 20,000 people and all demanded the ending of or reduction of taxes in a time of depression and threatening famine. The more radical of them carried hammer and sickle flags,* and demanded distribution of food and land and as many as twenty-four specific requests. Simultaneously, activists accelerated the formation of Red Workers Unions (of which there were said to be 312 members at Vinh, and 9,000 elsewhere), Red Peasant Associations (with up to 28,861 members), as well as legal organizations, such as mutual aid societies, sports associations, youth (816 members) and women's (864 members) organizations.

In late May a second wave of bigger demonstrations began, and continued throughout the summer with a general strike in July. There was a new intensification of the movement after late August and, on September 1, an estimated 20,000 demonstrators set fire to government offices in Than Chuong prefecture. Another large demonstration occurred September 7–9 in Ha Tinh, and in Nam Dan, Thanh Chuong, Anh Son, Nghi Loc, Hung Nguyen, Can Loc, and Huong Khe (the last two in Ha Tinh), and other districts, activists in Party cells and the Red Peasant Associations established their own local administrations, or soviets, as these structures were called after their Russian model. (The French preferred the term *régimes bolshevik*.) In all, soviets were set up in sixteen villages and nine districts of the two provinces embracing, according to the Communists, 50,000 or even 100,000 people and, according to the French,

*The yellow star on a red background later adopted by Vietnamese Communists as their national flag first appeared in the Mekong Delta uprising of November 1940.

affecting up to 60 percent of the inhabitants in various parts of the two provinces, with those mentioned having the most Communist activists and followers. The Party called for the seizure of communal lands, and a few agricultural cooperatives were established briefly.

As the revolutionaries were stepping up their actions, the French began to strike back in greater force, and in early September, hardly for the last time, killed dozens of demonstrators by bombs dropped from the air. Then on September 12, the date that came to be taken as the anniversary of the Nghe Tinh soviet movement, occurred the largest incident of all. Troops and airplanes broke up a demonstration of some 20,000 peasants and workers from Hung Nguyen district marching on the city of Vinh and killed about 217.[14]

Nonetheless the movement continued, and in places the Communists struck back with what the French called the "Red Terror," recalling similar events in China where, in the peasant movements of Hailufeng, of Hunan, Jiang Xi, and other parts of South China in the 1920s and 1930s, and of North China in the late 1940s, activists rallied villagers to denounce local "tyrants" and, if necessary, to execute them. Some eleven notables of a village near Vinh were executed in May 1930 and perhaps fifty persons in all, including thirteen Communists, accused of treason. More positively, the Red Peasant Associations abolished taxes, redistributed rice and land, continued to organize, and undertook irrigation and other economic projects as well as literary and educational campaigns.

These activities were the heart of the movement, although naturally the more rebellious acts and counterterror got the headlines. The Party Central Committee newly established in Saigon also decided, but of course for different reasons, that the movement had gone too far too fast. In late September, it declared the actions in Nghe An and Ha Tinh "not appropriate to the situation in our country because the Party and the masses in the country have not yet reached a sufficient level of preparedness and because we still do not have the means for armed violence. Violence in a few isolated areas at this time is premature and is an adventuristic action."[15] In short, according to Party leaders, the revolutionaries could not possibly protect their movement, and hence should not have started it. Nonetheless, since action had already been taken by local activists, they also stated that measures such as redistribution of rice and land, and the abolition of taxes should be continued in order "to keep the struggle alive" and so that people would remember.

Party Central's judgment that revolutionary power could not be maintained proved correct. The French undertook a series of measures that, together with growing famine in the region, effectively ended the Nghe Tinh soviets and other movements by mid-1931. The French rushed in reinforcements (they had had only a few dozen troops there at the start), set up a series of security posts (68 in Nghe An, 54 in Ha Tinh), required the carrying of statements of loyalty, and began to offer the peasants free food. Above all they stepped up the suppression of revolutionaries all over the country, and especially in the rebellious provinces of Annam. It is estimated that repressions took the lives of some 2,000 in the two provinces, and throughout the country thousands were arrested, bringing the total of political prisoners to 3,000–4,000 in 1931 and to 10,000 after 1932. As a result, the Party admitted that "certain organs . . . were provisionally destroyed by the police" and, in one document of the period, estimated that in places 99 percent of its leadership was under arrest.* In all, up to 50,000 leftists were reported arrested and 10,000 of them kept in jail until the mid-1930s.

Those arrested in this first great wave repression faced by the Communists included not ony the Party leaders of Annam, but first Party Secretary-General Tran Phu, who died in prison, reportedly of torture, later in 1931, and many, many others, including most of the Central Committee arrested in the Saigon area in March–April 1931. The 1930s arrests also included those of future leaders, Le Duan (who would spend about eleven years in jail), Truong Chinh (about six years), Pham Van Dong (about seven years), Pham Hung (about fifteen years), Vo Nguyen Giap ("only" about two years), and Ton Duc Thang (about sixteen years). In short, almost every top Communist leader spent years in prison, and many did not survive. In view of their triumph despite this appalling history, Communist leaders would claim that the prisons had been "revolutionary schools," where adversity "tempered them as fire fuses gold," and as "jade is polished." They studied Communist texts printed on

*Most top Party leaders of Annam, including Nguyen Phong Sac, who had been sent as a special representative of the central leadership to the area as early as June 1929, were arrested in April and May 1931. The arrests in Saigon reportedly followed information given out after the arrest of one Le Quang Sung, and later of Ngo Duc Tri, a member of the Central Committee's "permanent bureau" in Saigon.

toilet paper, and at times were even able to publish news and ideas in the *Prison Review*. Ho Chi Minh's statement on the thirteenth anniversary of the Party, when there were forty-two full members and twenty-nine alternate members of the Central Committee, provided more somber details: "speaking merely of the comrades in the Party Central Committee, fourteen have been shot, guillotined or beaten to death in prison . . . [since 1930, while another] . . . thirty-one of the comrades now (1960) in the Central Committee were given altogether 222 years of imprisonment . . . ."[16] Ho Chi Minh himself was arrested about this time, but in Hong Kong, not in Vietnam. This occurred in June, and was one of many examples of the fascinating but very obscure and difficult personal side of the underground struggle between international communism and its enemies. These episodes, far more numerous in the 1920s and 1930s than later, involved surveillance and intrigue, constant flights, changes of address, payments for information, tortuous plots, and great numbers of arrests and releases. The actors were men and women of many nationalities and organizations engaged in every imaginable activity to pursue their ends of intelligence and counter-intelligence.

In the spring of 1931, Ho Chi Minh became one of the victims of the results of an arrest made by British police in Singapore of the French Comintern agent Serge Lefranc, alias Ducroux. Lefranc had visited Ho in Hong Kong in April 1931 and then spent a month in Vietnam prior to his arrival and almost immediate apprehension in Singapore. Papers seized from Ducroux, together with information extracted from a Chinese Communist police chief arrested in April, led to the arrests in June of Ho's superiors as directors of the Comintern's Far Eastern Bureau in Shanghai, the Swiss couple Gertrude and Paul Ruegg (alias the Noulens couple), and of the Secretary-Generals of the Chinese and Vietnamese parties Hsiang Chung-fa and Tran Phu, and of many others. In China, Zhou Enlai reportedly ordered the execution of the entire family of a defector, down to some thirty-two cousins, as a brutal countermeasure to stop such leaks about the Party's apparatus.

The French requested Ho's extradition after his location by British police in Hong Kong on June 6 and arrest on the twelfth. But the British themselves tried Ho, identifying him as the head of the southern section of the Comintern Far East Bureau. They sentenced him to jail, pending deportation, a modest penalty in comparison with the death sentence given in absentia by a French court in Vinh. But the appeals dragged on, and Ho became ill. Indeed, he was reported dead of tuberculosis by both the English and the world Communist press in August 1932, and also by the normally well-informed French Sûreté. In all, the European press would report Ho's premature death ten more times prior to his triumphal entry into Hanoi in late 1954.

But in December 1932, following appeals by the Red Relief Association, and unlikely rumors of deals made to work for British Intelligence, London ordered Ho released. After another brief arrest in January in Singapore, he made his way to Shanghai from which, with the help of some visiting French comrades, he was able to book passage to Moscow via Vladivostok.[17] In Moscow, Ho furthered his Bolshevization together with, among others, the Chinese Communist leader Li Li-san, held responsible for Communist setbacks in China in 1930. There were even reports that Ho himself was under surveillance at times during the Stalinist purges of the 1930s and, apart from assisting at the Institute for the Study of National and Colonial Questions in Moscow, his activities remain something of a mystery, prior to his arrival at Mao Zedong's base of Yenan in northwest China in late 1938.

Meanwhile the Party was recognized as a "national section" of the Communist International in April 1931, binding it to the strict Comintern rules and reportedly entitling it to a monthly subsidy of 5,000 French francs or about 1,250 dollars per month.[18] But Moscow could affect events in distant Vietnam indirectly at best, and that primarily through a common ideology and training of Communist leaders.

CHAPTER THREE

The Lean Years

AFTER THE NEAR EXTERMINATION OF THE PARTY in the early 1930s, as in China after 1927, leadership of the Communist movement passed to a group of Russian and French "returned students." They retained leadership of the Party until the outbreak of World War II, the subsequent release from prison of younger leaders of the first generation (such as Pham Van Dong, Truong Chinh, and Vo Nguyen Giap in North Vietnam, Le Duan in Central Vietnam) and above all until the return of Ho Chi Minh to the northern border area in 1940. Before that, Party activities in the 1930s were dominated by returned students who included Tran Van Giau, Duong Bach Mai, and Nguyen Van Tao, working more or less openly in the Saigon area, and Le Hong Phong, Ha Huy Tap, and others working mostly underground from various locations in South China and Vietnam. Some biographical data on these men will demonstrate the historical complexity of the Vietnamese Communist movement and facilitate discussion of the complex events that followed the repressions of 1931.

One of the principal leaders of the recovery of communism in South Vietnam following the repressions of the early 1930s, Tran Van Giau, was born in Ta Nan, south of Saigon, in 1911, but early went to study in France, mostly at Toulouse where he reportedly earned a doctorate in history. From there he joined some three to four dozen Vietnamese students at the University of the Toilers of the East in Moscow, also known simply as the Stalin School. They included early Party Secretary-Generals Tran Phu, Ha Huy Tap, and Le Hong Phong, all of whom were among some twenty-two returnees arrested by French police in the next decade. Tran Van Giau returned to Saigon about early 1933 to take over leadership of the Party's Executive Committee, established the previous April but almost all of whose leadership also had been arrested, as Giau himself would be briefly in 1933, 1935, and 1939. Giau, nonetheless, survived and went on to direct the first months of the war against the French in Cochin China after August 1945. He was replaced in early 1946, supposedly because of his lack of finesse in the liquidation of erstwhile allies, such as the Trotskyist leader Ta Thu Thao. Thereafter he worked among Vietnamese in Thailand, and after 1954 became a prominent historian of the Communist movement, a perhaps unique distinction for a "purged" Communist leader.

Like Giau, Duong Bach Mai was born in Cochin China (in 1904) and educated in France and the Soviet Union, where he was known as Comrade Bourov. He returned to Saigon about 1931 and was prominent in local politics and journalism before he was arrested in 1938. Then after seven years on Poulo Condor, he headed the permanent Viet Minh delegation in Paris until his expulsion from France after March 1946. This occurred following a riot caused by his presence at a March 1946 session of the National Assembly in Paris, where he was denounced as a terrorist and "wolf in sheep's clothing." He died obscurely in Hanoi in 1963.

Another southerner prominent in Communist activities in Cochin China in the early 1930s, Nguyen Van Tao, even became a member of the Central Committee of the French Communist Party in 1928. In April of that year he founded a Vietnamese Communist group in Paris, and in the summer argued before the Sixth Comintern Congress in Moscow the needs of the developing revolutionary situation in Vietnam, especially the importance of the peasant movement. He also returned to Saigon in 1931 following seven months in a Paris jail for "disturbing the peace," and went on to become minister of labor in Hanoi, dying about 1970.

In the mid-1930s, before the renewed suppression of the Party accompanying the outbreak of World War II, Giau, Mai, Tao, and other activists rebuilt the Party in the South to over seven hundred members backed by thousands of sympathizers.

They did this on two levels. On the one hand they carried out propaganda and organizational work, both openly and underground. In Cochin China they were able to work effectively in open "legal" work so long as their identifications were in order and they observed strict rules of behavior. Hence, in the early 1930s, those

Communists who escaped arrest not only were able to publish some dozen clandestine Vietnamese-language journals, such as *Neutrality*, *Red Flag*, and *Communist Review*, but also were able to distribute legally the French-language journal *La Lutte*. Even more surprisingly, they were able to use the protection provided by French law governing the direct colony of Cochin China to take some part in the political process. Nguyen Van Tao won a seat in May 1933 on the Saigon Municipal Council, and Tao and Duong Bach Mai, together with the Trotskyites Ta Thu Thao and Tran Van Thach, won seats on the same council in the spring of 1935 and 1937. There were especially notable Trotskyist successes in elections to the Colonial Council in 1939. These elections and other Communist activities naturally led to great consternation among the some 5,000 French citizens of Saigon, even though they controlled the election of twelve seats on the Municipal Council, while the several hundred thousand Vietnamese of the city could elect only six.[1]

Paradoxically, a reason for the greater freedom of maneuver enjoyed by the Communists in the south after the crackdown of 1930–1931 may have been the greater power of the French there, in contrast to the more loosely controlled protectorates of Annam and Tonkin. In the latter areas the French *résidents supérieures*, in theory at least, worked with the Nguyen imperial court in Hue, and from 1937 to 1945 with Bao Dai's chief minister Pham Quynh. But in effect, as the Vietnamese had no real power, this meant the French police could more or less do as they liked, where in the colony of Cochin China, they were to some extent subject to French law and guarantees of freedom of speech. Important also was the support, even if limited, of the French Left and the Communist Party for Vietnamese revolutionaries, for example, their consistent work for amnesty for political prisoners. Moreover, while as later events would show, the colons of the south were among the most reactionary of Frenchmen, they were divided among themselves and frequently attacked the colonial administration, thereby lessening pressure on the Communists. Nonetheless, even in Saigon, Communists were constantly harassed and top leaders like Tran Van Giau (in 1933, 1935, and 1939), Nguyen Van Tao (in 1937), Duong Bach Mai and Ha Huy Tap (in 1938) faced constant, if temporary arrests. And in the countryside, as in Nguyen Thi Dinh's Ben Tre province, the Party was virtually liquidated in the early 1930s.

Another extraordinary aspect of the 1930s growth of Vietnamese communism despite all obstacles, and especially in the Saigon area, was the unique collaboration that occurred between Stalinists and Trotskyists. Duong Bach Mai could say as late as June 1937 despite his Stalinist education: "We do not overvalue the Trotskyists. However, while at the same time recognizing their errors, we also recognize that until the new order, they remain anti-Imperialists who merit all our support."[2] The cooperation between the two groups, so much at each other's throats elsewhere in the world, apparently was possible because of the remoteness of the country and the relatively few people involved, as well as because of the obvious fact that, following all the arrests, the Communists needed all the help they could get in order to survive. Therefore leftists of all descriptions cooperated in the early 1930s despite occasional criticisms at the time of what in 1951 Ho Chi Minh would say had been "unprincipled cooperation" with the Trotskyists.

In fact there were numerous Trotskyist groups, as well as other groups of non-Stalinist radicals in the south. The first opposition Communist group in Vietnam, which would soon be labeled Trotskyist was founded in December 1930 at Ca Mau in the far south by a former member of the Thanh Nien. The group soon moved to Saigon, and joined with other Trotskyists arriving from France. But these soon split, leaving at least three Trotskyist factions by 1931, the most famous under the leadership of Ta Thu Thao. Despite their own internal differences, the Trotskyists of Vietnam, as to some extent also in China, generally argued what ironically would become Moscow's own principal criticism of Maoism in China and of "rightism" in Vietnam, namely, that the orthodox Communist leaders represented petty bourgeois overreliance on the peasants and on nationalism. But just so, conditions in these Asian countries dictated concentration on the problems of the peasantry and anti-imperialism. And despite their criticisms of the reformism of the Stalinists, the Trotskyists too participated in elections, winning seats on the Municipal Council from 1933 on, and virtually sweeping the elections for the Colonial Council in 1939 with 80 percent of the Vietnamese vote. Despite their stress on work with the relatively small proletariat of Vietnam, the Trotskyists claimed a membership of 3,000 by 1939, which though undoubtedly exaggerated, probably made them more influential and numerous than the orthodox Communists in the Saigon area at the end of the 1930s. The Trotskyists, however, were never strong in the center and north and, more than the Stalinists, suffered from the renewed crackdown after 1939. Probably only several hundred Trotskyists survived the war and, as we shall see, these were then struck down by the Stalinists after 1945.

Besides Communists and Trotskyists, the best-known revolutionary in Saigon was the nationalist, Nguyen An Ninh. Where in the 1920s he refused to join the Thanh Nien, in the 1930s he demonstrated the spirit of cooperation among revolutionaries by joining with both Stalinists and Trotskyists in the publication of *La Lutte*, the journal that came to be taken as the symbol of all revolutionary activity in Saigon in the 1930s. After its founding in April 1933 and resumption of publication in October 1934, its editorial board came to consist of three nationalists (headed by Nguyen An Ninh), four Stalinists (including Duong Bach Mai and Nguyen Van Tao), and five Trotskyists (headed by Ta Thu Thao). Its 2,000 or so copies were published in French, which could be read by possibly 100,000 Vietnamese throughout the country, while journals in Vietnamese were published clandestinely in quantities of 4,000 or so copies.

Outside of Saigon, most other well-known Vietnamese revolutionaries in the early 1930s were either in prison or forced to operate abroad. In early 1932, after five years of study in Russia, Le Hong Phong arrived in Long Zhou, Guang Xi province, where he helped set up an External Direction Bureau of the Communist Party of Indochina. He and his group published the official journal of the Party *Bon So Vich* (Bolshevik) and attempted to restore Party work in North Vietnam, as well as among Tho, Nung, and other minorities, and in Laos. Another headquarters of Vietnamese Communists abroad after 1931 operated from Thailand (at times from Ban Mai near the Laos border), and was particularly active in promoting revolutionary work in Central Vietnam.[3]

BY EARLY 1934, the Exterior Bureau had moved to Macao, while in June of that year at an undisclosed location in Vietnam, a national congress of leading cadres of the Party decided to reconstitute the Party on a national scale. Later in 1934, Party leaders decided to convene the First National Congress of the Communist Party of Indochina, but security dictated that the congress be held abroad at Macao. Delegates from the five areas of Indochina, as well as from the groups in Thailand and South China, met in Macao, March 27–31, 1935. The Party had resumed its growth after about 1933, when only perhaps 200 members survived outside of prison. By 1935 the Party was said to consist of some 700–800 members in 150 cells, with several thousand sympathizers, and grew rapidly later in the 1930s to over 2,000 members, and at least 40,000 sympathizers.

Then following renewed tribulations, the Party supposedly numbered 5,000 members by the time of the August Revolution of 1945.

The Macao Congress was later termed "one for the unification of the forces of the Party," but curiously neither of its most important members, Ho Chi Minh or Le Hong Phong, was present. Again there is a Chinese parallel, as neither of the supposed founders of the Chinese Communist Party, Ch'en Du Xiu or Li Da Zhao, was present at its first congress in 1921. In any case, Ho Chi Minh (so far as is known) remained in Russia until 1938, and Le Hong Phong was apparently on his way to Moscow at the time of the 1935 Macao congress. Ha Huy Tap was elected secretary-general of the Central Committee of nine, including also Tran Van Giau, Nguyen Van Cu, and Phung Chi Kien, while Ho remained the senior Vietnamese representative of the Communist International in Moscow, and Le Hong Phong soon returned to Vietnam as Comintern representative, then as secretary-general of the Party. A bureau of the Vietnamese Party was established at Shanghai to maintain contact with Moscow, and an executive committee was established in Saigon, headed publicly by Tran Van Giau, and clandestinely by Ha Huy Tap and Le Hong Phong.

According to French Intelligence, the Party in Vietnam itself organized about this time "country" committees for Tonkin, Annam, and Cochin China, as well as for Cambodia and Laos. The committee for Annam was reportedly subdivided into northern (based at Vinh), central and southern committees (based at Quang Ngai, with branches in Binh Dinh and Nha Trang). In the south, Party work was even more highly organizd. In 1934, Tran Van Giau reportedly guided the subdivision of the southern committee into regional committees for east and west Cochin China, five provincial committees (including those for Gia Dinh, Cho Lon, Ben Tre and My Tho), and six other local committees. Hence Party organization as of the mid-1930s, at least in Cochin China, rose from village, factory, and residential cells, to district or other local committees, to provincial committee, to regional committee, to country committee, to an executive committee in Saigon, the external central committee then at Macao, and a liaison committee with the Comintern at Shanghai.

The early 1930s were the most leftist period in the history of the Vietnamese, as of the Chinese Communists, and at Comintern direction radical policies remained in effect throughout 1935. While continuing to propound the ten points of 1930, the Macao

Congress *Manifesto* placed greater stress than before on "armed violence, the most elevated form of class struggle, which alone is capable of delivering us from absolutism. . . ." It repeated the appeal stressed by the Party's 1932 "action program" for Vietnamese support for the struggles of the minority peoples. But in line with Stalinist efforts of the period for Bolshevization, the Macao *Manifesto* criticized excessive emphasis on alliances with non-Communist nationalist groups and, according to a Soviet source, also criticized excessive reliance on the peasants at the expense of proletarian leadership. In December 1934, the Party journal *Bon So Vich* (Bolshevik) even criticized Ho Chi Minh to the effect that while he had rendered "remarkable services to the Party . . . he did not understand the directives of the Communist International . . . and advocated erroneous reformist and collaborationist tactics . . . (based on his bourgeois nationalism)."

This doctrinal leftism on the part of the returned students, however, would soon change, forced by the dangerous rise of Nazi Germany and militarist Japan. To defend against that mortal danger, vulnerable but influential countries such as France and China sought to create "popular fronts," which could rally their populations more effectively, and the Communist International sought to organize Communist responses to the new challenge in areas such as Indochina. Accordingly, the Seventh World Congress of the Comintern, convened in Moscow, July 25–August 20, 1935, dictated a shift, to use the Communist terminology, from a "united front from below" to a "united front from above." For Vietnam, this meant a dropping of calls for the "immediate overthrow of capitalism and installation of socialism" in favor of rallying a "large popular front comprising patriotic and democratic groups and diverse sections of the population for action against fascism, the immediate and principal enemy." The old slogan "confiscate the landowners' land for distribution to the tillers" was dropped in the effort to woo moderate nationalists, including even landlords, into an "Indochinese Democratic Front." Even anti-Fascist Frenchmen and Vietnamese "national bourgeois" were invited to cooperate. As Ho Chi Minh explained about that time:

> At the present time the ICP should not make excessive demands (independence, parliament, etc.) so as not to fall into a snare prepared by the Japanese fascists. The Party must limit itself to demanding democratic rights, freedom of organization, assembly and press; general amnesty for political prisoners . . . struggle for the right of legal

> activities . . . (and) to unite not only the local population of Indochina but progressive French forces, (and) not only the working class but also representatives of the national bourgeoisie.[4]

The drastic changes of the mid-1930s in world politics came home to Vietnamese revolutionaries with the triumph of the Popular Front in France under Socialist leader Léon Blum in May 1936. The new government appointed Marius Moutet a "relatively sympathetic" minister of colonies, and he in turn directed the new governor-general of Indochina, Jules Brevie, who arrived in January 1937, to institute various reforms. These included the eight-hour working day and, most importantly for the Communists, the release of political prisoners, who were reduced in number from 10,000 to 3,000 by early 1937; and those released included most of the present leadership of Vietnam. Most released prisoners, however, had to be carefully screened for fear they had become double agents, and one Communist source in 1934 charged that only one in one hundred former prisoners could still be trusted.

Many Vietnamese Communists, understandably, were not happy with the new orders to tone down the struggle against arch-enemy France in the interests of the struggle against more distant Fascists, all the more so as, still in 1937, even the French Communist Party, while agitating against colonial abuses, favored a union of the colony with France, and not the outright independence demanded by all Vietnamese radicals. The Comintern and Party leaders, however, would insist on the execution of the new line. Le Hong Phong, who had been elected an alternate member of the Comintern Executive Committee at the Seventh World Congress, had returned to Vietnam to "directly lead the revolutionary movement together with the Central Committee" in effecting the necessary changes of policy. To this end, in July 1936, he convened the First Plenum of the 1935 Central Committee, and other plenums were held in mid-1937 and 1938, in part to criticize the "sectarianism" of those who hesitated to cooperate with the Popular Front. At the urging of Moscow, the Party also stepped up criticism of Vietnamese Trotskyists.

The proposal by the Blum government for a commission to study conditions in the French colonies gave the Party its first concrete opportunity to try to widen the United Front. Emulating the French colonies in Africa and spurred by the proposals of radical journalist Nguyen An Ninh, the Party in mid- and late 1936 proposed the creation of an Indochinese Congress that, in the tradition of French history, would send complaints and proposals (*cahiers générales des voeux*) to the Colonial Commission. The Party proceeded to organize some 600 "action committees" toward this end, and also claimed to lead over one-half of the 420,000 workers who staged 400 strikes as well as the 50,000 peasants who carried out 250 incidents between mid-1936 and mid-1937.

In short, the Communists continued effective work with the masses in this "second upsurge" of the Vietnamese Revolution, but their efforts to broaden the Indochinese Democratic Front to work for an Indochina Congress and for more effective resistance to Japan soon foundered. In the first place, the Blum government never sent a colonial commission to Indochina, only its minister of labor, Justin Godard, who was duly greeted with widespread demonstrations on his arrival in early 1937. More significantly for the Communists, efforts to achieve cooperation with such men as the Constitutionalist Party leader, Nguyen Phan Long, led to the breakdown of some old alliances as well as to the formation of new ones. The Trotskyists further divided among themselves but generally attacked the treason of Communist wooing of bourgeois enemies, while moderate nationalists for the most part refused Communist overtures. Moreover, the Blum government soon developed second thoughts about its policies in response to increased French political opposition. In May 1937, authorities in Saigon closed down the journal *La Lutte*, already torn by dissension between Stalinists, Trotskyists, and nationalists, and stepped up the arrest of radical leaders.

During these years, however, and before renewed French crackdowns after September 1939, the Communists made important progress, especially in United Front and propaganda work. Following lines laid down by the French Socialist Party for the Popular Front against Hitler, for example, Vietnamese Communists affiliated with branches of the French Socialist Party in attempts to influence colonial policies. These were the *Fédération Socialiste du Cochinchine* in the South and the *Fédération Socialiste du Nord Indochine*, the latter group claiming some 500 members in nine groups as far south as Tourane (Da Nang). In addition to the election campaigns after 1933 in Saigon, after 1936 Communists participated in elections for the "chambers of representatives of the people" in the center and north of the country, as well as for other advisory bodies in various locations. And where before 1936, May Day rallies generally could only be held in the south, on May 1,

1938, Communist agitators supposedly turned out over 20,000 demonstrators in Hanoi.

Nonetheless, in the 1930s, in contrast to the situation later, communism remained far stronger in the south than in the north of the country. Thus the journal *Le Travail* (Work), published in Hanoi, on September 16, 1936, praised the example of our "comrades in Cochin China" and appealed for "their support of our struggle. . . ." As late as late 1954, a French journalist could still write, "the Viet Minh here (in the south) is much stronger than in the North, for it lives completely among the people, while in Tonkin there is a certain divorce between the people, the army and the Party."[5]

In Tonkin, before 1945 in fact, French oppression was much stronger. In late 1930, French police estimated that only 146 Party members remained active in Tonkin, 58 having been arrested and 258 "frightened" into leaving the movement by "fear or repression." In 1931, they claimed that Communist activists had been eliminated from all but fourteen districts of the north, and in February 1936 the arrested chief of the Tonkin Party Committee, a woman named Hoang Dinh Giang, admitted to her captors that the Party in her region had been virtually wiped out. Then, however, following the arrival in Tonkin of some thousand Communists released from prison in 1936, radical activity in the region picked up, all the more dramatically in view of the Party's recent difficulties.

As WE HAVE SEEN, a reason for Communist strength in Saigon and other areas of the south, paradoxically, was that they were able to use the protections provided by a more direct application of French law to build a sort of legal Communism through their participation in local elections after 1933 and in publication of *La Lutte* and other journals. Therefore, the late 1936 movement for an Indochina Congress and other such efforts also were stronger in the south, even though the location of Cao Dai and after 1939 Hoa Hao religious organizations there dictated special techniques of United Front work. Hence the Party in the south in the early 1930s to some extent pioneered the techniques, not only of underground clandestine work, but of legal propaganda and United Front Work. When the possibility of such legal work was extended throughout the country, thanks to the victory of the Popular Front in France in

1936, Communist opportunities greatly increased. As a 1971 Party history explained:

> The fact that the Party could use legal forms of activities, including . . . representative assemblies and regional councils, constituted a great victory for Communists in a colonial and semi-feudal country like ours where there were more prisons than schools, where the people enjoyed no democratic freedoms. . . . Our Party achieved another great success in carrying out the struggle for democratic freedoms [and] improvement of living conditions. The mobilization and education of the masses, who became a "popular political army" comprising millions of people in the cities and in the countryside, brought about an extensive political movement during which a host of cadres were trained for revolutionary activities in our country.[6]

On the other hand, it was in the north that most of the work so important in view of later developments took place, with some of the close to fifty minorities who made up about 15 percent of the Vietnamese population. As early as 1926, Youth League activists had begun propaganda among the Thai-speaking minorities of northern provinces contiguous to China, and there was considerable radical activity there in 1929 and 1930. The Party stepped up such work after 1932 and in that year its *Action Program*, published in December, elaborated on earlier statements of support for the struggles of the minorities against the French and their Vietnamese allies. The French Sûreté noted the dangerous significance for them of the fact that some Thai-speaking Nung and Tho peoples were beginning by 1934 to join Communist-organized farmers' and workers' unions, and such organizations soon spread to the Yao and Meo peoples living at higher altitudes. A Tho leader, probably Hoang Van Thu, was elected to Party Central Committee in March 1935.

In propaganda, the authorization for the first time after 1936 of radical publications in Vietnamese of course immediately greatly enlarged the Communist audience. A list of some of the titles will hint at their content. They included: the Party's official journal, *Dan Chung* (The Masses) and *Le Peuple* in Saigon; *Dan* (The People), *Khoa Hoc Kach* (The Science of Revolution) and *Dan Ngheo* (The Proletarian) in Annam; and *Tin Tuc* (The News), *Hon Tre* (Soul of Youth), and *Le Travail* in the north. By the early 1940s the stress on nationalism became even more apparent with titles such as *Cuu Quoc* (National Salvation), *Hou Nuoc* (Soul of the Country) as well as *Gia Phong* (Liberation), *Lao Dong* (Labor), *Notre Voix* (Our Voice), and *Tien Phong* (Avant-Garde).

Working on these journals, as well as in other radical activities, in the north and center of the country were four younger but later famous Party leaders. They were Pham Van Dong, Troung Chinh, and Vo Nguyen Giap in Tonkin and Le Duan in Annam, all of whom had spent long and bitter years in prison in the aftermath of the 1930–1931 uprisings. The present premier of Vietnam, Pham Van Dong, for example, emerged from seven years on Poulo Condor to make his way to the north sometime in 1936. Born thirty years previously, March 1, 1906, of mandarin parents in Quang Ngai province on the south-central coast, Dong studied in Hue at the same French lycée as had Ho Chi Minh fifteen years earlier. His father served as a minister of the Emperor Duy Tan and then briefly as head of the National Academy in that city until 1917, when the French temporarily closed the academy for "subversive activities." A few years later the young Dong initiated his own long career of radical politics, organizing student strikes and demonstrations until arrested by the French. On this occasion, soon released, he made his way to Canton, about 1926 where he became one of the first to join Ho Chi Minh's Revolutionary Youth League and participated in a class of the famous Whampoa Military Academy. Returning to Vietnam, he organized underground labor unions and became a member of the Executive Committee of the Youth League before being arrested once more in 1929.

Truong Chinh, who became known as the Party's leading theoretician, is perhaps the most northern of the top Communist leaders, by temperament and by birth. He was born in 1909 of schoolteacher parents in Hanh Thien in the Red River Delta province of Nan Dinh and joined the Youth League and its activities in that region in 1928. Expelled from school, he transferred to and received his baccalaureate from the Lycee Albert Sarrault in Hanoi, the most prestigious French school in the country. Subsequently he continued his studies and also earned a living in the region as a teacher, as did both Pham Van Dong and Giap. Arrested in November 1930, in the wake of the uprisings of 1930–1931, Truong Chinh spent most of the next six years in Son La prison. Then, reappearing in Hanoi, he became a leading Party journalist and editor, using the pseudonym Qua Ninh, during the late 1930s. After a brief rearrest in 1939, he showed up in South China, and there was elected Party secretary-general in November 1940. Apart from Ho Chi Minh in exile and Tran Van Giao in Saigon, neither of whom served as secretary-general, Truong Chinh was virtually the first nominal leader in the Party's first decade to escape arrest and execution, the fate of predecessors, Ngo Gia Tu, Tran Phu (secretary-general, 1930–1931), Le Hong Phong (secretary-general, 1934–1938), Nguyen Van Cu (secretary-general, 1939) and Ha Huy Tap (secretary-general, 1940).

Of all Vietnamese leaders after Ho Chi Minh and Pham Van Dong, the one who probably contributed most impressively to the success of the Communist movement was Vo Nguyen Giap. Certainly, as leader of the incredible military victories over the French and then the Americans, Giap, long Vietnam's minister of defense, is the most famous. But Giap was far more than a general and, according to writers who have interviewed him, was, with Ho, the most impressive personality of the movement. Born of a literate peasant father just north of the seventeenth parallel in Quang Binh province, he became a brilliant student after 1923 at the National Academy, Quoc Hoc in Hue, the same school attended by both Ho Chi Minh and Ngo Dinh Diem, as well as by Pham Van Dong. There he took part in student strikes in the turbulent years 1925–1926, and joined first the revolutionary organization Tan Viet, and in 1930 the Party.

In 1930, Giap also was arrested in the wave of crackdowns accompanying the insurrection of that year, but was released well before the expiration of his three-year term. He made his way to Hanoi for further studies and graduated from the Lycée Albert Sarrault a few years after Truong Chinh. While teaching at a private school, he continued his studies at the university there and received a degree in law in 1937. As had Mao Tse-Tung a decade and a half earlier in China, he married a daughter* of a favorite professor and taught history at a private school where, among other Communists, Le Duc Tho was a student. Increasingly Giap became known as a principal contributor to the leftist journals that began to appear in Hanoi, especially after 1936, although until 1945 he was known by his pseudonym Van Dinh.[7] In 1937, together with Truong Chinh, Giap coauthored a work that would become a basic text for Vietnamese Communist work with the peasants, *The Peasant Question*, and as such will be discussed again in Chapter Six.

---

*Nguyen Thi Minh Giang, who also was a Communist and the sister of another Communist, Nguyen Thi Minh Khai, who married Le Hong Phong. Both women would die in the White Terror of the early 1940s, as had Mao's wife and sister, a decade earlier in China.

In Annam (Central Vietnam) French police complained of a revival of Communist activity in 1933 and 1934 and of a further acceleration of that growth after the 1936 prison releases. Le Duan, the future Party leader, for whom some information was given in the preceding chapter, played a key role in the later step-up of radical activities in Annam. In 1936 on his release from six years on Poulo Condor, he opened a bookstore in Hue that served as a principal outlet of Party propaganda. The following year he became secretary of the Party's Trung Bo (Central Vietnam Committee) and, prior to his rearrest in 1940, led a considerable expansion of Party work in the region. Both Le Duan's native province of Quang Tri, just north of Hue, and even more so Pham Van Dong's native Quang Ngai to its south, became centers of the next stage of Communist activity in the early 1940s.

The gains of the Communists in the "second upsurge" (from 1936 to 1939) in all regions of the country, predictably, could not be maintained. It was probably true, as the Party claimed in January 1938, that they had become "the strongest, best disciplined and most faithful defender of the peoples of Indochina." Even the French Sûreté admitted about the same time that only the Communists were "dynamic enough to lead large numbers of the masses" and that there was a general upsurge of spontaneous rebellious activity across the country after 1936. According to the French, the Party had over 2,000 members and 40,000 followers by the end of the decade.

But in view of the strains caused by the politics of the Popular Front and especially by the steady march toward World War II, a renewed crackdown by authorities was inevitable. It came in stages as with the closing of *La Lutte* in June 1937, in Saigon, and of *Tin Tuc* in Hanoi in September 1938. Then after Hitler's invasion of Poland in September 1939, the French outlawed the Party the following month and soon arrested about two thousand alleged Communists, including a little later one-time Party Secretary-Generals Le Hong Phong, Nguyen Van Cu, and Ha Huy Tap, as well as the two sisters who became wives of Le Hong Phong and Vo Nguyen Giap. All of these died in prison, while Le Duan, also arrested about this time, was only one of fifteen survivors out of one hundred prisoners in his section at Poulo Condor, from 1940 to 1945. Pham Van Dong, Vo Nhuyen Giap, and Truong Chinh had better luck, making their way to South China where, with Ho Chi Minh after the spring of 1940, they would change the course of history.[8]

In a sense, the struggle of the Communists by the end of the 1930s had come full circle. The revolutionary upsurge of 1930–1931 had been followed by a transitional period from 1932 to 1936, characterized by the activities of *La Lutte* in Saigon and underground rebuilding of the Party throughout the country and abroad in close coordination with Moscow. Then, during the period of the Indochina Democratic Front from 1936 to 1939, the Party had been able to undertake semilegal activities to try to win over sections of the Vietnamese elite while continuing largely clandestine activities among the masses, but this in turn was followed by a new retreat to an underground illegal existence after 1939. As the momentous changes in world politics forced the switch from radical to moderate politics in 1936, so the outbreak of full-scale war in the late 1930s ended the temporary Popular Fronts in Vietnam as elsewhere. By 1938, the Blum ministries had given way to that headed by Edouard Daladier in France, and the following year Stalin carried out the most startling of all diplomatic revolutions, alliance with Hitler in August 1939, an abnormal situation that ended in turn with Hitler's invasion of Russia in June 1941. Before that, Hitler had forced France's capitulation and the creation of the collaborationist Vichy government.

But, in Asia it was Japan that forced the shape of politics. Following its full-scale invasion of most of China after July 1937, and the continued resistence of nationalists and Communists in western areas of China, Japan decided to step up pressure on Indochina to the south, both to close off a principal route of supply for anti-Japanese forces in China and to procure resources for Japan's Greater East Asia Co-Prosperity Sphere. By September 1940, three months after Hitler's overrunning of France, Japan had also forced the Vichy government to allow the stationing of Japanese troops in Indochina, and a year later, U.S. protests against such ever-increasing Japanese actions led to the Pearl Harbor attack of December 7, 1941, and the American entry into the war. For the Communists of Vietnam, these developments led to what they called the "double yoke," not only of French colonialism, but of Japanese imperialist militarism. Yet World War II also opened the way to the first Communist conquest of power in Vietnam, in August 1945.

CHAPTER FOUR

The First Communist Victory

THE COMMUNISTS OF VIETNAM first established sustained bases of power in the northern part of their country in the midst of the Second World War. As in Russia before 1917 and China before 1949, the worsening of general conditions helped the revolutionaries.

Why? Because in these three greatest revolutions of the century, war further inflamed long-simmering revolts and at the same time greatly weakened the old order, thereby intensifying the revolutions involved. It was not so much a question of the Communists carrying out the "politics of the bad,"* hoping that would increase their chances, as that only the Communists in this century have seemed consistently able to organize effectively enough to turn terrible situations to their advantage. In Russia in World War I, and in China, Vietnam, and notably also in Yugoslavia in World War II, the Communists organized all the more effectively precisely because of extreme conditions, while other groups showed inability to act until conditions and security improved. And by then it was too late for the Communists to be stopped.

So it was in Vietnam, after the Japanese partially moved into the country in 1940 in the wake of their takeover of most of China after mid-1937, which precipitated the wider war the following

*In fact, such an approach usually backfired, perhaps most notoriously when the Comintern Executive Committee declared, three months after Hitler's seizure of power in early 1933, "the establishment of an undisguised fascist dictatorship . . . accelerates Germany's march towards Revolution."

year. On the one hand, Japan fatally weakened the French enemies of the Communists, while simultaneously strengthening nationalist beliefs in the possibility of defeating Europeans. And on the other hand, the Communists used lessons learned in the bitter history of Vietnam, as well as from the Chinese and Russian revolutions, to forge what proved to be an unstoppable force.

In 1945 they used their organization and the double opportunity provided, first by Japan's complete expulsion of the French in March, and then by the subsequent defeat of Japan in August, to create the first national Communist government in the history of Asia, some four years before that of China. Those events, which would become known as "the August Revolution," were signaled five years earlier by the largest uprisings since the Nghe Tinh soviet movement of 1930–1931, and it is therefore with the revolts of 1940 that this chapter commences.

THE FIRST OF THE 1940 REVOLTS was triggered by the Japanese defeat of the French garrison of Lang Son province on the Chinese border. Faced by French opposition to Japanese demands since June 1940 to close off supplies to Chiang Kai-shek's China and secure the stationing of their troops in Indochina, in September the Japanese decided to administer "a lesson" to the French by invading the northern border area known to the Communists as the Viet Bac. On the twenty-second, striking together with a few Japanese-sponsored Vietnamese nationalists (mostly members of Prince Cuong De's Phuc Cuoc or Restorationist Society) the Japanese quickly routed the French garrisons in the area. But their action set off an uprising of the Tho-ti and Nung minorities, who immediately seized several areas of Bac Son district, southwest of Lang Son.

Then by September 27, local Communists of both minority and Vietnamese origin used their superior organization to take the lead of the spontaneous Bac Son uprising. But they did so without the knowledge of higher Party authorities. The first Communist leader in the area, the Tho, Hoang Van Thu, who had set up Party cells in Bac Son in 1933, was with the Party Central Committee near Hanoi at this time, and local Regional Secretary Chu Van Tan, a Nung, left Bac Son immediately to consult with Thu and the Central Committee. Meanwhile the French absorbing their lesson, quickly agreed to the demand for the stationing of Japanese troops in Indochina, and with Japanese cooperation proceeded to suppress the uprising by mid-October, 1940.

The Communist leadership, as ten years before, faced a dilemma as well as benefits with the conditions arising from the uprisings and their suppression. In November 1939, meeting in Gia Dinh just outside Saigon, under the leadership of Secretary-General Nguyen Van Cu, the Party's Sixth Plenum of the 1935 Central Committee called for a more militant "anti-Imperialist National United Front," and for greater attention to the peasants, as well as for the preparation of armed uprisings to take advantage of the world crisis. But it also agonized over how many risks the newly endangered Party might properly take. Then, in 1940, with the arrival of Ho Chi Minh in the Chinese-Vietnamese border area, the Bac Son uprising of September, and the general development of the war, the Party decided on what proved the decisive move to establish a more permanent revolutionary base in the Viet Bac area. From there, sanctuary could be sought across the border in China, and the Party could exploit contradictions and border limitations between China, Japan, and the French. And to go along with the formation of the Viet Bac base area, the Party leadership decided to form, from the survivors of the Bac Son uprising, the first units of what would become the formidable Vietnamese Communist armed forces.

In addition to Ho Chi Minh, Pham Van Dong, and to Giap, who would soon take over overall leadership of the military effort, three other men played especially important roles in carrying out the decisions to form the base area and military units. They were the Tho minority leader, Hoang Van Thu, and the other top Party minority leader, Chu Van Tan, a Nung, who was sent back to Bac Son to form a military unit out of one group of twenty-four survivors. The third was Phung Chi Kien, born in Nghe An in 1905 and especially important in liaison work between the Vietnamese and Chinese Communist Parties. Arriving from South China, Kien developed a second armed group in the area, and in February 1941 the two groups became known as the National Salvation Army. Kien was killed in a French ambush in July of that year, but Chu Van Tan slowly built his forces and became the principal military assistant of Giap in the early 1940s. Hoang Van Thu also soon returned to his native area, charged with setting up a guerilla base area with the Bac Son-Vo Nhai region as the center, until he was captured in 1943 and killed by the French the following year.[1]

While these events were taking place in the north, an at first more imposing rebellion than that of Bac Son broke out far to the south in November 1940. But it was repressed with greater ferocity and posed additional political problems for the Party. Following the Sixth Plenum's call in the autumn of 1939 for "the creation of conditions for violent action and national liberation revolution," and a renewed call in July 1940 for "armed insurrection," activists in the south decided to strike. They included comrades of Nguyen Thi Dinh, then herself recently jailed.

They sought to take advantage of a temporary vacuum of power caused by the French sending of troops into Cambodia to meet the threat of Japanese ally Thailand's expansion eastward against Cambodia and Vietnam, which actually came in January 1941. Some government militia sent to fight the Thai, rallied to the Communists, and the Party claimed the support of up to one-third of the population of Cochin China. But the Party's Seventh Plenum meeting in early November 1940 near Hanoi, judged that in view of the suppression of the Bac Son revolt and other factors, conditions for general revolution were still unfavorable, and the uprising should be postponed. The delegate from Cochin China was to hurry south to see to that, but was arrested on the way, in Saigon, and the uprising therefore took place as scheduled, on November 23.

There were attacks for about a month on local authorities in the Saigon area and in eight provinces of the south, where at the time there were said to be up to 3,000 active Communists who organized some 15,000 others for the uprising. In My Tho province, 54 of 100 communes took part in the uprising, and Soc Trang and Bac Lieu further south were seized, with other revolutionary activities in Tan An, Vinh Long, and Can Tho, highways blocked, and several dozen "reactionaries" killed. For the first time, revolutionaries used what became the Communist national flag, a yellow star on a red field. The French, however, apparently again forewarned by informers, were able to strike back hard, despite the diversion caused by the threat from Thailand. They arrested more than 6,000 about this time, including Party leaders Ha Huy Tap, Nguyen Van Cu, Le Hong Phong, and Le Duan and, according to Communist sources, killed tens of thousands. The Communist movement in the south was gravely set back after the suppression of the 1940 uprising, an upsurge of the Hoa Hao movement taking advantage of the new situation. Surviving Communists then purged their own ranks, condemning several to death on the accusation of being double agents. Much later, on the seventeenth anniversary of the uprising, the former chairman of the Viet Minh Committee of the south,

Tran Van Giau, cited the November 1940 example as a warning to militants to bide their time against Diem's repressions, lest a premature uprising in the south be crushed in 1957 as in 1940.

On January 13, 1941, there was a soldier's mutiny at Do Luong near Vinh, Nghe An province, somewhat reminiscent of the Yen Bay revolt of February 1930. Despite its even quicker suppression and the lack of popular or Communist participation, the Party's *History of the August Revolution* listed it, together with the Bac Son and Delta uprisings, as the "first shots heralding the general insurrection and the beginning of an armed struggle of the Indochinese people."[2]

THE REAL BREAKTHROUGH of the Party, however, came in the northern areas of Vietnam, and in neighboring China. And it was Ho Chi Minh who once more, after a ten-year absence, would play the key role in many developments, and continue to do so until his death in 1969.

Following five years in Moscow, Ho arrived in the Chinese Communist capital of Yenan, northwest China, late in 1938, and after some months in Guiyang, Guilin, and elsewhere in southwest China, arrived in Kunming, Yunnan, north of Vietnam, in early 1940. There, and in nearby Guilin, Liuzhou, Nanguang, Longzhou, and especially at Jingxi, China, and at Pac Bo, Vietnam, just across the border, Ho, Pham Van Dong, Vo Nguyen Giap, Phung Chi Kien, and some forty Communists in all worked out the organizations and programs that would enable the Party to seize power for the first time five years later. Where the returned students who dominated Party leadership in the 1930s had criticized Ho's "excessive" nationalism, the 1935 change in the line of the Communist International to call for wider United Fronts against fascism, and the triumphs of the Popular Front in 1936 in France, facilitated Ho's return to Party leadership. The many Communists recently released from prison and surviving returned students now recognized the need for the greater flexibility provided by Ho's "Marxist nationalism." And with the Party again very much on the run with the renewed crackdowns after 1939, there was increasing recognition of the need for more experienced leadership. Two other skills of Ho also were much in demand. First of all, his language skills enabled him to deal more easily with Chinese authorities, and also to translate Maoist works on Party and army building into Vietnamese. In the spring of 1941, Ho even wrote a widely circulated letter on the new program of the Party in Chinese characters, which reportedly greatly impressed more traditional-minded Chinese.

Still more important was Ho's diplomatic genius, which not only neutralized as much as possible the foreign enemies of the Vietnamese Communists but, equally important, enabled the widest possible United Front among contending Vietnamese groups for the Communist revolution. Indeed, if the development by other Communist leaders of effective political and military organization provided the essentials of Communist power in Vietnam itself, it was Ho Chi Minh's diplomatic skills that as far as possible protected and advanced that power. At this time, Ho's work promoted the cause, both by working out deals with Chinese Nationalist generals enabling greater room for maneuver by Vietnamese Communists on both sides of the border, and by working with, and then outmaneuvering other groups of Vietnamese nationalists.

Both aspects were revealed already in the setting up of the Vietnam Liberation League among several hundred Vietnamese nationalists in the Chinese border town of Jingxi in late 1940 and early 1941. Dominated by Ho, Dong, Giap, and others, the League nominally was headed by a Nationalist (VNQDD) and included representatives of what would become in October 1942 the Revolutionary League, or Dong Ming Hoi, and other nationalist groups. It wooed the Chinese by pledging to unite with them on the basis of Sun Yat-sen's *Three Principles of the People* (which Ho Chi Minh translated in 1943 into Vietnamese), and to fight Japan and France "on an equal footing and in a spirit of mutual assistance." The Communists, however, quickly proceeded to eliminate more rightist members of the group, all the while utilizing the group's good offices with Chinese generals Zhang Fakuei, Li Jishen and others to organize training classes to build up their forces. In January 1942, Chinese authorities, increasingly worried by their own struggle with the Communists and angry at Communist propaganda, closed down the Liberation League. But the Communists had made a good beginning at winning over other nationalists and at training further their own elite. Furthermore, most of their activities were able to continue and even accelerate at Jingxi and elsewhere.

Going hand in hand with this building of their forces in China under cover of collaboration with the war effort of Chiang Kai-shek went further organizational efforts among Vietnamese and minority populations in the border area. From the winter of 1940, from shifting headquarters around Pac Bo, Cao Bang province, Ho Chi Minh and his followers, notably Vo Nguyen Giap, organized "national salvation associations" among workers, peasants, youth, and women, now backed by the fledgling National Salvation Army under Phung Chi Kien and Chu Van Tan. The "mass line," much discussed since the late 1920s, and already attempted wherever possible, now enabled the Communist "take-off" of the 1940s.

Effective mass organization work always required close contacts with local people in order first to win their confidence, then to learn intelligence about their region, develop sources of supplies, and above all to recruit and organize activist youth. At this time Ho Chi Minh also developed his version of Mao Zedong's "three major disciplines" and "eight point rules" for the behavior of Communist activists and military personnel. Ho's "four recommendations" were to help with daily work, learn local customs, and languages, and to show correct attitudes and discipline, while his "five interdictions" were to prevent damage, forced requisitions, breaking of promises, violation of local customs, and the divulging of secrets.

Activists gave great attention to mastering minority languages as well as Chinese, the lingua franca of the area. Giap, for example, sought to learn Tho and two other local languages. And as Mao Zedong also was stressing at this time, and as Ho Chi Minh had been advocating since the 1920s, the Vietnamese Communists emphasized simplicity of style and explanation in order to communicate better with local people. The position of such minority leaders as the Nung military leader, Chu Van Tan, and the Tho, Hoang Van Thu, who became the Party regional secretary for the northern provinces prior to his arrest in 1943, obviously greatly facilitated work among the minorities in an area where the use of Vietnamese, especially the accent of Central Vietnam, led to immediate suspicion. The fact that the Communists succeeded brilliantly in this work is shown by the striking fact that by the end of the war against France, up to 5 percent of the Tho population made up about 20 percent of Communist regular armed forces.[3]

AS THIS ILLEGAL AND LARGELY CLANDESTINE WORK of organizing political and military activists proceeded within Vietnam, the semilegal work, partly allowed by local Chinese authorities, to broaden the United Front among all Vietnamese who would join the liberation struggle, took on ever more importance. Ho and other leaders believed, correctly as it turned out, that recent developments had created still more favorable conditions than had existed in 1936 for the formation of a truly Popular Front, directed now against both France and Japan, and led by themselves. Indeed, because of the special problems faced by the Party in Vietnam itself, it became absolutely necessary to Communist survival, let alone victory, that the core leadership develop a strategy, not only for organizing the masses, but for manipulating what Marxists would call the "superstructure," that is, elite non-Communist nationalist groups, and where possible French, Japanese, and Chinese leaders. After all, the fiercely effective suppression of Communists by French and Japanese police, especially in the cities, forced activists to concentrate their in-country work in an area of the far north inhabited by only about a million people, four-fifths of whom were minority peoples. For example, the Party's Hanoi Committee was broken up five times between 1940 and 1945, and the real take-off of work in the more populous areas of the lowland coastal plains, though based on principles already learned in earlier struggles and Marxist studies, would have to come after 1945, then to the stupefaction of France and the United States. But now in the 1940s, the trick was for the remaining leadership to survive and to develop new bases of operation, both in northernmost Vietnam and in southern China. This they did with a vengeance, and the master stroke was the creation of the organizational vehicle, the Viet Minh, which would go on to unite what proved an unstoppable combination of Vietnamese nationalism and communism.

The first step was taken at the Eighth Plenum of the Party, held at Pac Bo village, Cao Bang province, beginning on May 10, 1941. There, joined by Truong Chinh, who became secretary-general, Hoang Van Thu, Hoang Quoc Viet, Phung Chi Kien, and four others,* Ho Chi Minh proclaimed the founding of the Vietnam Doc Lap Dong Minh, or as it universally came to stand for the entire movement, the Viet Minh. A resolution of the conference made unmistakably clear the priority of nationalism and the consequent possibility and necessity of the unification of all groups for the "survival of the nation and race":

> The problem of class struggle will continue to exist. But in the present stage, nation is above all; thus all demands of Party which would

*Pham Van Dong and Vo Nguyen Giap arrived from China just afterwards.

> be beneficial to a particular class but would be harmful to the nation should be postponed . . . [Therefore, even] landlords, rich peasants, native bourgeoisie . . . with the exception of a few running dogs who flatter and fawn on the Japanese enemy . . . [can] become the reserve army of the revolution. . . .[4]

Accordingly, and most importantly, land reform was scaled down to include confiscation only of the land of "traitors," together with calls for the reduction of rents and interest. As Ho Chi Minh would put it several weeks later in his celebrated "Letter from Abroad" of June 6, 1941:

> National salvation is the common cause of our entire people. Every Vietnamese must take part in it. He who has money will contribute his money, he who has strength will contribute his strength, he who has talent will contribute his talent. . . .
>
> The hour has struck. Raise aloft the banner of insurrection and lead the people throughout the country to overthrow the Japanese and the French. The sacred call of the fatherland is resounding in our ears, the ardent blood of our heroic predecessors is seething in our hearts. The fighting spirit of the people is mounting before our eyes. Let us unite and unify our action to overthrow the Japanese and the French. The Vietnamese revolution will certainly triumph. The world revolution will certainly triumph.

The plenum also stressed anew the need for armed insurrection and the importance of harnessing peasant discontent. According to William Duiker, the instructions of the Pac Bo meeting thereby "turned guerrilla warfare into an integral element of [Communist] revolutionary strategy," with its stress on the formation of National Salvation Associations and self-defense units, and amounted to "final abandonment of the lingering reliance on the Bolshevik model" of revolution.[5]

Yet, not only the Communists were wooing Vietnamese nationalists. The Japanese and their secret police, the Kempetei, actively sought to recruit Vietnamese who might be useful to them. This was the moment when logically Japan might have set up a pliable government under Prince Cuong De, the descendant of the founder of the Nguyen dynasty who Phan Boi Chau had fostered from Tokyo after 1905 as a potential leader of a reformist dynasty. But the Japanese evidently preferred to continue to play a double game, weakening but not entirely replacing France. Accordingly, Japan continued to keep Cuong De in the wings while encouraging the growth of his Phuc Quoc (Restorationist Society) and of various more or less pro-Japanese groups making up the party known as the Dai Viet. They also wooed other non-Communist nationalists, including Ngo Dinh Diem and members of the Constitutionalist Party before settling on an amenable professor, Tran Trong Kiem, to head the brief Japanese-sponsored government from March to August 1945.

More importantly, in the early 1940s, the Japanese worked with the religious sects, the Cao Dai and Hoa Hao, to try to build up their popularity. The French, in their general crackdown following the outbreak of war, tried to break both groups, closing Cao Dai temples in 1940, exiling its leaders the following year, and in August 1940 sending Huynh Phu So, who had founded the Hoa Hao in 1939, to a psychiatric hospital. The Japanese, however, intervened to enable the Cao Dai to rebuild their forces in Tay Ninh and simultaneously gave protection to the Huynh Phu So of the Hoa Hao, who became known as the "mad bonze" after converting his hospital psychiatrist to the faith. Released in May 1941, the Hoa Hao prophet continued his mission until assassinated, apparently by Communists, in April 1947.[6]

Most Vietnamese quite correctly distrusted the Japanese, who among other things were expropriating increasing quantities of rice from the country—585,000 tons in 1941, 1,023,000 tons in 1943, and 900,000 tons in 1944. By the latter year, the most terrible famine in Vietnamese history was raging in the north and would cost over one million lives. Given such conditions, increasing numbers of Vietnamese nationalists made their way to China, rejoining or joining the Nationalist Party (VNQDD) and the newly founded Dong Ming Hoi (Revolutionary League). Increasing numbers of others also joined the French bureaucracy, as the Vichy government belatedly recognizing the weakness of its position in Indochina, doubled the number of Vietnamese able to work in the government bureaucracy, and began to reduce the number of French civil servants. For the first time significant numbers of Vietnamese became province chiefs, and their salaries rose to near equality with those of the French. This was a great change, since previously it was said that a French sargeant earned more than a Vietnamese general, and that a French doorkeeper at the University of Indochina earned three times the salary of a Vietnamese professor. After mid-1940, the new governor-general, Jean Decoux, also initiated an expansion of the little education available to the population and an ambitious youth and sports program. But, ironically, Communists rapidly infiltrated the French-sponsored youth and sports programs, while most Vietnamese realized that the reforms were not fundamental, and that in any case other government policies further exacerbated the extremely severe conditions.[7]

Accordingly, most of these developments played into the hands of the Communists, who were able to expand, though with continuing difficulties, the power of the Viet Minh Front. In 1943, a new Democratic Party was founded among the "national bourgeoisie" to join the Viet Minh, while the Communists' "new culture" program won adherents among intellectuals. This involved further infiltration and organization of the youth programs above all in the south, and in the north, a variety of literary and reform movements for land, legal, and tax systems. Above all, in the coastal lowlands, Communists led and profited from the struggle to organize the peasantry to deal with the developing famine, organizing seizures of government rice storages, and in places distributing sweet potatoes, seeds, and cloth.

The greatest progress of the Party, however, came in the building of core organizations in three areas of North Vietnam and in southernmost China. The Central Committee itself, under Secretary-General Truong Chinh, Hoang Quoc Viet, and others, continued to try to work as close to Hanoi as possible despite continuing arrests, as of Hoang Van Thu in 1943. In the northern mountains, two bases were developed that became the core area from which Viet Minh power would expand.

The first was the Bac Son-Vu Nhai area of Bac Can (or Bac Thai) province. It was almost eliminated by the French in pacification sweeps in 1941, and in July of that year Phung Chi Kien was killed in an ambush. Co-leader Chu Van Tan was forced to take surviving troops to China in 1942, but these returned in the winter of 1942–1943 and resumed a more organized expansion. The other northern base was in Cao Bang province, about fifty miles further north, right on the Chinese border. There, from shifting headquarters around Pac Bo, a mile or so inside Vietnam, Ho Chi Minh, Pham Van Dong, Vo Nguyen Giap, and others put out the journal *Viet Lap* (Independent Vietnam), developed training courses for Communist activists, and by late 1941 controlled about one-third of the province. By 1943, together with Chu Van Tan's forces to the south, they succeeded in linking the two areas of the Cao Bang and the Bac Son base areas and also in expanding further southward into the Thai Nguyen area, eastward into Lang Son, and establishing

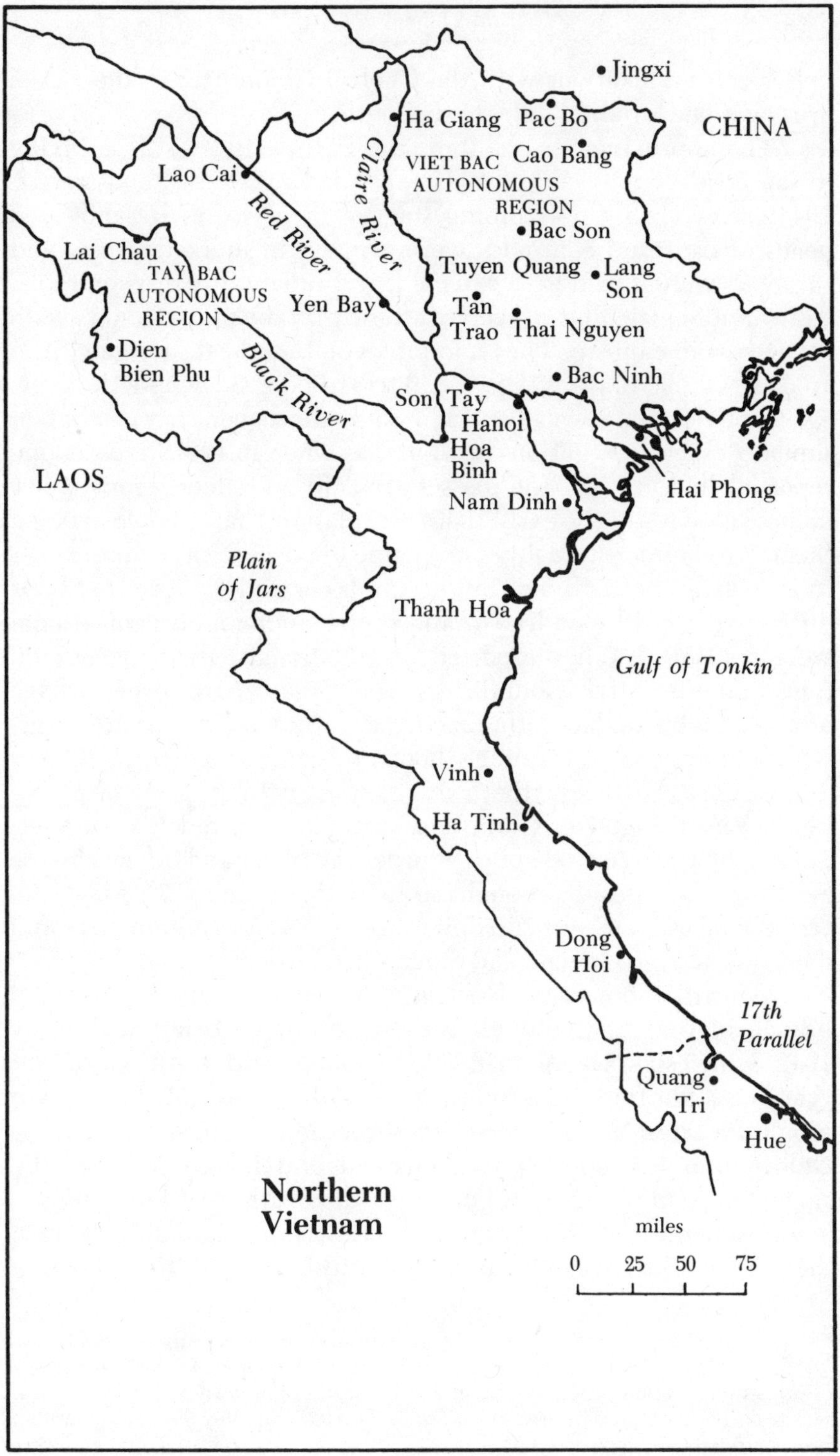

Jingxi
Ha Giang
Pac Bo
CHINA
Cao Bang
VIET BAC
AUTONOMOUS
REGION
Lao Cai
Red River
Claire River
Bac Son
Lai Chau
TAY BAC
AUTONOMOUS
REGION
Tuyen Quang
Lang
Son
Yen Bay
Tan
Trao
Thai Nguyen
Dien
Bien Phu
Black River
Bac Ninh
Son Tay
Hanoi
Hoa
Binh
LAOS
Hai Phong
Nam Dinh
Plain
of Jars
Thanh Hoa
Gulf of Tonkin
Vinh
Ha Tinh
Dong
Hoi
17th
Parallel
Quang
Tri
Hue
Northern
Vietnam
miles
0 25 50 75

better communications with the Central Committee in the Hanoi area over one hundred miles to the south.

The approximately one thousand Party activists still surviving in the north by the end of 1941 expanded to several thousand by 1944, but only by overcoming staggering pressures. Decapitated heads of captured comrades were exposed in market places, and survivors were forced to live in cold, wet mountain areas, on roots, fruits, and maize, and to keep constantly on the move from cave to cave to avoid capture. They had prices on their heads ranging from 1,000 to 20,000 piastres (about $50 to $1,000 U.S., where the average annual income was less than $50). Moreover, reminiscent of similar desperate situations in China, as when in 1928 Mao Zedong reported that at first "the masses are cold and aloof," some Vietnamese activists of the early 1940s complained that "people avoided them," and understandably some came to advocate a temporary retreat to await better times. But militants correctly judged that their difficulties would soon lessen, and propaganda and organizational work continued. They reported that National Salvation Associations and Viet Minh Committees were organized in every village and gradually replaced the enemy government in various areas, while numerous new training schools and groups were formed.

Activists in the northern areas, most notably Ho Chi Minh, Pham Van Dong, and Giap, constantly kept in touch with Vietnamese on the other side of the border, at Jingxi and other Chinese localities. At times they sought security there, and with some success as well as many ups and downs, they sought to obtain arms and recognition from Chinese and other allied leaders.

Toward those ends, Ho Chi Minh had set up the Vietnam branch of the International Anti-Aggression Association in early 1942, which soon claimed 200,000 members, and in August of that year he set out for China to seek aid for his movement. But he was promptly arrested and placed in succession in prisons in Jingxi, Guilin, and Liuzhou.* Often chained and forced to wear the cangue around his neck, Ho observed the death of at least one fellow prisoner during these terrible months, and as had already been the case in 1931, was widely believed to have died himself. Only

*According to some sources, Ho had unsuccessfully disguised himself as a blind peasant, according to others as a journalist, at the time of his arrest for lack of proper papers for himself and his guide. Later, an inquirer mistook the Chinese words *shih lo* (yes, he is in prison) for *Ssu lo* (he died), thereby leading to another premature mourning of Ho Chi Minh.

several months later did Party leaders receive a message handwritten on a newspaper smuggled into Vietnam. The message also contained the poem:

> The clouds embrace the peaks, the peaks embrace the clouds,
> The river below shines like a mirror, spotless and clean.
> On the crests of the Western mountains, my heart stirs as I wander,
> Looking toward the Southern sky and dreaming of my old friends.[8]

Ho was released on September 10, 1943, paradoxically because of the incompetence and bickering between pro-Chinese and pro-Japanese factions on the part of some of his Vietnamese enemies. This came about after Chinese General Zhang Fakuei allowed the organization of the Vietnam Dong Ming Hoi in October 1942 as an umbrella group for diverse Vietnamese Nationalist organizations. But the Chinese soon became disgusted with divisions between members of the Vietnamese Nationalist, Restorationist, and other parties making up the league, and at their lack of leadership and inability to supply effective information and support for the struggle against Japan. It appeared that only the Communists could supply information from within Vietnam, and Xiao Wen, a deputy of Zhang Fakuei, succeeded in getting the support of his boss and of Chungking for the idea of making Ho Chi Minh a leader of the Dong Minh Hoi, even though that organization had sought to exclude Communists altogether. Accordingly, although his Communist background was well known—despite his change of name from Nguyen Ai Quoc to Ho Chi Minh at this time—Ho was released. In 1944 he became an active participant in the Revolutionary League, at a swoop obtaining a 50,000 Chinese dollar subsidy, and the use of the name of an important non-Communist organization. Then in the middle of the year, further impressed by Ho's "fine qualities, honest and sincere," "energetic and hardworking," and by his good knowledge of "Chinese, English and French," Chinese authorities decided to allow Ho to return to Vietnam to further anti-Japanese efforts.

IN HO'S ABSENCE from the country, his comrades had not been idle. Committee meetings in November 1942 and February 1943 both in the Highlands and in the Delta, established new Party organizations and called for the organization of village activists into what became "The People's Committees" of the August 1945 Revolution.

The French repressions of 1941 and 1943, as well as efforts to create dissent by the infiltration of so-called ABs, or anti-Bolshevik agents, disrupted but did not stop the growth of Communist political and military organization. As Chu Van Tan put it in his 1971 reminiscences:

> The task of mobilizing the people in the Bac Son region was pushed ahead and produced good results. National Salvation Associations and Viet Minh Committees were organized in every village, and gradually replaced the enemy government. The people supplied the guerillas quite adequately from all points of view and helped the revolutionary armed forces to expand continuously. Side by side with the expansion of the Army for National Salvation, self defense and combat self defense units were set up along the length and breadth of the base area. . . .[9]

A May 1944 meeting called for further "preparation of an insurrection," and at another late July and August meeting Party leaders decided the time had come to strike in the north, where "conditions are ripe for starting guerilla warfare" in Cao Bang, Bac Can, and Lang Son provinces. Ho Chi Minh, however, escorted back from Jingxi by Giap and Dong just after this, succeeded in persuading his colleagues to postpone the uprisings as premature and as incorrectly limited to the northern provinces. He called instead for further preparations: "The period of peaceful development of the revolution is over, but the time for nation-wide uprising has not come yet . . . it is time to move from political to armed struggle, but at present the former is still more important than the latter. So an appropriate form should be found . . . [to combine political and military struggle]."[10]

The new form in fact was to be a further development of the work that had been proceeding under torturous conditions since the suppression of the Bac Son uprising four years before. Most important was the Vietnam Liberation Army Propaganda Unit, formed in December 1944, under Vo Nguyen Giap. The unit's instructions spelled out the gist of Communist propaganda and tactics of the time:

> Because ours is a national resistance by the whole people we must mobilize and arm the whole people. Therefore, when concentrating our [regular] forces . . . we must maintain [also] the local armed forces . . . [and] gather their cadres for training . . . maintain liaison, and co-ordinate military operations. Considering tactics, we will ap-

> ply guerilla warfare, which consists in being secret, rapid, active, now in the east, now in the west, arriving unexpectedly and leaving unnoticed.[11]

Starting with only forty-four men, Giap's unit immediately overran two French outposts, captured weapons, and then rapidly expanded based on the principles outlined above.

Such military units, together with those formed earlier, such as that under Chu Van Tan, which by the spring of 1945 numbered some 3,000 men, backed by an ever more skilled political apparatus and diplomatic leadership, placed the Communists in a good position to profit from the decisive developments of 1945.

Oddly enough, the Communists were helped as well at this time by the United States, which as during World War I had begun to talk of backing the independence of subject countries. While the United States early in the war pleaded ignorance in order to avoid concrete actions, when for example asked by the Viet Minh to help free Ho Chi Minh from a Chinese prison, it soon came to look with favor on Vietnamese nationalism, and recommended a United Nations "trusteeship" for Indochina.

With no crystal ball to inform him of later developments, as early as December 21, 1941, Ho Chi Minh called for cooperation with Washington and Chungking, and by the end of the war, Ho reportedly manifested "unrestrained affection for all Americans." In late 1944 he sought to escort an American pilot, a Lieutenant Shaw, shot down in the northern mountains back to the U.S. Offices of Strategic Services (OSS, the forerunner of the CIA) base in Kunming, southwest China. Although that pilot and two others were able to return to their bases separately, Ho was rewarded, by being appointed OSS Agent number 19 (with the code name of Lucius), charged with sending back information from Vietnam about Japanese troop movements and general conditions. Moreover, Claire Chennault, general of the famed Flying Tigers, on March 29 asked Ho to organize a rescue and coordination team for other Americans, one of whom later praised Ho as "an awfully sweet guy." The OSS also gave Ho six 38-caliber revolvers, the first of perhaps 5,000 U.S. weapons air-dropped in 1945 to the Viet Minh for supposed use against the Japanese. Along with this ironic beginning of relations between the United States and the Vietnamese Communists, the English airlifted some supplies and exiled Vietnamese Communists into the country, and even some French officers toyed with establishing contacts with Ho's forces. In September, Ho declared "the great American Republic is a good friend of ours," and from October to February 1946, wrote at least eight letters to President Truman and his secretary of state appealing for American aid against the French, requests that Washington let drop with obvious consequences for the future.[12]

The actions of the allies in early 1945 to further contacts with the Viet Minh, of course, were precipitated by developments in the war against Japan. Even as the Americans were rolling back their forces in the Pacific, the Japanese made a final effort to finish off Chiang Kai-shek in west China with a large-scale offensive in mid-1944 that took over large new areas, including much of neighboring Guangxi.

FAR MORE DECISIVE FOR EVENTS in Vietnam was Japan's March 1945 coup d'état against the French, predicted by Ho Chi Minh since September 1944. It was an act of desperation. Because of increasing defeats, such as the loss of Burma, the Philippines, and Iwo Jima in February 1945, Japan decided to increase its control over Indochina and simultaneously to forestall a threatened Free-French and allied offensive there.

The result of this last-ditch Japanese effort, however, was to give the Communists the chance they had been awaiting for years. On August 6, 1944, a Party document had forecast:

> Zero hour is near. Germany is almost beaten, and her defeat will lead to Japan's. Then . . . Indochina will be reduced to anarchy. We shall not even need to seize power, for there will be no power. . . . Our impending uprising will be carried out in highly favorable conditions, without parallel in the history of our country. The occasion being propitious and the factors favorable, it would be unforgiveable not to take advantage of them. . . .[13]

On the same night as the Japanese coup of March 9, while Ho Chi Minh was on another aid-seeking mission to China, Party Secretary-General Truong Chinh called an emergency "enlarged conference of the standing bureau of the Party Central Committee" about fifteen miles outside Hanoi. The conference's instructions stated that the new situation decreed further "preparations for the general insurrection to seize power in the whole country." The primary enemy temporarily had become Japan, but Vietnamese had to be "on guard against the Gaullist intention to re-establish [French] domination in Indochina." A month later, a Party journal criticized the view of some that "we should make use of the Japanese coup d'état to eliminate the French," but in fact that was exactly what the Communists did.

The Party also astutely used the terrible economic situation of the times to turn even more to their advantage an increasingly favorable political situation. The Japanese expulsions and arrests of the French after March 9 coincided with the peak of the horrendous famine ravaging the north and north-center of the country. Communist activists therefore declared "the central task for mobilizing the masses" to be to "seize paddy stocks to save the people from starvation," with a view "to launching a powerful movement of struggle against the Japanese fascists for national salvation." In addition to seizures of foodstuffs, which still did not prevent the deaths from starvation of up to two million people according to Communist estimates, activists urged "non-cooperation . . . strikes . . . sabotage . . . and guerilla warfare" against Japan.

The Japanese in fact had basically just replaced the French. Although they nominally decreed the independence of the country in line with their propaganda for a Greater East Asia Co-Prosperity Sphere, it was obvious to all that their 30,000, then up to 100,000 or more, troops held real power. As had the French, they directly ruled Cochin China. In Hue, they induced Emperor Bao Dai to replace the long-discredited government of Pham Quynh with one led by a respected professor, Tran Trong Kim; but only pro-Japanese members of the Dai Viet and Phuc Quoc Parties, of the religious sects, and a few others paid it much attention.

While the French, then the Japanese, held the principal cities, the Communists accelerated the building of their power, especially in the northern border regions of the Viet Bac. In the spring of 1945 they launched repeated attacks on remote outposts and jails, and stepped up Party and Army building. In the same area, Giap and Chu Van Tan reported up to 90 percent of local youth volunteered for their forces, while National Salvation Army soldiers patrolled to the verses:

> Onward march the Viet Minh troops
> sharing a common desire to save their country.
> Their footsteps
> resounding on the long and rugged road.[14]

In more and more areas, activists formed National Salvation and Viet Minh committees, preparatory to the election of the "people's committees" that would establish revolutionary power across most of the country at the time of the August Revolution. Simultaneously, peasant seizures of land accelerated and facilitated the formation of "people's committees."

On April 16, the Viet Minh National Committee transformed into the Vietnam National Liberation Committee, declaring itself the Provisional Revolutionary Government of the country. At the same time, a conference of the Revolutionary Military Committee, at Hiep Hoa, Bac Giang province, under the leadership of Secretary-General Troung Chinh, proclaimed the merger of the various military forces into a Vietnam National Liberation Army of over 3,000 men under Generals Vo Nguyen Giap, Chu Van Tan, and Tran Dang Ninh. At the same time as a new national army came into being, lower-level forces and local militia, the formidable three-tiered Vietnamese military organization of "all the people," was further developed. And the growing military forces were becoming increasingly well supplied by occasional airdrops from U.S. and British aircraft, and especially with weapons captured from the French after the March 9 coup, as well as later from the Japanese. The Communists also stepped up their own manufacture of crude but effective mines, grenades, and other primitive weapons.

In early May 1945, Ho Chi Minh arrived from his latest trip to China at Tan Trao, Tuyen Quang province near the southern edge of the northern guerilla areas, which became the new headquarters of the Party. Although falling gravely ill, assisted by Giap, Ho declared the creation of a Liberated Zone, comprising most of the six provinces of Cao Bang, Bac Can, Lang Son, Ha Giang, Tuyen Quang, and Thai Nguyen, and parts of four other provinces in the north. The Liberated Zone was said to bring a "new life" to over one million people, while in three areas of Quang Ngai province on the south-central coast, "anti-Japanese resistance bases" were created in March and May 1945. A conference of the Viet Minh National Committee under Ho and Giap confirmed all of these decisions on June 4, and declared the ten major policies of the movement:

1. The elimination of Japanese, traitors and criminals (after the defeat of Japan, transformed into a proposal for revolutionary government).

2. The confiscation of properties of the above and their distribution to the poor.
3. Universal suffrage and basic human rights and freedoms.
4. The arming of the masses and support for the guerillas and armed forces.
5. The organization of land reclamation, production and the economy.
6. Restrictions of work hours and days, and relief work.
7. Redistribution of communal lands, reduction of rents and debts.
8. The replacing of previous taxes and corvees with a light progressive tax.
9. The combatting of illiteracy, and providing of military and political education.
10. Equality for minorities and women.[15]

This program with later refinements and the two leading slogans, "national independence" and "seize paddy stocks to save the people from starvation" were likened to the 1917 Bolshevik slogan "bread, peace, and land," in their effects on the revolutionary situation. At the same time, even French negotiator Jean Sainteny termed the Viet Minh's five points of July (condensed from the ten policies) "very moderate and perfectly acceptable."

The surrender of Nazi Germany in early May 1945, and the accelerating allied campaigns against Japan opened the way to the first Communist seizure of power, known as the August Revolution. When Japan surrendered August 15 following the dropping of atomic bombs on Hiroshima and Nagasaki and the invasion of Manchuria and Korea by Soviet troops over the preceding nine days, the Party had already begun the climactic actions of that month.

From August 13 to 15, a Party Congress met at Tan Trao and called for a "general insurrection for wresting power from the hands of the Japanese fascists and their puppets before the arrival of Allied troops." It designated a National Insurrection Committee under Truong Chinh, with Giap and others, and convened a People's Congress of over sixty delegates of "all political parties, mass organizations, nationalities and religious communities." Hurriedly assembled on August 16, this congress confirmed the establishment of the National Liberation Committee under Ho Chi Minh, and that this in effect was to be the new government of Vietnam. Seeking to give reality to Ho's words "unity is strength . . . and only a united struggle will bring us independence," half the members of this committee were non-Communist, but manifestly, Ho, Giap, Dong, and three other Communists were its driving force. It adopted the national flag of a yellow star on a red field, first used in the Mekong Delta uprising of late 1940, and the national anthem sung by Viet Minh soldiers. And it refined the ten points of the Viet Minh adopted in June, stressing a call "to seize power" and "to arm the people and develop the Vietnam Liberation Army." Elections of People's Committees were to establish revolutionary power wherever possible.

Even before the Japanese surrender, the Kim government had resigned in Hue, on August 7, and Communist-led uprisings occurred at Ha Tinh on August 11 and at Ba To, Quang Nghai province on August 13. In the latter province, the Communists claimed to have organized over 100,000 members of National Salvation Associations. To the north after August 16, Giap's forces took over remaining areas of Thai Nguyen and other provinces. But it was August 19 at Hanoi that occurred the real explosion of the August Revolution. On that date, some thousand Viet Minh entered Hanoi and one hundred thousand demonstrators effectively took over the city to the slogans "support the Viet Minh" and "complete independence for Vietnam." There, already at the beginning of 1945, the Party had claimed to organize over 3,000 proletarians for the Revolution. As news of the August Revolution at Hanoi spread, an estimated 150,000 demonstrators took over Hue, on August 23, and a still greater crowd of up to half a million marched in Saigon on August 25. In the wake of these massive demonstrations of popular support in all regions for the Viet Minh, Emperor Bao Dai abdicated on August 24 to "hand over power to the Democratic Republican Government" in order to avoid "further suffering."

In the wake of these tumultuous events, on September 2, 1945, in the center of Hanoi, Ho Chi Minh proclaimed the establishment of the Democratic Republic of Vietnam, and to an enthusiastic crowd of over half a million people read a Declaration of Independence:

> All men are created equal, all men have a right to life, liberty and happiness . . . [above all, Vietnam, which has] courageously opposed French domination for more than eighty years . . . has the right to enjoy freedom and independence and in fact has become a free and independent country . . . [It will sacrifice all] to defend the right to freedom and independence.[16]

In case any one missed the last point, Ho added that "Vietnam will fight to the bitter end against any attempt by the French colonialists to reconquer the country."

Ever the master tactician and diplomat, Ho Chi Minh chose to begin with the opening words of the American Declaration of Independence of 1776 and in the presence of American officers and military men then in Hanoi, in part in order to woo the support of the United States against France and now also China for the protection of Vietnamese independence. There were reports of a perhaps accidental fly-over by American aircraft, but where President Roosevelt had condemned France for leaving the Vietnamese "worse off than they were at the beginning" and recommended a United Nations Trusteeship for the country (supported at first by the Soviet Union), Washington was rapidly becoming more concerned with postwar power realities than with libertarian principles. Still less would the British block the return of the French, nor as it turned out would the Chinese.

Assigned by the Potsdam Conference of July 1945, to "accept the Japanese surrender" south of the sixteenth parallel (near Da Nang, south of Hue), England was contending with Gandhi's very different type of liberation movement in India, and hence not only authorized the return of the French to the south but as well used remaining Japanese troops for several months "to keep order." China, charged with accepting the Japanese surrender north of the sixteenth parallel, in a curious parallel with Soviet behavior in China's own northeast, seemed far more interested in looting than in working with Ho Chi Minh's newly installed government. Rather it actively but futilely promoted the pro-Chinese Nationalist Party and other groups.

Hence, as World War II ended, the Communists had established partial power in all sections of Vietnam, but almost immediately were faced with the return of the French, backed by the British, the growing hostility of the United States, and with "a friend like China." To the complicated interaction of these foreign powers after the Japanese surrender on the equally complicated chessboard of Vietnam we must now turn.

CHAPTER FIVE

The French War

THE BEGINNING OF THE THIRTY YEAR WAR in Vietnam dates back to September 1945, and it began as it ended in 1975, in Saigon. While the situation in the north was increasingly tense and would explode into the larger scale warfare between Viet Minh and French forces in late 1946 that is more commonly taken as the beginning of the First Indochina War, fighting was continuous in the south from September 1945 on.

The Viet Minh had established partial control over Saigon on August 25, 1945, a week after they had done so in Hanoi. But even before the French evicted them from the city a month later, the Viet Minh had greater problems in Saigon than in the north. They had to deal with various contentious groups as well as fight the French. First of all, to the left were their turbulent allies of the 1930s, the Trotskyists. Although still split, at most several thousand strong in the south, and hurt more by French and Japanese repressions than by the better-organized Communists, leaders such as Ta Thu Thao nonetheless remained very influential and apparently so troublesome to the Communists that the southern Party felt compelled to execute Thao and some other Trotskyist leaders in late 1945 and 1946.

More important competitors to Viet Minh control of the south were the Cao Dai and Hoa Hao sects, which were stronger than ever in 1945, having enjoyed a certain, if complex, Japanese support against the French. The Hoa Hao in effect controlled most of southwest Cochin China, and the Cao Dai their headquarters province of Tay Ninh and parts of the southern delta. Although without strength in the north, the Hoa Hao would claim a million and a half and the Cao Dai two million members in the south by 1955. Both groups had cooperated to varying degrees with the Communists in the 1930s and then to some extent with Japan. With the latter's defeat, the sects again maneuvered between the Communists and their enemies. In the immediate aftermath of Japan's surrender, some Cao Dai groups had basically allied either with the Viet Minh or with the Trotskyists. But in June 1946, the commander of the Cao Dai armed forces (in 1945 numbering some 3,000 men and claiming 45,000 later) made a deal with the French, confirmed by the French release of Cao Dai leader Pham Cong Tac. By 1947, the sect was completely hostile to the Communists.

The Viet Minh break with the Hoa Hao also came in stages but was far stormier. On September 8, 1945, Communist and Hoa Hao forces clashed over a contested march of some 15,000 Hoa Hao on Can Tho, with many dozens killed. Then, in spite of Hoa Hao participation in the Viet Minh's National United Front in 1946, the Communists denounced hostile action by the sect and decided to eliminate the "mad bonze" Huynh Phu So, its charismatic founder. Thereafter, much of the Hoa Hao movement, like the Cao Dai, allied directly with French against the Viet Minh.

In Saigon, of special importance also was the secret society organization, the Binh Xuyen. In the late war period and its aftermath, it took control of the part of Cho Lon after which it was named and other sections of the metropolis. Then after a fierce clash with the Viet Minh in 1948, its colorful leader, Bay Vien, struck a deal with the French to support them in Saigon in return for permission to run such profitable enterprises as the infamous gambling house known as the Grand Monde and other affiliated drug and prostitution networks. There were also far less important representatives of the Nationalists, Restorationist, and Dai Viet Parties in Saigon, although as we shall see they played a more substantial role in the north, where they received Chinese help.

Yet among all these groups in the south, the Communists were the best organized. Although at first numbering only several hundred actual members, they established a "vanguard youth" organization after the March Japanese coup, and claimed to organize through it 200,000 followers in the Saigon region and a million others throughout Cochin China. At the time of the August 25 takeover of the city they established a nine man Provisional Executive

Committee of the South under the leadership of Tran Van Giau, supported by longtime Communist colleagues Duong Bach Mai and Nguyen Van Tao, as well as at first by a half-dozen non-Communist nationalists. Then after the mid-August Central Committee meetings near Hanoi, the Party sent Executive Committee member Hoang Quoc Viet to the south, and Ton Duc Thang and Le Duan, just released from prison, also joined the southern leadership, which established headquarters in My Tho province and then by 1946–1947 in Quang Ngai.

On September 2, the Committee of the South again organized hundreds of thousands of residents of Saigon to support the new republic, proclaimed that same day in Hanoi by Ho Chi Minh. But the demonstrations in Saigon were marked by disunity, and by violence that took the lives of five Frenchmen and of dozens of Vietnamese. Predictably, conservatives cited this and other breakdowns of order, most notoriously the slaughter of some one hundred and fifty Frenchmen in an outlying area on September 25, to call for a return of the French, while the revolutionaries argued on the contrary that such incidents were caused by French agents provocateurs. The Communists, in fact, aware of their precarious position in the south, argued the necessity of keeping order and for temporary negotiations with the foreign powers. Communist Minister of Security Doung Bach Mai increasingly used force to silence criticisms of Communist policies by Trotskyists, and by Cao Dai, Hoa Hao, and other Nationalist groups. Also about this time, and prefiguring the city's change of name thirty years later, southern leaders spoke of Saigon as "the city of Ho Chi Minh." But the Viet Minh soon lost control of the city's Committee of the South, as it was expanded to thirteen, later adding still more non-Communist members.[1]

FRANCE, which did not disguise the intention to restore its prewar rule over Indochina, above all was the foreign power with which Vietnamese nationalists, first in the south and soon throughout the country, would have to reckon. On March 24, 1945, two weeks after the Japanese coup of March 9, and reiterating a statement of "Free France" in December 1943 from Algiers, the government of Charles De Gaulle issued a Declaration from "liberated" Paris to the effect that it would work for the restoration of the five "countries" of Cochin China, Annam, Tonkin, Laos, and Cambodia in an "Indochina Federation" but supposedly with greater rights and autonomy than before the war, under the formula "a free state within the French Union." In the wake of the Japanese surrender of August 15, Free French groups operating from Calcutta and Kunming returned with difficulty to Vietnam, and proceeded to try to restore their power. In the north, they were frustrated in this effort by Chinese opposition to the return, and by their temporary failure to secure the aid of the United States. But in the south, with the help of the conservative British commander, General Douglas Gracey, they partially succeeded.

Already on August 27, a meeting was held between Viet Minh leaders and the French, but it only revealed the growing gulf between the two sides. While in late July, the Viet Minh proposed a "five point program" allowing five to ten years for the achievement of full independence and other moderate provisions, developments and extremists on both sides maximized differences. In late August, the Party's Central Committee directed resistance to the return of France, while following the September 2 events and growing lawlessness in Saigon, the French succeeded in winning Gracey's decision for the eviction of the Viet Minh from the city. This occurred during the night of September 22–23, when some 1,400 French troops, just released from Japanese prisons and backed by 2,800 English-officered Gurka troops, moved against Viet Minh positions in the city. When the Viet Minh fought back and the war began in earnest, Gracey then commanded further use of Japanese troops still in the country to "keep order." As historian Joseph Buttinger put it, "the scandalous fact [was] that the British, instead of disarming the Japanese, ordered them to help the French in the war against the Vietnamese. . . ."[2]

Following a brief truce and negotiations among contending forces, the newly arrived 35,000 French troops under Resistance hero General Jean Leclerc proceeded to undertake the "pacification" of the south in a series of bloody campaigns of guerilla warfare and scorched-earth policies on both sides, lasting from October 21 until the capture of Ca Mau at the southern tip of the country in early February. French colons of the south and their leaders rejoiced at this new lease of life and sought to resume their former lives of colonial ease and its symbols, for example, restoring the name Rue Catinat* to the most fashionable street of Saigon (Tu Do

*The name of the ship that shelled Da Nang in 1856 to begin the French conquest of Indochina.

Street), which the revolutionaries had briefly named the Street of the Paris Commune.

But the lull would prove artificial, as Communist leaders and local activists such as Madame Nguyen Thi Dinh whose provincial capital of Ben Tre had fallen to the French on February 7, continued to survive in the underground they already knew all too well. Guerilla warfare, now carried out by some 20,000 troops under Nguyen Binh, who replaced Tran Van Giau in early 1946, would continue with varying degrees of violence and types of action in up to two-thirds of the south for another entire generation. As General Giap put it on a visit to a southern resistance base near Nha Trang in January 1946, the French were faced already with "an indestructible steel fortress constituted by a population who refused to return to their life of slavery."

Communist leaders in Hanoi took immediate note of the alarming turn of events in the south. On September 26, 1945, Ho Chi Minh declared that his "government and all our compatriots throughout the country, will support the combatants and population of the South with all our force . . . to save independence . . . . " Then, on November 5, Ho made a statement that with variations would be repeated over and over again for thirty years: "The French colonialists should know that the Vietnamese people do not wish to spill blood, that it loves peace. But if it must sacrifice millions of combatants, lead a resistance for long years to defend the independence of the country, and preserve its children from slavery, it will do so. It is certain the resistance will win."[3] The Communist Party would continue to lead this resistance and the concomitant struggle for the national and social revolutions of Vietnam until their final victory in 1975. In late 1945, for example, they sent numerous northern soldiers, especially from the central provinces, on a "southward march" to bolster Viet Minh forces in the south, and such northerners came to comprise up to 80 percent of the regular Communist troops in the south at various times during the French war.

Yet in another page unique to Vietnamese Communist history, the Party actually declared itself dissolved on November 11, 1945. This was done only on paper, and "the organization" as Ho Chi Minh later called it, of "Marxist Study Groups" and the "people's committees," which Communists set up to install revolutionary government at the local level, continued to exist. Nonetheless, the remarkable fact is that between late 1945 and the Second Party

Congress of February 1951, when it was restored under the name of the Vietnam Workers' Party, there was not an official Communist Party in Indochina. This maneuver of course aimed primarily to appease the Chinese Nationalists then occupying the north, and to lessen the "fear of communism" of various groups of Vietnamese Nationalists so as to create the most effective united front against the French. Similarly in the interest of the widest possible united front, the Viet Minh in the late 1940s concentrated its propaganda almost entirely on the national struggle against France under Ho Chi Minh's slogan, "we would rather die as free men, than live as slaves." While privately confessing their long-term commitment to the Marxist revolution, and pushing drastic reductions of taxes by 20 per cent, and abolition of hated government monopolies on salt, alcohol, and opium in "liberated" areas, they avoided talk of the Communist "social revolution," emphasizing always the "anti-Imperialist revolution."

Despite such Communist flexibility in varying the stress between the national and social revolutions, many remained suspicious and hostile. The Hoa Hao and Cao Dai were, in places in the south, stronger than the Communists, and thereafter became increasingly allied with the French, especially after the assassination of Hoa Hao leader Huynh Phu So, in April 1947. And well before that, Communists had turned to the use of force against rival leaders they felt were interfering with their larger goals, as when they executed Trotskyist leader Ta Thu Thao shortly after the end of the war. In mid 1946, Ho Chi Minh was quoted as stating, Ta Thu Thao was "a great patriot and we mourn him," but as quickly adding, "all those who do not follow the line which I have laid down will be broken." Already in 1939, Ho had denounced the Trotskyists as "agents of Imperialism," but officially the Viet Minh criticized such "excesses" in the use of terror as well as in the carrying out of land confiscations. In early 1946, for reasons presumably related to such criticism, they sent south former Nationalist (VNQDD) leader Nguyen Binh to replace longtime southern stalwart Tran Van Giau on a reorganized Committee for the South. Giau's purge may also have been related to reported criticisms at this time of the inconsistency of Soviet policies toward Vietnam.[4]

The terror also continued, and from mid-1945 through 1946, the Communists did away, not only with Ta Thu Thao and Huynh Phu So, but with five other Trotskyist leaders—with Pham Quyhn, Bao Dai's prime minister from 1932 until March 1945; with the founder of the Constitutionalist Party, Bui Quang Chieu; with Ngo Dinh Diem's brother Ngo Dinh Khoi; and with various other non-Communist Nationalists. Some sources speak of Communist executions of some 5,000 and imprisonment of another 25,000 Nationalist rivals at this time, but according to Troung Chinh, the Party should have eliminated more "enemies of the revolution" than it did. In September 1946, he wrote that, except in Quang Ngai province, revolutionaries had been "conciliatory to the point of weakness, forgetting [Lenin's dictum] that a 'victorious power must be a dictatorial one,' " and adding that "for a new-born revolutionary power to be lenient with counter-revolutionaries is tantamount to committing suicide."[5]

More pacifically, Ho Chi Minh and Viet Minh leaders continued to woo Vietnamese nationalists, criticizing the discredited alliance of the Phu Quoc and Dai Viet with now defeated Japan, and of the Nationalists (VNQDD and Dong Ming Hoi) with the Chinese forces that were then ravaging the north of the country. The VNQDD in particular had taken over certain provinces of lowland North Vietnam where they had retained considerable influence, but in late 1945 they were all too dependent on China's backing. In order to show up the unpopularity of these groups and their own popularity, Ho Chi Minh called for a Government of National Union with the VNQDD and Dong Ming Hoi and for elections on January 6, 1946, to determine its representation. On the insistence of the Nationalists, and of China, the VNQDD and Dong Ming Hoi were to be guaranteed 70 of 380 seats in the General Assembly and substantial representation at the ministerial level in order to ensure their survival since, as foreseen, the Viet Minh swept those elections, claiming 97 percent of the votes. But true to their promises, the Communists took only five of eleven posts in the new government established February 24, 1946, although Ho Chi Minh continued as president of the republic.

Members of the VNQDD and Dong Ming Hoi remained a problem for the Viet Minh until their Chinese backers left the country in the spring. Outbreaks of violence continued throughout 1946, and were not always precipitated by the Communists. At one point, for example, the Nationalists even kidnapped Giap and another Communist leader, thereby forcing their removal from the February 24 government in exchange for the release of those leaders. In any case Giap remained in effective control of the Viet Minh military, as head of its National Liberation Committee, and during the summer of 1946 proceeded to close Nationalist organizations and newspapers and finally to destroy most of what was left of the non-Communist Nationalist movement. Ironically, they were helped in this by the French, who recognized that the Communists had more control over their followers than the Nationalists, and accordingly were less responsible for breakdowns of order and anarchistic attacks on the French.

The Catholics, who controlled up to 20 percent of Tonkin and northern Annam, however, continued to expand in parts of the northern delta in 1947–1948, as did the Dai Viet, at times with French support. Many Catholics, especially in the north, however, at first supported the Viet Minh after the August Revolution, including at first the brother of Ngo Dinh Diem, Bishop Ngo Dinh Thuc. The Church's hierarchy noted its approval of the new government on September 23, 1945, in a letter to the Pope, asking the "blessing, good will, and prayers of your holiness" for the country's newly won independence.[6]

Therefore, the Communists were able to stay on top of the complicated contest with other Vietnamese Nationalists, using a mixture of ploys, persuasion, and force, and maintained their image as upholders of "militant nationalism." In May 1946, they established a new front organization, still broader than the Viet Minh which in name it later absorbed, known as the Lien Viet.* Then in November the National Assembly created a new constitution and government, dominated by the Communists although they conceded a majority of the ministries to non-Communist leaders of the Lien Viet.

EQUALLY IMPORTANT for the leaders of a small country like Vietnam as the monopolization of nationalism was the handling of relations with the powers. And in this also, the Viet Minh succeeded brilliantly, first using contacts with Americans to advance their position, then in the spring of 1946 using the French against China, and finally turning all their forces against France. Given the complex of forces in 1945, it is possible that more skillful diplomacy by France, and also by the United States, might have taken advantage of Ho Chi Minh's relative diplomatic moderation to work out an arrange-

*Until the mid-1950s, however, the Communist movement in Vietnam continued to be referred to as the Viet Minh.

ment with some form of "Titoist" Vietnam that would not have allied so closely with the Soviet Union, nor with China. For in late 1945 Moscow and the Communist Party of France advised the Vietnamese, as well as the Chinese Communists, to avoid "premature adventurism," lest it complicate the achievement of Soviet goals in Europe, which had priority.

Indeed, in July 1945 Ho had spoken of waiting five to ten years for independence while undertaking relatively moderate reforms, temporarily under a French governor and with continuing economic and other concessions for France. And a few months later, on March 7, 1946, he queried, "Why should we sacrifice fifty or 100,000 men when we can achieve independence within five years through negotiations?" But a failure of leadership by all concerned and the pressures of the time prevented compromise, except briefly in 1946. Ho later denied that he had ever offered such generous terms to France and, despite the abolition of the Party in November 1945 and other gestures, the conservative French, who made their country's policies, mostly believed, as one stated, that "Ho Chi Minh in no way is a patriot. He is above all a rootless, mean man whose loyalty goes only to international Communism and who will govern only through terrorism."[7] This was little different from the statement introducing the colonial Sûreté's 1933 history of the Communists, that they were "pseudo-intellectuals and misfits," representing the worst of Vietnamese society. For their part, most Vietnamese expressed what a journalist called a "living, leaping" hatred of the French. Given such animosities, war between the still colonialist rulers of France and the now fiercely independent Vietnamese could be avoided only with the greatest of statesmanship, and this was not to be.

A third major actor, China, further complicated relations between Vietnam and France during these critical months. Over 150,000 Chinese troops entered Vietnam in September 1945 to accept the Japanese surrender north of the sixteenth parallel as agreed to by the Potsdam Conference, and installed a permanent garrison of some 50,000, who remained until the following spring. As they came without supplies, the Chinese troops were forced to live off the land, and this at the very time that the Viet Minh was launching "an all-out campaign against famine," which had already cost over one million lives. The Chinese troops also were very badly disciplined and clothed, with the result that they committed more than the normal amount of soldierly looting and pillage. And at the same time that organized soldiers and accompanying carpetbaggers were stripping the country of virtually everything in sight, they forced a scandalously exploitative exchange rate on the Vietnamese, with the Chinese currency overvalued at least tenfold. To partially pacify the Chinese while continuing to strengthen their control of the population, the Viet Minh proclaimed a "gold week" in September to procure arms, and to produce some of the payments demanded by the Chinese generals, including a gold opium smoking set that Ho Chi Minh ironically presented to Chinese Commanding General Lu Han. The Chinese also set up representatives of the VNQDD and Dong Ming Hoi Parties, apparently trying to establish their satellites in a neighboring area, in still another curious parallel with Soviet actions at the time. But where the Chinese were estimated to have fleeced Vietnam of 500 million piastres, Soviet actions in Manchuria reportedly stripped away the far greater figure of some 2 billion U.S. dollars.

The Chinese, however, while adding enormously to the already great problems of postwar Vietnam, were also extremely useful to the Viet Minh to the extent that they blocked the advance of the French to the north during a crucial period. By the time that occurred, as permitted by the Chinese-French treaty of February 28, 1946, the Viet Minh had substantially strengthened their political and military position. And even then, Ho Chi Minh's diplomatic genius, further transformed the situation to the advantage of the Viet Minh, although he could not prevent the widening of the war with France later in the year. Essentially, Ho first negotiated with the French to get rid of the Chinese in the spring of 1946, and then undertook further negotiations with Paris, which failed but which nonetheless won another half year for the continued strengthening of the Viet Minh position and virtual elimination of their Nationalist rivals.

The principal actors after the departure of the Chinese were Ho Chi Minh, as always after 1940 closely backed by Giap and Pham Van Dong, and the chief of the French mission in Hanoi, Jean Sainteny, backed by the commander of French forces in the south, Jean Leclerc. In brief, by the late winter of 1946, Ho and his followers felt compelled to work out a compromise agreement with arch-enemy France because, among other reasons, Viet Minh troops were on the run in the south, the Chinese and their Vietnamese Nationalist allies were causing great trouble in the north, and especially because China had just signed an agreement permitting the return of French troops without any reference whatsoever to Ho Chi Minh's government. For his part, Sainteny had come to recognize the strength of the Viet Minh in the north and to realize as did Leclerc that, short of a new mobilization that war-weary France could not afford, France would have to come to terms with Ho Chi Minh. Accordingly with much last-minute bargaining, and after a high-level Party meeting the day before, Ho and Sainteny worked out and signed on March 6, 1946, in the presence of "counselor" Vinh Thuy, the former Emperor Bao Dai, what was undoubtedly the most promising of all agreements between the Commuists and their enemies in Vietnam.

In the March 6 agreement, France recognized "the Republic of Vietnam as a free state," but also called it "part of the Indochina Federation and French Union," while the Viet Minh agreed to "amicably receive the French army" on its arrival in the north. These units were not to exceed 15,000 French and 10,000 Vietnamese soldiers under their command, and they were not to remain in Vietnam later than 1952. The Viet Minh also accepted the French interpretation of Doc Lap (independence) as "free" but not yet independent, while France agreed, though in fact it never carried out, to "ratify the decisions taken by the population consulted by referendum," regarding the unification of Cochin China, Annam, and Tonkin. The details of the accords were to be worked out by the "opening of immediate, frank and friendly negotiations."[8]

This brave but deliberately vague compromise came unstuck almost immediately. First of all the Chinese commander of Haiphong harbor temporarily upset the arrival of the French troops with an exchange of gunfire for several hours, claiming he did not have authorization for the landing despite an agreement of February 28. That agreement incidentally had given China special rights in Vietnam even as France agreed to end its "unequal rights" in China in return for the transfer of authority to the French. That amounted to what King Chen called "China's first unequal treaty" with another country, and the last Chinese troops did not leave Vietnam until June 1946.

The fact that Leclerc and the French troops were already on the way to the north after the February 28 treaty was the most compelling reason for Ho's acceptance of the March 6 accord, together with the fear that a new Chinese-French arrangement would completely shut out the Viet Minh. Then Ho had to overcome the arguments against compromise with the French by Party militants like Troung Chinh and Hoang Quoc Viet, and later Giap, and also by the conservative Nationalists who accused him of a sell-out. Accordingly on the day after the March 6 agreement, he and Giap explained to a crowd of 100,000 people in Hanoi their reasons for the compromise with their slogan "independence or death." Privately, Ho used the earthy expression, "It is better to sniff French dung for a while than eat China's all our lives," which Giap later explained more helpfully, "We agreed to allow 15,000 French troops to enter the North for a specific period of time in order to boot out 180,000 brutal soldiers of Chiang Kai-shek." Giap further specified that the agreement aimed to "obtain a breathing spell to prepare for the new struggle and coordinate it with the struggle of the French people," the latter a reference to a hoped-for victory of the French Left in elections of autumn, 1946. To the rally, Giap also referred to Lenin's Treaty of Brest-Litovsk with Germany in the last days of World War I in order to protect the Bolshevik Revolution. The huge rally finally was won over completely by Ho Chi Minh's moving statement, "I have spent my whole life fighting for our country's independence. You know I would sooner die than betray the nation. I swear I have not betrayed you." Nonetheless, other Vietnamese continued to attack Ho as a traitor for his excessive concessions.[9]

THE MARCH 6 AGREEMENTS, however, were done in, not by Party militants or other Vietnamese critics of the Viet Minh, or by the Chinese, so much as by French policy makers. While far-sighted men like Sainteny and Leclerc strove valiantly to create a compromise with Ho Chi Minh, whom they came to respect as Sainteny put it, as a man "of the highest caliber . . . [with] his intelligence, his vast culture and total unselfishness," conservatives opposed all negotiations with the "terrorists." Ho Chi Minh was largely correct in his divided feelings about the French. He told Jean Lacouture at this time, "A race such as yours which has given the world the literature of freedom will always find us friends . . . if only you knew, monsieur, how passionately I reread Victor Hugo and Michelet year after year. . . . So different on the other hand [are . . .] the Frenchmen who have misrepresented your country here. . . ." Similarly, a Viet Minh directive of the time declared, "our main enemy is the French reactionary element . . . [but] we must collaborate unreservedly with those Frenchmen who are sincerely democratic. . . .[10]

Indeed, it seems clear that the conservative French bureaucrats, who believed that the grandeur and glory of France were as tied to the fate of their empire in 1946 as in 1896, and the colons, especially of Saigon, who wished to guard at whatever cost the privileges and charms of colonial life, must bear the primary responsibility for the failure of the March 6 accords.

The new high commissioner for Indochina, Admiral Georges Thierry D'Argenlieu, a Carmelite monk for over fifteen years before becoming a close associate of De Gaulle during the war, and *résident* in Saigon from October 1945 to March 1947, brought the pressures of both groups to bear on the scuttling of the March 6 agreement. First of all, backed by Commissioner for Cochin China Cédile and others, D'Argenlieu refused to apply the agreement at all to the south, arguing it applied only to Annam and Tonkin. The Saigon French had already set up a new Advisory Council for Cochin China on February 4, and on March 26 decided to form a provisional autonomous government for the south, which was officially declared June 1, at the very moment Ho Chi Minh was on his way to Paris for the most crucial stage of the negotiations to fulfill the March 6 accords. Although D'Argenlieu agreed to meet with Ho on a French cruiser in Ha Long Bay on March 24, 1946, his delegates to the conference at Dalat in late April and early May only underlined the worst fears of Communist delegates Giap and Doung Bach Mai, rather than, as intended, preparing the way for meaningful negotiations. Furthermore, D'Argenlieu's men proceeded to organize parts of the Southern Highlands into an "autonomous region" for the montagnards of the area in a further display of their intentions to continue policies of "divide and rule." In 1948, the French similarly set up an "autonomous federation" of Thai peoples in the north, though as we shall see, with effects less favorable for them.

Hence when Ho Chi Minh and his party arrived in France in June 1946 to work out the details of the March 6 agreement, only extreme optimists could hope for success. And as so often during these years, as later during the American war, the domestic politics of the enemies of Vietnam played a disturbingly disproportionate role, as if Vietnamese made up a large part of the opposition parties of France and the United States. Thus, even as his plane was over Damascus on the way to France, Ho Chi Minh learned of D'Argenleiu's June 1 proclamation of the separate Republic of Cochin China, and then was told he could not disembark in Paris until after the completion of elections for a new French government. Accordingly, Ho spent several weeks of forced vacation in fashionable Biarritz before arriving in Paris following the installation of the new government of Georges Bidault.

One of fifteen such governments between 1945 and 1954, Bidault's then insisted that the talks be held at Fontainebleau, an hour's drive to the south, rather than in Paris, where it was feared the Communists would draw support from the active Parisian Left. Even that would have been far from certain, as the French Communists themselves were sharply divided over the question of Vietnamese nationalism. While by 1950 Party leader Maurice Thorez strongly campaigned "against the foul war in Vietnam," in April 1946 he was quoted as saying in the interest of French politics that he "ardently hoped to see the French flag flying over every territory in the French Union," and that if the Vietnamese did not live up to the French understanding of the March accords "we will take the necessary measures, and let guns speak for us if need be." On March 18, 1947, Communist delegates to the General Assembly joined the majority in voting war funds for the then Ramadier government.

Yet, in mid-1946, Ho Chi Minh apparently still hoped to win over "progressive" French to accept a fully independent Vietnam under his leadership. The French government, perhaps fearing just that, refused to assign any full ministers or very important political figures to the Fontainebleau conference, with the result that Ho Chi Minh turned over the direction of his delegation to the trusted Pham Van Dong. Not surprisingly, no progress was forthcoming. The basic problem was summarized a few months later by the chief French negotiator, Max André: "The French regarded the agreement of March 6 as an end [in itself], the basis of a stable and lasting situation: the Vietnamese thought of it only as a first step by France toward totally and definitively renouncing Indochina." For the Communists, Giap basically agreed, but of course gave a different emphasis. In 1970, he reflected that with the March 6 agreement, "the enemy had retreated one basic step. But to us, this victory was only the beginning . . . . Not too long afterward, the French reactionary colonialists betrayed all the terms they had signed."[11]

Nonetheless, for two months after July 6, the two sides exchanged statements and counterstatements at Fontainebleau, while Ho Chi Minh continued to charm more open-minded French with what Robert Shaplen called his "wit, his oriental courtesy, his savoir-faire, his mixed profundity and playfulness . . . his open love for children, above all his seeming sincerity and simplicity." Where in Biarritz he had chatted with peasants and fishermen and visited Lourdes, in Paris Ho was installed in unaccustomed luxury at the Hotel Royal Monceau, and in August at a villa outside the city. He presented flowers to the ladies, on occasion slept on the floor, did his own laundry, spoke excellent French, and debated the existence of God, the truths of Christianity and Buddhism with a French priest with whom Ho said he got on famously "as we are both idealists." He also declared: "Everyone has the right to his own doctrine. I studied and chose Marx. Jesus said two thousand years ago that one should love one's enemies. That dogma has not been realized. When will Marxism be realized? I cannot answer . . . ." Ho reportedly went to mass on Christmas Eve 1945.[12]

More immediately, Ho got no proper response to the very Asian query, "Is the French Union to be round or square?" In August, D'Argenlieu had held a second Dalat Conference further sealing his intention to keep Cochin China separate, and finally, on September 9, Pham Van Dong signaled the end of his delegation's patience with French obstinacy. Most of the Viet Minh party sailed for home, while Ho Chi Minh decided to yield even further in order not to "go back empty handed." Late on the night of September 14 he insisted on going to the residence of Socialist Minister of French Overseas Territories Marius Moutet, who, already in his pajamas, signed with him the "Modus Vivendi" of that date. Basically repeating the terms of the March 6 agreement, the September 14 document in addition gave further economic rights to the French in the north, while the French promised to be more "democratic" in the south, without, however, agreeing to the referendum promised on March 6.

HO ARRIVED BACK IN HAIPHONG on October 20 on the French warship *Dumont d'Urville*, which a month later was involved in the biggest act of violence yet, and the final torpedoing of the March 6 accords. This came about when French military officers demanded military control of Haiphong and, on the pretext of Viet Minh delays, on November 23 opened fire on the city. The action was ordered by the commander in chief, General Jean-Etienne Valluy, over the objections of local commander, General Louis-Constant Morlière, in order, as Valluy put it, "to give a harsh lesson to those who have treacherously attacked us . . . . By every means at your disposal, you must take control of Haiphong and bring the government and the Vietnamese army to repentance . . . ."[13] By subsequent French admission, over 6,000 Vietnamese were killed during this "lesson"—the Viet Minh claimed 20,000—surely one of the worst examples of Western imperialist gunboat diplomacy. In this instance, the ratio of Vietnamese to foreigners killed was close to 1,000 to one, as about 5 French had been killed in ambush and another 6 taken prisoner on November 20. Overall during these difficult months, and indeed for the entire thirty-year war, the ratio of Communist supporters and their enemies killed was on the order of 4 to 1 and, at times during the American war, 10 to 1 or more.

In the aftermath of the carnage of November 23, military preparations accelerated on both sides, although Ho Chi Minh and the new French government of Léon Blum desperately sought last-minute compromises. Ho told a French correspondent in mid-December, "This war is something we wish to avoid at all costs. We long passionately for independence but for independence within the French union. War doesn't pay." He appealed directly to the French National Assembly in similar terms about the same time.

It was too late, especially as messages back and forth between Hanoi and Paris, and even last-ditch personal efforts by Sainteny and Marius Moutet, were delayed by intransigent French officials in Saigon. On the night of December 19, hours after the issuing of French demands for disarming the Viet Minh in Hanoi, Communist forces took the initiative with attacks throughout the city. Most of the 50,000 regular Viet Minh forces had already withdrawn to the mountain fastnesses of the North, and to two new base areas in Tuyen Quang and Hoa Binh provinces, but some fought on in Hanoi until February 1947. The Communists also maintained strength on the central coast, in Quang Ngai and Binh Dinh provinces, and in mid-1946 launched offensives south of Saigon, increasing their control to almost three-quarters of Cochin China. In all parts of the country, they claimed a militia of almost one million by this time.

Hence, even as the Viet Minh yielded initially before superior French forces, they stepped up the resistance whose incredible tenacity in the end would defeat two of the world's greatest powers. Ho Chi Minh predicted as much in his famous appeal of December 20:

> Compatriots, all over the country!
> As we desire peace we have made concessions. But the more conces-

> sions we make, the more the French colonialists press on, for they are bent on reconquering our country.
> No! We would rather sacrifice all than lose our country. Never shall we be enslaved!
> Compatriots, stand up!
> Men and women, old and young, regardless of religious creed, political affiliation and nationality, all Vietnamese must stand up to fight the French colonialists and save the Fatherland. Those who have rifles will use their rifles; those who have swords will use their swords; those who have no swords will use spades, hoes or sticks. . . .
> The hour for national salvation has struck! We must shed even our last drop of blood to safeguard our country . . . with our determination to face all sacrifices, we are bound to win.

About this time also, Ho elaborated, "We are not unaware of what is in store for us. France disposes of terrifying weapons. The struggle will be atrocious, but the Vietnamese people are willing to endure everything rather than give up their freedom." Giap said the same in February 1946: "We shall not let ourselves be stopped by any loss, any violence, any destruction."[14]

With equally chilling prescience, Ho had told Sainteny a few months earlier, "If we have to fight, we will fight. You will kill ten of our men and we will kill one of yours. In the end, it will be you who will tire of it." At other times, Ho used images worthy of La Fontaine to make the same point. In September 1945, "If ever the tiger pauses, the elephant will impale him on his mighty tusks. But the tiger will not pause, and the elephant will die of exhaustion and loss of blood." Or of Lao Zi, as in June 1947:

> The enemy is like fire and we like water. Water will certainly get the better of fire. [He explained:] The enemy wants to win a quick victory. If the war drags on, he will suffer increasing losses and will be defeated. That is why we use the strategy of a protracted war of resistance in order to develop our forces . . . we use guerilla tactics to wear down the enemy forces until a general offensive wipes them out. Each citizen is a combatant, each village a fortress. The twenty million Vietnamese are bound to cut to pieces the few scores of thousands of reactionary colonialists.

Then, in February 1951, he used another striking animal image: "The discrepancy between our forces and the enemy's was so great that at the time some people likened our war of resistance to a fight between a 'grasshopper and an elephant'. . . . Yes, it's now grasshopper versus elephant, but tomorrow the elephant will collapse."

And in the 1960s, Ho likened the American war machine to a fox who, with his hind feet caught in the trap of South Vietnam, lunged his front feet into the trap of North Vietnam.

It is too bad that French and American policy makers did not appreciate these quotations, although some of their nationals did. Even in the 1930s, a French woman had noted, "The more the government shoots and kills and imprisons, the more the revolutionary movement rises up, like a nest of ants." And after several years of war, a French lieutenant complained, "We kill scores and scores of them. But there are always just as many left—in fact more. There's an inexhaustible supply. And then it's not always the real, full-blown Viet that we kill. . . . Often they are just villagers, people's militia, half or even only a quarter Viet." Another officer admitted twenty years before Americans made similar remarks, "What is a Viet Minh? A Viet Minh, he is a dead Vietnamese." But commanding General Henri Navarre in October 1953 would also state: "It is certain that the great force of the Viet Minh lies in the conviction (true or false) that it alone has inspired in its people (a sense of) equality and social justice. That is the principal reason for the combat qualities of the Viet Minh soldier. . . ." Most French generals and politicians on the other hand apparently believed what the French Chief of Staff, General Famin had said in 1915, "The Annamites do not possess the vigor and physical resistance necessary to fight a European type war."[16]

THE FRENCH LIEUTENANT WAS CORRECT for the late 1940s as well as for twenty years later. Despite the greatest use of force on a similar area in the history of warfare, the Vietnamese revolutionaries kept coming. The 5,000 Communist activists of the time of the August Revolution of 1945 increased to 20,000 in 1946, 210,000 in 1949, and to over 760,000 by 1951. The armed forces under Vo Nguyen Giap expanded from about 30,000 in September 1945 to perhaps 60,000 by the time of the start of full-scale war in December 1946, to over 168,000 in 1948, to over 350,000 (including over 120,000 regulars) by the time of the defeat of the French in 1954. They were backed by many more supporters in front organizations, such as the Vanguard Youth, which claimed one million members, and above all by the Viet Minh, which in 1946 claimed 500,000 members (200,000 in Tonkin, and 150,000 each in Annam and Cochin China) as well as another 500,000 sympathizers. In 1948, there were some 820,000 members of Viet Minh-sponsored peasant associations, and by 1952, the Lien Viet claimed 8 million members. These Communists and their supporters opposed over 40,000 regular French and Foreign Legion troops and some 18,000 Vietnamese troops at the beginning of the war. The French forces passed 200,000 in 1950 and by 1954 doubled again, although only some 54,000 of these troops were French citizens. They commanded 20,000 Foreign Legionnaires, 30,000 North Africans, and over 300,000 Vietnamese troops.

As throughout the thirty-year war, their enemies controlled the most populous areas, and all the major cities and communications lines. But by about 1950 the Communists controlled over half of the countryside, and up to three-quarters of the south as well as over half of the northern delta. In many of these areas, as would the Americans later, the French claimed control, but it was extremely limited, depending on temporary sweeps by their military units largely during waking hours. At night and in the absence of government troops, or most of the time, many villages followed the Communist-led resistance forces, closely integrated with local activists in contrast to the more "foreign" government sweeps by "outside" troops.

The Communists continued to draw political activists, military recruits and supplies and labor from this "sea of the people," and they constantly propagandized, especially among "workers, peasants, youth and women," using local actions, agitation, and journals. The main military forces of the Communists, however, concentrated early in the war in the northern mountainous provinces of Bac Can, Ha Giang, Tuyen Quang, and Thai Nguyen, known as the Viet Bac. At first retreating before superior enemy forces according to the principles of the first stage of the Maoist formula for guerilla warfare, Viet Minh forces nonetheless prevented the hoped-for quick victory of the French in late 1947, although at one point French units apparently came within an hour of capturing Ho Chi Minh and other leaders, after a parachute drop in Bac Can province. Communist base areas were reduced and the French were able to form an alliance with a local Tai minority group. The French command in 1947 claimed to inflict over 10,000 casualties on the Viet Minh, while suffering themselves 1,000 dead and 3,000 wounded.

After a standoff between the opposing forces in 1948 and 1949, with the arrival of newly victorious Chinese Communist forces at the Vietnam border in 1950, for the first time the Viet Minh began to receive a regular supply of arms, many of them American weapons captured from Chiang Kai-shek's armies the year before, and from 30,000 Nationalist troops who retreated into Vietnam in 1949. The United States, with the outbreak of the Korean War in June 1950, however, also began to send arms to French forces and would eventually supply some $4 billion of the total expenses of the French for the war, estimated at $7.5 billion. By 1954 the United States was footing 78 percent of the French war bill, certainly a far greater external support than the Viet Minh received.[17]

EXPANDING RECRUITMENT AND EQUIPMENT enabled the Viet Minh to move from their "first stage" of guerilla warfare, which, as outlined by Mao Zedong, Ho, Giap, and others, "aimed at preserving and increasing our main forces," to the "second stage" of "active contention with the enemy and preparation for the general counteroffensive from 1948 to 1950. The general counteroffensive would mark the victorious "third stage" of the revolutionary war, which in Vietnam grew almost imperceptibly out of phase two.

Already by the spring of 1948, the Viet Minh were reversing the loss of northern strongpoints to the French fall 1947 offensive. The "terrifying weapons" of which Ho had spoken in mid-1945, as would be the case with American arms twenty years later, could capture territory but, given Communist skill at mobilizing the population, could not hold it without a far greater commitment of troops than either France or the United States would give.

There were Viet Minh offensives even in the south in the late 1940s and early 1950s, although on a smaller scale than in the north, and most Communist main force southern units were forced to retreat to the Plain of Junks, southwest of Saigon, and to the southernmost point of Ca Mau. In contrast to the 1930s, Party growth now lagged in the south, primarily because of greater competition from the sects and a greater French presence. Of up to 180,000 Party members reported in 1948, only 23,000 were said to be from the south, and 30,000 or 50,000 according to various estimates in 1954. About this time there were also reports of considerable political dissension among the southern Communists. Nguyen Binh, for example, may have been assassinated on Party orders in September 1951, following criticisms of the failure of offensive actions he had prematurely ordered, and of his lack of discipline and arrogance. Others believe rather that he was ambushed and killed by the French. In any case, there then developed differences of opinion between Nguyen Binh's successor as Communist leader of the south, Le Duan, and his deputy, Le Duc Tho. Frustration with such problems undoubtedly figured in Ho Chi Minh's 1949 complaint about excessive individualism and selfishness among the southerners. Nevertheless, in the south as well, the Communists maintained a steady pressure, and in renewed offensives toward the end of the war expanded their control to some 60 percent of the territory of what would become the anti-Communist Republic of Vietnam.

In the north, in February 1950, Giap began an offensive named after martyred General Le Hong Phong (who had died in prison in 1942) to push overextended French forces completely out of the northern provinces bordering China along Colonial Route 4. Starting with the capture of Lao Kay, Viet Minh forces went on to take Dong Khe and Cao Bang in the spring and summer of 1950 and, in October, Lang Son. These victories gave the Communists complete control of northern Tonkin and cost France what Bernard Fall called the "greatest colonial defeat since Montcalm died at Quebec."[18]

In 1951, however, Giap overreached himself with a premature move of his best units into the lowlands in battles in the northern Red River Delta from January to April, and in May south of Hanoi in Thanh Hoa province. It was premature because the Communists were not as yet capable of withstanding French firepower in the open, and because the French "Douglas MacArthur," General Jean de Lattre de Tassigny, before his death of cancer in January 1952, succeeded temporarily in reversing the tide of events. This was primarily accomplished by his bolstering of the morale of French forces, but his so-called De Lattre Line of 1,200 strong points had no more success than the McNamara Line sixteen years later in stopping the Communist secret weapon of small-scale attacks and recruitment of new activists. The fall of Hoa Binh, south of Hanoi, to Communist forces in February 1952 was a sign of things to come.

After Giap withdrew his main force units into the Viet Bac to recover from the set backs of 1951, he set the stage for the final showdown, with drives westward into the northern Vietnam-Laos Highlands in late 1951 and 1952 and in the spring of 1953. The Communists already had made substantial progress in organizing the Tai (Thos) and other minorities there and hence were in a good position to accept the challenge of the new French commander, Henri Navarre, when in November 1953 he established a forward position at Dien Bien Phu, in order to try to destroy Communist units in open combat, as had been done in the 1951 campaigns. But now the opposite happened. In November 1952 Navarre's predecessor, General Raoul Salan, had suffered a severe defeat in North Vietnam; and following the Viet Minh capture of Sam Nua, Laos, in April 1953, and menacing thrusts toward Lai Chau and Luang Prabang several months later, another important French goal in creating the Dien Bien Phu base became to try to protect Laos from further Communist inroads, with the consequent linking of the resistance movements of the three countries. Laos had been retaken by the French in the spring of 1946, several months after they had recaptured Cambodia. Only Laos among the former Indochinese states had willingly signed accords for joining the French Union. Hence Paris judged its security particularly important.

BEFORE GOING AHEAD with description of the defeat of the French garrison at Dien Bien Phu and its aftermath, it is necessary to mention some highlights of the extraordinarily complex international politics of the time, which so affected Vietnam. First of all, as cold war tensions between the United States and the Soviet Union intensified and as the Communists began to go on the offensive in China, the French decided in 1947 to try to work out the so-called Bao Dai Solution. In part this effort was designed to answer earlier American arguments against "racist" colonialism, and thereby to put their reconquest of Indochina into the framework of the world wide struggle between "free" and Communist states. It was in October 1947 also that former U.S. Ambassador to Paris William C. Bullitt visited Bao Dai, then in Hong Kong, and wrote an influential article advocating such a policy. The French, in brief, hoped that Bao Dai, the heir of the nineteenth-century Nguyen dynasty, would do what the Communists had refused to do, namely settle for less than full independence within the French Union, and thereby create the semblance of a sovereign Vietnamese state, seeking French help against the Communists.

At first Bao Dai insisted on firm guarantees of independence and, it should be remembered, he had abdicated in favor of Ho Chi Minh in August 1945, serving for several months as Ho's "special adviser." But after great pressure from non-Communist Vietnamese intermediaries as well as the French, in March 1949 Bao Dai signed what became known as the Elysée agreement.* In it, at least three years too late, French conceded that Cochin China was to be merged with an "independent Vietnam, an Associated State of the French Union," and the French agreed to end their direct administration of Hanoi, Haiphong, and Da Nang. But as in 1945 and 1946 and throughout the war, there was continued basic disagreement as to what constituted independence. The French insisted on keeping complete control of foreign policy, their Vietnamese-staffed army, and on maintaining very unequal economic concessions.

Further negotiations over these and other problems dragged on interminably, and as late as July 1953 there was new talk of "perfecting the independence and sovereignty of the Associated States of Indochina." On the very eve of the final French defeat, in early June 1954, yet another (the fifth) treaty for "total independence" was signed. Not long after the official creation of his State of Vietnam in July 1949, Bao Dai himself was forced to admit, it is not a "Bao Dai solution . . . but just a French solution," that is, another ploy to try to broaden France's base of support while nonetheless retaining its privileges.

It was another classic case of too few reforms, too late. Had the French offered in 1945 and 1946 what, under military pressure, they partly gave in 1949 and later, there might have been a chance to salvage a moderate, pro-French Vietnam.

Even had the French given greater and earlier concessions toward Vietnamese nationalism however, there still would have been required far greater dedication and leadership for the creation of a moderate republic than ever appeared among Vietnamese groups other than the Communists. Rather, for the most part, non-Communist Vietnamese demonstrated short-sightedness, factionalism, and corruption, and in addition were considered either too pro-French (as the Constitutionalists), too tied to the Chinese (as the VNQDD), or the Japanese (as the Dai Viet). The Cao Dai and Hoa Hao had almost made deals with France in the late 1940s, and the Binh Xuyen did so unabashedly. Nor did the various prime ministers of Bao Dai (Nguyen Van Xuan, Nguyen Phan Long, Tran Van Hu, Nguyen Van Tam, Buu Loc) exhibit more than fleeting

*Named after the Paris residence of the president, then Vincent Auriol. In September 1947 at Ha Long, the French had set initial terms for Bao Dai's return, and a Provisional Central Government under Bao Dai and his minister, Nguyen Van Xuan, appeared in April 1948.

moments of effective, independent leadership. Furthermore, as in the American war, corruption became ever more evident, especially in the manipulation of overvalued piastres, which were exchanged for greater numbers of francs, officially pegged at seventeen francs the piastre until 1953, then ten to one, but about seven to one on the black market.

Given this lack of statesmanship and leadership on the part both of the French and their allies, the Viet Minh continued to enjoy by far the greatest popular support. Members of Bao Dai's staff referred to them as "our heroes," and even future U.S.-backed Saigon leader, Nguyen Cao Ky, would declare a quarter of a century later, "to all of us, Ho Chi Minh was, until 1946, a great patriot. As a schoolboy, I happily joined the chanting of a chorus, 'no one loves Ho Chi Minh more than the children.' " In the words of historian Joseph Buttinger:

> The Viet Minh over the years had succeeded in creating an image of itself as an anti-French, anti-Japanese, anti-Chinese force. Nobody liked the war, but it never occurred to the people to put the blame for it on the leader of the Viet Minh . . . [who] had never betrayed the aims of militant nationalism. By choosing armed resistance rather than any further retreat, Ho had proved himself the most determined patriot in the nationalist camp.[19]

This judgment was confirmed by an eminent French scholar and diplomat on the occasion of the last direct French effort to avert full-scale war before the launching of Valluy's general offensive in October 1947. This was when Paul Mus, special counselor to Emile Bolleart, successor to D'Argenlieu as high commissioner for Indochina, met with Ho Chi Minh in the jungle on May 12, 1947. Presenting terms demanding the free entry of French troops throughout Viet Minh territory that Mus knew to be tantamount of a demand for surrender, he reported Ho's famous reply: "There is no place in the French Union for cowards. I would be one were I to accept."[20]

During these years, indeed, Ho was reported frequently under attack for his concessions in 1946 by militants Hoang Quoc Viet and others, including at times Giap. During these years also Ho was frequently ill with malaria, was nearly captured in 1947, and on many occasions between then and late 1954 was rumored dead in the European press.

Ho in fact was very much alive and presided over the Party's Second National Congress, February 11–19, 1951, held at Vinh

Quang, Tuyen Quang province (after the First held at Macao in March 1935). It was at this time that the Party was officially reconstituted as the Vietnam Workers' Party (Vietnam Lao Dong Dang), following its formal dissolution in November 1945. Paradoxically, the Second Congress also declared that the Viet Minh had been dissolved into the still broader United Front organization, the Lien Viet, which had been created in May 1946.

The 211 delegates and alternates to the Congress, representing over 760,000 Party members, elected Ho Chi Minh chairman, Troung Chinh secretary-general, and a Central Executive Committee (Political Bureau) of nineteen, also including Le Duan, Vo Nguyen Giap, Pham Van Dong, Le Duc Tho, Hoang Quoc Viet, Chu Van Tan, Ton Duc Thang, and Pham Hung. The Congress declared itself guided by the "doctrinal thought of Marx, Engels, Lenin and Mao Tse-tung," and committed itself to "drive out the imperialist aggressors, to gain genuine independence and unity for the nation, to remove the feudal and semi-feudal leftovers, to give land to the tillers, to develop the people's democratic regime, and to lay foundations for socialism."[21] The Party was to work for these goals with "iron discipline," "democratic centralism," and by the use of "criticism and self criticism," the latter in turn leading to the campaign for the "three rectifications" and some purges in 1952. Ho Chi Minh's important *Political Report* to the Congress summarized "the experiences of twenty years of struggle of the Party" and noted that the second stage of the resistance war would soon pass to the third stage of the "general counteroffensive," although he refused to predict its exact beginning.

Of extreme importance for this final stage of the war against France was the triumph of the Chinese Communists, who moved to their own third-stage "general counteroffensive" in the summer of 1948. The defeat of Chiang Kai-shek's armies came in Manchuria and North China late in that year, while already in the extreme south isolated Chinese Communist units on two occasions in 1947 and 1948 had crossed into Vietnam from Guang Xi province. Then with the arrival of Lin Biao's armies on the border of Vietnam in late 1949 came a great increase in Chinese aid for the Viet Minh, up to 4,000–6,000 tons a month by early 1954. And by the time of the decisive battle of Dien Bien Phu, a Chinese staff headed by Wei Guoqing, with up to seven other generals, helped to coordinate that aid and the final offensive.

THE FINAL PHASE OF THE WAR was not long in coming. Viet Minh units, following victories along the northern border in 1950 and temporary setbacks in 1951, began moving into northwestern mountain areas, especially after October 1952. Then, when the Navarre Plan backed by the United States led to the parachuting of the first of some 16,000 men into Dien Bien Phu on November 20, 1953, in an effort to both protect Laos and to draw the Viet Minh into open combat, Giap accepted the challenge on both counts.

First of all, shock brigades involving up to 200,000 porters* were able, to the surprise of the French, to transport heavy artillery and other weapons and supplies by bicycle, foot, and animal cart across 500 kilometers of extremely difficult mountain terrain, and thereby create attack positions on thousand-meter peaks surrounding the village of Dien Bien Phu. Where the French commanders, and in February visiting American General John W. O'Daniel, declared themselves "enthusiastic" for the coming battle, they were in fact surrounded in a hopeless position.

There followed several months of offensives elsewhere, notably the Christmas Day Communist capture of Thak Hak, Laos, on the upper Mekong, which cut northern Indochina in two, and further preparations around Dien Bien Phu, including massive stockpiling of supplies and the digging of up to one hundred kilometers of tunnels to the very edges of French headquarters. Then on March 13, 1954, the Communists opened their attack, almost exactly twenty-one years to the day before the final offensive against Saigon. With violent bombardments and "human wave" offensives, they captured two important outposts the first three days of battle, a third on the eighteenth, and another series in early April. The airstrip was put out of action on March 28, and thereafter the garrison had to be supplied by parachutes, 82,296 of which, according to Bernard Fall's graphic description, "covered the battlefield like freshly fallen snow. Or like a burial shroud." The fortified position was slowly but steadily being choked to death.[22]

When the U.S. Congress and England refused to go along with the plans of Secretary of State John Foster Dulles, Vice-President Richard Nixon, and Chief of Staff Admiral Arthur Radford, for American airstrikes—including, it seems, hints if not outright pro-

*Who used an estimated three million workdays in several months, according to Party histories.

posals for the use of tactical atomic weapons—to try to save the outpost, Dien Bien Phu was doomed. A final series of Communist attacks led to the surrender of the 11,000 survivors, the pride of the French expeditionary force. They had lost over 1,500 dead and 4,000 wounded in this battle, and the Communists 23,000, of whom 8,000 were killed, out of an attacking force of 49,500 with another 55,000 support troops. They were the most dramatized casualties of a war in which the French suffered 20,685 men killed, and their French Union forces, composed of other nationalities, over 50,000 more dead and about 100,000 wounded. Total casualties of the French war have been estimated at up to a half million dead and one million wounded. In addition to the fighting around Dien Bien Phu in early 1954 there were larger than ever attacks on French positions by local guerillas throughout the country, especially along the central coast, in the Central Highlands, where the Viet Minh scored another striking victory at An Khe in June, and in the southern delta.

The game was up, as the French were increasingly aware. Massive American aid, and hints of armed intervention in the belief that stopping the Communists was "essential to the security of the free world, not only in the Far East but in the Middle East and Europe as well," helped French conservatives to continue the war as long as there seemed the slightest hope of stopping Ho Chi Minh and "containing Chinese communism." They argued that militarily the tide was about to turn, but even before the fall of Dien Bien Phu, Paris had come to realize it must end the war. As early as October 1953, it spoke of France's interest in a settlement and immediately after Dien Bien Phu, Socialist Pierre Mendes-France came to power on June 17, 1954, with the promise to "conclude an honorable peace by July 20," a deadline he would just meet.

For their part, the Communist powers, if not their Vietnamese comrades, were also interested in a renewed effort for peace. The death of Stalin in March 1953 accelerated a shift by both Russia and China toward a politics of "peaceful competition" and in July 1953 came the armistice ending the Korean War by reverting to a post-1945 division at the thirty-eighth parallel between the Communist north and the non-Communist south. The partition of the country between the Communists and their enemies became an obvious idea also for Vietnam, but the indigenous Communists of Vietnam were far stronger than those of Korea, which fact explains much subsequent history. Nonetheless, after eight years of war against a militarily vastly superior enemy, Vietnamese Communist leaders also had reasons to negotiate. On November 26, 1953, Ho Chi Minh declared he would be "ready to examine French propositions," provided they recognized the independence of his country.[23]

NEGOTIATIONS OVER THE FUTURE OF VIETNAM came with the transformation of the Geneva Conference on the problems of Berlin and Korea, which had begun on January 25, 1954, into a conference on Indochina. In February and March, the French General Assembly declared its desire to negotiate and then the Battle of Dien Bien Phu served as an opening fanfare. Although the United States continued to object, the conference duly began to consider Indochina on May 8, the day after the fall of Dien Bien Phu. Great Britian and the Soviet Union, represented by their foreign ministers, Anthony Eden and Vyacheslav Molotov, were declared cochairmen of the conference, which was attended also by reprsentatives of the People's Republic of China (Zhou Enlai), Laos, and Cambodia, as well as by representatives of the United States (Bedell Smith), and Bao Dai's State of Vietnam, headed by Ngo Dinh Diem after his accession to the premiership on June 16. But the negotiations were primarily between the Democratic Republic of Vietnam, represented by Foreign Minister Pham Van Dong, and France, after June 17 represented by delegates of new Premier Mendes-France.

After weeks of complex and difficult negotiations, the conference produced the Geneva Accords of July 20, actually signed by France and Communist Vietnam in the early morning of July 21, but with the clock unplugged to meet the deadline of Mendes-France. Although the contending sides would claim their own interpretations of the documents, it seems clear that essentially the Geneva Accords represented a face-saving formula for the French, recognizing the Communist victory in the north, but dividing the country temporarily at the seventeenth parallel, with the French and anti-Communists to be guaranteed haven in the southern part of the country until "free" elections two years later, in July 1956, which supposedly would reunify the country. All expected, whether they feared or hoped, that if such elections were to be held, Ho Chi Minh would win them, while elections in 1955 in Laos and Cambodia would presumably go to moderate nationalists in those countries.

Considering the popularity of Ho Chi Minh throughout the country and the military strength of the Communists even in the south, where they controlled over half the territory and up to one-third the people, it seems evident that Pham Van Dong, pressed by Russia and China in the interests of their worldwide policies, made the greater concessions. A leading authority of South Vietnam after 1954 stated that "what is surprising [about the Geneva Accords, considering the respective positions] . . . is that the French came off so well."[24] However, it is also true that the Viet Minh were much weakened militarily by their all-out effort at Dien Bien Phu, which undoubtedly caused them losses heavier than the 10 percent casualties suffered by the French. In April, at the same time the French were seeking a last-minute rescue by the United States, the Viet Minh were also appealing for greater Chinese Aid.

The most important of the Viet Minh concessions were the agreement to the division of the country, which specified that the division be as far north as the seventeenth parallel, and that elections be held two years later rather than six months later. The last two concessions were apparently agreed to by Zhou Enlai and Molotov in late June and early July, and forced on the Vietnamese Communists. For when Pham Van Dong first spoke of the possibility of a division of the country on May 25, he said that this could be done only temporarily, and subject to elections within several months which, as in 1946, it was thought Ho Chi Minh would certainly win.* And Dong argued that any such division should be as far south as the thirteenth or fourteenth parallels (south of Quang Ngai), since even the postwar division for the acceptance of the Japanese surrender had been at the sixteenth parallel (south of Hue). Indeed it is certain, although few details have come to light, that many Party militants like Nguyen Thi Dinh would have gone on fighting to win over remaining areas of the south.

Pham Van Dong made another compromise, apparently at Zhou Enlai's insistence, when on June 16 he agreed to drop earlier insistence on representation for the revolutionaries of Laos and Cambodia in return for promises of the neutrality of these two smaller neighbors. There was also a Communist concession on the replacement of war material while banning reinforcements, since the anti-Communist side was incomparably better armed. Finally,

---

*Eisenhower later wrote that most felt "possibly 80 percent of the population would have voted for the Communist Ho Chi Minh as their leader, rather than Chief of State, Bao Dai," at least as of 1954. Pham Van Dong, however, reportedly admitted control of not more than one-third of the population of the south in 1954, and by 1956 conditions had changed further in ways that might have changed earlier estimates.

Dong agreed to a three-way division among neutral India (as chairman), capitalist Canada, and Communist Poland for the International Control Commission (ICC) to supervise the accords, instead of the earlier insistence on reserving that duty for the adversaries, France and the Democratic Republic of Vietnam. Twenty-five years later, Hanoi charged it had been ready to go on to final victory after Dien Bien Phu but was forced to compromise by the Chinese.[25]

THE MOST IMPORTANT TERMS of the Geneva Agreements were for a cease-fire, followed by the regroupment within 300 days of Communist forces to the north of the seventeenth parallel and of anti-Communists to its south (articles 1, 2, 10). Some 80,000 to 100,000 Communist sympathizers went north and about ten times that number, mostly Catholics, went south, points to which we will return. This first "Agreement on the Cessation of Hostilities," signed by representatives of France and the Democratic Republic of Vietnam, also banned the introduction of foreign troops and arms from the three countries (articles 16–19), called for exchanges of prisoners (article 21), specified the duties of the International Control Commission (articles 28–47), and noted that the division at the seventeenth parallel was "provisional," "pending the general elections which will bring about the unification of Vietnam" (article 14).

Then a "final declaration" of the Congress concluded several hours later and dated July 21 further "noted" (although it was not signed) that the division at the seventeenth parallel was "provisional, and should not in any way be interpreted as constituting a political or territorial boundary," and that "general elections shall be held in July, 1956" to determine the future of the country, (Final Declaration, clauses 6 and 7). Furthermore, the Final Declaration declared that the Vietnamese people shall "enjoy the fundamental freedoms, guaranteed by democratic institutions established as a result of free, general elections by secret ballot" (clause 7), and that there should be no "individual or collective reprisals against persons who had collaborated in any way with one of the parties during the war" (clause 9).

On the day following the close of the conference, Ho Chi Minh declared that the Geneva Accords represented a "great victory for our diplomacy," given the expulsion of France and presumably in expectation of the complete unification of the country under his government in 1956. About the same time, the Sixth Plenum of the Party Central Committee confirmed support, while warning of consequences of noncompliance with its interpretation of the agreement. But, in striking contrast, the newly installed Saigon government of Ngo Dinh Diem declared the agreements "catastrophic and immoral" and that it would reserve "complete freedom of action" with regard to them. For the United States, Bedell Smith stated that his government would "refrain from the threat or use of force to disturb" the accords, but also that it was "not prepared to join in the declaration . . . such as is submitted," that is with the provisions referring to the "provisional" nature of the division at the seventeenth parallel and the call for elections in July 1956. President Eisenhower declared on the same day that the United States "did not take part in the decisions of the Conference and is not bound by them."

Hence, neither the Saigon government nor the United States, who together would thwart the unification of Vietnam by the Communists for another twenty years, signed the Geneva Agreements. Nonetheless, they recognized that the alternative to them was the continuation of the heavy fighting then in progress, and hence pledged not to disturb them. But the United States already indicated the shape of things to come by declaring on June 29 that it would seek "free elections supervised by the United Nations," that is, a type of election in 1956 that the Communists could hardly be expected to accept in an era where United Nations forces led by the United States had just stopped the Communist conquest of South Korea. In February 1954, also with Korea very much on his mind, Eisenhower had declared, "I can conceive of no greater tragedy than for the United States to become involved in an all-out war in Indochina." The president had refused to go along with the Dulles-Radford-Nixon plan for such intervention in April, but as yet insensitive to the contradiction between American desires and possibilities for Vietnam, in that same month agreed with the "falling domino principle," which held that the loss of Vietnam to the Communists would be followed by similar results elsewhere and, therefore, would not be acceptable to the United States.

In order to prevent such hypothetical falling dominos, in the decade after Geneva, therefore, the United States proceeded to undertake, as earlier had the French with Bao Dai, all possible measures to stop the progress of Communism in Vietnam. Washington stopped the publication of favorable reminiscences of mid-1945 encounters with Ho Chi Minh by OSS agent Archimedes Patti (finally published in 1981). Above all, it supported Diem's scuttling of the compromise agreed on at Geneva which, in return for a temporary division of the country giving the French time to depart, had agreed to elections which would lead to unification, undoubtedly under Ho Chi Minh. Thus Saigon, backed by the United States, blocked the elections of 1956, carried out systematic reprisals against supporters of the Viet Minh who remained in the south, and increased American economic and military involvement until Eisenhower's "tragedy" . . . of all-out war in Indochina" became a reality in the 1960s.[26]

For the Communists of the south, there was no peace in the 1950s either, and to further background of their struggle we shall now turn.

PART TWO

Communist Strengths and Establishment Weaknesses

CHAPTER SIX

Nationalism and Ideology

BEFORE CONTINUING THE CHRONOLOGICAL NARRATIVE of the further decades of war that followed the events of 1954 and that so heavily and tragically involved the United States, more analysis is needed of the background for the astonishing survival and victories of the Communists. About twenty years after the victory of Dien Bien Phu, in his 1972 "to arm the Revolutionary masses, to build the peoples army," Vo Nguyen Giap would write:

> The war of the Vietnamese people has become the legendary, historical event of the twentieth century. Our people have demonstrated a striking truth: in our era, a people, even if small . . . and poor, if it is united and resolute, if it possesses a just revolutionary line, if it knows how to apply creatively Marxist-Leninist principles of the revolution of all the people and people's war . . . can defeat an aggressor many times more powerful than it.[1]

Discussion of several ideas of this quotation dominate this and the following chapter, namely, characteristics of Vietnamese nationalism that inspired the Communist leaders and how they organized that sense of nationalism, added social commitment, and created a people's war that indeed did become one of "the legendary historical events of the twentieth century."

First of all, it is evident that nationalism was intimately tied to the development of communism in Vietnam from the beginning. The patriotism that inspired Ho Chi Minh and his disciples developed into a "national communism" from the 1920s on. And paradoxically, France played an enormous role in the development of this revolutionary Vietnamese nationalism, both negatively and positively. There was the understandable reaction to the new difficulties posed by French rule which, for example, quadrupled the land under cultivation between 1880 and 1930, but exported and taxed the Vietnamese so much that per capita food consumption declined in the same period. And the economic growth and accompanying expansion of the urban middle class unleashed by the French colonization of Vietnam naturally led to a parallel expansion of revolutionary ranks from among the better educated, often more frustrated, younger generations.

The ideas of the great French Revolution played an equally important, but positive role. With supreme irony, the official stationery of the Colonial Ministry and even the walls of some prisons were headed by the famous slogan "Liberté, égalité, fraternité." And while school children were taught about "nos ancetres, les Gaulois," it was hardly surprising that more and more Vietnamese, even as they were urged to celebrate the victories of Joan of Arc over the English in the fifteenth century, thought instead of their own Trung sisters, who had led a revolt against Chinese occupation some 1,400 years earlier.

Therefore, in reaction to the French, Vietnamese turned to their own examples of resistance to foreign invaders, and as twentieth-century patriots never tired of pointing out, their history was full of such exploits. In addition to the Trung sisters, who rebelled against China, A.D. 40–43, dozens of other early heroes fought the Chinese, and the Vietnamese were among the few peoples to defeat the Mongol armies, which they did on four occasions in the late 1200s. Just before his death in 1300, Tran Hung Dao, perhaps the greatest leader of those wars, stated principles of a resistance war that were especially dear to the Vietnamese Communists: "The enemy relies on numbers. But to oppose the long with the short—there lies our skill. If the enemy makes a violent rush it is easy to defeat him. But if he shows patience . . . then . . . as in a chess game . . . the army must be united and of one mind, like father and son. . . ."[2]

Such an extremely rich, millenarian tradition of resistance to foreign invasion joined with other characteristics of the Vietnamese people to create an extraordinary spirit of "endurance, sacrifice, patriotism," and sense of solidarity of family, village, and country. Various Vietnamese proverbs graphically propose, "It is better to die in honor than live in disgrace," "A single tree cannot make a forest," "When pirates come into the house, even women must take up arms," and "Our hearts are like iron and stone, they will never tremble." Vietnamese repeated such Confucian injunctions as "If one knows the way to live, one also knows the way to die," "To serve men with all one's heart is to serve the gods as well"; "Study the way, as the worker shapes his stone. Improve oneself as the artisan polishes jade; without study, men cannot know the principle of things"; and "Every day, three times a day, I examine myself to see whether I may have failed to serve others, failed to keep my word to my friends, or forgotten to apply the principles I have been taught." In short they learned some of the sources of strength of Imperial China, and went on to use these lessons as necessary against their teachers, and in the twentieth century, of course, against France and the United States.

Vietnamese also believed in the Buddhist concept of karma—that one's future is shaped by one's actions, as well as in general Buddhist concepts of dedication, poverty, and simplicity. Clearly, therefore, traditional Vietnamese responsiveness to fate and the will of heaven, often characterized as simple fatalism, did not preclude effective action. It has been described better as "pragmatic fatalism," or the desire to change what can be changed while accepting what cannot be changed. Such concepts and the sense of community anchored in the some 30,000 hamlets of the country made the Vietnamese a strong and dynamic people. As French scholar Paul Isoart put it in 1961, the Vietnamese were "habituated to suffering . . . insensitive to pain, tough in the face of hardship to the point of stoicism, although also pitiless to the point of cruelty" toward their enemies.[3]

Such a people, numbering about twenty million by 1940, in such a land promised great achievements in the modern age, but only if they could be mobilized and directed in new ways. Here numerous other questions arise for the historical interpretation of how that mobilization and direction proceeded, and how it was that the Communists came to guide it.

First of all, we must note the qualitative change from earlier patriotism to the nationalism of the twentieth-century leaders. Modern nationalism requires a well-reasoned conception of the future, which in the West did not come until after the eighteenth century. In Vietnam, as in most of Asia and the Third World, it was not until the twentieth century that nationalist leaders could formulate conceptions of a new, "modern" nation. Patriotic bravery was there for two millenia, and late nineteenth-century patriots in that tradition could accurately state, "We swear to fight [foreign invaders] forever and without respite . . . there will be men to resist the aggressor [France] as long as grass grows on the soil of this country," and the "courage of our mandarins, . . . as of our people and simple soldiers cedes to none in bravery to the death."[4]

But there was a qualitative change from this traditional patriotism, unmatched as it was to twentieth-century nationalism. In the early decades of the century, well before Ho Chi Minh, men like Phan Boi Chau and Phan Chu Trinh, inspired by similar spirits in China and Japan, went beyond their patriotic ancestors to advocate a new nationalism, calling not only for the expulsion of France but also for the creation of a new kind of society and state.

Here rises again the important question of why the non-Communist successors of the two Phans ceased to lead effective nationalist movements after the 1920s, except as the creatures of foreign powers. The answers to this are many and difficult. There was the question of timing. The earlier writings of men such as the two Phans and the actions of earlier anti-French terrorists were necessary to form a wider base of modern nationalists, committed and angry enough for the further growth of still more revolutionary groups. Then, the French themselves played an unwitting but important role in striking down non-Communist nationalists, especially the Vietnamese Nationalist Party (VNQDD) after 1930, and then helping the Communists to eliminate almost completely the VNQDD, Dong Minh Hoi, and Dai Viet parties after the departure of their Chinese supporters in mid-1946.

Even more, the way for the Communist takeover and radicalization of Vietnamese nationalism was cleared in the early 1940s by World War II and the Japanese expulsion of the French while also encouraging pan-Asian nationalism. And the religious sects, the Cao Dai and Hoa Hao, who in the south at least, at times organized more people than the Communists, nonetheless lacked consistent political programs and leadership.

Yet, as in sports, so in history, opportunity only creates chances, and far more than luck is required to take advantage of these chances. In the case of Vietnam, the chances given to the Communists by the progression of history, the suppression of other nationalist groups and the actions of France, Japan, China, and the United States were surely more than offset by the extraordinary pressures those foreign powers and their Vietnamese allies used against the Communists. Recall Ho Chi Minh's statement of 1960 (see Chapter Two) that fourteen of the Party's Central Committee members had died violently in the course of the Revolution and another thirty had passed collectively 222 years in jail, surely a record for a surviving revolutionary movement. This of course did not refer to the tens of thousands of other Communist victims up to that time, and came before the Second Indochina War took the lives of up to two million more Vietnamese.

How then explain the triumph of the Vietnamese Communists? In addition to nationalism, two words above all have to be analyzed further—organization and ideology, the latter of course including nationalism. Communist mastery of organization was most important of all, as no other Vietnamese group was able even to create a consistently coherent leadership, let alone the "steel fortresses" of village activists that would withstand decades of unprecedented violence directed against them. Such organization, therefore above all, enabled Communist leadership of Vietnamese nationalism. The role of ideology is more difficult and controversial, but certainly was itself a key to the effectiveness of Communist organization. It is no accident that the closest parallels to the history of the Communist revolutions of the twentieth century are those of religious movements. Nationalism joined with Marxism, like some secular religion, to provide an essential cement and reinforcement for the "steel fortresses" Communist activists built.

THE EARLY WRITINGS OF HO CHI MINH provide the best means to begin the exploration of Communist mastery of organization and ideology in Vietnam. The son and grandson of participants in the older-style resistance to France, Ho first of all called attention to the necessity for the awakening of youth to the necessity for a new-style revolution. In a passage reminiscent of the famous appeal to youth made a decade earlier by the founder of Chinese communism, Chen Du-xiu, Ho concluded his *French Colonization on Trial* (first published in Paris, 1925) with a section devoted "to the Annamese youth" and the sentence, "Poor Indochina! You will die unless your old-fashioned youth comes to life."

It was also no accident that the journal of the Revolutionary Youth League, as in China, stressed "Youth" (*Thanh Nien*) in its title. But the question, of course, was how to "come to life" and for what. For Vietnamese and Chinese revolutionaries the answer was both nationalist and Communist, that is, to adopt Marxism-Leninism to "save the country." Paraphrasing Lenin's famous phrase "without a revolutionary theory, there can be no revolutionary movement," Ho Chi Minh wrote in late 1924, "To make revolution, it is necessary to have a correct political line, adequate strategy and tactics, strict organization and to avoid blind actions." He elaborated these ideas as the editor of the journal of the Youth League (*Thanh Nien*) and in the pamphlet that became the bible of Vietnamese revolutionaries after its publication as *The Road to Revolution* in Canton in 1926. There he stated, "to carry out revolution . . . there must be a revolutionary party . . . the party must have a doctrine . . . [and the] most revolutionary is Lenin's."

Like the Chinese Communists, however, Ho gave more stress than did Lenin to morality, as against theory, as the key to organization. This was a natural development given the history of the two countries, where for many centuries good Confucians believed that only the most moral of men could organize and govern effectively. Hence an early training manual required that cadres be "thrifty, show justice, avoid self interest, be humble and have a sense of sacrifice." The 1925 regulations of the Youth League, similarly declared "the League member vows to sacrifice his own will, his own interests and his own life in order to first carry out national liberation [overthrowing French colonialists and restoring independence to the people], and later carry out the world revolution [overthrowing capitalism and achieving socialism]."

Later statements of the journal of the Youth League elaborated: "It is better to die for liberty than to live in slavery"; "Party members must have a discipline of iron and carry out the orders of superiors even at the risk of their lives"; and "A revolutionary must be patient, loyal, sociable and brave to the point of sacrifice . . . he must obey the general will and die if need be for the community . . . all revolutionaries undergo a thousand vicissitudes . . . and victory will depend in great measure on the fighting spirit of the revolutionaries." Thirty years later (1958) in an essay titled "On Revolutionary Morality," Ho Chi Minh summarized many of these ideas, adding an attack on "the worst and most dangerous vestige of the old society, individualism." He reaffirmed the belief that "the prime criterion of a revolutionary is his resolve to struggle all his life for the Party and the Revolution."

Therefore, Vietnamese Communist publications showed an almost Confucian social ranking to describe Vietnamese society in terms of students, scholars, peasants, workers, artisans, merchants, and soldiers. Yet their differences with the old society and values were far more important. Where traditional China and Vietnam were noted for their stress on Confucian morality and for a relatively high degree of political organization, the twentieth-century revolutionaries preached new doctrines centered on the materialistic dialectic and class struggle, instead of on the Confucian preaching of social harmony. Above all, there was commitment to work with the masses through a new type of social organization based on cells of local activists, and it was their development of this type of Leninist organization of the masses that most distinguished the Vietnamese Communists.

The first issue of the journal of the Revolutionary Youth League on June 21, 1925, declared that revolution is not the work of "a few people, but of the union of thousands and thousands of individuals . . . [in which] the union of [all] revolutionaries is essential." Succeeding issues specified, "There is only one way, and that is to organize the proletariat for revolution," and "It is necessary for all the people and not one man or group, to rise up."

Because of this stress on organizing the masses and in reaction to the relatively isolated actions of other nationalists, in the 1920s the Vietnamese Marxists opposed individual terrorism, "because our enemies are numerous and if one falls, he is immediately replaced by another." Therefore, "Assassination is not a revolutionary means. On the contrary, it is an obstacle to the progress of the revolution." On the other hand, as the journal explained (November 14, 1926), "Violence is the only means to destroy capitalism and imperialism," but it must be organized class violence and not individual terrorism. Thus the revolt of the VNQDD at Yen Bay in February 1930 failed, according to a Party analysis a month later, because it was carried out only by a few soldiers, it "was not well organized and did not have the support of the peasants and workers. The revolution can only triumph if it has popular support, above all of the peasants and workers."

It was the Youth League and after 1930 the Communist Party that were to organize the people in Lenin's phrase as "the midwife" of revolution. As the journal of the Youth League stated on September 18, 1927, "A directing Party is necessary to organize revolutionary groups . . . and must introduce agitators in all factories, schools and public and private establishments in cities and villages . . . to counsel and direct." That and other statements frequently referred to the Party as the "doctor of the revolution," who must understand the needs of the people as the doctor understands the causes of illness. Reflecting not only the Western revolutionary tradition of Rousseau and Robespierre, here the Vietnamese made almost a direct paraphrase of "the Chinese Machiavelli," Han Fei (third century B.C.), in the statement, "Revolutionaries are like doctors, and oppressed peoples like the ill. As a doctor feels the pulse of a sick person, diagnoses his sickness and prepares necessary remedies, so the revolutionary sounds out weak and oppressed peoples and indicates the revolutionary panacea and how to use it." And where the doctor gives bitter medicine to cure an illness, so the revolution may cost "a great number of lives," but it will establish a better society. And foreshadowing Ho Chi Minh's 1946 statement "All those who do not follow the line which I have laid down will be broken," the journal stated that in order to "avoid the sabotage of our revolutionary work, we must pitilessly crush all false revolutionaries." Like good Confucians, however, they also paraphrased the Analects and stated, "If you want to cure the illness, first heal yourself," insisting that all revolutionaries maintain high moral standards and share the hardships of the people.

The publications of the Revolutionary Youth League in the late 1920s therefore showed relatively sophisticated understanding of the need for propaganda and for organization. Issues of February 29 and May 8, 1927, explained, a "precondition is to explain that the true interest of the people is revolution . . ." and "without organization there can be no revolution." Issues of September 25 and November 1, 1927, stated the essential principles of what would become known as the Mass Line, noting the need to understand the needs of the people, to make plans, and then to "organize, educate and discipline [the masses] and prepare them for combat." In sum, as "your twenty million compatriots are plunged in an ocean of misery . . . the sole means for deliverance is [for them] to make revolution, and throw the capitalists and French imperialists into the sea." As a Communist leaflet found near Saigon in September 1930 put it, "Struggle and we shall live. Abstain from struggle and we will die."[5]

Following the setbacks of the Chinese Communist Party after April 1927 and increasing repression in Vietnam, especially after the 1930–1931 uprisings, the Vietnamese revolutionaries became increasingly concerned with more Stalinist types of ideology and organization. This Bolshevization of the Party, carried out mostly under the leadership of students returned from Moscow, such as Le Hong Phong and Tran Van Giau, gave way in turn to renewed flexibility and tolerance with the development of world United Fronts against fascism after 1935, and under Ho Chi Minh's leadership once more after 1938. The mature Indochinese Communist Party, as elsewhere, of course, absorbed and refined both hard-line and flexible tendencies, and gave different emphases at different times according to the dialectic of party politics and historical change.

During the period of Bolshevization from the late 1920s to the mid-1930s, special attention was given to the question of the class backgrounds of Party members. Could they adequately serve the masses if they themselves came from an elite background? Marx had referred to "far-sighted" leaders of the previously dominant class crossing over to lead the revolution of an ascendant class, and this presumably could explain Lenin's and Ho Chi Minh's leadership of a "proletarian revolution" even though they were of mandarin or at least upper-middle-class background, while Mao Zedong was of rich peasant, or lower-middle-class background. But the predominantly petty-bourgeois (peasant rank and file, intellectual leaders) origins of the Chinese and Vietnamese parties have come under constant attack from Moscow, from the Trotskyists, and back in the early 1930s from those parties themselves. As a Communist publication wrote on December 30, 1933, "In the epoch of Imperialism, a revolutionary movement cannot triumph unless workers play the principal role, have political hegemony . . . are the majority of the Party . . . and guide the others . . ."[6]

As early as June 1929, therefore, in order to reduce their peasant and intellectual composition, some Vietnamese Marxists adopted the slogan "Proletarianize to mobilize the proletariat." Before that, Ho Chi Minh and his comrades spoke primarily of the "workers and exploiters" in vague terms and defined the proletariat simply as "the most oppressed class . . . with the greatest revolutionary resolve." But, with the new emphasis, in at least one province (Nam Ha near Hanoi), according to a recent study, Party membership was proletarianized to the extent that workers rose from 24 percent in 1927 to 40 percent of membership in 1931, with peasants reduced to 35 percent and petty bourgeois intellectuals to 20 percent.

Hence, there have been constant efforts to proletarianize the Vietnamese Party since the late 1920s, although in an overwhelmingly peasant country, not surprisingly, most members have remained petty bourgeois in origin. But the Vietnamese, like the Maoists of China, and with good Confucian idealism, generally have taken the fundamental point to be the willingness of Party members, even intellectuals or peasants, to work for a more proletarian and industrialized society. You could be proletarian if you thought proletarian.

YET, OBVIOUSLY, "THE MASSES" of Vietnam meant overwhelmingly the peasants. As early as 1926 and 1927, a series of articles on the "peasants and revolution" in *Thanh Nien* pointed out that since in Vietnam "95 percent of the population work in agriculture," the only way to carry out revolution was to mobilize the peasants in order to "expel the French and overthrow capitalism." Although somewhat naive in holding up the example of the happiness of Russian peasants after the Bolshevik Revolution, these articles indicated some essential aspects of "preparing the masses for revolution." Cadres were instructed to inform themselves of the situation in a given village and then to try to teach the peasants "little by little to understand [that they must change a situation in which] . . . you work all year, you sweat blood and water, you are always badly fed and clothed . . . while the French do nothing, parade in their automobiles and are richly clothed . . . [so] why work for those who are neither Vietnamese nor friends?" There were special appeals also to women, "Oh, my sisters, who do you submit to this iniquitous oppression?" which added to all the other exploitations of the poor by the rich and the French the curses of scorn and rape.

But it was Ho Chi Minh, only a year or so after Peng Pai began work with the peasantry of Hailufeng, China, and before Mao Zedong did so, who expressed above all early Vietnamese comitment to organizing the peasants. As a youth of eighteen, Ho reportedly participated in student demonstrations in support of the 1908 peasant uprisings in Central Vietnam. In June 1923, he attended the Congress of the Peasants International (Krestintern) in Moscow, which elected him to its executive committee in October. In January 1924, he published a short article in *La Vie Ouvrière*, on the peasantry of his country who the French "oppressed as Annamites," and who in addition were "exploited, expropriated, and ruined as peasants" by French and Vietnamese landlords. And in June that year, he told the Fifth Congress of the Communist International in Moscow: "The revolt of the colonial peasants is imminent. They have already risen in several colonies, but each time their rebellions have been drowned in blood. If they now seem resigned, that is solely for lack of organization and leadership. It is the duty of the Communist International to work toward their union. . . ."[7]

Although as explained later by Erich Wollenberg, a German participant in some of these events and an acquaintance at the time of Ho in Moscow, "the Comintern took lightly the Krestintern and even joked about it." Yet subsequent history would show that the idea of organizing the peasants for revolution was anything but a joke. After his expulsion from China with Borodin in mid-1927, Ho wrote a chapter in a classic Communist work, *The Armed Insurrection*, first published in 1928. In it, he stated the two essential points—that the "victory of the proletarian revolution . . . in agricultural and semi-agricultural countries is unthinkable without the aid . . . of the peasantry . . ." and conversely, that peasant movements "could not succeed without the leadership of the working class." Therefore, the proletarian party "must take direction of the movement, organize and mobilize the peasant masses around certain class slogans conforming to the character of the revolution, in a word, direct the movement towards the realization of these slogans . . . and co-ordinate the peasant movement with the goals and revolutionary operations of the proletariat in the industrial centers." After discussion of recent revolutionary history in China, Russia, and Europe, Ho continued that in agrarian societies "the essential condition for the lasting success of Communist movements is solidity of liaison with the peasant masses." And based on sound intelligence and analysis of the region in question, the struggle of the Communists "must reflect the interest of the peasant masses like a mirror in order for it to succeed."[8]

It can be seen from these citations and from those in *Thanh Nien* that Ho and some of his followers already in the late 1920s showed genuine if still somewhat vague, understanding of crucial elements of what would become their real secret weapons by the 1940s, as it was for the Chinese Communists—the ability to organize the peasants for their revolution. Party publications also showed increasing understanding of another crucial element in the development of the Mass Line, the links btween the national and social revolutions. In the late 1920s, *Thanh Nien* repeatedly, if again vaguely, called not only for the expulsion of the French but also for the destruction of native capitalism and feudalism. For example, the issue of August 7, 1927, called for the "overturning of the domination of the capitalists and big landowners, and the collectivization of the means of production."

According to a Party history, the program of the Party's First Congress in 1930 "for the first time explicitly joined the national question to the peasant question," and linked together the "overthrow of French Imperialism, Vietnamese feudalism, and the counterrevolutionary bourgeoisie," with further demands for land confiscation, nationalization of industries, abolition of taxes and corvées, and more equitable working and social conditions. In the 1930–1931 uprisings, the Party specified actions to abolish or lower taxes, debts, and forced labor, and the redistribution to the poor of rice and communal land, and the reduction of rents to one-third. A Communist tract seized by the French at Vinh in March 1931 stated: "What is the goal of Communism? It is to abolish private property, caste divisions [between rich and poor]. . . , the oppression of men by men, and to establish a regime of equality, liberty and fraternity among men of all countries. In order to attain this goal, it is necessary to overturn capitalist society and found a communist society . . . by preparing revolutionary war based on the workers and cultivators. . . ."

The Party's December 1932 restatement of the 1930 ten-point program, besides advocating further proletarianization, again began with stress on the overthrow of French imperialism which has "brought us only humiliation and suffering. Our entire country is locked in a vice of iron, loaded with the chains of slavery [and] . . . is drowning in blood" under the "white terror." But the 1932 program went on to give still more attention to the social revolution of agrarian and urban reforms. It denounced the neglect of land reform by the VNQDD and other groups and their "lack of faith in the revolutionary struggle of the masses," and stated that by contrast "the Indochinese Communist Party provides fundamental tasks of the revolution in order to . . . mobilize the popular masses toward revolutionary insurrection for the freedom of the Indochinese people. It is only through struggle that Indochinese workers will obtain satisfaction, so that our struggle may be victorious, we must be organized. It is important to strengthen the mass revolutionary organizations, principally the red trade unions and peasant unions. . . ."

Party publications of the 1930s are full of similar instructions, and of criticisms of the insufficiencies of work to mobilize the revolutionary anger of the peasants. There were also criticisms of the opposite error—of excessive faith in the peasants—with admonitions to stress the necessity for proletarian leadership of the peasant majority.

But the first lengthy and detailed Party discussion of the peasant question that has survived is the essay of that name written by Truong Chinh and Vo Nguyen Giap in 1937. Because of the changes in party policies after 1935, the authors proceed with relative caution in order to avoid disruptions of their current work for an anti-Fascist front. But their sympathies are clear, as they give a graphic picture of the abuses suffered by Vietnam's peasants, who

> make up 90 percent of the population . . . work very hard out in the fields for a small number of well-fed, satiated and snobbish people who are indifferent to the miserable and wretched plight of the masses. The unlucky and simple-minded peasants accept their wretched fate because they do not understand the cause of their misery. They feel all they can do is implore heaven, pray to Buddha, and hope their children and grandchildren will endure less suffering. . . . However, when they cannot bear it any longer they suddenly wake and see reality. Then they put all their dreams aside and become angry. . . . They leap into battle, determined to wage a decisive struggle against their exploiters . . . they fight as though they would rather die than continue to endure such suffering.[9]

The authors predict "the hour has come" when the peasants will "leap into battle" and after lengthy descriptions of the abusive inequalities and taxation that made "the cost of living 15 percent higher for the Indochinese people than for the other peoples of the Far East." They demand the raising of "the people's standard of living," and an end to exploitation and corruption, and restate the Party position that "the key to the Indochinese peasant problem is to give the peasants land to till."

At least since the 1930 Party program, therefore, the Vietnamese Communists advocated confiscation of "lands of the imperialists and Vietnamese counterrevolutionary landlords," the abolition or lowering of rents and taxes, and social revolution. But in contrast to the Chinese Communist experience and primarily due to the strength of French oppression during their first decade, they had few opportunities to create bases where they could try to carry out these policies. The uprisings of Nghe Tinh in 1930–1931 and in the Mekong Delta in late 1940 were quickly suppressed and given the overwhelming strength of their enemies, the Party was careful especially after 1935 to avoid antagonizing potential allies. In concrete situations throughout, and in propaganda from 1936 on, activists talked primarily of redistributing the communal land [which made up 3 percent of the land in Cochin China, 25 percent in Annam, and 20 percent in Tonkin], and the lands of proven enemies, rather than of land in general, which would have alienated others, such as rich peasants, who the Party hoped to recruit for its fight against France.

Then in the late 1940s, in the expanding areas under its control, the Party revolutionized the old system of allotment of communal lands, in order to deprive village notables of their power to monopolize the benefits of the system, and to equalize distribution of both communal and abandoned lands. Moreover, rents were lowered to 25 percent, debts abolished, and taxes made progressive instead of regressive. However, until at least 1952, although the Party consistently advocated reduction of taxes, interest, rent, and selective confiscation and redistribution of property, it continued to place priority on building the United Front against France, and hence limited the attack on "feudal landlordism" in all its aspects in order to minimize the hostility of landed groups. The extent to which this relative moderation may have cost support among the most deprived and angry peasantry is problematical, as above all it was the constant arrests and military sweeps by the French and their allies that limited revolutionary activity before 1945.

There was also the question of peasant political apathy, which had moved Karl Marx to say the peasants were "conservative, nay reactionary" and as difficult to mobilize as a "sack of potatoes." A French agent of the Sûreté in Vietnam stated similarly in April 1938 that the "great majority of the population of this country are almost completely apolitical . . . lost in the peaceful pursuit of their agricultural occupations."[10] But here again the Vietnamese, like the Chinese Communists, succeeded brilliantly in proving that the Asian peasant was, if anything, more revolutionary than the European proletariat that inspired Marx and Lenin. And like the Chinese Communists, the Vietnamese broke new ground in training their cadres how to get around such apathy and fear as existed, among other things, by teaching simple and relevant forms of communication, learning local dialects and minority languages, and convincing significant numbers of their countrymen of the necessity to strike at the roots of their misery. This work began in a rudimentary way in the 1920s, gathered force in the 1930s even as the Party struggled with unprecedented oppression, and then took off in the 1940s. By 1958, Le Duan could justly state that the Vietnamese revolution was "basically a peasant guerilla war. . . . The peasants have contributed most to the revolution."

BEFORE PROCEEDING WITH FURTHER DISCUSSION of the Communist mobilization of the Vietnamese peasants, another series of problems must be explored, with references to events in later years, especially concerning land reform. The logical culmination of the social revolution after the seizure of power—the nationalization of the economy—while satisfying to the Communists, was bound to clash with fundamental self-interests of large numbers of others. On the one hand, the mobilization of the masses became possible only with an almost religious preaching of both nationalism and radical social change, the one to complete the other. But on the other hand, the very fervor that enabled Communist cadres to be so uniquely effective in such propagandizing, organizing, mobilizing, and organizing to seize power easily led later to excesses that temporarily would swing the pendulum back from extremist revolution toward greater moderation.

This contradiction became most evident concerning the question of land reform, and was especially crucial since Communists and non-Communists alike recognized the peasants' yearning for land as the most important single issue in the carrying out of the social revolution. Accordingly, it is necessary here to carry forward the history of land reform in Vietnam beyond our chronological coverage of political and military events.

Until near the end of the French war, the Communists did not emphasize their commitment to end private property beyond beginning land redistribution in areas they controlled and making general statements about the "overturning of the domination of the capitalists and big landowners, and the collectivization of the means of production." Then when they did have a chance to carry out the socialist revolution in agriculture, many became frightened at the prospect, as they did in Russia in the 1930s and about the same time in China. This was in 1953, when the Viet Minh felt sufficiently sure of their victory over the French and in control of large enough areas of North Vietnam to launch a general land reform for the first time.

Following decisions by the Party, on December 1, 1953, the National Assembly decreed the carrying out of the land reform of the national, bourgeois, democratic revolution, under the slogans "land to the tiller," and "rely on the poor and lower middle peasants, unite with the middle peasants and restrict and finally eliminate the rich peasant enemy. . . ."

As had Mao Zedong in China five years earlier, Party leaders linked the land reform directly to the war effort since "the two tasks of the anti-Imperialist and anti-feudalist struggle are inseparable." In his report to the National Assembly, Ho Chi Minh elaborated, "We must push forward the war of resistance to ensure success for land reform. We must strive to implement land reform in order to secure complete victory for the war of resistance . . . . To carry out land reform is aimed at securing victory for the war of resistance."[11]

After the August Revolution of 1945, the Communists had stepped up "radical rent reduction" not to exceed 25 percent of the crop, redistributed some 310,210 hectares of land to about 17 percent of the peasant households, primarily in the north, and began to form mutual aid teams and cooperatives. But, in order not to antagonize the peasants, they moved very cautiously in speaking of the ultimate Communist goal of nationalization and collectivization of the land. As an important southern cadre explained at the time, even though they were opposed to the system of private land holding, they were "obliged to stick to it because our entire political action among the peasants is based upon the right of each to individual property. We would have risked losing their support had we stopped breaking up landholdings."[12] Nevertheless, in 1953, as their increasing powers enabled them to in the north, the Communists initiated more sweeping land reform, as well as rectification campaigns, before curtailing both campaigns temporarily in the interests of the final war effort. A year after victory over the French, in 1955 and 1956, the reforms resumed and were extended to 72 percent of the rural population of the north, with some 810,000 hectares or about one acre each distributed to two million rural families, who also received access to farm tools and animals.

Once this "bourgeois democratic" phase of the reform had been completed in 1956, which caused some "excesses" in the destruction of "feudalism," as will be discussed further, the north undertook the socialist phase of the collectivization of agriculture and by July 1961 claimed that 88 percent of the peasant homes of the north had been integrated into mostly lower-stage agricultural cooperatives with another 10 percent in other forms of cooperative enterprises. By late 1962, in the second year of the First Five Year Plan, "collectivization and irrigation and drainage works were to all intents and purposes complete" for the first stage of socialist land reform, and food production was said to be growing at an impressive rate of 4 percent per year. Finally in 1969, it was declared that 94.6 percent of the people were in "higher stage cooperatives," although as in Russia and China, with about 5 percent of the land still farmed as "residential land," or privately.

So far, so good. But the excesses of these reforms alarmed many non-Communist Vietnamese on two counts: first, its socialist abolition of private property and, second, the "leftist excesses," especially the erroneous description of too many as "landlords" in the effort to destroy "the feudal landlord class."

During the earlier "bourgeois democratic" phase of land redistribution to the poor, leftist activists perpetrated what has been called "classism," where poor peasants were considered uniformly virtuous and landlords the incarnation of evil. In the process, even landlords who had fought the French were condemned and peasants who had been apolitical during the previous decades were promoted, and an atmosphere was created in which, according to one writer, "people do not dare to greet each other when they meet in the street," and where those who were labeled landlords were "boycotted, shunned . . . became creatures, at whom children were encouraged to throw stones, . . ." and often starved to death as a result.[13]

The same writer and subsequent analysts charged that up to 50,000 people were killed in the land reform of 1955–1956, which, if true, would have been proportionately perhaps twice the number executed in the Chinese land reform a few years earlier, or on the order of 1 in 300 North Vietnamese overall, as against 1 in 600 in China, where up to 1 million out of some 600 million apparently died in the land reform there in the early 1950s.

Careful later studies, however, have estimated that the true figures for those executed in the northern land reform may have been more like 1,500, plus 1,500 jailed according to one, or possibly up to 15,000 killed according to another, and therefore that most of Saigon's propaganda on the subject was exaggerated if not a "total fabrication."[14] In any case, it is clear that considerable violence was used in the northern land reform, which is scarcely surprising given the commitment to destroy the previously dominant "feudal landlord class."

Aside from the violence involved, the main effect of the passions raised by the campaign was to intensify other aspects of the Revolution, particularly economic ones. For a basic problem of the reform, as for the economy of North Vietnam in general, was the paucity of land and the density of population, which reached as many as 3,800 inhabitants to the square mile in Nam Dinh province, as against about sixty in the United States, on the average. Therefore, when the Party divided the population into landlords, rich peasants, upper-, mid-, and lower-middle peasants, poor peasants, and landless agricultural workers, there were bound to be artificial designations since big landlords (with more than 50 hectares) made up only one-tenth of 1 percent of the population, and 60 percent of all land was held in units of about one acre.

In this situation, it was not surprising that the tens of thousands of cadres who mobilized for the land reform committed leftist excesses, especially since Ho had instructed them: "Land reform is a revolutionary task . . . it is a glorious and heavy task. The fighter is not only the man who kills the enemy at the front. You are fighters too, fighters on the anti-feudal front. . . ."[15] Thus primed, these cadres, as did their counterparts in China, led Special People's Tribunals to give public trials of landlords and village tyrants "who for thousands of years had exploited and oppressed them." Shouting "Down with the traitorous, reactionary landlords and exploiters of peasants," they often meted out summary justice on the spot, and the passions released by such actions can easily be imagined.

Ho Chi Minh stated in February 1957, "the land reform law . . . aimed at abolishing the system of feudal ownership, which has hamstrung the onward march of our people, and at restituting land to millions of toiling peasants . . . [It] has overthrown the feudal landlord class and given land to the tillers." But Ho also admitted that "serious mistakes were committed . . . [which] we must resolutely correct. . . ." On August 17, 1956, Ho had demanded the rectification of "errors" that were later revealed to have wrongly classified up to 30 percent of those designated as landlords, to have "relied on false documents to purge and jail many innocent . . . people," and to have taken unnecessary numbers of lives.

The correction of these errors came too late to stop a peasant revolt against the Communist leadership that was doubly embarrassing as it came in early November 1956 at the very time Soviet tanks were suppressing the anti-Russian revolt in Hungary, and especially as it occurred in Ho Chi Minh's own native province of Nghe An. As in 1930 against the French, thousands of peasants marched on Vinh to demand changes in policy, while the Communists, with greater efficiency even than the French in 1931, struck back, reportedly killing up to 1,000 and deporting another 5,000. They also accelerated the "correction of errors," abolishing the Special People's Tribunals and releasing some 12,000 political prisoners. The Party Central Committee's Tenth Plenum in September 1956 had replaced Truong Chinh as secretary-general of the Party (succeeded by Ho Chi Minh, then Le Duan) and dismissed two members of the Political Bureau because of their responsibility for the excesses of the land reform. There were other smaller revolts against the Party, and about this time also there was a Vietnamese version of China's "One Hundred Flowers" policy with early liberalization followed by renewed tightening of policies toward intellectuals. But by 1957 political conditions in the north had returned to the norms of "democratic centralism" or a Party-led "dictatorship of the people," with the collectivization of the land well under way by the following year.

The land reform of the mid-1950s, therefore, by bringing to a head many of the questions of the social revolution, produced the biggest crisis ever faced from within by the Vietnamese Communists. This crisis revealed more clearly than ever the harsh dictatorial side of the Party in power, and in a way grew out of the very strengths of tight organization of activists that gave the Communists such enormous staying power in their long struggles for power. But before the Communist victories, for most of the people in a country whose per capita income in 1955 was estimated at ninety dollars, questions of democracy and freedom were evidently secondary to problems of survival and to perceptions of inequality and injustice. Nor, of course, was there freedom in the anti-Communist areas, a problem that became increasingly severe during the American war.

SOME OTHER RELATIVELY LESS IMPORTANT ASPECTS of Communist mastery of the mobilization of the masses for their revolution can be touched on before returning to the heart of the matter, with a closer look at themes and techniques of village organization after the

1930s, and during the American war. First of all, to return briefly to the question of the proletarianization of the Party in a largely agrarian country, it is evident that the Vietnamese Revolution was marked by greater activity in the cities than was the case in the Chinese Revolution. There were the impressive electoral victories of Communists and Trotskyists in Saigon in the 1930s, Communist control of Hanoi and other cities from August 1945 to early 1946 in the war against the French, and numerous strikes and revolutionary actions in Saigon, Hue, and elsewhere during the American war, especially during the Tet offensive of 1968. Communist historians, therefore, have said that, concerning the balance between urban and rural revolutionary work, the Vietnamese Communist revolution came somewhere between the primarily urban French and Russian revolutions, which also had important peasant rebellions, and the almost entirely peasant-based revolution in China after 1927.

Certainly, the Vietnamese continued to stress the "proletarian line." As Giap stated in 1969, "The working class possesses the highest revolutionary spirit and is both the leading class and the force that together with the peasants and laborers forms the main force army of the revolution. . . ." But he also called for "coordination between building firm strongholds in the rural areas and building revolutionary bases in the urban areas."[16]

Then there is the question of the originality of Vietnamese people's war, or, to turn it around, of Chinese and Russian influences on Vietnamese techniques of people's war. The Chinese, like the French in the formation of modern Vietnamese nationalism, had both positive and negative impact. As part of their Chinese heritage, many Vietnamese were familiar with Sun Zi's *Art of War*, which, before the Chinese invasions of Vietnam after the third century B.C., had established some principles of guerilla warfare, calling for effective intelligence of the enemy, mobility, and use of surprise. Then over the centuries, the Vietnamese added their own ideas to turn such lessons against the Chinese and Mongols with astonishingly effective results. As summarized by Georges Boudarel, "War of movement based on the guerilla, generalization of the resistance, optimum use of the terrain and local factors, of protracted and wearing combat, flexibility of tactics to choose the opportune moment without ever losing sight of the relation of forces and political realities of the war, such in brief are the directing ideas which inspired the great figures of Vietnamese military history in the feudal epoch."[17]

It is evident that, in intensity if not in size, the Vietnamese have at least matched Maoist achievements in mass organization for people's war in the twentieth century, as in earlier centuries they at times more than matched Imperial Chinese military accomplishments, frequently defeating far larger Chinese and Mongol armies. In Canton, in the 1920s and elsewhere in China later, important Vietnamese Communist leaders gathered direct knowledge of Chinese Communist theories and practices of organizing people's war.* Then when Ho returned from Russia to Mao's base in North China in 1938 and to South China in succeeding years, he set about increasing still further his and his comrade's knowledge of Chinese doctrines, immediately writing, for example, three works on guerilla tactics and experiences of guerilla wars in Russia and China.

But the increasing quantity of Vietnamese writings on people's war not only reflected Soviet, and especially Chinese, teaching on the subject, but at least equally their own earlier studies and experiences. They expounded ideas already discussed in the 1920s on the necessity for the formation of militants as the "vanguards of revolutionary action," and on the "organization and mobilization of the peasant masses around certain class slogans," and went beyond them to stress the necessity for political and ideological controls for the soldiers, and the creation of soldiers' committees and political representatives for the army. "The military without the political is like a tree without a root," said Ho Chi Minh, and it was about this time, as seen in Chapter four, that Ho and Giap worked out their versions of Mao's rules for the behavior of their soldiers toward the masses, as well as for the formation of their version of rural bases, or "war zones." The establishment of Giap's Armed Propaganda units in 1944 effectively stressed this potent combination of the use of politics and force "to mobilize and arm the whole people," in order to "combat the long with the short." As Giap wrote in 1959,

> the long term people's war in Vietnam also called for appropriate forms of fighting . . . of an economically backward country, stand-

*Phung Chi Kien, Hoang Van Hoan, and Ho Tung Mau were three early Vietnamese Communist leaders who were long-time members of the Chinese Communist Party. Others such as Ly Bin and Nguyen Son participated in the Long March of the Chinese Communists from 1934 to 1936.

> ing up against a powerfully equipped and well-trained army of aggression. Is the enemy strong? One avoids him. Is he weak? One attacks him. To his modern armament one opposes a boundless heroism to vanquish either by harassing or by combining military operations with political and economic action [and] . . . initiative, flexibility, rapidity, surprise, suddenness in attack and retreat.[18]

The Vietnamese also elaborated their versions of the Maoist formula, "people, not weapons decide wars." As one Vietnamese put it in the 1960s, "In this war, the decisive war is the people. Weapons are dead things. By themselves, they cannot function. It is the people who use the weapons and make them effective."[19]

The learning from China was especially intense during the Thanh Nien period of the late 1920s, when so many of the senior leaders were in Canton, and again in the 1940s and 1950s. By the end of the French war, some 40,000 Vietnamese soldiers were estimated to have received training in China, and some thirty to forty basic writings of Chinese communism had been translated into Vietnamese. Ho himself translated Sun Yat-sen's "Three Principles of the People," and Mao's theoretical works, "On Practice" and "On Contradiction." The creation of the Armed Propaganda units in 1944 is reminiscent of Peng Pai's use of the same term to describe his work twenty years earlier in South China at a time when senior Vietnamese leaders were working nearby in Canton. Vietnamese also must have observed and studied the tunnel systems developed in North China Communist bases during the resistance against Japan. They went on to build extensive underground bases that greatly offset superior enemy fire and airpower, especially in the American war.

There was also continuous attention to the study of the Marxist and Leninist classics, and especially important must have been such Comintern instructions as that of its Sixth Congress, which in August 1928 called for the "use of all kinds of conflicts and contradictions within society . . . to link them with peasant demands to propagandize and mobilize the masses . . ." Yet, in February 1927 Ho could also repeat the argument of two years earlier by a Chinese Marxist, Guo Mo Ro, that there was no basic conflict between Marxism and Confucianism. Ho imagined that, if reborn, Confucius would be "a worthy successor of Lenin." And fifteen years before Mao's famous 1941 attack on the "eight legged essay," Ho stressed the need to avoid what he called the "spinach style" of overly literary and complex sentences in order to better reach the people.[20]

Parallel with the study of Marxist and Chinese doctrines and practice, there was review of earlier Vietnamese history and experiences. In the 1930s, numerous articles in Party journals stressed the necessity of mass organization and the use of Marxist analysis to learn from their country's history and developments, especially to study the Nghe Tinh soviet movement of 1930–1931. In 1947 Truong Chinh's *The Resistance Will Win* and in 1950 Giap's *The Military Responsibility for Preparing the Counter Offensive* were especially important for the propagation of the military principles mentioned above, and for such other ideas as the development of the war from primarily political to a combination of political and military, to primarily military struggle. Then, at the beginning of the French war on December 22, 1946, the Viet Minh announced that they would follow Mao Zedong's concept of the three stages of strategic retreat, stalemate, and counteroffensive, with varying combinations of guerilla, mobile, and positional warfare according to the situation. The Vietnamese works of the time show especially well the combination of learning from their own history, and learning from the experiences of Russia and China, as does Truong Chinh's 1946 analysis of the previous year's August Revolution.

Just how close Vietnamese and Chinese doctrines were, at least until the 1970s, can be seen by a comparison of Vietnamese works on the subject with Mao's December 25, 1947, list of the ten principles of people's war, and with the most famous later exposition on the subject, that of Lin Biao in 1965. Mao outlined "the main methods the People's Liberation Army has employed in defeating Chiang Kai-shek," which I have paraphrased for greater succinctness as follows: (1) attack small, isolated enemy forces first, stronger ones later; (2) take the countryside and small cities first, bigger cities later; (3) concentrate on destroying the enemy's strength, not on holding cities or territory; (4) use superior force in each battle, even if inferior in overall strength, and avoid battle if outnumbered in a certain situation; (5) avoid battle unless sure of winning and adequate preparations have been made; (6) use special strengths of courage and stamina; (7) use mobile tactics; (8) seize weakly defended cities and strong points first, strongly defended ones later; (9) use captured arms and personnel as sources of supply; (10) "make good use of (short) intervals between campaigns to rest, train and consolidate our troops."[21]

In September 1965, Lin Biao cited Vietnam as "the most convincing current example . . . [using] the power of People's War . . . against the U.S. colossus. . . ." But the occasion was also the twentieth anniversary of the surrender of Japan, and most of Lin's analysis naturally was drawn from the history of the Chinese Revolution and its war against Japan.[22] Lin stressed Mao's advocacy of "relying on the peasants and establishing rural base areas," with the creation of a "people's army." This was necessary since "political power grows out of the barrel of a gun," and the Communists were forced to use military tactics for a situation in which "our strategy is 'to pit one against ten,' while our tactic is 'to pit ten against one' . . .," and such principles as "enemy advances, we retreat; enemy halts, we harass; enemy tires, we attack . . . ."

In the actual situation of the American escalation of the Vietnamese war, Lin predicted that the "countryside" of the Third World would surround the cities of Europe and North America, but he was also explaining why China would not intervene directly on behalf of the Vietnamese against the United States, since people's war, by definition, is based primarily on local grievances and energies. Lin himself disappeared in September 1971 as part of the post-Cultural Revolution purge of the left wing of Chinese communism, but his 1965 work not only provides the most succinct resumé of Maoist principles of people's war in a worldwide setting, but is very similar to Vietnamese writings on the subject referred to in this book.

THE MOST COMPLETE VIETNAMESE EXPRESSION of these principles in reference to Vietnamese history has been given in the last major published work of Vo Nguyen Giap, who overall has been matched only by Mao Zedong in the theory and practice of people's war. That work is *To Arm the Revolutionary Masses; To Build the People's Army*. (The passages cited are taken from the French edition.) Published in 1972, the work appears to reveal an increasing distrust of the Chinese. It presents the origins of the theory of people's war as coming primarily from classical Marxism and Ho Chi Minh's early writings, and its practice in the Vietnamese case as coming from a combination of that theory with the rich native tradition of resistance against the Chinese and Mongol invasions of earlier centuries. There is only passing reference to Mao's revolution in China, while Giap expounds at much greater length on the Marxist classics and

Vietnamese history. He cites a late nineteenth-century quotation of Engels showing the relevance of classical Marxism for the subject: "A people who wishes to conquer its independence, will not limit its methods to ordinary warfare. Insurrections of the masses, revolutionary wars, detachments of guerillas everywhere, this is the only method by which a small nation can defeat a bigger nation, and a small army oppose a bigger, better organized army."[23]

According to Giap, therefore, Marx and Engels after the 1850s were "the first to lay down the fundamental theories of the problem of military organization of . . . the working class, and the replacement of the permanent army with the people in arms . . ." while Lenin developed further the idea that the "Red Socialist Army must be built on the base of the armed people." Elsewhere Giap cited approvingly Lenin's statement, "To conduct a war, it is necessary to mobilize all the people's forces, to turn the entire country into a revolutionary bastion . . . ," and Lenin's belief that "In the final analysis, victory in any war is determined by the willingness of the masses to shed blood." While he noted that the "Chinese people set up a Red Army of workers and peasants, and realized 'the mobilization and armament of all the people' to win a striking victory," he implied that the history of Vietnam was even better for understanding the principle of "the armament of the revolutionary masses and the building of the revolutionary army . . ." and that what Marx and Engels had hoped for concerning

> the insurrection of the entire people and the war of the people in nineteenth century Europe, occurred frequently enough a thousand years ago in the feudal epoch of our country . . . . As against several Western countries where the creation of the nation was tied to the birth of capitalism, our nation was formed and developed from very ancient struggles against foreign, feudal aggression and domination. Numerous national uprisings and national wars successively broke out in the course of different centuries of our history . . . [where] the history of European wars of the middle ages is that of slaughters of different feudal groups with mercenary armies, the history of the wars of our country at that time is essentially that of national insurrections and wars, of insurrections and wars of the people.[24]

Giap claims that the Vietnamese "troops of the just cause" in ancient times developed the conceptions of "each inhabitant a soldier" and "villages of resistance" during the early wars against the Chinese and Mongols. They, therefore, carried out "truly a war of the people during the feudal epoch." Therefore, according to Giap, the

> history of insurrections, wars, and military organization of our country, show the heroic traditions of struggle against foreign aggression . . . of a small country, tightly unified and using all of its forces to fight and defeat much more powerful aggressions . . . and put in practice very early the principle of "everyone a soldier" and the leading of large masses to participate in different forms of combat . . . [in order] to "conquer the big with the small," "oppose the few to the many," "neutralize the long with the short," and "get the best of the strong with the weak."[25]

In the twentieth century, however, Giap stresses that "there were created new forms of struggle to assure victory," namely, a "high class consciousness," still more flexible forms of struggle combining political and military, clandestine and semilegal struggle, the ability to seize the right moment to fight, and procuring the help of other socialist countries for modern arms and political support. "The invincible strength of the people's armed forces" in the twentieth-century wars, above all "proceeded from the direction of the Party," a new type of political organization representing the new vanguard class of the proletariat, which "armed the entire people . . . [organized] three categories of regular, regional troops and popular militias." Hence,

> the new development in our Party's line of revolutionary war . . . has been . . . the application of the fundamental principles of Marxism-Leninism concerning war and armed forces to the concrete conditions of our country. Our people have promoted to a higher level the traditional indomitability, the heroism, and combat skill of a people who have defeated powerful aggressor armies in the course of their long history.[26]

Therefore, Giap argued in 1969, Vietnam had creatively adopted:

> the revolutionary violence viewpoint of Marxism-Leninism, of considering revolution an undertaking of the masses, and of regarding revolutionary violence as the violence of the masses . . . combining the masses' political forces with the people's armed forces and armed struggle with the masses' political struggle, thus turning them into uprisings and a war of all the people.

He further elaborated:

> To conduct a people's war, it is necessary to adopt a correct line in the building up of forces. This is the line of mobilizing, arming and motivating the entire people to participate in all types of uprising and war, and in building up a widespread mass political force . . . with the three categories of people's armed forces as the nucleus . . . to stage a nationwide struggle against aggression . . . [which] inherits and develops to a new level the tradition of nationwide anti-invasion struggle, in which everyone must be a soldier and every woman must fight the enemy when he invades her home . . .
>
> To conduct a people's war, it is necessary to mobilize the entire people . . . the problem that our Party faced was how could our people—barehanded without an inch of free land as a base, with only a small country and population, and with a backward agricultural economy—struggle to liberate themselves and to build firm bases and rear areas for the people's war to defeat the imperialist aggressors . . .
>
> Our Party creatively solved this problem, . . . it learned to rely completely on the people and to proceed from building the masses' political bases to building bases and rear areas, . . . our sole prop was the revolutionary organization of the people and their already enlightened patriotism and boundless loyalty toward the revolutionary undertaking. Relying on this patriotism, our Party did its best to conduct a revolutionary drive to educate, mobilize and lead the masses in the various forms of their political struggle . . . and following this . . . advanced toward guerilla warfare and the phased armed uprising and building of . . . Liberation Zones . . . [and] guerilla bases . . . .
>
> [Therefore] the main points of our people's formula for waging war [are] first to wage a comprehensive war of all the people and to associate military forces with political forces, armed struggle with political struggle, and armed uprisings with revolutionary war . . . to carry on people's war in mountains, lowlands and cities, closely coordinating attacks . . . to rely mainly on one's own forces and simultaneously endeavour to win over international support . . . .
>
> If coordination of the armed forces with the political forces, armed struggle with political struggle, and armed insurrection with revolutionary war is the main content of the formula for carrying out the all-out war of all the people, then in the field of armed struggle and in the waging of guerilla and regular wars, the coordination of guerilla war with regular war is the most fundamental part of the art of sending all the people headlong into the fight . . . .
>
> Guerilla warfare is a form of armed struggle by the masses of the people.[27]

In other works, written just before the U.S. escalation of 1965, Giap declared that by developing the "fighting spirit and hatred" of the people, and "relying on our absolute political superiority, on the righteousness of our cause, and on our people's unity in struggle, it is possible to use what is weak to fight what is strong, to defeat the most modern weapons with a revolutionary spirit." This was how they had defeated the French, and why "the United States jet helicopters, amphibious cars, ultrarapid submachine guns, flamethrowers, automatic mines, noxious chemicals, unsinkable landing craft and other modern weapons cannot save the puppet army [of Saigon] from repeated failures."

The history of the thirty-year war in Vietnam proves that behind much of Giap's rhetoric about people's war lay important truths, at least for the Vietnamese. But still the question remains, how did they do it?

Above all, wrote Giap, it was a question of forging a correct political line, and this could only be done by a Party formed on Marxist-Leninist principles. "Once the question of 'why and for whom' is clarified . . . victory is certain."

> The Party's leadership of the uprising of all the people and people's war has been reflected primarily in the way it determines the correct political and military lines, sets forth the tasks and the basic and urgent goals of the revolution, and determines and leads the implementation of revolutionary methods, the forms for organizing forces, the methods and tricks involved in the struggle . . . only our Party can correctly combine class interests with national interests, the class factor with the national factor, and genuine patriotism with lofty international proletarianism.[28]

With such beliefs, "many outstanding Party members and cells . . . led the people in combat and production, . . . [to create] the steel fortresses, the efficient general staffs of people's war . . ." Thereby they formed "the line of the people's revolutionary war . . . [linking] the two revolutionary tasks, the national and the democratic . . . mobilizing and organizing the entire people, particularly . . . the large mass of peasants under the leadership of the working class."

Therefore, Giap continued,

> the uprising of the entire people in our country was a new development of revolutionary struggle: combining political and armed violence, and carried out simultaneously in the countryside and the cit-

> ies, the principal means being the political strength of the masses . . . organized into a broad united front based on the alliance of the working class with the peasantry . . . .
>
> [This] practice of revolutionary struggle in our country in new historical conditions has made an original contribution to Marxist Leninist theory on revolutionary armed struggle, according to which revolutionary struggle is a dialectic combination of political struggle, sometimes the form of a long revolutionary war, sometimes the form of an entire people's uprising and sometimes combining all of the above forms.

In his famous 1961 essay, "People's War, People's Army," regarding the French war, Giap had asked: "Why were the Vietnamese people able to win? . . . [They] won because their war of liberation was a people's war . . . the work of an entire people. Therein lies the key to victory . . . [and] our army is a people's army because it defends the fundamental interests of our people, in the first place those of the toiling people, workers and peasants . . . .[29]

As much as Mao Zedong in China, Giap realized the link between the need for military protection and the Mass Line. Writing together with Van Tien Dung, after the final victory of 1975, he said "We applied both the law governing war and that governing armed uprising, and firmly grasped their interaction . . . ," and applied as well renewed coordination between regular and "people's forces" with "attacks by our regional armed forces and uprisings by the masses . . . in coordination with the military attacks of our regular units . . . [We] seized the opportunity to hit the enemy . . . in conformity with the characteristics of uprisings in a revolutionary war . . . ."[30]

Giap also refined the conception of the three-phase war with reference to the relation between the political and military sides, so that in the first phase of retreat in the face of superior enemy strength, the Party stresses political struggle. In the second phase of stalemate, political and military struggle are equally stressed and, in the final phase, military force temporarily becomes dominant until the final victory over the enemy. To ensure the application of these ideals in the Communist armies, up to 40 percent of the troops and over 90 percent of the officers were to be members of the Communist Party, the case by 1954.

It was almost as Giap had said in 1966, " . . . in the military field, apart from the great invention of the atomic weapon, there is a greater invention, the people's war . . . ." Obviously atomic weapons and people's war cannot be compared directly, but it is also true that the Communist revolutions of Asia have shown indeed that "men, not weapons, decide wars." Given the conditions that existed in Vietnam, and despite the awesome power thrown against the Communists, the statement of Premier Pham Van Dong in April 1965 has also been proved correct. He stated, ". . . we have an invincible and powerful ideological weapon, that is the theory of people's war."[31]

MANY OF THESE IDEAS as seen earlier were hinted at as far back as the 1920s in the writings of Ho Chi Minh and in *Thanh Nien*, and developed in the 1930s and especially in the 1940s in North Vietnam. They were first presented in a more systematic form in the 1940s by Truong Chinh. In his "The August Revolution" in 1946 he wrote that "we conquered power, the direct aim of every revolution, because it was the work of a whole people united in the struggle under the leadership of the Indochinese Communist party." In 1947, "The Resistance Will Win" elaborated on the Chinese phrase "the people are the water and our army the fish." Truong Chinh wrote that,

> To achieve good results in guerilla and mobile warfare we must mobilize the people to support our armed forces enthusiastically and to fight the enemy together with them. The people are the eyes and ears of the army, they feed and keep the soldiers . . . constitute an inexhaustible source of strength for the army . . . . We must act in such a way that wherever the enemy goes, he meets the resistance forces of the entire Vietnamese people, who arms in hand, fight against him, ready to die rather than return to slavery.[32]

He also used an East Asian variation of the Italian Fascist symbol of bonding together bands (*fascia*) for strength, stating "To wage a long resistance war, the entire people must be united and singleminded. It is the same with our people as with a bundle of chopsticks. If the chopsticks are bound together, it is difficult to break them. But if they are separated, nothing is easier than to snap them one by one . . . .Therefore, "Our resistance war is a people's war [in which] regular army, militia, and guerilla forces combine and fight together . . . thus catching the enemy between two fires . . . ." And in 1948, Truong Chinh spoke of "the most conscious elements . . . who see the direction of society . . . and in the course of struggle create a revolutionary doctrine that they diffuse among the masses, using all legal and illegal possibilities. . . ."

By the time of the American war, the present secretary-general of the Party, Le Duan, had become another principal spokesman of people's war. In late 1956, explaining to southern revolutionaries the need for restraint despite the failure to hold the 1956 elections and Diem's increasing repressions, Le Duan declared that "Those who lead the revolutionary movement are determined to mingle with the masses, to protect and serve the interests of the masses and to pursue correctly the mass line." And he argued that since they had become "indistinguishable with the masses," it would be no more possible for the "U.S.-Diem" regime to destroy the revolution in the south than it had been for the French in the 1930s and 1940s. About the same time Tran Van Giao even stated, "any revolution is a revolution of the people, for the people and by the people."

In late 1958 a Party "Directive for the South," however, admitted that still more mass work was necessary, and that a "considerable number of Party members do not yet understand" the Party line of restraint in the face of growing repression and "significant losses" suffered in the south. It criticized the leftist deviation of individual assassination and careless attacks and premature advocacy of armed uprising, which were preventing a "truly broad . . . vast" mass movement. But the Party called for continuing and stepping up the peaceful struggle, and then in 1959, at the urging of Le Duan and other spokesmen of the southern militants, for the use also of military struggle, in combination with political struggle. A decade later, given the Communists' tenacity in the face of the American escalation, on the fortieth anniversary of the Party, Le Duan could state with much justice, that all our successes "are the result of the invincible line of the people's war," and that the "people's war in the South is a war 'for the people and by the people' . . . it prescribes using both [political and military] forms of struggle, attacking the enemy in all three strategic areas [mountains, lowlands, and cities], coordinating the combat actions of the three types of armed forces with uprisings by the revolutionary masses . . . and calls for a protracted war, gaining strength as it fights . . . ."

He also stated:

> Revolution is the work of millions of popular masses standing up to overthrow the ruling classes, which command powerful means of violence together with other material and spiritual forces. That is why a revolution is always a long term process . . . [and] necessarily goes through many difficult and complex stages of struggle full of twists and bends . . . A revolution is not a coup d'état. It is not the outcome

> of plots. It is the work of the masses . . . to realize this task, one must mingle and be active with the masses in everyday life, even within the enemy organizations . . .

Le Duan also singled out the two problems with which we began this discussion of the roots of the extraordinary Vietnamese Communist achievements in people's war—organization and ideology. In the "Directive for the South," he wrote,

> On the road to the seizure of power, the only weapon available to the revolutionary masses is organization. . . . All activities seeking to bring the masses to the point when they will rise up and overthrow the ruling classes revolve around this point; organize, organize, organize . . .
>
> The purpose of political propaganda is the organization of the masses . . . for combat . . . [and] through combat they are further organized and educated . . . therefore propaganda, organization and struggle go hand in hand . . . organization and struggle, struggle and organization, again struggle . . . one battle leads to another . . .

While late in 1969, the Party headquarters for the south (COSVN) could still acknowledge problems of insufficient attention to the "mass character . . . of People's War," on the eve of the final victory in 1974, Le Duan could properly claim "our strength lies in our organization." And like Ho Chi Minh forty years before, he cited Marx and Lenin on the need for ideology in order to strengthen organization. Most of all he stressed the primacy of organization: "To carry out revolution we must have a revolutionary ideology and also a revolutionary organization. Organization ensures the realization of ideology . . . that words are matched by deeds . . . without revolutionary theory and revolutionary ideology, there can be no revolutionary actions . . . if an ideology is to be put into practice, there must be organization." And like both Ho and Mao Zedong, Le Duan stressed the responsibility of each cadre for "learning . . . not only through books and newspapers, but also in practical life":

> We should never forget that learning and the whole system of education must combine the need of raising our consciousness and knowledge with that of raising our Communist qualities and morality, and that "Communist morality is based on the struggle for the consolidation and completion of Communism" . . . the ideal for which we have so many times risked our lives and for which our people have consistently and loyally followed the Party, trusted and loved us, the ideal for which our people have shed and are shedding so much

sweat and blood even though its complete realization is still a long way off and many privations and hardships are ahead . . . .

[Therefore] we must link learning with struggle, struggle against ourselves and struggle for the revolutionary realization of our revolutionary tasks.

Above all, Le Duan, like Giap, developed the stress of Lenin, Mao, and Ho Chi Minh on Party organization, and most characteristically on the Mass Line. Ho had already stated in 1958, the masses "must be led by the Party . . . . At the same time the Party must stay close to the masses and skillfully organize and lead them if the revolution is to triumph. Revolutionary morality consists in uniting with the masses in one body, trusting them and paying attention to their opinion . . . ." Le Duan in 1974 elaborated on this in a passage reminiscent of Mao Zedong's famous 1943 statement of the Mass Line:

The strength of the Communist Party, of the Communists, always lies in their close relations with the masses . . . cadres build up a movement and in return the movement gives birth to cadres . . . cadres must mingle with the masses in this movement, march in the van to set an example for the masses, persuade and organize them, understand their feelings and aspirations, and concern themselves with their everyday moral and material life. They must show modesty and simplicity, listen to the opinions of the masses, gather the masses' experiences and knowledge to complement their own experiences and knowledge. They must constantly place themselves under the control of the masses . . . .[33]

Speaking of work among the northern mountain minorities in the 1940s, the Nung military leader Chu Van Tan, in his 1971 reminiscences, described principles of mass organization that would apply equally in the lowlands, with perhaps less emphasis on kinship although that was important everywhere:

Cadres from the minorities were recruited usually through family or friendship ties, trained in short courses, and then sent back to their areas of work. When a cadre moved into a settlement, if he did not have any relatives or friends in the village, he set about winning the sympathy and trust of a villager, then contacted other families through this person.

The most ardent sympathizers were trained to become cadres and to lead the local movement. After that the cadre moved on to another settlement where he could count on the kinship and friendship

> ties of the people he had recruited in the previous settlement to gain an entry into the area. At the same time, the villagers he had recruited would proselytize their own relatives, and friends scattered in various villages. In this way the network spread . . . .[34]

At the time of which Chu Van Tan was speaking, the Vietnamese Communists were developing their movement along these lines, stressing guidelines for Communist cadres who were to practice the "three withs" of living, eating, and working with the people of the area in which Communists worked, They also refined means of educating and advancing local youth within their own areas, thereby channeling the powerful force of personal ambition to work for the ideals of the revolution. Thus, as of the mid-1960s after interviews and research in eighteen villages of the delta and central lowlands Samuel Popkin noted that in sharp contrast to the lack of opportunity given by the government, on the Viet Cong side "a peasant can progress as far as his capacities permit." Moreover, although one peasant reported in 1967, "the Viet Cong collect higher taxes, they know how to please the people; they behave politely so people feel they are more favored . . . they do not thunder at the people like the government soldiers . . . ." In other situations, the Communists also used considerable coercion, reportedly forcing one-quarter to one-third of their recruitment in both the French and American wars. As will be seen again in succeeding chapters, they also developed to as high a degree as did the Chinese Communists principles of the United Front to "unite with all those who can be united and neutralize the rest," and developed "everywhere" mass organizations according to the slogan, "unite proletarians, peasants, youth and women."

In all these ways, therefore, the Vietnamese Communists developed extraordinarily effective means, as did their then Chinese comrades, for the organization of the masses. And like the Chinese Communists, they sought to prevent arrogance, lapses of discipline, and other faults that would vitiate this work by promoting "criticism and self criticism." In January 1949 Ho Chi Minh said, "To make the revolution, one must first and foremost remould oneself . . . there are two ways to achieve ideological unity and inner cohesion: criticism and self criticism. Everyone from the top down must use them to achieve ever closer unity and greater progress . . . [and] an iron discipline . . . ." In 1945, Ho attacked "very serious mistakes" of the "violation of legality," abuse of power, corruption, favoritism, sowing of discord and arrogance" among People's Committees, and in 1952–1953 there was a "thought reform campaign" for some 15,800 cadres.[35]

THIS LONG PRESENTATION OF QUOTATIONS of Vietnamese Communist leaders aims to give some understanding of what the men who organized history's most intense guerilla war believe were the keys to the mass organization that made it possible. While many parts of such statements were necessarily designed to project confidence and inspiration to their revolutionary work—only such inspiration and confidence would fulfill their predictions of the "invincibility of people's war"—the fifty years of struggle of the Communist Party of Vietnam, especially their twenty years of brutal warfare against France and the United States, have more than shown their validity.

Even so, one is still left with a sense of mystery as to how the Vietnamese Communists vanquished perhaps the greatest odds in the history of warfare. A final quotation offers perhaps the best explanation, namely, that the Vietnamese victories were a product of a skill, similar to that of the judo expert, who can turn the strengths of his opponent against himself. In "The Judo Lesson," Nguyen Khac Vien, a leading spokesman of Hanoi's causes who before writing this article in 1961 had spent twenty-five years in France, graphically wrote:

> The puny little man was wracking his brain trying to figure out a way to overcome his opponent's mass of muscle and brawn . . . . The judo teacher arrived . . . [and] explained . . . it is in the movement [of your enemy], not in your own strength, that you must find the force to defeat your opponent. Grab his moves at the end of their thrust, prolong them and you will lure your adversary into a fall which he himself has precipitated . . . .
>
> For many long years, I witnessed the highly emotional, historically important judo match taking place in my country, . . . My first memories go back to 1930. I was a schoolboy in Vinh. People were dying by the thousands . . . . We were weak and poor. A single plane could disperse crowds. [Even] the technique of manufacturing nails escaped us completely. All of this obsessed me for years and years. I saw that neither of those two elder Asian statesmen, Gandhi or Sun Yat-sen, could teach me how to silence an armed plane . . . .
>
> [But] Ho Chi Minh and Lenin showed us . . . . The notion of internal contradictions within Imperialism is crucial . . . . Study the

makeup of your country well and study how different social classes behave toward foreign domination . . . . Pay particular attention to workers and poor peasants. When these people acquire national consciousness and class consciousness, the match will be won. The critical strength of the revolution lies in them . . . .[36]

CHAPTER SEVEN

Organization and Practice

A CLOSER LOOK AT EVENTS in the three adjoining southern provinces of Ben Tre, Long An, and My Tho in the 1950s and 1960s will clarify how the Communists acted on the principles just outlined.

In Ben Tre province (called Kien Hoa after 1956) there had been considerable opposition to the French in the late nineteenth century. Then Communists took leadership of the 1930 and 1940 uprisings in the area, and were subsequently hunted and arrested without letup, as in 1940 were Madame Nguyen Thi Dinh and her husband who died in jail. Still, where possible, Madame Dinh and her colleagues distributed clandestine journals, founded cells of militants, and worked to organize mass organizations for youth, women, sports, and other groups, as well as radical workers and peasant unions. As another militant reminisced later, "Repression or no repression . . . each militant was required to establish contact with several villages, propagate a certain number of ideas and watchwords, and do his best to establish nests of sympathizers." A Party statement of December 1933 had maintained, "The deeper the influence of the Communist Party among the propertyless and poor elements in the countryside, and the more the Party can organize them, the surer the victory . . . . " "Whatever the difficulties, we must base our work on the masses."

With the French reconquest of most of the south in late 1945 and 1946, this became harder than ever to accomplish. By the early 1950s, Madame Dinh related, they had lost control of almost all of Ben Tre province.

> This was the most dangerous and the most difficult period for Ben Tre during the nine years of resistance. On some days we did not even have enough rice gruel to go round. Sometimes we had to shed blood to obtain drinking water . . . [and] enemy repression was fiercer than ever before. Within a short time, one by one the Secretary of the district committee Party committee, the commander of the district local force, and a relatively large number of village and hamlet cadres were either killed in combat or captured and liquidated by the enemy. I myself came close to being killed many times. . . . [Yet Madame Dinh kept going, and for another twenty years, as she wrote in her 1966 memoirs, feeling she was a "small tree" who came to realize] we had to have the strength of the whole forest in order to be able to stay the force of the strong winds and storms . . . . [Therefore] we relied on the people for support . . . the main thing is for us to have confidence in the masses and to stay close to carry out the struggle. If we do this, we'll achieve success.[1]

The "enemy" who almost destroyed the Communist movement in Ben Tre province in the early 1950s was led by Jean Leroy, a land-owning native of the province with a Vietnamese mother, who became a colonel in the French army. His memoirs, published as *Fils de la Rizière*, form an interesting, and not always predictable, contrast with those of Madame Dinh. He led the pacification of Communists in the area where he had grown up, An Hoa, the northernmost of the three islands making up Ben Tre province by 1947, and then mobilized a largely Catholic army of about 12,000 men, which pacified the other two islands of the province in 1950 and 1951.* Leroy admitted that "to successfully combat the Viet Minh . . . it was necessary to apply the same methods as they," which meant, he explained, "living in the midst of the population like a fish in water," fighting at night instead of the day, keeping troops constantly among the people, and above all, once security was achieved, lowering land rents, building schools and hospitals, and giving a sense of ideals and concern for the people. In the process, he came into conflict, not only with the Communists, but with landlords, who in some cases were trying to collect rents that the Communists had abolished early in the war.

In 1951 and 1952, Leroy expanded his work to other areas to the south and west of Ben Tre, but with less success than in his home province. Moreover, because of his high-handed and inde-

---

*Many Catholics, however, supported the Viet Minh for a time after 1945, including at first the brother of Ngo Dinh Diem, Bishop Ngo Dinh Thuc.

pendent methods, representatives of Bao Dai and the French increasingly accused him of running his territory like a private fief, and began to replace his units with other Vietnamese and French troops. Leroy in effect then was kicked upstairs and sent to the prestigious war college (*Ecole de Guerre*) in France in April 1953, while Communist activists like Madame Dinh soon resumed their work in most villages of Ben Tre.

The success of Leroy's efforts were a relatively solitary exception, perhaps proving the rule that virtually the only Vietnamese willing and capable of organizing the masses for both fighting and construction were the Communists. Leroy admitted that, until he turned around the situation in Ben Tre, most of the people admired and followed the Communists, and it is clear that, basically backed by the French, Leroy and his men did not face hardships comparable to those faced by the Communists. His troops, for example, were paid about 500 piastres (then officially about twenty two dollars a month), whereas, even in the early 1960s, Communist soldiers received about 100 piastres (then officially about three dollars, in fact about one dollar). This contrast in dangers faced and material rewards between the Communists and their enemies held true also when their situations were compared with those faced by the Cao Dai, Hoa Hao, and other groups. Leroy had to fight French bureaucracy and jealousies, but not French, much less American, weapons, blockades, and surveillance. For their part the Communists called Leroy the "butcher of Ben Tre" and a "drinker of blood," as he increased the number of military posts in the province from 98 to 564. Leroy in fact was proud of the aggressiveness of his efforts to turn the tables on the Communists who, he claimed, put a price of 20,000 piastres on his head and used "pure terror" in the name of false and hence empty promises. He claimed to "understand the peasant [Nhaque] personality," and maintained that no one truly followed the Communists of their free will or wanted union with the north and did so only if forced.[2]

Leroy, therefore, presents a very different picture of Ben Tre province from that presented by Madame Nguyen Thi Dinh. But in view of later events, one is inclined to have more confidence in the Communist version of the "mind of the people" than in Leroy's. Perhaps many different Leroys might have made a profound difference in Vietnam, but the fact was that over the years, despite all the billions spent by France and the United States to cultivate anti-Communism in Vietnam, very few successful competitors to the

Communists came forward. Leroy was almost the only one during the French war, and after his departure in 1953, the Communists almost immediately recouped their losses, and controlled virtually all the province except the capital and 8 of 137 villages in the province by July 1954. Because of their renewed successes, Madame Dinh reported that militants were "frustrated and annoyed" at being forced by the Geneva accords to lay down their arms.

After 1954 numerous Communists left Ben Tre province for the north—for example, Madame Dinh's son—but others like Madame Dinh remained and sustained a Communist presence despite incredible new hardships inflicted on them by Diem and the Americans. By 1958, according to a later Communist source, the authorities had killed 2,000 activists, destroying 85 percent of the revolutionary apparatus in the province. However, after rapid growth in 1959, the Communists were able to take over parts of Ben Tre province, January 17–24, 1960, in an action that many mark as the real beginning of the Second Indochina War.

In 1962, Diem appointed as governor of the province, under its new name of Kien Hoa, former Viet Minh combatant Pham Ngoc Thao, whose brother was a high official in Hanoi, but who had switched to Diem's side in 1955. Considered one of the most capable of the southern commanders and with obvious knowledge of his Communist enemies, Thao in theory should have been as effective in pacifying Ben Tre as had been Jean Leroy a decade earlier. Instead his attention was almost immediately diverted to the November 1963 overthrow of Diem, of which he was a leading participant. Thereafter, Thao attempted two further coups, and was himself killed by rival generals in July 1965, accused of continued plotting against the government, and apparently also of advocacy of a third force of "human socialism." Then in 1968, the province was bizarrely immortalized by the statement of an American officer who stated of Ben Tre City in March 1968, we had "to destroy the town to save it," after his forces had killed an estimated 550 and wounded another 1,200 of its 75,000 inhabitants during the Tet offensive of the Communists.[3]

The province came under even heavier attack in the first six months of 1969 when Operation Speedy Express of the U.S. Army's Ninth Division used "awesome firepower," including napalm, antipersonnel weapons, B-52 raids, and artillery at a level "impossible to reckon," to kill an estimated 10,883 "enemy" in Kien Hoa (Ben Tre) and Dinh Tuong (My Tho) provinces. Since only 748 weapons were retrieved, it was reported that one official estimated that perhaps half the casualties had been civilians, while residents reported the wholesale destruction of villages by artillery, air strikes, defoliants, and "burning down with cigarette lighters." Although some 120,000 inhabitants who had been living in Communist areas supposedly came under government control, still, in 1970 the United States estimated as "secure" only 37 percent of Kien Hoa province.

It appears that American decision makers in the 1960s agreed with the controversial French journalist Lucien Bodard, who stated in the aftermath of 1954 that the Americans might save what the French had lost, since "the Americans would never have fought as we did. They would have fought a different war. And by crushing the country and the people under a hail of bombs and dollars, they might very well have had more success than we."* Thus, in February 1966, at a time when U.S. forces were climbing beyond 200,000, and when literally millions of tons of explosives were being used against Communist forces, the American specialist on the Viet Cong, Douglas Pike, wrote:

> The Viet Cong today finds itself in a doctrinal box with all three of its possible routes to victory—the socio-political, the military, and the diplomatic—closed to it. Consequently it has fallen back on the sterile thesis of the protracted conflict that will be won because the enemy, the United States, will tire of the whole affair and withdraw. But this does nothing for its own morale. Guerillas living in swamps, without adequate food or medical care, far from their families, cannot be expected to fight on indefinitely.[4]

While Pike reported that at that time there were an estimated half million active supporters of the 55,000 Communist soldiers, 115,000 guerrillas, and about 40,000 political cadres in the south, he believed that "the whole concept of victory on the battlefield is being called into question in Viet Cong ranks." Half of the political officers were northerners, as were some 15,000 of the troops. Therefore Pike believed "the Viet Cong have lost the close identification with the people that marked their earlier days," and only about 10 percent of the people in the south were "true believers," with perhaps another 20 percent wavering, as against the 38 per-

---

*Indeed, where the French on the eve of their defeat in 1954 employed some 300 odd propeller-driven aircraft, by 1966, the United States already was using over 3,000 ultra modern airplanes, including 800 spotter aircraft and transports, 1,200 helicopters and 1,000 combat jets.

cent estimated by George Tanham to have truly believed in the Viet Minh cause during the French war. Where 25 percent were said to oppose the Viet Minh, some 70 percent reportedly opposed the Viet Cong.

Such remarks, among other things, reflect ignorance of the principles of people's war as outlined by its Vietnamese practitioners. If 10 percent truly supported the Communists to the extent of risking their lives daily for the cause, that, in fact, was a large number. In more stable situations, extremists willing to do that seldom reach 1 percent, as, for example, with the Red Brigades and other terrorist groups in Italy. Even in the French wartime resistance against the Nazis, participation apparently reached only about 1 percent of the population. Therefore, it takes a very "revolutionary situation" for as many as 10 percent to undertake the rigors of trying to lead a people's war. "The people" are not so much the majority, as the activists, in Truong Chinh's words of 1948 cited above, "the most conscious elements . . . who see the direction of society," and act to move the majority in that direction. Only when in power, as in Vietnam for the first time in the January 1946 elections, have the Communsits been willing to undertake "democratic" votes to determine majority opinions. Far more important for people's war than such votes has been the recruitment of activists, who, even if a minority, could determine the course of events for the majority.

This reliance on activists is the essence of the doctrine of the Mass Line and people's war, and one has to say that all history, depending on the local circumstances, has followed similar rules. Contrary to the statements of their enemies, the Communists believed, correctly as it turned out, that their greater understanding of people's war more than offset the vastly superior armament and financial strength of the United States and its allies in the Second Indochina War. A leading commander in the south, Tran Van Tra, stated that although "the second [war] was much more painful, more cruel [than the French war] . . . we had still better chances of victory. We had deepened our contacts with the masses and our revolutionary strategy. To increased means, we opposed increased skill." Madame Nguyen Thi Dinh agreed, declaring in 1966, that compared to

> the nine year resistance . . . there were many more factors in our favor . . . [By the early 1960s] the masses understood the revolution and had acquired a definite level of consciousness, and their hatred

> of the enemy was very deep and intense. The ranks of the enemy were rent with dissension and a number of them had links with the revolution. We were supported by a strong and reconstructed socialist north . . . .[5]

A CLOSER LOOK at a second southern province during the American war will further clarify some of these issues. Long An, a province of some 350,000 people just south and west of Saigon, had been typical of many areas in the south during the French war, with government control of the cities and much of the countryside during the day, but with a substantial Viet Minh presence also, established through village "committees of resistance and administration," and guerilla patrols and tax collections at night. Then, following the departure for the north of several hundred Communist activists after 1954 and the arrests of many others during the repressions of the mid-and late 1950s, the Communist presence in the province was reduced to perhaps 400 activists. As a Party member captured in 1962 declared: "By 1959 . . . almost all their apparatus had been smashed, the population no longer dared to communicate [even] with their relatives in the movement . . . the southern regime with American assistance was becoming stronger and not collapsing as had been predicted." In many places in Long An, as in neighboring provinces, up to 90 percent or more of Party activists were arrrested or killed, and yet, at first in the hope of the elections of 1956, and then in recognition of the unfavorable balance of forces, the Party advised sticking with political struggle rather than armed counterattacks, "to lie patiently in ambush, gathering one's forces, waiting to strike at the right moment." "Because of this situation, Party members were angry at the Central Committee and demanded armed action," this informant continued, as reported by Jeffrey Race:

> Toward the end of 1959 . . . if you did not have a gun you could not keep your head on your shoulders. . . . There was no place where Party members could find rest and security. Almost all were imprisoned or shot or were forced to surrender. Some village chapters which had four or five hundred members during the resistance [against France] and which had one or two hundred members in 1954 were now reduced to ten members, and even these ten could not remain among the people but had to flee into the jungle to survive.[6]

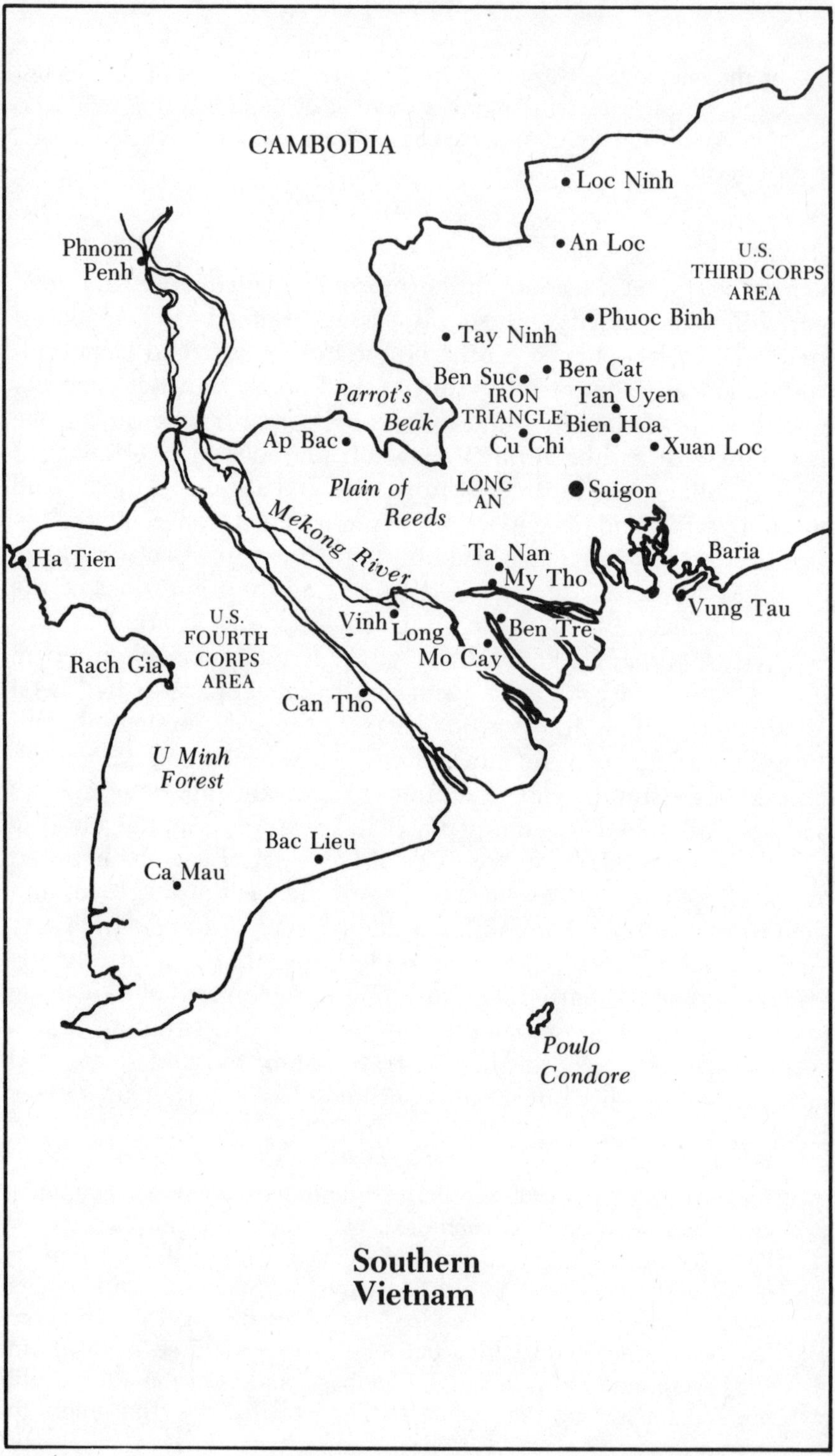
CAMBODIA
Loc Ninh
An Loc
Phnom Penh
U.S. THIRD CORPS AREA
Phuoc Binh
Tay Ninh
Ben Suc
Ben Cat
Parrot's Beak
IRON TRIANGLE
Tan Uyen
Bien Hoa
Ap Bac
Cu Chi
Xuan Loc
Plain of Reeds
LONG AN
Saigon
Mekong River
Ha Tien
Ta Nan
My Tho
Baria
Vung Tau
U.S. FOURTH CORPS AREA
Vinh Long
Ben Tre
Rach Gia
Mo Cay
Can Tho
U Minh Forest
Bac Lieu
Ca Mau
Poulo Condore
Southern Vietnam

Finally, due to the pressure of events and anguished pleas from below by surviving cadres, the Party leaders after January and May 1959 authorized the formation of new armed units in the south to "use revolutionary violence to combat counter revolutionary violence, and carry out insurrection to conquer power for the people." As a result, by late 1959, the few surviving Communists throughout the south were able to accelerate their recruitment and go on the attack. Significantly, the first approved armed action, which according to the Communists signaled the beginning of the "second resistance," took place in Madame Nguyen Thi Dinh's neighboring province of Ben Tre on January 17, 1960. As she wrote six years later,

> The time finally came when the ardent aspiration of our people and cadres was at last satisfied . . . . [The Party's new policy] called for the mobilization of the people all over the south to carry out political struggle in conjunction with military action . . . . [And on January 17] the enemy's machinery of control in a number of villages crumbled . . . the people became the complete masters of a number of hamlets and villages. Our task on January 18 and the following days was to track down and arrest the remaining tyrants, beseige the posts, take over the remaining hamlets and villages, destroy the roads, cut down trees to build roadblocks, and get ready to fight if the enemy brought in troops to attack us. We organized meetings of peasants to discuss the equal distribution of the ricefields we had seized . . . .[7]

During this uprising, the Communists seized some one hundred weapons, "mostly French muskets," from government troops, giving them about one to three rifles per village, where before they often had fought with "their bare hands" and farm implements. These attacks in Ben Tre and others in Long An and elsewhere reversed the situation of the late 1950s and the decline of the Communist movement in the south. Although the confirmation of the change of line from political struggle to military resistance took months to reach the village level and was not confirmed until November 1959, Communist military actions resumed by the end of the year, and increased thereafter.

As will be seen in more detail in the next chapter, there were widespread uprisings in most provinces of the south and December 1960 saw the founding of the National Liberation Front. Until the mid-1960s, these efforts were carried out almost entirely by southerners. In Long An province, for example, the "infiltration" of northerners into the province was estimated at 10 per year in 1960, and 100 in 1965, whereas by 1968 there were 3,100 American troops and 14,550 government troops in that province alone. And yet, despite still greater counterforce used against them, the Communist-led units once more, as in 1930 and 1945, began to increase in number—in Long An, for example, from the surviving 400 cadres of 1959 to 800 in 1962, to 2,200 in 1965, and 3,100 in 1968. By mid-1964, these activists controlled all but 30 of some 260 hamlets in the province and virtually all of the population except the 22,000 residents of the capital of Tan An, and an equal number in the 6 district capitals.

Again one faces the question, how did the Communists resume their growth, now in a situation where the government had designated Long An a "model province," and where by 1968 the United States was spending possibly 600 million dollars a year and using thousands of tons of explosives against lightly armed Communist soldiers, who were paid on the order of one dollar a month.* At one point in 1966, a Communist source estimated that American forces expended up to three tons of bombs for every man, woman, and child in one hamlet in Long An province.[8]

According to the study by Jeffrey Race, on which most of this discussion of Long An province is based, the Communist victory there came about largely because the Viet Cong represented the interests of the local society, and not those of distant Saigon and Washington. That of course makes for still another inversion of the anti-Communist propaganda, which argued that it was the Communists who fought for utopian ideals at the behest of Moscow and against local interests. Even where there were only one or two Communist activists in the average hamlet, Race argues, "The revolutionary movement was able to develop greater forces than the Saigon government in rural Vietnam . . . through the development of social policies leading to superior motivation . . . policies redistributive of wealth and income, policies redistributive of power and status, and policies of provocation and protection." In that situation, "the lone guerilla represents a monopoly of force in his hamlet, except for a few hours a month during which the government battalion is sweeping through," since the guerilla was generally a native of his village and remained there in contrast to government troops who, as a matter of policy, were sent out of their home prov-

*The average American soldier's pay was over $300 a month, and the government soldier's about $20 a month.

ince. "In the same sense, artillery and air power . . . may represent a much weaker force than a single man on the ground in the right place." Thus, whereas the *Marine Corps Gazette* in a review on the back cover of Race's book *War Comes to Long An* could state, "Mr. Race does not appear to espouse views either for or against the American effort . . ." the author in fact stated:

> The new society [advocated by the Communists] conformed to majority local interests, whereas the existing government organization was objectively the pawn of "outsiders"—both in the sense of place and sympathy with the local area, and in the sense of following life styles and economic interests different from those of the majority of the rural population.

Race explained that the Communists used land reform and other crucial economic and social programs to give power and benefits to the local community and its activists. They thereby persuaded most of the rural population that if "the government came back, the peasants would return to their former status as slaves. Consequently, they must fight to preserve their interests and their lives." Therefore,

> to occupy roles in the revolutionary movement was perceived by major segments of the local population as defending its interests, while to occupy government roles was seen as being manipulated by outside forces in opposition to local interests—not to mention that it sometimes involved cooperation with and protection of criminal and corrupt elements within the government . . . .

And where the government tried to explain "why the Communists were bad and why the people must follow the government," even officials were forced to admit "the villagers just didn't listen to us," and recalled instead that "during the resistance, the Communists had been the only ones in the village to fight against the French," and that the Communists had redistributed land, taxed the poor less, favored the poor for recruitment and promotion, and even used less violence than the government against poor villagers. Consequently the Communists were seen as "close to the people . . ." while the government "cannot possibly represent [their] interests."

In the late 1960s, the government at least partly missed its last chance to carry out the reforms necessary to change this situation. With analogies to the activities undertaken by Colonel Jean Leroy in Ben Tre province in the early 1950s, another colonel, Nguyen Be, who had fought on the Viet Minh side in the French war before switching sides to become commandant of the National Training Center at Vung Tao in 1968, proposed a "kind of Communism without class warfare" to win over the peasants. But where Be stressed a real return throughout the south of power to the people of the villages, with far-reaching political, educational, and landholding reforms, the highly publicized Rural Construction Program launched in 1968 in Long An province, according to Race, "ignored the redistributive issues and concentrated instead on 'development' and on certain suppressive and intelligence functions . . . ," a sort of "highly organized public welfare or public works effort."[9] Even with the more far-reaching land reform launched in March 1970, it was not enough, and came far too late.

TWO STUDIES OF A THIRD SOUTHERN PROVINCE in the 1960s, My Tho,* between Ben Tre and Long An, give further evidence of missed government opportunities and Communist strengths. As in Ben Tre and Long An, the Communists were very much on the ropes by 1958, as in one village where all twenty Communists had been arrested. But a minimum number of Communists managed to survive, often using an elaborate series of hiding places. They struck back after the winter of 1959–1960 and intensified a mixture of criticisms of the government, selected assassinations (which peaked in 1963), effective organization, land reform, and local government. In January 1963, Communist forces there scored an important victory at Ap Bac, as will be described in Chapter Eight, and by 1965 they had increased their control to an estimated 60 percent of the province despite continuing heavy losses of cadres. Communist use of the essential strengths of the Mass Line of "struggle by the whole people" created a situation in which according to the study by David Hunt, although

> once proud institutions enrolling hundreds of peasants were effectively reduced to a handful of cadres . . . Yet US-GVN authorities could bomb and shell for years . . . but if they did not succeed in wiping out the core of NLF strength, . . . as soon as the bombing stopped . . . the refugees . . . would stream back to their villages . . . [and] the cadres would begin once again to build up their "infrastructure". . .
>
> American escalation rested on assumptions which seemed plausible enough. Amidst the bombing and shelling, with homes and

*Also called Dinh Tuong and, after 1975, Tien Giang province.

> fields in ruins and villages emptied of peasants, with the ranks of the NLF split by defections and its methods of operations sabotaged in a thousand ways, surely the insurgents would lose faith in the Front and gradually give up the struggle. But the cadres did not give up . . . they persisted with their activities and thereby prevented the United States from winning the war.[10]

In 1959 a provincial Party document had reiterated techniques for maintaining and rebuilding their infrastructure in My Tho province. William Andrews reported in his study that it called for:

> First, investigation of the military, political, economic and social situation . . . conducted by covert agents. Then propaganda work . . . third, organizational work. . . . Finally . . . the population was enmeshed in the Party organizations . . . [and] led into various mixes of military and political actions against the South Vietnamese government.[11]

Using such techniques, within a few years in one village of about 3,000 people, a Party secretary was able to write that the Party had increased to "twenty-six members . . . [its] Youth, thirty, the Farmers Association, 274, the Liberation Youth Group, 150, the Liberation Women's Group, 119. Two thousand people or two-thirds of the villagers take part in Party-led activities."

Similarly, in Kien Phong province west of Saigon in 1962, journalist Denis Warner found that a small number of Communist and Youth League activists, together with ten times that number enrolled in various youth, peasant, and women's mass organizations, had effectively taken control of a certain village, even though the activists made up only about 1 percent of the population of the village. Although "the people were not interested in Communism," effective land reform, education, and health work, backed by the ability to call on armed forces of some 500 men, enabled the Communists to firmly install themselves in the village.

Yet, it was precisely such Communist gains that led to the U.S. escalation in 1965. Then, as Hunt noted: "this relentless shelling of the countryside, the creation of free fire zones in areas where hundreds of thousands of people lived and work, [became] after 1965 the central reality of the war in My Tho." In one village, for example, the population was reduced from 3,000 to 142 persons, and "even the most dedicated cadres were shaken, as the full weight of American power made itself felt." Many came to the conclusion "that it will be difficult for the Front to win this war, because the

U.S. is too rich and powerful . . . ." "Some said, 'I am looking at your face today, but tomorrow we might never see each other again.' . . . They all seemed very confused and demoralized." But others felt that although "we ought to expect to be killed, if we decide to fight for the revolution . . . our death will serve our children's interests . . . ." And because the oppression was so general that "whether they worked for the revolution or not, they would be arrested, jailed and beaten up by the enemy, . . . therefore they had better join the Front to help fight . . . ." Moreover, in sharp contrast to their enemies, the Party "institutionalized close communications between its organizations and their constituencies by such enforced working principles as "Criticism and self criticism," "From the masses to the masses," the "Higher ups go down," and the employment and promotion of local people in their own locales.

The result of all this, at least in Long An province, was that half or more of village youths were estimated to actively support the revolutionary movement, which was five to ten times the number who supported the government, despite its vastly greater resources and firepower. In short, Race reported, "the revolutionary movement had won in Long An by 1965 . . . it had all but extinguished the government presence in the province . . . and had the ability based on internal forces, to smash the remaining units at will . . . .[12] Despite all the efforts that had gone into pacifying Long An, the killing of at least 4,000 of Communist supporters in 1968 alone, for example, the estimated 2,000 activists who remained forced the Americans in that year to rank Long An as "least secure" of all forty-four provinces of the south except for two at the extreme southern tip of the country, An Xuyen and Chuong Thien. The entry of more government troops and American soldiers and airpower, and above all belated reforms, especially a new "land to the tiller" government land reform proclaimed in March 1970 temporarily reversed the situation again in Long An with Communist forces there reduced to about 400 men in the early 1970s. Similarly, to the north, in a village of some 7,600, about seven miles south of Hue, a study by James Trullinger found that although the Communists were forced to lay low after the establishment of an American base nearby in early 1968, they still retained support of one-third to one-half of the population. That support increased again to over two-thirds by 1973–1974, even though the government, which was supported only by an estimated 10 to 15 per cent of the village, continued to place the area in a B or "safe" category. Thus by the mid-

and late 1960s, it seemed simply too late for the anti-Communists of Vietnam, and the victory of their enemies was just around the corner.

Before returning to a more chronological overview of events after 1954, when Washington and Saigon believed there was some hope for the survival of a non-Communist South Vietnam, some further analysis of two of the most important questions explaining Communist strength in provinces like Ben Tre, Long An, and My Tho is required, namely, the questions of land reform in the south and the use of force and terror.

AT ABOUT THE SAME TIME in the 1950s as the land reform in the north was revealing the full scope of the Communist revolution in Vietnam for the period of the transition to socialism, with its destruction of the "feudal landlord class" and creation of cooperatives, the Diem government in the south lost its best chance to create an equitable private landholding system for the 85 percent of its citizens who then lived in the countryside. This was a grievous mistake, as all agree that the lack of adequate land reform was undoubtedly the single most important factor determining the degree of revolutionary unrest in the country. As the leading American advisor for land reform, Wolf Ladejinksy, an architect of the successful agrarian reforms in Japan and Taiwan after the war and in Saigon from the mid-1950s until 1962, put it in 1961,

> In predominantly agrarian Asia the new order of things, economic or political or both, depends primarily on the solution of the land question, namely land for the landless. In a different setting, the Russian Communists exploited this . . . [and] Nationalist China was defeated not so much by force of arms as by the Communist tactic of promising land to the poverty stricken, landless, hopeless peasantry.[13]

Already in the last years of the Bao Dai governments there had been much talk of the necessity for land reform, and some action. Leroy's successes in Ben Tre province in 1951 and 1952 were attributed to the fact that he had reduced rents by one-half or more, leading "the Annamites of the province to fight to defend their new riches." After all, only one-quarter of 1 percent of the rural population owned about 40 percent of the rice land of the south in 1954, and 80 percent of the peasantry were forced to rent their land at exorbitant rents, often exceeding 50 percent. In Central Vietnam, as in the north, the problem was the equally difficult, but very different one, of the smallness of holdings, as well as of interest rates often exceeding 100 percent per year, high taxes, and other problems. There were some 400,000 tenants in Central Vietnam and 600,000 in the south, and there was a clear challenge for the Diem government to give them the land that would make these former tenants "fight to defend their new riches." The opportunity was there, and at one point in late 1954, the United States attempted to insist on effective land reform as a condition of further aid. But events would show the overoptimism of Ladejinsky's claim of 1961:

> Seven years after the country's independence they [the peasants] are measurably better off . . . [and] in his efforts to deal with rural problems President Ngo [Dien Diem] and his government have not resorted to force, setting class against class, or using any of the methods used by the Communists to impose their brand of agrarianism. This is in striking contrast to the somber realities across the seventeenth parallel . . . of subduing the peasantry through murder and bloodshed. . .
>
> The chagrin of the North Vietnamese is the greater because the non-Communist Asians cannot help but make comparisons between the enfranchisement of the peasantry in South Vietnam and their enslavement in North Vietnam. . . .
>
> In the company of some other non-Communist nations, Free Vietnam is demonstrating anew that where there is a will to redress the injustices of an agrarian system, a way can be found, and without paying the price of the tragic upheaval of Communist agrarianism.[14]

The reality was very different, and Ladejinsky would have been more accurate to stress that in the end only ten percent (109,438) of the million tenants of the south received land, and even worse, that that minority were forced to pay for what they often already considered theirs. This was because the Communists after February 1946 had already distributed some 600,000 (of about two million) hectares, of land in the south, where there had been a 57 percent tenancy rate. By 1960, they were again advocating a radical land reform of rent reductions (to usually about 15 percent), and confiscations through "purchases of land . . . in excess of a given area . . ." (often fixed at from two to five hectares, or one-tenth or less of the government land limit). They claimed to distribute 1,546,275 hectares (averaging about a half hectare or just over one acre per family) in their "liberated areas." Therefore the government's far more modest reforms seemed all too often to serve the interest of restoring the "landlord power" that had been largely ended by the Viet Minh before 1954.

Diem's early 1955 laws setting a maximum rent of 25 percent seemed reasonable until many peasants realized that, in former Viet Minh areas where they had ceased to pay most rents, they would be forced to pay landlords who had already been evicted by the Viet Minh. Furthermore, the limit of 25 percent was almost universally disregarded by landlords who frequently demanded 40 to 50 percent of the crop, and rents still averaged 34 percent in the late 1950s. The limiting of landholding to 100 hectares (about 250 acres), as fixed by Ordinance 57 in October 1956, was an even more inadequate measure for an area where the average holding was half a hectare, and even less in Central Vietnam. Diem's reforms aimed to redistribute about one-quarter of the cultivated land, and did involve confiscations of the property of some 2,000 big landlords, who were compensated 10 percent in cash and 90 percent in government bonds. But in many places, confiscated lands went to other rich owners or to the government, or after 1965 for the building of U.S. military bases. In one case reported in 1966, for example, the Americans paid off the owner of a tract of land in order to build a military base. The richly compensated owner reportedly returned to a life of ease in Hong Kong, while the farmers of the area were simply forced out of their homes, often undoubtedly to make their way to Communist areas.

In any case, as of 1961, at least two-thirds of the cultivated land of the south was still farmed by tenants, who almost always were forced to pay more than the legal 25 percent rent. Incredibly, it is said that with the exception of Ladejinsky and a few others, "U.S. officials did not believe that land based grievances were important," and as late as 1968, "allied support for land reform was uncertain at best." As Robert Sansom put it, "the Americans offered the peasant a constitution, the Viet Cong offered him his land and with it the right to survive." Therefore, concluded Sansom, "the 'old realities' of the Delta Economy . . . served as the basis for the success of the Viet Cong movement."[15] Hence, as the limitations of the tsar's "emancipation of the Russian serfs in the 1860s had helped set the stage for the Bolshevik Revolution, so Diem's land reforms served mostly to make Vietnamese peasants more conscious of and angry at their situation.

In addition to the problems of the limitations on and lateness of the reforms for rent reduction and land redistribution, the Diem government committed another grave error by ending the sacrosanct powers of the village councils. In traditional times, the autonomy of the village was expressed in the saying, "The laws of the Emperor yield to the customs of the village," reminiscent of the Chinese saying "Heaven is high above, and the emperor is far away," while the French generally were forced also to work through village elders. But in mid-1956, Diem replaced elective village and municipal councils with officials appointed by his government on the basis, not of loyalty to their village interests, but of loyalty to Saigon. Where there were always tensions between the village poor and rich notables, now there was an additional antagonism between the villagers and representatives of distant conservative Saigon.

Nor did Diem's various reorganizations of the countryside, the agrovilles of 1959–1961 and strategic hamlets of 1962–1963, as will be seen in greater detail in the next chapter, bring greater security as intended. Rather, as much as the failures of the land reform, the reorganizations antagonized the peasants who were to be relocated into about 100 fortified agrovilles, and then into some 11,000 strategic hamlets. But only about one-fifth were ever completed, and the Communists were able further to mobilize peasant anger against such forced dislocations.

Still another grievous error came with the treatment of the mountain minority peoples, into whose areas the government moved over 100,000 lowland Vietnamese, many of them refugees from the north. This considerably worsened traditional hostilities against the government by many of the close to fifty montagnard tribes of the south, and was fanned further by increasing Communist activity and promises of autonomy in the early 1960s. In January 1959, the Kor tribe overran a government outpost, and in November 1960 the Jarai rebelled near Plei Ku. In September 1964, there was a larger scale attack by the Rhade on the government and on U.S. positions in the Central Highland, and another in December 1965. By that time, the Communists claimed control of 95 percent of the Central Highlands.[16]

Nor did other trappings of the Diem government produce gains in legitimacy. Various elections in 1955, 1956, 1959, 1961, and 1963 were patently rigged, and "morality laws" banning fortune telling, cockfights, contraceptives, gambling, "sentimental songs," divorce, and even dancing in public only made more blatant the lack of democracy and rampant corruption. It was small wonder that the issuing of millions of new identification cards, the arrest of tens of thousands, and other efforts did not win popular support.

To return to the central concern of this section, the most important failing of Diem was the failure of the land reforms. As a former Party southern regional committee member told Race:

> The majority of the peasantry [were] angry at the government. The peasants felt that they had spilled their blood to drive the French from the country, while the landlords sided with the French and fought against the peasants. Thus at the very least the peasants' rights to the land should have been confirmed. Instead, they were forced to buy the land . . . and . . . felt victimized by the government. . . . Hence, the use of land redistribution was an integral part of the party takeover in rural areas [such as] Long An, the promise of land being one of the major themes of Party propaganda in the years from 1956 through 1959. Now [in the early 1960s] with the disappearance of the local government authorities, meetings would be called by the Party sponsored Farmers' Association . . . to distribute land without charge under the guidance of the village chi bo [cell]. . . .[17]

The result was a steadily increasing Communist influence and presence in the agricultural areas of the south in the 1950s and early 1960s, followed by a forcing of many of these cadres from their rural homelands into the mountainous areas to the west and north. Thus, communism in South Vietnam was not imported from the north, but rather, according to a later study by Jeffrey Paige, there was "a peasant based guerilla insurgency moving from its natural base of support in the Delta to the safer military terrain of the central highlands," in response to government and U.S. pressure.

Finally, in still another Vietnamese example of reforms coming much too late, the government of Nguyen Van Thieu began at last to come to grips with the land problem. Rural Construction Programs were launched with fanfare, although little effective reform, in 1968. But then, more meaningfully, in March of 1970, a "land to the tiller" law was enacted reducing the maximum holding from 100 hectares to 15 (from about 250 acres to 37), and the proportion of the agricultrual population who still were tenants was reduced from 60 percent to 34 percent in 1972 and reportedly to 16 percent by 1973, with powers also restored temporarily to the village councils. Had the anti-Communists enacted such a law in 1930 or 1945 or 1955, or even 1965, it might have prevented many Communist gains.

The pressures of the war itself also could not help but contribute to this belated and as it turned out temporary progress of the government in the late 1960s and early 1970s. As American specialist Samuel Popkin explained in 1970 after extensive interviews in eighteen villages of the south:

> Under the pressures of war the Vietcong were no longer able to deliver social benefits to the population, while the GVN living on American resources was able to begin flooding the countryside with schools, fertilizers, Hondas, infirmaries and hundreds of thousands of non-agricultural jobs. The peasants, although they often realized the superior quality of Viet Cong government, were nonetheless attracted by the better and safer living conditions in GVN controlled areas.
>
> The peasant population adjusted to the war by avoiding it. They chose to live in villages with the most economic advantages and ideally on the side that would predominate in the end. As Viet Cong forces became more and more strained, they demanded more and more commitment to the struggle, willing or not. [Thus as a peasant stated in a 1967 interview] "Viet Cong were very good people but forced [the people] to participate in struggle movements, [to the extent that] after life under the Viet Cong, government is now preferred."[18]

Indeed Communist recruitment appeared to have fallen markedly in the south in the wake of the offensives of 1968 and government reforms thereafter. In Long An province, for example, Communist activists appeared to have been reduced from over 2,000 to perhaps 400 by 1970. But the final Communist victory of 1975 undid these belated developments in summary fashion, and the southern Communists' "organizational core outlasted U.S. escalation," with evident results.

THE QUESTION OF THE USE of terror and violence reveals another reversal in the case of Vietnam of the usual conservative belief that it is the Communsits who use most terror and violence and, therefore, must be stopped by the legitimate government. In Vietnam, it was more often the other way round.

The Vietnamese Communists indeed used terror, but used it purposefully. As the Youth League journal had put it already thirty years earlier, "Assassination . . . [can be] an obstacle to the progress of the revolution . . . [although] violence is the only means to destroy capitalism and Imperialism," because only organized class violence, not individual terrorism, can be effective. The organization of this "revolutionary violence" meant the channeling and controlling of hatreds and desires in ways that would serve the Revolution. During the Nghe Tinh soviet, a Party provincial committee circular of October 9, 1930, stated:

> The violent means we have employed has strengthened our power and inspired fear among the notables, rich, and police . . . . But violent means cannot be envisaged until after a profound study of the situation of the mind and capacity of the masses . . . [only then] choose one or two important people among the . . . agents . . . chiefs and sub chiefs of the cantonal police to assassinate. But it is necessary to have our authorization before any execution . . . .[19]

In the 1940s, the Communists were estimated to have executed over 5,000 reactionaries, and in September 1946 Truong Chinh spoke of supplementing armed demonstrations and guerilla warfare with "the elimination of traitors in towns and country by picked detachments." These techniques succeeded so well that by the 1940s the Vietnamese Communists had organized their people to the extent that by far the greater violence would henceforth be used against them. Their violence, therefore, usually was on a smaller and more informed scale than that of their enemies, and most of the time aimed primarily at trying to stop the arrests, executions, and unprecedented firepower being used against them.

With regard to the land reforms of the 1950s, there was much violence associated with the "destruction of feudalism" and the cooperativization of agriculture in the north, but in the south it was the anti-Communist government that used the greatest violence to try to undo the Communist programs. Race's study of Long An province put it this way:

> The revolutionary land program achieved a far broader distribution of land than did the government program, and without the killing and terror which is associated in the minds of Western readers with Communist practices in land reform . . . the principal violence was brought about not by the Party but by the government in its attempts to reinstall the landlords . . . .[20]

In the south after 1954, the Communists also used much terror to be sure, assassinations rising from over 400 a year in the late

1950s to over 5,000 a year from 1967 through 1970. But their targets were "officials, traitors and tyrants," as against all who sided with the Communists, whom the latter naturally termed "the people," who it would appear suffered much, if not most, of the violence inflicted by the government. Furthermore, after 1954, the Communists did not begin to strike back at all until 1957, and in a big way until 1959 and 1960, whereas Diem's military and police actions against the Communists began in 1955 and 1956. The American authority on the Viet Cong, Douglas Pike, wrote in 1966, "Armed combat was a GVN [Saigon] imposed requirement; the NLF was obliged to use counter-force to survive."[21]

Therefore, while both sides used terror and violence in the situation in which Vietnam found itself after 1925, the Communists could use it far more effectively, against "enemies of the people," whereas the anti-Communists trying to stop the Communist gains, felt forced to use indiscriminate violence, often against substantial concentrations of population accused of harboring the Communists.

The essence of the contrast between the two sides' use of violence in Vietnam again comes down to organization; that is, the Communists learned to withstand the violence used against them, and then to use it themselves, but more skillfully. Nowhere can this be shown more clearly than in Long An province. There the Communists confirmed their increasing takeover of much of the province with the assassination of some twenty-six enemies in the third week of January 1960, whereas they had assassinated three officials in all of 1959. But in 1959 the Communists had suffered an average of twenty-six arrests (at least of suspected Communists) and another nine killed or captured every month, averages that climbed to fifty-five arrested and ten killed or captured each month in 1960. On the government side, total losses of cadre killed and captured from various kinds of enemy action averaged 1.8 and 14.6 per month in 1959 and 1960 respectively, as against 36.7 and 66.4 on the Communist side for the same periods. Thus, in 1959 the Communists lost 20 times as many men as the government, and 4.5 times as many in 1960. Yet the Communists were judged to have succeeded virtually in taking over the province several years after this, since the Communist assassinations were "sufficient to cripple the government apparatus at the village and hamlet level," and since despite its far greater losses, "the movement's adherents multiplied much faster than the movement's losses."[22] There could be no clearer demonstration of Communist strength and government weakness in adverse situations.

One important factor in the vastly greater effectiveness of Communist, as against government, terror, undoubtedly was the unpredictability of the Communist strikes, which in that sense perhaps did "strike more terror" against people who did not know when or how it would come, than did the more plodding efforts of the government. But as will be discussed in Chapter Nine, this changed with the air war in 1960s, although there is continuing controversy, for example, over such episodes as how many of the 4,700 killed in the Battle of Hue in February 1968 were victims of Communist terror as against U.S. firepower. In any case, the contrast in numbers is striking testimony to the fact that, whatever terror and violence the Communsits used, was exceeded many fold by their enemies.

A recent study by Guenter Lewy estimates that the Communists assassinated at least 36,725 people from 1957 to 1972,only 20 percent of whom were government officials and police. But the same source then estimates that total deaths in the comparable period of the American war came to 1,313,000 from 1965–1974, including 365,000 civilians.[23] Other sources commonly give figures of two or even three million killed during the American war, and another ten million made refugees, while the French war took perhaps a half million lives. During the Diem years, up to 170,000 are estimated to have died violently, while officially the government spoke of arresting 20,000 to 30,000 Communists in the 1950s.

Something like one in perhaps twenty Vietnamese, therefore, died from war-related causes from 1945 to 1975, not to speak of many more wounded and made refugees because of efforts to dispute the successive victories of the Communists. If the August Revolution of 1945 had been allowed to stand, the Communist government no doubt would have killed many, and "reeducated" and uprooted many more in the processes of the Communist Revolution from above, as was the case after 1954 and 1975, but overall the numbers killed would surely have been far less than those killed by France, the United States, and their allies trying to stop the Communist Revolution from below for over thirty years. As it was, the proportion seems about equal to the numbers of Russians who were victims of Stalin's "revolution" of the 1930s. If the "end" of "freedom" undoubtedly was something to fight for, it is nonetheless a very sobering thought that the "means" of fighting for it, paid for overwhelmingly by the United States, had effects as catastrophic for Vietnam as the "means" Stalin used to consolidate the "end" of communism in Russia.

As if it were better to be "dead than red," in the decade after 1964 the United States used in all some 14,392,302 tons of explosives (about half bombs, and half munitions) in Vietnam, in all the equivalent of close to 720 Hiroshima-style atomic bombs. These dry figures encompass the use of some 400,000 tons of napalm, an additional 18,850,000 gallons of herbicide (11,220,000 gallons of which was the notorious Agent Orange, and an estimated 550 kilograms of which were deadly Dioxin), and left over twenty-five milion craters in an area about the size of California. Most of the bombs (about four million tons) and virtually all of the munitions and defoliants were unloaded on South Vietnam, about half of whose forests were destroyed. By the late 1960s, the United States was estimated to be spending 400,000 dollars for every Viet Cong killed, and using some 300 pounds of explosives a year for every man, woman, and child of the south. At times, the figures were even more staggering, as in the estimated use of up to seventy-three tons of explosives for every Communist killed in one fortified position, and of more than 648,000 pounds of bombs against one unfortunate village in Quang Ngai in January 1969. The Communists claimed that another village, in Long An province, received three tons of bombs per inhabitant in 1966.

At that point, terror was obviously far more apt to come from the sky than from the Communists. The American sociologist Philip Slater put it this way: to argue that the U.S. was trying to stop "Communist terror" is "a little like saying that when an elephant steps on a mouse, the mouse is an aggressor when it bites the elephant's foot."[24]

Non-Communist sources estimate that over 100,000 civilians a month were being killed or wounded by the late 1960s, primarily by the vast American expenditures of firepower. Communist forces increasingly used Soviet and Chinese heavy weapons, but even in 1973 after the departure of American troops, Saigon forces used eighteen times as many shells as the Communists according to one estimate, not to speak of the aviation that it alone employed.

The dropping of candies and propaganda to "win hearts and minds" could hardly have been much consolation. Nor the messages that often accompanied the bombs and troops. As reported by Jonathan Schell, one message in Quang Ngai, declared: "The U.S. forces have come to help the Government of Vietnam rid your village of the Viet Cong who enslave you. If you allow the Viet Cong to hide in your hamlet, you can expect destruction from the air . . . Do not let your hamlet be destroyed. Point out the Viet Cong who bring death and destruction to you and your home. . . ."[25] Another leaflet showed a "field of rubble," its caption saying "If you support the Viet Cong . . . your village will look like this." Its text stated, "If the Viet Cong in this area use you or your village . . . you can expect death from the sky. . . ." Another leaflet prepared in early 1967 for use in Operation Cedar Falls, described its theme as "scare." It declared in part:

> Each day, each week, each month, more and more of your comrades, base camps and tunnels are found and destroyed. You are shelled more often. You are bombed more often. You are forced to move very often. You are forced to dig deeper. You are tired. You are sick. Your leaders tell you victory is near. They are wrong. Only death is near. Do you hear the planes? Do you hear the bombs? These are the sounds of death: your death. Rally [to the government side] now to survive . . . .[26]

The reporter who related these devastating evidences of American tactics was describing military operations between January and August 1967, first in Ben Suc village about thirty miles northwest of Saigon, and then in Quang Ngai province on the central coast. The operation in Quang Ngai uprooted over 7,000 people and destroyed two-thirds of the homes in the area, in the evident belief of one of the captions that "We must destroy the Viet Cong to have peace," and of an American civilian advisor who said that since the "Viet Cong use villages as protection the way a gangster uses a hostage . . . you just can't get them but to level the villages they are located in . . . but we give them an opportunity to get out and go . . . ."

In any case, if the "Viet Cong gangsters" lived in their areas and knew who they were killing if they chose to asassinate someone, the Americans did not. As one pilot put it: "We are going four or five hundred knots and we can't see much ourselves. I've never seen a body or a person yet, and I've been on over a hundred missions. It's virtually impossible to see any movement on the ground . . . ."[27] A Saigon general visiting a destroyed area said, "Good, Good! They are all Viet Cong. Kill them," while an American sergeant was less discriminating, declaring, "What does it matter? They're all Vietnamese." Only one American in the Ben Suc operation was heard to communicate in Vietnamese.

In 1967 the United States used more than two million tons of bombs and munitions in Vietnam; and in the "Cedar Falls" operation of January against the area in which the village of Ben Suc was located, eleven B-52 strikes and 400 sorties of other aircraft backed some 30,000 U.S. troops in operations that displaced close to 6,000 persons. An Associated Press dispatch related: "Ben Suc has disappeared systematically before the American bulldozers. Houses of three stories are no more than heaps of rubble . . . . houses are in flames, children are crying, women crazy, the rice field ruined . . . ."[28]

One recalls the statement about Ben Tre City during the Tet offensive of early 1968, "It became necessary to destroy the town to save it," or another statement in May 1969 about an American military operation near Da Nang, which used some 750,000 pounds of bombs against a Viet Cong stronghold that was "converted from a densely populated, heavily wooded area into a barren wasteland, a plowed field." In that case, the operation was called "a success." Of 1,017 "enemy" killed, only 129 weapons were recovered. A list of some thirty massacres allegedly committed by American soldiers from 1965 to the end of 1969, compiled by Gabriel Kolko and L. Schwartz, states that 300 "innocents" lost their lives in this episode, as against 500 at the far more infamous My Lai (Son My, Quang Ngai province, March 1968, where the official figure given of noncombatants killed was 347). They estimate that from 32 to 1,500 were killed in each of the other 28 massacres.[29]

The uses of overwhelming firepower in such operations and almost everywhere in the "free fire zones" of the countryside largely produced yet another statistic, surely unique to the Vietnam war—the most rapid urbanization in history. As late as 1964, South Vietnam was over 80 percent rural, but by 1969 at least 50 percent lived in towns of over 25,000 people, and by 1972 the urban population was placed at 65 percent. Vast numbers of these people lived in hastily constructed slums in appalling conditions, even as sizable numbers of their daughters plied a lucrative trade as prostitutes (over half a million according to the Communsits) for the some 60,000 American civilians in Saigon and a half million soldiers throughout the country as of 1968–1969.

For American advisors this unprecedented urbanization was no accident. As the well-known Harvard professor, Samuel Huntington, wrote in June 1968:

> The depopulation of the countryside struck directly at the strength and potential appeal of the Viet Cong. . . . For if the "direct application of mechanical and conventional power" takes place on such a massive scale as to produce a massive migration from the countryside to city, the basic assumptions underlying the Maoist doctrine of revolutionary war no longer operate. The Maoist-inspired rural revolution is undercut by the American sponsored urban revolution. . . .[30]

THE AREA JUST NORTHWEST OF SAIGON known as the Iron Triangle had been a center of Viet Minh activity during the French war, and in June 1962 the Communists ambushed a government convoy near Ben Cat. Thereafter, despite the fact that Diem's army had an outpost in Ben Suc and that in the 1960s the Americans built an airbase to its east at Ben Cat, and carried out almost continuous military operations like Cedar Falls, the Communists continued strong in the region. To describe how they managed this, perhaps Giap's term "steel fortress" would be a more appropriate term than Ho Chi Minh's "brass wall," or the "iron" of the Iron Triangle.

It surely took a "steel" will to survive. For example, at the extreme south of the Iron Triangle in the Cu Chi area about twenty miles northwest of Saigon, the Communists were able to survive massive bombings and military sweeps only by building by hand an incredible complex of over 150 miles of tunnels up to 30 feet deep, on two or three levels, linked by corridors often only 2 feet by 2 feet, and by living in these hideouts, as others did elsewhere, for years. The German journalist Horst Fass, visiting Cu Chi in October 1977, was told by a forty-five-year-old survivor, "We literally dug for thirty years, usually in the dark, squatting down. We carved out about a meter every eight hours, and women distributed the earth on the surface hiding it under fallen leaves . . . we always moved in the dark, saving our candles and torches for emergencies. Our amputees lay in the dark sometimes for months."[31] At times American troops were directly above these tunnels, and used flooding, tear gas, dogs, and "tunnel rats" (specially trained GIs) to try to flush the Communists out of their holes. But even the use of the 60,000 pounds of bombs dropped from each B-52, which fell unannounced as the plane was so far overhead and could penetrate at

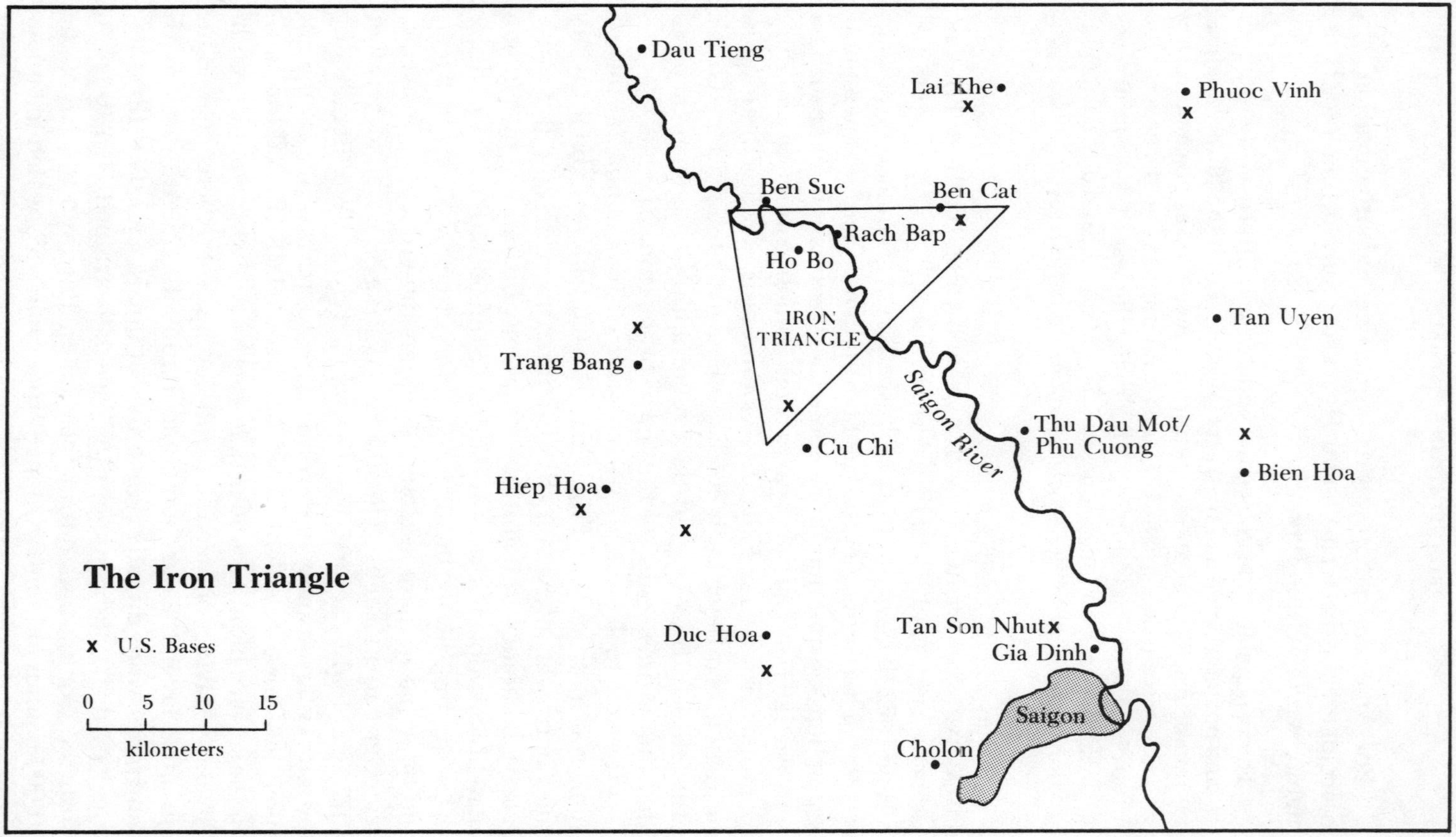
The Iron Triangle
x U.S. Bases
0 5 10 15
kilometers
Dau Tieng
Lai Khe
Phuoc Vinh
Ben Suc
Ben Cat
Rach Bap
Ho Bo
IRON TRIANGLE
Tan Uyen
Trang Bang
Saigon River
Thu Dau Mot/ Phu Cuong
Cu Chi
Bien Hoa
Hiep Hoa
Duc Hoa
Tan Son Nhut
Gia Dinh
Saigon
Cholon

times up to fifteen feet underground, of incendiary and "high explosive fragmentation" bombs thrown into the tunnels, or of flamethrowers and napalm to suck oxygen out of them, did not stop the Communist underground.

The Vietnamese had built such hidden fortifications and escapes to withstand the vastly superior military power of their enemies as early as the late 1880s against the French, but by the 1940s much more elaborate systems were constructed. By the early 1950s, for example, a tunnel system of seven kilometers of tunnels and trenches was developed in a village of about 4,000 persons some fifteen miles north of Hanoi. A local revolutionary later said that this "gave [us] an immense advantage, permitting movement without being seen and attacks on the adversary in unsuspected places," as during a decisive battle against the French in May 1954.

Later, still larger underground complexes were built both in the south and north against the U.S. air war, and eventually totaled, it is said, over 30,000 miles of tunnels. By 1969 one village just north of the seventeenth parallel had 100 miles of underground trenches linking its hamlets with neighboring villages. In 1964, journalists Wilfred Burchett and Madeleine Riffaud were shown some of the tunnels near Saigon and reported the difficulties they had in surviving many minutes where some Communists were forced to live for years, and where "the greatest pleasure in those days was to stick one's head out to the surface and just breathe air."[32]

But just how important these undergrounds were to the Communists was further revealed by Truong Nhu Tang, the revolutionary government's minister of justice from 1969 to 1975, after he sought refuge in France in the spring of 1980. He related how A-frame type, reinforced underground shelters, improved after 1965 to house the Communists' southern headquarters, had been able to withstand the most destructive U.S. bombs if they fell no closer than about one hundred meters (300 feet). Returning from higher studies in France to become a director-general of the Vietnamese Sugar Company, Tang had participated in the founding of the National Liberation Front in December 1960. Twice arrested, in 1964 and 1967, in February 1968 he was freed in exchange for three captured American officers, and able to reach Communist areas northwest of Saigon.[33]

Asked in an interview in Paris on November 7, 1980, how the revolutionary government had survived the enormous tonnages of bombs and military sweeps directed against its long-sought headquarters—at first located northwest of the Iron Triangle near Tay Ninh, then further west near Mimot and Kratie in Cambodia, from 1970–1972 along the Waico River near the southern border of Laos, and then again in the south near Loc Ninh about ninety miles northwest of Saigon—Tang agreed that it was indeed "incredible" and "terrifying," so much so that on one occasion a group of visiting Russian specialists had all "pissed in their pants" as bombs fell overhead. But virtually all the top leaders had been able to survive through the use of the underground shelters and superior intelligence, although many lower-ranking cadres, especially when "on mission" had been killed, and many others had drowned when they fell into bomb craters filled with monsoon rains. He reported that Communist information was good enough—through agents at all levels of the Saigon government, radioed reports from sympathetic Vietnamese living near U.S. air bases in the south and in Thailand, and from Russian ships that monitored bomber takeoffs and routes—to move, often by bicycle, some ten kilometers away from projected B-52 trajectories. In quiet periods, they could sleep in hammocks between trees and retreat underground as necessary.

The tunnel systems developed by the revolutionaries were therefore as indispensable as they were extraordinarily difficult to build and to tolerate. So were more comfortable but no less dangerous refuges in homes, concealed places, even Buddhist temples. One southern activist explained to Wilfred Burchett that in the delta town of My Tho:

> Every . . . [important] Committee member had at least ten . . . hiding places in which he or she could seek refuge at any time. . . . That is what we mean when we say we were protected by the people. There were cases when the owners of such shelters were arrested, tortured—in some cases to death—without betraying the secrets of the revolution. Our people understood very well the necessity of protecting the cadres.[34]

And to the B-52s and other weapons, the Communists opposed mines, homemade and captured weapons, skillful camouflage, pitted traps, "air forces" of hornets, frogs to trigger false warnings, and "long haired" armies of protesting women, and then by the later 1960s and early 1970s increasingly modern arsenals of AK-47 rifles and other sophisticated Soviet and Chinese weapons. They fought hand to hand and at night where possible to prevent or minimize the threat of U.S. airpower.

The complex of hundreds of miles (150 in Cu Chi alone) of underground tunnels and communications trenches in the Iron Triangle, described by GIs as "like the New York City subway system," was not only the most amazing such complex for which documentation exists, but also had the most astonishing results. It enabled the maintenance of the Saigon Party Committee and an advanced combat headquarters at the very doorstep of Saigon throughout the war, despite the vast tonnage of bombs and military sweeps thrown continuously against it. In the concluding days of the war in late April 1975, Commanding General Van Tien Dung and political bureau members Pham Hung and Le Duc Tho joined southern military commander Tran Van Tra there to direct the final assault on Saigon. This "forward headquarters" was between Cu Chi, Ben Cat, and Ben Suc,* near the center of operations of the "Cedar Falls campaign. Burchett reported in 1978:

> One of the best kept secrets was that the Vietnamese People's Army kept its advanced headquarters in . . . the Iron Triangle throughout the war . . . [although] probably the most bombed, burned, shelled and raked over area in all of South Vietnam . . . . I asked Ba Huyet, a lean greying cadre who had helped set up and defend the base, how it was possible to hang on? He replied: "When we got orders to set up a secure base here, the first thing we did was to start digging thirty kilometers of underground tunnels. It was in 1960. Not only was this one of our closest outposts to Saigon, but it was our advanced command post throughout the war . . . ."[36]

While developing these incredible projects to demonstrate the axiom that "Men, not weapons, decide," the Communists also had to wrestle with an almost total lack of communications until late in both wars. Giap described the advantage of establishing telephone contact with Ho Chi Minh following the capture of a telephone set in 1945, and by the end of the French war, only some two to three days were required to transmit messages from the Central Committee in the north to village committees in the extreme south. But af-

---

*The higher-ranking headquarters of COSVN and the PRG was forced further west and north, from near Tay Ninh, into Cambodia, then near the southern border of Laos, and after 1972 back to near Loc Ninh about sixty miles north of Ben Cat. General Bernard W. Rogers, assistant commander of the First Infantry Division, which took part in Operation Cedar Falls, described the discovery of an "extensive tunnel complex" along the stream (the Rach Son), between the Ho Bo Woods and the Filhol Plantation, some six miles north of Cu Chi, near the hamlet of Rach Bap. That must have been an early location of part of the "forward headquarters," apparently reorganized after the departure of Operation Cedar Falls.[35]

ter 1954, as a member of the National Liberation Front related to Georges Chaffard, "We were totally cut off from the north and dispersed in separate guerilla areas [maquis]," and it required up to several months to transmit messages from one area of the south to another, with the locations of key committees often disrupted by arrests and military sweeps. Messages had to be encoded in private letters or delivered by hand, and even the highest Party committee in the south (COSVN) often communicated with Hanoi via Pnomh Penh from its location, at times in the Iron Triangle, near Tay Ninh, to its west near or occasionally in Cambodia near Mimot, north of Tay Ninh.

In terms of the military links between the north and Communists in the south, the so-called Ho Chi Minh trail was crucial. Begun in 1959, in conjunction with the decision to fight back in the south, by the final victory of 1975, the system had been expanded to over 12,000 miles, moving out of North Vietnam through parts of Laos and Cambodia and back into western parts of South Vietnam.

As will be discussed in greater detail in Chapter Eight, by 1964 it was estimated that in all over 30,000 "northerners" had moved south over this network, and of course normal communications between the two Vietnams were blocked after 1954. But until 1964 nearly all such "northerners" were ethnic "southerners" who had gone north after 1954 and were returning south, and most were political, not military, personnel. As of March 1965, when the United States began its rapid escalation of the 21,000 American troops then in Vietnam, the highest estimates spoke of 5,800 armed "northern troops" among at least 25,000 southern Communists. Then in late 1968, when Americans in Vietnam numbered over a half million, the highest estimates of northern combat troops in the south was near 80,000 or, if political and support personnel are included, up to 200,000 of the estimated total southern Communist strength of 300,000. According to other sources, a half million "northerners" moved south in all from 1965 to 1968, but about 5 percent died on the way, as did hundreds of thousands of others in the south. Even during the build-up and final offensive of 1975, American sources estimated the number of northern troops invading the south at about 178,000.[37]

Such statistics, together with the history of the country, made American charges of northern "aggression" against the south via the

Ho Chi Minh trail "laughable," to use the word of Georges Chaffard, who also noted that the North Vietnamese using the Ho Chi Minh trail were forced to carry an average load of twenty-five kilos (fifty-five pounds) on a trip that took usually from six weeks to two to three months under a hail of U.S. bombs. A North Vietnamese wrote of the trail, "Whoever passed . . . cannot forget the image of the columns of combatants moving along the track, some of them carrying stretchers, climbing mountain passes roughly cut into thousands of steps, then across bridges dangling high above torrents, and finally stopping over at some liaison station where they would take their frugal meals, sometimes consisting of nothing but salt and bamboo shoots." General Van Tien Dung in the wake of the final victory described the changes and vast improvements by 1975, when some 10,000 trucks were able to travel a newly macadamized road equipped with fuel lines. He also noted the burial mounds of those who along the trail "sacrificed their lives . . . and challenge us to score victories befitting the memory of our fallen comrades . . . ." It was "one of history's great military engineering feats . . . ." But above all, the Ho Chi Minh trail was another example of the incredible resilience of the Communists' effort to unify their country.

Even before the Communist "general spring offensive" of Tet 1968, American officials like Secretary of Defense McNamara were beginning to express increasing doubts that Communist infiltration of arms and troops into the south could be stopped. It was estimated that while the United States was destroying some 10 percent of the supplies being sent south by the labor of some 300,000 northern troops and laborers, close to one-third of southern military needs was still reaching the south. There Communist strength was increasing, not decreasing, despite the vast tonnage of bombs used against the trail and the McNamara Line of mines and electronic sensors constructed in 1967 across northernmost South Vietnam. It was estimated that less than 100 tons a day of supplies was sufficient for the Communsit guerilla war in the south, a figure, if prorated, about one-fiftieth of the over two million tons of bombs the United States expended there every year from 1967 to 1970. In 1967, Hanoi was said to import about 5,800 tons of supplies a day from all sources.[38]

Despite growing doubts abouts its effectiveness and eight different bombing halts of the air war against parts of North Vietnam from 1965 to 1969, the bombing of the Ho Chi Minh trail continued and increased, counting for about a quarter of the total of up to 7.8 million tons of bombs dropped on Indochina by 1975.

NOR DID EFFORTS to "copy" the Communist use of terror against the enemy political apparatus, such as the infamous Phoenix Program, produce desired results for the anti-Communists. In the 1950s there had been numerous efforts to "learn from the enemy," from Leroy's restructuring of Ben Tre province during the French war to Ngo Dinh Nhu's "passion for imitation of Communist methods" in organizing his brother's police and political networks. But none of these efforts contained the slightest notion of the Mass Line that made the Communist "carrot and stick" organization of the people so effective. Not only did the anti-Communists, with the exception of Leroy and a few others, not practice the "three withs" of living, eating, and working with the people, but in all too many cases, they followed the mock-serious GI slogans of "If he's running, he's VC," and "The only good dink is a dead dink." Ngo Dinh Nhu was reported as complaining in 1961, in glaring contrast to Communist statements cited above, that: "If GVN cadres merely went out among the peasants to ask what they wanted and then tried to satisfy them, they were 'submerged with demands' and could do nothing. The only thing that could be done . . . was to issue orders and 'back them up with imprisonment.' "[39]

The Phoenix Program, in which some 650 Americans from 1968–1972 supervised Saigon's efforts to "eliminate" the political infrastructure of the Communists in the south, was said to have killed 20,987, jailed 28,778, and "re-educated" 17,717 "Communists," or according to many non-Communist as well as Communist writers, caused the death of over 40,000 (or even 100,000), which alone was close to the total of 36,725 reportedly assassinated by the Viet Cong from 1957 to 1972. Some other sources speak of lower totals, but also indicate that at times only 6 percent of those killed were "targeted" or thought certain to be Communists, while the others were killed "in the course of operations" and presumably as with other casualties of the war, considered "if dead, a VC." The Saigon police, it was frequently reported, also honored the slogan for captured prisoners, "If they are innocent, beat them until they are guilty."

As apparently did the Communists at times, the Phoenix Program also fixed quotas of "agents" to be eliminated, registered and reregistered twelve million people, and used paid informers against their enemies, offering up to $11,000 at one point for a live Communist, half that if dead. But the endemic corruption of South Vietnam, which enabled anyone with money to "purchase his freedom," the inadequacy of information on higher-level political cadres, and other problems, condemned these operations to ineffective as well as reprehensible police sweeps. In all, a largely sympathetic study by Guenter Lewy concluded that "while the Phoenix program undoubtedly made some contribution to the weakening of the enemy's strength in the countryside . . . the program failed to accomplish a decisive attrition of the Viet Cong infrastructure . . . ." The same could be said of various other programs and random assassinations engineered or carried out by the U.S. military and the CIA and their allies.

The sources of Communist strength at the village level—attractive-sounding programs and local activists to argue for their implementation while staffing Party political and military organization—therefore survived, even if understandably shaken by the unprecedented firepower used against them, by U.S.-financed operations such as the Phoenix and Rural Construction programs, and then especially by belated reforms, such as the "land to the tiller" law of 1970. But over all the years of war, the Communists kept close roots in the villages of the country and were able to inspire the idealism and ambitions of sufficient numbers of youth, educating and organizing them to supply a continuous source of manpower and energy despite continuing enormous losses of cadre. As a young Communist of Madame Dinh's Ben Tre province told Madeleine Riffaud in 1964, "When one of us falls there are more than ten new recruits to replace him."[40] This was an exaggeration if applied overall, but the fact was that the Communists of the south were still holding out at the time of the 1975 invasion, despite the greatest opposition ever faced by a revolutionary movement.

The gearing up of that opposition with the establishment of the Diem government and a brief chronology of events after 1954 is the next subject.

PART THREE

The Second Indochina War

CHAPTER EIGHT

The Diem Years

GIVEN THE WEAKNESSES AND DIVISIONS of non-Communist nationalists, the retreat of the French, and the strengths of the Communists, virtually everyone after the Geneva Conference believed that Ho Chi Minh's government would soon unite the divided country.

But they reckoned without Ngo Dinh Diem and the United States.

Together Diem and his supporters almost succeeded in establishing an eduring state south of the seventeenth parallel where none was intended. Yet, within a decade, Diem had created a dictatorship so unpopular as to lead to his own overthrow and murder on November 1, 1963, and to a situation so precarious as to require the introduction of a half million American troops to try to stop new Communist advances.

DIEM'S BIOGRAPHY REFLECTED much of the diversity and contradictions of his country and time and helps explain his dramatic rise and fall. By striking coincidence, his ancestral, or real home to East Asians who counted their ancestry back for centuries, was the same as that of Vo Nguyen Giap—Quang Binh province, just north of the seventeenth parallel. Moreover, Diem attended the same lycée in Hue (Quoc Hoc) as had Ho Chi Minh before him, and as would Giap and Pham Van Dong after him. There is debate as to whether his place of birth, on January 3, 1901, was Quang Binh or Hue, but in any case Diem spent most of his childhood in the old imperial capital. There he observed the first generation of modern nationalists—Phan Boi Chau, Phan Chu Trinh, Prince Cuong De, and others who often joined discussions at his home; for his father had become minister of rites and grand chamberlain to the Emperor Thanh Thai before the French deposed the latter in 1907 for anti-French activities. And Diem's family not only bore witness to the enduring Confucian traditions of the country and the rise of anti-French nationalsim but also was one of the first to have been converted to Catholicism, as early as the seventeenth century.

Given this background and his subsequent career, a leading authority would write in 1962, "It remains an open question whether Diem is basically a Confucianist with a Catholic overlay, or vice versa," or equally, whether he became a revolutionary republican or an absolutist monarch. For in a European context, as Bernard Fall pointed out, Diem came to promote a Spanish-style Christianity with the "ruthless efficiency of the Grand Inquisitor," as well as a Spanish-style "absolute monarchy without a king," like some Asian Franco. Another biographer, Denis Warner, called Diem the "last Confucian" and described a career often resembling that of "a monk living behind stone walls," who at the age of fifteen had spent several months in a monastery and took an early vow of celibacy. But throughout his career he was also very much a Vietnamese nationalist, a "mandarin Catholic nationalist" perhaps compared with the "Communist nationalists."

In 1921, Diem graduated first in his class from the French-run School of Law and Administration in Hanoi, and eight years later became governor of Phan Thiet (or Binh Thuan) province on the coast northeast of Saigon, where the Communists accused him of savage repressions of the 1930–1931 uprisings. When Diem was thirty-two in May 1933, Emperor Bao Dai appointed the brilliant young man minister of the interior. But Diem resigned the post three months later, charging betrayals of Vietnamese nationalism. He spent most of the next twelve years in Hue, talking and writing of plans for an independent Vietnam on the American model. After 1940, he refused to work actively for the Japanese, although he happily accepted their protection against the French.

Shortly after Ho Chi Minh's August Revolution of 1945, Diem was briefly arrested by the Viet Minh, who about that time apparently murdered his eldest brother, who had been governor of Quang Nam province. Another elder brother, Catholic Bishop Ngo Dinh Thuc, surprisingly supported the Viet Minh briefly after the

August Revolution, as did other Catholic nationalists. But not Diem, although despite his refusal to cooperate, he was released from Communist confinement following the March 6, 1946, accords. Thereafter, he was active in discussions of the Bao Dai Solution, but also refused an offer to head such a government in 1948 and 1949, charging correctly that the French had attached too many strings to their offers. Leaving the country in 1950, Diem spent much of 1951–1953 at Maryknoll seminary in Lakewood, New Jersey, with frequent American political contacts, and much of the year before May 1954 at a Benedictine monastery in Belgium.

With France's belated concession of full independence to Vietnam on June 4, 1954, and promises of expanded powers for himself, Diem decided to accept a new offer by Bao Dai and was appointed prime minister on June 16. Returning from Paris to an unenthusiastic reception in Saigon ten days later, he formed his first cabinet on July 7, just in time to refuse to sign the July 20 accords ending the war and creating two "temporary" zones for the north and the south. He revealed perhaps more than he intended with his remark at the time, "Vietnam looked like France at the time of Joan of Arc."[1]

Indeed, given the challenges faced, and the universal expectation of his failure, which was perhaps why a hostile Bao Dai had appointed him, Diem achieved startling successes during his first years in power. First of all, in the autumn he was able to overcome a challenge to his authority by the military chief of staff, General Nguyen Van Hinh, who boasted he could overthrow Diem with a dial of the telephone. Then in the spring of 1955, he was able to divide and defeat the powerful religious and secret society sects of South Vietnam, and in October of that year to replace Emperor Bao Dai as head of state in name as well as in fact. Based on these early successes, Diem went on to ignore Hanoi's overtures for better relations, avoided the holding of the promised 1956 elections to unify the country, and undertook the attempted elimination of all followers of Ho Chi Minh remaining in the south.

WITHOUT U.S. SUPPORT, none of this would have been possible. While it is too simple to charge that Washington forced its man on Bao Dai and thereafter on the Vietnamese people—there were very few other non-Communist choices—it soon moved to bolster anti-Communist positions in the south in such a way as to ensure a fatally close alliance with Diem. Secretary of State Dulles's long-planned sequel to NATO, the Southeast Asia Treaty Organization (SEATO) was formed in Manila on September 8, 1954, and pledged to "meet the common danger" that would arise, not only from armed attack, but from "subversive activities directed from without." Thereafter, SEATO formed the basis for increasing military support while American economic assistance to South Vietnam held at over two hundred million dollars a year before mounting astronomically in the 1960s. In the 1950s, Washington paid for some two-thirds of government expenses (80 percent by late in the war), even as Hanoi's aid from Russia and China was declining from about two-thirds of the North Vietnamese budget in 1955 to 21 percent in 1961. Direct foreign investments in South Vietnam, however, remained small (and more French than American), and as late as 1959 made up only one-sixth of total capital investments in the country. In other words, it would be more correct to say that the United States controlled the government than the economy, the reverse of the classical Marxist argument. In any case, future President John F. Kennedy could justly state on June 1, 1956, "If we are not the parents of little Vietnam, then surely we are the godparents. We presided at its birth, we gave assistance to its life, we have helped to shape its future." Then on the very day of his own death, November 23, 1963, Kennedy went further to state, "Without the United States, South Vietnam would collapse overnight." As for the Communists, more predictably, they simply spoke of "the My-Diem regime," or the U.S.-Diem Government," with the United States conspicuously placed first.

On October 1, 1954, for the first time President Eisenhower specified that this increasing commitment was for the moment tied to Diem himself, as the best if not the ideal choice to "save Vietnam from Communism." Subsequent messages and actions increased that commitment although until mid-1955 Washington hedged its bets somewhat for fear Diem could not survive.

During the last half of 1954, the United States stepped up its military aid to an anti-Communist South Vietnam. It upgraded the Military Assistance Advisory Group (MAAG), established to oversee American aid in late 1950, by enlarging it to the maximum 385 men allowed by the Geneva Accords. Its commander was General John ("Iron Mike") O'Daniel, and President Eisenhower appointed another general, Lawton Collins, as his "personal representative" and ambassador to Saigon. In December, Collins reached agreement with the head of the French forces still in Indochina, General Paul Ely, that the United States would replace France in all its functions beginning January 1, 1955, and the last French soldier left the country in April 1956.

Meanwhile, an initial core of a dozen U.S. Central Intelligence agents, organized in a so-called Saigon Military Mission under Edward G. Lansdale, was increasingly active after June 1954. It carried out missions ranging from sabotage and adverse astrological predictions in the north, to training, intelligence, and bribes in the south. According to French sources, without the help of the Lansdale group, and a little later that of a group of Michigan State University professors and "counselors" (including CIA agents) headed by Wesley Fishel, and the agricultural expert Wolf Ladejinsky,* not to speak of other more open U.S. aid, "Diem would have been swept away" immediately. They also state that American military personnel in Vietnam soon numbered, not the 385 allowed, but 1,600 surreptitiously dispersed in three organizations under the control of MAAG.[2] In addition, activists like U.S. Navy doctor Thomas A. Dooley, who later inspired an important philanthropic organization in Laos and other countries of Southeast Asia, toured the United States to drum up support for Diem's efforts against the "organized godlessness" of the "new Red Imperialism." The American diplomatic mission in Saigon† soon grew to become the largest in the world, and by the late 1960s directed some 11,509 American and 110,000 Vietnamese employees, supporting a half million American troops.

USING THIS GROWING U.S. SUPPORT and an "uncanny ability to divide his enemies by a series of intricate maneuvers," Diem proceeded to eliminate the French-trained and -supported chief of staff, General Nguyen Van Hinh. In September 1954, Hinh came close to toppling the government, inducing initial support from France and the sects,

*Like Landsale, Ladejinsky was well known as an adviser to President Raymon Magsaysay in the early 1950s suppression in the Philippines of some 15,000 Communist guerillas known as the Huks.

†Headed successively by Ambassadors Donald R. Heath (October 1950–November 1954), G. Frederick Reinhardt (May 1955–February 1957), Elbridge Durbrow (April 1957–May 1961), Frederick E. Nolting, Jr. (May 1961–August 1963), Henry Cabot Lodge (August 1963–June 1964), Maxwell D. Taylor (July 1964–July 1965), Henry Cabot Lodge (July 1965–March 1967), Ellsworth Bunker (April 1967–March 1973), Graham Martin (June 1973–April 1975).

and the resignation of over half of Diem's cabinet. But with U.S. support, Diem succeeded in splitting and reportedly bribing the sects, thereby undermining Hinh. In November, Bao Dai replaced Hinh, although a rising younger Saigon military leader, Tran Van Don, would later state, "At the time this seemed a major error because Hinh was probably the best officer we had. If he had remained in charge, I feel we would have had a much better chance of defeating the Communists."[3]

It was Diem's spring 1955 defeat of the powerful Cao Dai and Hoa Hao religious sects (claiming up to two million and one and one-half million followers respectively) and the smaller but well-organized Binh Xuyen Society that most convincingly persuaded skeptics both in South Vietnam and the United States that Diem was accomplishing the seemingly impossible task of consolidating his control over the south. In January, Diem served notice that he intended to eliminate all such rival power centers when he refused to renew the license for the Binh Xuyen to run their infamous gambling casino, Le Grand Monde, and its associated enormous brothel known as the Hall of Mirrors, where "some 1200 girls serviced their patrons around the clock." As he had accomplished in September in the Hinh affair, Diem at first was able to use competition between the sects, and the ambitions and venality of some of their leaders, to prevent effective action against him. But in March, core groups of all three sects, encouraged by Bao Dai and the French, formed "a spiritual union" and again induced a resignation of a majority of Diem's cabinet. Moreover, General Collins now came to agree that Diem must go.

Yet once again, by skillful maneuvering, Diem survived. He used the backing of Lansdale and other Americans, new defections of sect leaders,* and above all the loyalty of the army, won by key promotions, including those of Generals Tran Van Don and Duong Van Minh ("Big Minh"), who would overthrow him in 1963, to defeat this, his gravest challenge of the 1950s. After a month of stalemate, on April 28, 1955, his army went on the attack and by May 1 in furious combat drove most of the 2,500 Binh Xuyen troops, plus the Saigon police and "thugs" they controlled, out of Saigon. The Cao Dai troops, once 15,000–20,000 strong, had mostly already de-

*Including Cao Dai Generals Trinh Minh The and Nguyen Thanh Phuong, and Hoa Hao warlord Tran Van Soai, who between them allegedly accepted about eight of some twelve million American-supplied dollars paid in bribes during these critical months.

fected to the government side, and on September 19, 1956, the government occupied the Cao Dai "papacy" of Tay Ninh. The Hoa Hao, with a "federation" of core believers of 7,000–8,000, and claiming an army of 10,000–15,000, and 1.5 million supporters, was mostly dispersed from its southern delta strongholds by September 1955, though famed leader Ba Cut ("third finger severed") fought on until April 1956, when he was captured and decapitated. Some leaders and followers of all three sects went underground or into exile and later joined the Communist-led National Liberation Front.

Now Diem moved to remove the vestiges of power of the last Nguyen Emperor, Bao Dai. Beginning in May, he began to organize a plebiscite in which the electorate would be asked to choose between a republic headed by himself or a continuation of the monarchy headed by Bao Dai. In elections of October 23, 1955, it was announced that 98.2 percent had voted in favor of Diem. This was hardly surprising given Bao Dai's residence on the French Côte d'Azur, the government's blatant propaganda, stuffing of ballot boxes, and the nature of the ballot to be chosen. Diem's picture, for example, showed him surrounded by modern-looking young people against a red background, which was the traditional color of good luck in Vietnam, while Bao Dai was pictured wearing ancient imperial robes against a green background, the color of bad luck.

More commendable was the new Republic's handling of close to a million refugees resettled in the south after the Geneva Conference's division of the country. With close to $100 million aid from the United States and charities, resettlement went relatively smoothly, though with foreseeable problems of location and employment, and some perhaps unnecessary relocation of mountain minorities to make room for up to several hundred thousand new lowland refugees.

The most controversial aspect of the resettlements was religious. Up to three-quarters of the close to 900,000 refugees to the south were Catholic and mostly either rich or associated with the defeated French. The pressures on the Catholics to leave were enormous given the close organization between priests and laity and the fact that 72 percent of the clergy went south. Rumors even circulated to the effect that the "Virgin Mary has gone south." Nonetheless, although in 1954 some 40 percent of the Catholic population as a whole left the north, as of 1960 the Church still estimated that a majority of the 1,807,784 Vietnamese faithful remained in the north, as against some 793,000 in the south.

The influx of Catholics to the south greatly increased the already Catholic bias of the Diem government. The president himself was very religious and his brother Thuc was the archbishop of Hue. Although forming about 10 percent of the population of the south, during much of the Diem period Catholics held a disproportionate number of government positions, at times one-third or more of the cabinet posts, provincial governorships, and seats in the National Assembly. Diem was said to be "forced to find his political base among Catholic refugees," and organized progovernment demonstrations by them after September 1954. There was a similar disproportionate representation of officials from Diem's native Annam.

Still more problems stemmed from the nepotism of the Diem government. In the wake of the new resignation of the majority of his cabinet in April 1955, Diem governed almost exclusively through his brothers and their protégés. In addition to Archbishop Thuc, younger brothers Nhu and Can were extremely powerful. Nhu held the title of "adviser" and became the *éminence grise* of the administration, its principal theorist, political organizer, and director of the omnipresent police and secret service. Can, also an adviser, became in effect the absolute boss of the family's native Central Vietnam, and was said to run Hue "like a fief." Another brother became ambassador to London, and other relatives held various choice positions.

The wife of Nhu, Tran Le Xuan (Beautiful Spring) became the unfortunate symbol of this feudal atmosphere, serving as "official hostess" for her bachelor brother-in-law, Diem. According to Joseph Buttinger, Madame Nhu used her considerable energy and willpower to aid the regime as one might help "a drowning man by a rock tied to his neck." She created her own feminist political party, the Woman's Solidarity Movement, a private army, a paramilitary woman's corps, and became a deputy to the National Assembly. There, beginning in late 1958 she had passed a "Family Code" and "Law for the Protection of Morality," which declared illegal "polygamy, divorce, dancing, beauty contests, gambling, fortune telling, cockfighting, prostitution, and a hundred other things dear to the heart of Vietnamese men." By 1963, Mme. Nhu even forbade citizens to hear "sentimental songs" or be "seen in public with a person of another sex."[4] By then, a poster of some student demonstrators at a New York university seemed apt. It read "No Nhus is good news."

More serious, but in its way perhaps equally out of touch with reality, was the concept known as Personalism, worked out by Nhu and Diem from 1953 on. Almost as eclectic as the teachings of Cao Dai, it cited primarily teachings of the French philosopher Emanuel Mounier, but also a blend of Christianity and Marxism, Moral Rearmament, and other teachings ranging from Confucianism to Existentialism. It sought to harmonize "the material and spiritual aspirations of the individual with the social needs of the community and the political needs of the state and . . . a middle path between capitalist individualism and Marxist collectivism." This "vague mishmash of ideas" was limited, not only by the authoritarianism of the regime, but presumably by such facts as that Nhu was known to smoke opium. Nevertheless in 1956, Nhu started a Personalist Labor Party (Can Lao Dang), which claimed 70,000 members by the end of the decade, but it served "primarily as a political intelligence agency for Nhu." Similarly, Diem's own more loosely structured National Revolutionary Movement, founded in October 1954, and claiming a million and a half members by the early 1960s, together with other parallel organizations were primarily artificially created progovernment groups.

Athough much inspired by the successful Communist linking of ideology and organization the personalist groups almost totally lacked the dynamism of the Communist mass organizations since their adherents joined almost entirely for negative reasons, to avoid persecution and arrest. They were more comparable to Chiang Kai-shek's efforts in China in the 1930s, under the rubric of the New Life Movement, to carry out nonrevolutionary modernization through a kind of updated neo-Confucianism. Such efforts have succeeded in Asia only in Japan after 1868 and, given the gap between Communist and government efforts to organize the people in Vietnam and China, one has to ponder Mao's statement of December 1947 that "No army opposed to the people can use our tactics."

In any case, in Diem's Vietnam, in good Confucian tradition, no organization of the people could take place without government approval. There were only two choices, establishment organization or illegal organization. Meetings had to be approved, and seldom were, and all publications were subject to strict censorship, with the result that "South Vietnam is for all practical purposes a one-Party state." It was also increasingly, and admittedly, corrupt with widespread use of secret accounts and bribes practiced by many of the 138,000 government employees, if not by Diem himself. Nhu was reportedly "up to his ears" in corruption and according to Malcolm Browne, "Careers in the civil service too often are merely platforms for a lifetime of extortion."

As might have been expected, there was a natural reaction to this corrupt creation of a modern-day imperial state. Aside from the Communists, many sought to establish alternatives to Diem, but except for the Communists, none succeeded. In March 1956, a faction of the Dai (great) Viet Party, a conservative nationalist group formed about 1941 at first with close ties to Japan and which by late in the French war had become the strongest indigenous anti-Viet Minh group, rebelled briefly against Diem. The next year Diem narrowly escaped an assassination attempt, two new anti-Diem parties were founded, and the remnants of the sects formed a Front of National Union and Revolution.

By the early 1960s, it was increasingly apparent that the Diem government, which for anti-Communists had started so promisingly, had become a kind of neo-Confucian dictatorship, locked into a set of fundamentally impossible policies. In a revolutionary situation of rapid change, it was increasingly authoritarian, corrupt, and intolerant. Diem refused to countenance the slightest criticism, let alone opposition, and Nhu's secret police relentlessly tracked opponents, either to exile, jail, or open revolt.

In April 1960, eighteen representatives of the Dai Viet, surviving leaders of the sects, and dissident Catholic and military groups, including eleven former cabinet members, issued a stinging indictment of the regime, known as the Caravelle Declaration after a Saigon hotel where they met, charging antidemocratic elections in 1956, and 1959, leading to a rubber-stamp National Assembly, abusive censorship, and indiscriminate arrests. On November 11, 1960, a group of dissident military units in Saigon almost took over the government, but failed and new crackdowns followed. Most of the Caravelle group were arrrested, including three future prime ministers, and the then most prominent and respected opposition leader of the 1950s, Dr. Phan Quang Dan.

On February 27, 1962, two Vietnamese pilots destroyed a wing of the Presidential Palace, but missed Diem and Nhu. Regarding his escape from this latest assassination attempt, not as a warning lesson, but once more as due to "divine providence," Diem tightened his dictatorship still further. The result of all this according to Buttinger, a former principal foreign supporter of Diem, was that:

> Opposed by the intellectuals, despised by the educated middle class, rejected by businessmen, hated by the youth and by all nationalists

> with political ambitions, and totally lacking in mass support, the Diem Government had to rely for its survival on an apparatus of coercion . . . . Abuse of power, nepotism, corruption, contempt for inferiors and heartless unconcern for the needs of the people were the examples the "Family" set . . . [and while Diem] . . . no doubt despised [the widespread corruption] as a means of personal enrichment . . . [he] willingly embraced [it] as a means of maintaining himself in power.[5]

Yet Diem continued to have high-placed defenders. Frederick Nolting, the American ambassador to Saigon in the early 1960s, for example, could tell a British radio audience a decade later:

> This man was honest . . . dedicated . . . and [had] the best chances of rallying the nationalist spirit of the non-Communist South Vietnamese of anyone on the political scene. While he had his shortcomings . . . a stubborn streak . . . verbosity . . . he was autocratic and paternalistic in the mandarin sense [but not a western style dictator] . . . Diem was a dedicated, responsible leader. He had wide support among the peasants of South Vietnam . . . based on his reputation for honesty and justice . . . and his hard work for his people.[6]

Somewhat more succinctly, President Johnson was quoted as saying "Shit, man, he's the only boy we got out there."

DIEM'S TREATMENT OF THE COMMUNISTS of the south may be easily imagined given the judgment of a sympathetic observer that opposition groups had "less political freedom . . . than there was under the French." Yet, as in their already three-decades-old struggle for survival, Communist organization, willpower, and propaganda proved a match for new overwhelming efforts to destroy them. Barely, however.

Up to 90,000 Viet Minh sympathizers went north in the wake of the 1954 Geneva treaty, and probably an equivalent number were arrested or executed. The Party, variously estimated at 30,000 to 60,000 strong in the south in 1954, was reduced by reorganization as well as by repression to perhaps 15,000 in 1956 and less than 5,000 in 1959. Much larger numbers of sympathizers backed the core Communists, however, as will be discussed further.

In 1954, the Communists controlled up to two-thirds of the south and one-third or even one-half its people outside of the major cities and strongholds of the sects. The headquarters of the Nam Bo

Regional Committee* in 1954 was located at Ca Mau near the southern tip of the country. Sympathizers grouped there, in areas around Saigon and in Quang Ngai and Binh Dinh provinces on the central coast south of Da Nang for passage to the north.

There is debate as to what the Communists expected in South Vietnam after Geneva. Apparently some militants had been prepared to go on fighting for the complete conquest of their country, while others were willing to settle for a temporary division, in expectation of a peaceful unification with the victory of Ho Chi Minh in the promised 1956 elections. In the late 1970s dispute with China, Hanoi charged that its erstwhile ally had forced compromises over the location and timing of the division of Vietnam as well as over disposal of Cambodia and Laos, amounting to a "first betrayal by the Chinese leaders of the revolutionary struggle of the Vietnamese people." Certainly many Vietnamese Communists were skeptical of the promised elections, given "the crafty nature of U.S. imperialism . . . aggressive and bellicose" and its determination to "keep socialism from spreading throughout southeast Asia," in the words of Party statements of the early 1960s.

But in the mid-1950s, the conjunction of the post-Stalinist stress by both Russia and China on "peaceful transitions to socialism," together with the fatigue of the Vietnamese Communists after nine years of heavy warfare, and with Diem's initial consolidation of power in the south, all combined to force a Party decision to temporarily follow a "peaceful line" in the south, with priority to the "building of socialism" in the north. As Le Duan stressed to southern Party members in November 1956, four months after Diem's blocking of the elections, "Only the peaceful struggle line . . . [which as he explained] relies on the revolutionary political forces of the masses . . . can create the strong political forces . . . to defeat the scheme of war provocation and the cruel policy of the U.S. Diem [regime]"[7]

But events in the south forced a progressive change in the Party line by the late 1950s—from primarily political struggle to a combination of political and military struggle, and by the mid-1960s to

*Then headed by Le Duan, with Pham Hung and Le Duc Tho as deputies. After 1959, the Regional Committee, as from 1951 to 1954, again reverted to the Central Office for South Vietnam (COSVN), or the southern branch of the Party Central Committee. Below it were five (earlier three) interzone committees and a Saigon committee, provincial and district committees and, at the bottom, Party cells in residential and work areas.

primarily military struggle. With considerable evidence, the Communists argue that these shifts were forced on them by the actions of the "dictatorial, anti-Democratic, and extremely cruel" Diem government and its American backers, leaving them no choice but "the path of overthrowing the regime by force.

As already discussed, the Diem government ignored the provisions of the Geneva Conference calling for the setting up of national elections in July 1956 to unify and decide the nature of the country. Why? Because, as President Eisenhower speculated in 1963 with reference to the last years of the French War, "Possibly eighty percent of the population would have voted for the Communist Ho Chi Minh as their leader rather than Chief of State, Bao Dai." While some observers argue that, due to Diem's accomplishments, by 1956 the situation would have changed, given a choice between the new head of state and Ho, Diem took no chances. He ignored all calls for the establishment of preparatory committees for the elections in 1955, and staged instead his own referendum to replace Bao Dai as head of state.

Given the greater population of the Communist north, and the stress on the impossibility of free elections in a Communist state, Diem had the full backing, if not urging, of the United States in these moves. Already, in the middle of the Geneva Conference, Secretary of State Dulles secretly stated that elections must be delayed "as long after the cease-fire conference as possible" and "in conditions free from intimidation to give democratic elements their best chance." The result was the setting of a 1956 date for the elections rather than a date six months later as favored by the Viet Minh. In 1955, the U.S. National Security Council urged that "to give no impression of blocking elections while avoiding the possibility of losing them, Diem should insist on free elections by secret ballot with strict supervision. Communists in Korea and Germany have rejected these conditions: hopefully the Viet Minh would follow suit." And in the autumn of 1977, the secretary of state of the early 1960s, Dean Rusk, was equally frank to a much wider audience on British television: "I think one could make an argument that those elections should have been held, but . . . there was no possibility of free elections either in North Vietnam or in South Vietnam in 1955 or 1956 . . . [at] the same time, the Soviets were utterly opposed to free elections in Korea. So the question must have arisen why should we accommodate them in one spot if they wouldn't accommodate us in these places."[8] In other words, neither the United States nor Diem had any intention of holding elections that it was feared would be lost; and in Vietnam, Diem in all probability would have lost.

Even as it became clear that the two Vietnams would remain separate after 1954, Hanoi proposed peaceful economic and cultural exchanges, and mutual reduction of forces. Beginning in November 1954, Hanoi requested postal exchanges, and from March 1957 Premier Pham Van Dong broadened proposals to "reestablish economic relations between the two zones . . . bilateral reduction of armed forces . . . and trade exchanges . . . ." From 1954 to 1960, Hanoi claimed to send thirty-nine diplomatic dispatches, in addition to innumerable declarations, calling for increased contacts between the two sides, in part at least induced by its own troubles with land reform and declining aid from Russia and China. But Diem either ignored all such initiatives, or posed conditions such as his April 1958 demand that the north establish the same "democratic liberties" as "existed in the south," including the right to leave of an additional 92,319 people who allegedly wanted to emigrate to the south. In April 1960 Diem established a Special Committee for the Liberation of the North, while as late as May 1961 Hanoi spoke of possibilities of negotiations between the two zones, based on the neutrality of the south. The International Control Commission, while because of its composition and the local and international situation, was both generally anti-Diem and helpless to settle these disputes, nonetheless through February 1961 lodged 154 "violations" of the Geneva Accords against the Diem government, and only one against Hanoi.

MORE SERIOUS STILL for the Communists of the south than Diem's blocking of the 1956 elections were his actions in violation of the Geneva Accords (Article 14c, and Final Declaration, Article 9), specifying "Each party undertakes to refrain from any reprisals or discrimination against persons or organizations on account of their activities during the hostilities and to guarantee their democratic liberties." By contrast, Diem's brother Nhu told Jean Lacouture, "You do not coexist with those who want to exterminate you," and brother Can was reported even to have stated, "My hand will never tire of killing Communists . . . Everyone among you should offer the life of one red to your country. As for me, millions . . . ."[9]

Based on such thinking, an "anti-Communist denunciation campaign" was intensified after the suppression of the sects in 1955, and led to the detention in succeeding years of an estimated 50,000 to 100,000 suspects or, according to the Communists, even 800,000, with another 90,000 executed. Already by mid-1955, some 50 percent of Party cells were destroyed in Tay Ninh province and 90 percent by mid-1956, while in two districts near Saigon, the Party claimed only 6 out of 1,000 Party members survived the 1950s. In Long An province in 1959, an average of 26 persons accused of being Communists were being arrested each month and another 9 killed. In the district of Tam Ky south of Da Nang, an estimated 1 in 9 persons were killed, with 13,000 "disappearances" and 7,000 imprisonments out of a population of 180,000. By November 1957, a Communist source spoke of 2,148 of its supporters killed throughout the south with another 65,000 arrested. According to an anti-Vietnamese Cambodian Communist source, overall some 70 percent of the Party in the South was destroyed by 1959, with all but one member of the Central Committee in the south forced to leave the country, or killed or captured. Survivors were forced to hide in swamps and forests between Bien Hoa and Tay Ninh, and in the extreme southwest or Cambodia.

Borrowing from traditional Chinese as well as Communist practices, popular rallies were held to denounce Communists, while families, villages, schools, and places of work were organized to report all suspicious activities and post names and photos of all residents. By the early 1960s, all citizens were required to carry identification papers, and on May 6, 1959, was passed the most sweeping of the anti-Communist legislations, the infamous Law 10–59, which set up special military tribunals to carry out death sentences against anyone deemed "to hide a Communist or . . . become involved with a Communist . . . ."

It was not only the Communists who were affected by the government sweeps. One anti-Communist author P. J. Honey, in 1960, considered "The majority of the detainees are neither Communists nor pro-Communists," although Denis Warner in 1962 argued that of 20,000 Communist suspects in prison, no more than 300 were "genuine liberals." Yet some 3,000 Cao Dai, for example, were arrested, and the International Control Commission estimated in 1958 that at least 2,749 people had been "brutalized or killed" in violation of Article 14c of the Geneva Accords. The government announced in 1960 that it had arrested 48,200 Communists or suspects and had held 893,291 sessions to unmask Communists attended by 18,759,111 persons.

Partially offsetting these draconian measures against them from the Communist point of view, however, was the growing general disaffection with Diem, both because of the repressions and because of other policy failures. This was especially important in the countryside, where the vast peasant majority was generally unhappy with the inadequate or reactionary agrarian and village reforms announced in 1955–1956, and then increasingly angry from 1959 on at efforts to relocate entire populations into anti-Communist fortified villages.

As described briefly in Chapter Seven, the government land reform was perceived as a step backward for the many peasants who already had experienced Communist land reforms of sharply reduced rents or appropriation of abandoned lands during the French war, while Diem's mid-1956 decrees to appoint village officials alienated still more of the rural population that for centuries had had at least some say in the election of the councils that effectively governed life in the 2,560 villages of South Vietnam embracing about 15,000 hamlets. Then, in February 1959, the government decreed the grouping of peasantry in key areas into about 100 agrovilles or new "agrarian cities" which would guarantee better security against the Communists while offering improved facilities for electrification, irrigation, and the like. Ngo Dinh Nhu, who was considered the mastermind of this and subsequent efforts, explained that the new groupings would create a "a democratic civilization . . . of combatants and heroes" in the struggle against the Communists. In fact, Nhu was attempting to learn from the Communists' much longer experience in organizing villages as well as from British experience with similar anti-Communist villages in Malaya a decade before.

In Vietnam, however, unlike in Malaya where most of the 7,000–8,000 guerillas had been Chinese, the Communists and their domestic enemies were of the same race, and many if not most peasants not unnaturally opposed the government efforts to "let the water out of the pond to catch the fish," when that meant their removal from ancestral lands and tombs to new dwelling places that they were largely forced to build themselves.

Because of such opposition, bad planning, and lack of resources to speed the process, by late 1961 only twenty-two of the agrovilles had been completed, at which point the government decided to reform the program, with the substitution of "strategic hamlets" for the hated agrovilles. Retreating from the idea of constructing entirely new communities, the strategic hamlets of 1962–1963 were to fortify some two-thirds of the south's existing hamlets. Yet, if they involved less forced dislocations, the new measures still increased government demands on the peasants, ringed the hamlets with barbed wire, and increased security requirements to the extent that the Communists could easily propagandize against such "glorified concentration camps." There were reports of increased difficulties for the Communists to infiltrate the villages, and of a temporary reduction in the number of their supporters; but with the fall of Diem, the whole network of strategic hamlets largely collapsed. The Communists claimed to destroy some 1,662 of the strategic hamlets in the single month after the murder of Diem, and while the government in all claimed construction of some 7,000–8,000 units, at most a fifth were considered sound. Subsequent programs for "New Life Hamlets" in 1964–1966, and "Revolutionary Development" thereafter were scarcely more successful in breaking the Communist's near monopoly on village organization and peasant motivation.

THE COMMUNIST SURVIVAL of Diem's repressions was due, not only to the government's failures and mistakes, but as in earlier crises, to organization and high motivation, and to a lesser degree to external events and support. The organizational strengths of the Communists in turn derived, not only from their ability to recruit activists from the peasantry according to the principles of People's War as described in Chapter Six, but from their ability to organize other sections of the population according to principles of the United Front. With the Party and the army, the United Front to "unite all the people with whom we can unite" was for the Vietnamese, as for the Chinese, one of the three "magic weapons" of their struggle.

As described in Chapter Two, both for theoretical reasons to do with the national bourgeois revolution and for practical reasons of the necessity for allies, from 1925 on the Vietnamese Communists consistently worked at United Front problems. They applied a two-sided policy of allying with those groups they could lead and opposing those groups they could not lead. After varying degrees of attempted cooperation with nationalist groups and even the Trotskyists in the 1930s, by 1945 the Communists became strong enough to liquidate troublesome "third force" and Trotskyist leaders, and to induce most other patriotic Vietnamese to join the Viet Minh. In 1946 the still broader Lien Viet Front replaced the Viet Minh, and in September 1955, following instructions of the Central Committee's Eighth Plenum the previous month, the Communists organized the Vietnam Fatherland Front to coordinate the struggle of all peace-loving groups against American imperialism. Participants ranged from Buddhists, Catholics, and sects to International Friendship and Peace Groups, overseas Vietnamese, and "all nationalities, religions, democratic political parties, and people's organizations . . . ." Later in 1955, those Communist efforts, and continuing government oppressions, helped lead to the formation of a National Liberation Front, dominated by Hoa Hao, Cao Dai, and Binh Xuyen and dedicated to the overthrow of Diem.

In the villages and cities of the south, the youth, peasant, and women's groups, and "committees for peace" like that of Nguyen Huu Tho in Saigon, struggled to survive Diem's roundups and to coordinate with the Front headquarters in Hanoi. The Party's southern leadership naturally continuously debated other possible responses to their many dilemmas. Le Duan reportedly argued the necessity for the preparation of a resumption of armed struggle at a March 1956 meeting of the Party's Regional Committee for the South, which he headed until his transfer to Hanoi later in the year. In September 1956, Van Tien Dung, the commander of the 1975 offensive that took Saigon, visited the south as did Le Duan two years later. But Hanoi continued to dictate caution for the time being, following the advice of Moscow,* which sent Anastas Mikoyan to Hanoi in April 1956 about the time of the Ninth Plenum. Later in that year, however, after hearing Le Duan's proposals for "the Road to Revolution in South Vietnam," the Eleventh Plenum moved to advise southern militants to strike back against "corrupt officials, cruel tyrants and wicked landlords," in short, to step up "revolutionary terror" against "counter-revolutionary terror." Several hundred officials were eliminated in 1957, although in March 1957 the Twelfth Plenum reportedly offered to consider delaying reunification for ten to fifteen years if Diem would relent with his persecutions and untertake negotiations with Hanoi.

---

*Moscow apparently even considered proposing the entry of both Vietnams to the United Nations in early 1957, before Hanoi got the idea dropped.

THE LOW POINT FOR THE PARTY in the south came in 1959, when one of its few thousand surviving members told Jeffrey Race: "The situation in the South had passed into a stage the Communists considered the darkest in their lives. . . . Not only had the southern regime not been destroyed, it was instead destroying the Party . . . ."[10] Nonetheless, these few party militants, surviving especially in swamps and jungles south and west of Saigon, managed to hold out and keep contact with larger numbers of sympathizers in the various front organizations. Even the southern headquarters of the Party managed to continue work despite overwhelming efforts to destroy it, moving from Ca Mau in the extreme south in the early 1950s to locations northwest of Saigon, first near Tay Ninh, and by the early 1970s at times into Cambodia. In the late 1960s, COSVN reportedly was located in the village of Xa Mat, near the northwest border of Tay Ninh province and Cambodia, while the Saigon Party Committee and a forward military headquarters were only twenty odd miles north of Saigon, between Cu Chi, Ben Suc, and Ben Cat in the Iron Triangle. Midway in the French war, the Party's Nam Bo Regional Committee had been upgraded to the Southern Branch of the Central Committee (usually called Central Office for South Vietnam or COSVN. After 1954 it reverted to a regional committee and then in two stages in 1959 and 1961 was again upgraded into a section of the Central Committee, headed by Nguyen Van Linh (alias Nguyen Van Cuc),* then Nguyen Chi Thanh in the early 1960s, and after 1967 by Pham Hung. By the early 1970s, it was said to include some 2,400 leaders and guard troops.

In January 1959, the Party Central Committee's Fifteenth Plenum authorized southern militants to go on the offensive, to move from "a peaceful line" that "relies on the revolutionary political forces of the masses" to a "general uprising to seize political power . . . [and] overthrow the U.S.-Diem Government," whose "cruel terror and repression . . . has caused the Party a significant number of losses. . . ." Rising assassinations of government personnel and Communist-led uprisings, especially in Quang Ngai province in the autumn of 1959, and in Ben Tre in January 1960, signaled the rise of Communist aggressiveness in areas of the south. The leadership, however, until 1963 continued to be extremely cautious, stating in February 1960 that while under the new conditions "political strug-

---

*A protégé of Le Duan during the French War, Linh was born in the South in 1913 of northern parents.

gle and armed struggle must advance side by side . . . political struggle must still be fundamental and primary," and stop short of full-scale "guerilla war," except in the Highlands where "military struggle" had become "primary." This caution was dictated by fear that "the Americans would intensify the war by bringing in troops," and important Party meetings of January and May 1959 and the Party's Third National Congress of September 1960 still stressed efforts "to build socialism in the North and overthrow the U.S.-Diem regime in the South, and thus to achieve peace and unification by peaceful means" and thereby "avoid going down the road to complete war. . . ."[11] Then in December 1960, the Party created the National Liberation Front (NLF) followed a year later by the organization of the People's Revolutionary Party (PRP) and in 1969 by the Provisional Revolutionary Government (PRG).

This combination of gradually more aggressive Communist tactics, coupled with continuing United Front work and rising anger of the populace against the government, enabled the Party in the south to resume its growth from a low of under 5,000 in 1959, to more than double its effectives to 10,000 by late 1960. Thereafter, core elements increased to an estimated 16,000 in October 1961, 30,000 in 1962, and 35,000 by February 1965. Larger numbers of supporters swelled to an estimated 200,000 and then 300,000 by the mid-1960s with a passive following of up to one million. By then the Communists dominated up to one-third of the hamlets (one half in the delta), and three-fourths of the countryside of the south. Military units were comprised of locally recruited village militia, regional troops, and "main force units," the latter with increasing, but still minor, staffing by infiltration from the north. Assassinations of government officials also increased dramatically from about 500 a year in 1958 to several thousand a year after 1961 (a reported maximum of over 5,000 a year in 1968, 1969 and 1970), although the Party criticized "indiscriminate punishments" and throughout demanded the subordination of violence to its political objectives.

HOW MANY OF THESE COMMUNIST FORCES in the south came from the north? Contrary to U.S. Department of State publications of December 1961 and February 1965, a small minority did so, at least until after American escalation of the war. Despite their titles, "A Threat to the Peace: North Vietnam's Effort to Conquer South Vietnam," and "Aggression from the North: The Record of North Vietnam's Campaign to Conquer South Vietnam," Washington's own figures of 1965 admitted that "many of the lower level elements . . . are recruited within South Vietnam." The December 1961 document moreover cited CIA estimates that "about 10–20 percent of total Viet Cong strength consists of cadres infiltrated from North Vietnam . . . ," and predictably did not mention that Diem had arrested most of the southern Communists who had not gone north, or that most of the early "infiltrators" were in fact "regroupees" returning home after their transfer to the north in compliance with the 1954 Geneva Accords.

In all, perhaps 4,500 regroupees returned south in 1959–1960, and until 1963 nearly all such infiltrators were ethnic southerners. In 1964, the leading Saigon general, Tran Van Don, acknowledged that "no large scale infiltration of North Vietnamese Regular Units had yet occurred," and as late as November of that year, U.S. intelligence sources still admitted, "despite a large and growing DRV (Democratic Republic of Vietnam) contribution to the Viet Cong insurrection, the primary sources of Communist strength in the South remain indigenous . . . ." Just before beginning the greatest bombing campaigns in history to stop "aggression from the North," Washington also acknowledged that the greatest Communist strength in the south was below and west of Saigon, far from the north. It had access to captured documents that at least as late as 1960 stated that "the people must get their own arms" by capturing government supplies, and that the Communists had less than 1,000 firearms for all of the south at that time. In the province of Long An, the infiltration of northern Communists was estimated at 10 a year in 1960, and perhaps 100 a year in 1965, a "negligible" figure compared with locally recruited guerillas. In December 1963, Secretary of Defense McNamara estimated that in the first nine months of that year, some "1,000–1,500 Viet Cong cadres entered South Vietnam from Laos," and as late as January 1966, Secretary of State Rusk still was quoted as saying some 80 percent of the Viet Cong were southerners.

If, in fact, the north did control the policy of the southern revolution, until the American escalation of 1965, it seems that northern personnel made up even fewer than the 20 percent of southern Communist forces as charged by Washington. At that time, when there were already 23,000 American troops in the south, confidential sources estimated there were 5,800 northern soldiers, plus possibly 20,000–30,000 political officers, mostly regroupees, out of a total estimated Communist strength in the south of 180,700. American sociologist Philip Slater therefore concluded that the United States "attacked North Vietnam in part because we were unwilling to admit that we were fighting the people of South Vietnam."[12]

In 1967, the Saigon Ministry of Foreign Affairs gave the following figures of illegal infiltrators from the north to the south: 300 in 1959; 2,700 in 1960; 13,600 in 1961; 12,300 in 1962; 7,450 in 1963; 13,000 in 1964; and then 33,300 in 1965 and 73,900 in 1966, two-thirds of whom may have been political officers. Later estimates spoke of 90,000 northerners entering in 1967 and up to 300,000 in 1968, when 181,149 Communists were said to have been killed out of a total strength then of over 300,000. The figures for the infiltration of U.S. troops were of course far more concrete, and show that U.S. military personnel in South Vietnam increased from 875 in 1960, to 3,164 in 1961, 11,325 in 1962, 16,263 in 1963, 23,310 in 1964, over 180,000 by the end of 1965, and a peak of 543,000 in early 1969.

If against this background, American arguments of a northern invasion of the south are hardly convincing, Washington advanced better arguments to the effect that the war in the south was planned, or at least authorized, by Hanoi. Indeed, Hanoi was proud of that fact, as for forty years it had led the struggle for a unified and independent Vietnam. In that case, the U.S. White Paper of February 1965, was factually correct in stating that the "hard core [of the southern Communists] . . . were trained in the North," and received from there "many of the weapons and much of the ammunition." It was no accident that the new umbrella organization for the Revolution in the south, the National Liberation Front was made official in December 1960 in the wake of the Party's Third National Congress.

Growing out of Viet Minh successor organizations formed in 1954, 1955, 1958, and March 1960, on December 20, 1960, "in a liberated area" later revealed as at a rubber plantation in Tan Uyen district north of Bien Hoa, twenty representatives of "various classes, parties, religious groups, nationalities and women's groups," founded the South Vietnam National Liberation Front (NLF). Headed as president by Nguyen Huu Tho, who was shortly liberated from jail by partisans for the occasion, and by Huynh Tan Phat and others, including Ybih Aleo, chairman of the Communist-sponsored Western Highlands Autonomy Movement, as Vice Presidents, and with Party leaders Nguyen Van Linh, (Nguyen Van

Cuc), Tran Nam Trung,* Vo Chi Cong, Hoang Van Thai, Nguyen Thi Dinh, and later Nguyen Chi Thanh and Pham Hung holding important positions, the NLF sought to execute the Party's Third Congress appeal to "carry out its work in a very flexible manner, in order to rally all forces that can be rallied, win over all forces that can be won over, neutralize all forces that can be neutralized and draw the broad masses into the movement of common struggle against the U.S.-Diem clique."[13] Its ten-point program called for the overthrow of the Diem government, "lackey of the United States," but for a relatively moderate program of "democracy, land reform, independence, neutrality, peace . . . ." The NLF quickly established committees in thirty-eight of the south's forty-one provinces, and held its First Congress in February 1962.

The Party sought to provide the organizational and military muscle and overall guidance for this latest manifestation of the United Front in Vietnam. From Hanoi, the Party called on its 525,000 members to follow the order of the Third National Congress in September 1960† to do all possible to help "liberate the South from the atrocious rule of the United States and their henchmen," even while stressing that the "socialist revolution in the North" was then still the most decisive task. Just a month before the U.S. escalation of February 1965, the Party Central Committee pledged "to do whatever can be done to help the Southern Revolution," and called for preparations against possible "direct participation of American troops" and plans "to attack the North."

In the south, after the formation of the National Liberation Front, the next organizational step was to make official the "leadership of the Marxist-Leninist Party of the working class." However, to facilitate "drawing in the broad masses," including those who might fear the word *Communist*, this was disguised by creating a new name for the Party in the south, the People's Revolutionary Party (PRP). Announced January 1, 1962, with Vo Chi Cong‡ as its head, the PRP was ostensibly just another party making up the

*Trần Nam Trung, a veteran of the August 1945 uprising in Ba To, Quang Ngai province, headed the Party's Central Vietnam Regional Committee in the early 1960s and was a leader of the PRP.

†As against over 700,000 as of the Second Congress in 1951, 800,000 in 1966, and 1,553,500 at the time of the Fourth Congress in 1976.

‡Born near Da Nang in 1912, Cong was active in Party work in his native Annam after 1936 and imprisoned for several years after 1942. In 1976, he was identified as one of four new members of the Political Bureau, and served as minister of agriculture from 1977 to 1979.

NLF, along with progressive Buddhist, Catholic, and other organizations. In reality, it served as a cover for the Communist Committee for the South (COSVN) and as the organ of Party direction of the NLF and village-level front organizations, the youth, peasant, women, worker, religious, nationality, educational, cultural, National Salvation and other mass organizations.

In conjunction with the decisions from 1959 on for the southern Communists to utilize military as well as political struggle, and for the north to do "whatever can be done" to help that struggle, the Party also decided to construct the network of trails linking the north and the south, which would become known as the Ho Chi Minh Trail. Since all contacts across the Demilitarized Zone were blocked, these trails crossed into Laos and southward through parts of Cambodia to reach central and southern areas of the country. In May 1959, Hanoi formed a special military group to organize and keep open the trails that by 1966 transited south some 4,500 men a month (up to 20,000 in 1968) and up to 100 (or occasionally 300 or more) tons of supplies a day. In the early 1960s, however, smaller quantities were carried on the backs of the soldiers themselves or by bicycle, averaging a load of 25 kilos, and the trip took six weeks to two months over hundreds of miles of jungle, mountains, and mud, soon to come under a rain of bombs. Later, hundreds of trucks moved over an improved system that by the end of the war was said to embrace some 20,000 kilometers of roadway, while other supplies came by sea, along the coastlines of Central and South Vietnam and Cambodia. Trucks and boats were ingeniously camouflaged, trees shaped to cover the road system from the air, and portable bamboo bridges rolled up when not in use. It is nonetheless astonishing that so many "long marches" from North to South Vietnam could survive the hail of literally several million tons of bombs that fell on the Ho Chi Minh Trail from 1965 to 1973.[14] Yet, before 1972, American sources estimated that the bombing could destroy only perhaps 10 percent of the goods and 5 percent of the personnel moving south, and that at most about a third of total southern needs were supplied by the Ho Chi Minh Trail, with some other supplies arriving by sea, but most being procured or captured in the south.

THE SITUATION IN NEIGHBORING LAOS, through which much of the Ho Chi Minh Trail traveled, naturally greatly shaped the responses of both sides. One of the first American references to the possibility of bombing North Vietnam was triggered by Communist gains there, when on April 26, 1961, President Kennedy ordered the study of "strikes on intermediate bases in North Vietnam, and if necessary, strikes on bases in Red China which supply their operations against Laos." Such American considerations, and the actual sending of several thousand troops to Thailand the following year were reactions as well to the failure of the Bay of Pigs invasion against Castro's Cuba on April 17, 1961, and to the impasse between Kennedy and Soviet leader Khrushchev in Vienna in June 1961. But in Southeast Asia, the considerations were in response to the exceedingly grave situation in Laos, which Washington felt had developed after recent Communist and neutralist gains, helped by Russian airlifts of war materiel.

Laos, a country of some three million, about half ethnic Lao, the rest Thai and other nationalities, had won partial autonomy within the French Union in 1949. It maintained a shaky balance between neutralists, Communists, and anti-Communists from 1954 to 1958, when the Communist leader Souphanouvong and twelve other leftists won over half the seats in a special parliamentary election. Rightist leaders Prince Boum Oum and General Phoumi Nosavan, with U.S. support, proceeded to force the resignation of neutralist Prince Souvanna Phouma and arrested Souphanouvong the following year, triggering increased warfare after 1959. The situation was further complicated by a new rightist coup in December 1959 and a neutralist seizure of the capital of Vientiane in August 1960 by Parachute Commander Kong Le. The new polarization forced many neutralists, temporarily including Long Le, to side with the Communists, while the United States greatly increased its aid to the rightists lest a Communist victory create a "dagger pointed at South Vietnam" since in the words of Eisenhower, "Laos was the key to the entire area . . . ."

In the late spring of 1961, representatives of the three feuding factions, urged by Great Britain and Russia as the cochairmen of the 1954 Geneva Conference, opened a "second Geneva Conference," attended by fourteen nations to try to settle the problem of Laos. By the end of that year, there was agreement on the principle of a neutral government, which would end the war by representing all three factions and barring foreign troops and influence. The United States interpreted that to mean the withdrawal of North Vietnamese troops, estimated years later at 90,000 strong (plus 30,000

Chinese), while the Communists interpreted it to mean the exclusion of U.S. influence and "mercenaries" such as the CIA-appointed Meo army, which soon totaled 30,000–40,000. In any case, the agreement was delayed until after rightist opposition to it was broken by a Communist defeat of Phoumi Nosavan's forces at Nam Tha on May 6, 1962. That battle, likened to Dien Bien Phu on a smaller scale, led to the Declaration of the Neutrality of Laos on July 23, 1962, concluded also almost exactly eight years after the first Geneva Agreement. As in Vietnam, the peace that followed was relative and temporary. The new centrist government of Souvanna Phouma, formed in June 1962, moved closer to the positions of the rightists, as did Kong Le after the Communists drove him from the Plaine des Jarres in April 1963.[15] Thereafter, the Communists, with increasing Vietnamese presence, controlled most of the northeast and eastern border regions, ensuring their increasing use of the Ho Chi Minh Trail.

WHILE IN 1961–1962, the United States was also preoccupied with cold war problems in Cuba, Berlin, and Laos, it took fateful decisions to "make a stand in Vietnam" that would both demonstrate U.S. resolve to the Soviet Union and China, and at the same time show Third World revolutionaries what to expect if they resorted to armed insurrections of the Chinese and Vietnamese type. This was the time when the "best and brightest" of the American political intelligentsia, in the words of David Halberstam's best-seller of the period, developed the idea that Dulles's doctrine of "massive retaliation" to deter Communist aggression in the 1950s had to be supplemented by new counterinsurgency tactics, such as the use of mobile, elite units like the Green Berets, helicopters, and all sorts of modern technology, in order to stop insurrections like that in Vietnam. Led, with varying differences of approach, by President Kennedy's secretary of defense, Robert McNamara, Secretary of State Dean Rusk, presidential assistants Walt Rostow, brothers McGeorge and William Bundy, CIA Director William Colby, General Maxwell Taylor, and others, these men settled on Vietnam as the place to show, as Rostow put it, "that the Communist technique of guerilla warfare can be dealt with." The problem, they believed, was worldwide, but all "part of the same struggle" according to Secretary of State Rusk. Therefore in President Kennedy's words, since "we have a problem in making our power pertinent, . . . Vietnam looks like the place."[16]

Unfortunately, despite growing talk of the "other war" to win people's "hearts and minds," American planning for counterinsurgency showed little understanding of the real issues involved, namely, how to convince the peasant masses that the government was worth fighting for, and to organize them accordingly. Although some mostly lower-level diplomatic intelligence and military personnel, especially those who spent more than the usual one-year military rotation in Vietnam, came to recognize the imbalance between American objectives and Vietnamese realities, most decision makers appeared to agree with the statement of future Army Chief of Staff General Earle Wheeler, ironically made on the anniversary of the Bolshevik Revolution, November 7, 1962, that the problems were not primarily political and economic, but that rather the "essence of the problem of Vietnam is military."

Certainly, U.S. military actions, from the mistaken training of the 1950s for a Korean-style massive invasion from the north, to the 1960s use of unprecedented levels of bombing and modern weaponry, showed a vastly disproportionate emphasis, to the point that in 1968 Washington spent at least fourteen billion dollars on bombing and ground offensives and less than one-fifteenth that, or 858 million on economic aid, including "pacification." On February 8, 1963, the commander of the U.S. forces in Vietnam, General Paul Harkins, could state, "Vietnam has become for American troops a field of experimentation for anti-guerilla tactics." Policy makers apparently believed, as Secretary of State Kissinger would put it in September 1969, that American power could bring the breaking point for a "fourth-rate power like North Vietnam." Nonetheless, other Americans urged caution, and admitted that "the primary sources of Communist strength in South Vietnam remain indigenous," while Presidents Kennedy and Johnson repeatedly stated words to the effect that the war could be won "only by the Vietnamese people themselves."

In an attempt to straighten out some of this confusion, in 1961 President Kennedy sent three high-level missions to South Vietnam. In April, Vice-President Lyndon Johnson recommended increased support to show we "stand by our friends" in a "critical" area where Ngo Dinh Diem could be likened to the "Winston Churchill of Asia." Then the study mission of economics professor Eugene Staley of Stanford University in May and June, and above all the mission of General Maxwell Taylor, Walt Rostow, William Bundy, and others in October made more specific recommendations.

After considerable debate, these led to increases in the South Vietnamese Army to over 170,000 soldiers and 120,000 militia and increases in U.S. aid, and in the number of American advisers from 685 men to over 11,000 by the end of 1962. According to the Communists, these changes and the parallel shift from agrovilles to the strategic hamlets amounted to the declaration of a "special war" in which "troops of the satellite countries play the main role," but which were preparatory to a "limited war" in which American troops would become the main force.

In fact, the escalation of 1961 was the result of another ill-considered compromise. Caught between conflicting demands, ranging from opposition to "excessive" pressures on Diem by Ambassador Nolting and military assistance chief, General Paul Harkins, to advice to drop Diem altogether unless he changed his policies, as urged by Under Secretary of State Chester Bowles and Senior Adviser Averell Harriman, President Kennedy decided to follow the recommendations of the Johnson, Staley, and Taylor missions to increase both aid to the government and the demands for its reform. While Diem resisted the latter, and even balked on increasing the numbers of American troops lest his independence be further eroded, increases in the American presence continued willynilly, building on their own momentum, and in spite of all objections. Nor was there the hoped-for progress in pacification that would provide a base for the increased American commitment.

INDEED, THE WAR WAS VERY MUCH GATHERING MOMENTUM at the time of the fateful 1961 decisions of Washington to renew and increase its commitment to Saigon. The Party in Hanoi took decisions increasingly to "use revolutionary violence to oppose counter revolutionary violence" from January 1959 on, although the Communists of the south did not begin to strike back in force until close to a year later. But before that there were increasing antigovernment incidents, assassinations, and demonstrations, and revolts by some of the several dozen mountain minorities, totaling in all perhaps 700,000 of the people of the south. The Party later claimed to have trained over 1,000 southern minority cadres in Hanoi, and to have helped liberate over 100 villages in the Central Highlands by the end of the 1950s. In January 1959, the small tribe known as the Kor, revolted in mountains of Quang Ngai province, Central Vietnam, and the Hre and Bahnar further west did so in July and later in the same year. In the lowlands, the Communists increased their activities, forming "Committees of Resistance" in many localities after a congress of southern militants in March 1959, and especially later in the year with verification of Hanoi's decisions to strike back in the south was received.

Then came the beginning of the "second liberation war" with minority and other uprisings in 1959, especially the establishment of a "liberated zone" of several thousand people in Tra Bong and Son Tay districts, and also in Ba To and Minh Long districts, western Quang Ngai province, after August 28, 1959. More dramatic still was the seizure of much of Ben Tre province for a week after January 17, 1960. There, according to the Communists, "for the first time, a popular insurrection," led by Nguyen Thi Dinh and others, "won victory on a provincial scale," seizing 100 military positions and liberating 72 of 100 villages in Mo Cay district before being suppressed by government reinforcements after January 24. In February, a raid in Tay Ninh seized about 1,000 arms, said to be as many as the Communists possessed for all of the south in 1959, and in August a small Communist group seized a military outpost not far from Da Nang in "an area long famous for its lack of Communist activity." In November, another minority revolt occurred, this time by part of the relatively numerous Jarai tribe in the Central Highlands west of Quang Ngai. In May 1961, representatives of thirty southern minorities, chaired by NLF Vice-President Ibih Aleo, established a Central Highlands Autonomous Movement, and the NLF declared the area an autonomous zone in 1962. By 1963, less than a third of the Highland minorities were estimated still to be loyal to Saigon as the Communists stepped up activities in the Highlands and their promises of tribal autonomy. In September 1964, some 15,000 of the Rhade tribe revolted near Ban Me Thuot against the government and its American advisers, although in general the U.S. Special Force teams had made better progress in organizing the montagnards than their traditional enemies, the lowland Vietnamese.

In December 1960, the National Liberation Front had come into existence. The following year, in September, it made its presence felt with the brief seizure of the provincial capital of Phuoc Vinh only fifty miles north of Saigon, and in the same month, with the destruction of a military outpost near Kon Tum. In 1962, Communist forces apparently expanded from 16,000 to 30,000 despite "thousands" of anti-Communist operations and up to 50,000 air attacks, that were said to have killed some 30,000 people. That year also saw the first significant number (thirty-one) of American advisers killed.

Although the Communists suffered reverses in places, especially in parts of 1962 and 1963, they continued to gain in confidence, above all after what they claimed was their greatest victory yet—in January 1963 at the village of Ap Bac, My Tho province, forty miles west of Saigon—over a unit of 2,000 soldiers with fifty-one American advisers and advanced equipment and air support. The government force was partly destroyed, in part by a mistaken air strike, and lost five of its fifteen helicopters. In nearby Long An province also, the Communists used their growing military strength and above all their development of Party and mass organizations to "all but extinguish the government presence" by the end of the following year. Before the U.S. escalation of 1965, therefore, Jeffrey Race concluded, "the revolutionary movement had won in Long An," and by extension in much of the south.[17]

Reports of these government reverses and Communist gains, and the controversies over their causes, only served to highlight Washington's ignorance of the history and nature of the Vietnamese Revolution. And the next catastrophe for the anti-Communists of Vietnam came not from Communist advances but from the overthrow of the Diem government.

THE GATHERING NON-COMMUNIST OPPOSITION to Diem signaled by the Caravelle Declaration of April 1960, by the near coup of November 1960, and the bombing attack of February 1962, came to a head with the Buddhist revolt of 1963, which in turn forced leading generals backed by the United States to depose and kill Diem before the year was out.

Buddhism, divided among various Mahayana sects, was the religion of over two-thirds of the Vietnamese population. In general, the Buddhists resented the disproportionate influence in the Diem years of the 10 percent who were Catholics, but it was a series of government actions after May 1963 that moved activists to all-out struggle against Diem. The crisis erupted on May 7, when the government forbade the display of nongovernment flags in public, even though two days previously Diem's brother Thuc had celebrated the twenty-fifth anniversary of his bishopric with an elaborate display of Catholic flags. More importantly, May 8 was considered the 2587th birthday of the Buddha, and huge demonstrations with flags were organized in defiance of the unreasonable order. In Hue, police fired on the crowd, killing nine, and new and larger demonstrations followed in many places. Although retreating on the flag issue, the government refused to meet other Buddhist demands, especially for the punishment of those responsible for the May 8 killings, and instead with obvious falsity blamed the attack on the Viet Cong.

Demonstrations gathered intensity in Saigon especially after June 11, when an elderly monk burned himself to death before a horrified crowd and journalists who promptly flashed pictures of the tragedy around the world. Six other monks and one nun followed this ultimate act of protest through self-immolation, while Ngo Dinh Nhu and his wife further exacerbated the situation with appalling statements to the effect that "If the Buddhists want to have another barbecue, I will be glad to supply the gasoline." More demonstrations followed, such as on August 18, when 15,000 antigovernment protestors marched through Saigon.

On August 21, Nhu ordered the "settling of the Buddhist affair" by attacks on pagodas in Saigon, Hue, and elsewhere, leading to the arrests of over 1,400 and shooting of at least thirty bonzes. Predictably, new demonstrations followed, now joined by students of the University of Saigon and other schools, and there were dramatic resignations from the government by the foreign minister and others.

By late August, the situation had so deteriorated that some South Vietnamese generals, supported by some key Americans, decided to replace the Diem government. Most important in this denouement were the newly appointed Chiefs of Staff Tran Van Don and Duong Van Minh ("Big Minh"), both French-trained officers who had helped Diem overcome his enemies in 1954–1955, but who by July 1963, because of the handling of the Buddhist crisis, decided Diem had to be ousted. They coordinated with other opposition leaders, who had begun to think along similar lines at least a year earlier, and most importantly with American enemies of Diem, since obviously American economic and military support would continue to be essential to their own survival. Most importantly, they felt encouraged to act by State Department officials headed by Under Secretary of State George Ball, and the new ambassador, Henry Cabot Lodge, who arrived in Saigon the day after the pagoda raids of August 21.

On August 24, Lodge received a telegram in Ball's name to the effect that the "U.S. Government cannot tolerate a situation in which power lies in Nhu's hands . . . [and] cannot accept [their] actions against Buddhists . . . [and] would find it impossible to continue support . . . unless . . . Diem removes the Nhus . . . . If he remains obdurate, then we are prepared to accept the obvious implication that we can no longer support Diem, . . . [but would support] appropriate military commanders . . . in any interim period of breakdown of Central Government mechanism." Ambassador Lodge later stated that this telegram was revoked by Secretary of State Rusk immediately on his return from a trip, but the confusion of American policy at the time was aptly shown by President Kennedy's query on hearing conflicting reports from a new study mission, "You two did visit the same country, didn't you?"[18]

In any case, Saigon generals drew the proper conclusion that President Kennedy now agreed that Nhu had to go, and Diem as well, if he refused to break with his brother. When Diem refused just that on September 5, Generals Don and Minh initiated their final plans to oust the president. And in October, Ambassador Lodge, CIA agent Lucien Conein, and others informed "appropriate" generals that the United States would "not thwart a coup."

The Ngo brothers meanwhile were at least partially aware of these currents, and initiated two courses of action to forestall them. Nhu planned his own fake coup as a prelude to further arrests, and in September apparently opened secret negotiations with Hanoi, both to undercut his enemies, and possibly to open the way for a neutralist solution guaranteeing his and his brother's temporary participation in a new, more leftist government, along lines proposed by French President Charles De Gaulle and others since at least 1961.

On the afternoon of November 1, 1963, Generals Don and Minh struck, following weeks of complex preparations and maneuvers. Their troops surrounded the Presidential Palace, while Diem and Nhu, stalling on American offers of safe passage and asylum, were able to flee at night by an underground tunnel. Both were captured the next day, and executed several hours later, reportedly on the order of Big Minh.

Thus ended the decade of best hope for what, in 1956, then Senator Kennedy had called the "proving ground of democracy in Asia." For all the discussion and anguished politicking that preceded Diem's fall, few observers foresaw the still greater chaos and anguish that would follow.

CHAPTER NINE

The American War Escalates

THE EXPECTATION that the removal of Diem on November 1, 1963, would solve the weaknesses of the anti-Communists in Vietnam further revealed Washington's misconceptions of a revolution in which control of villages, far more than any coup d'état, was decisive.

In 1960, the Communists were estimated to control "at least half of the country, including most of the southern area . . . [and] their armed forces numbered about 10,000 despite heavy losses." By early 1964, "red areas" supposedly were reduced temporarily to about 40 percent, as the popular Big Minh government and new American support seemed at first to be eroding Communist support. But this was followed by new reversals, and declines in government control to less than half of the south by the end of 1964. A year after that, despite the massive American escalation of the war, Saigon strong man Nguyen Cao Ky admitted that his government controlled completely only 25 percent of the population. That was in November 1965, the same month that U.S. Secretary of Defense McNamara noted that the Communists were rapidly increasing "their forces . . . both by heavy recruitment in the South (especially in the Delta) and by infiltration of regular forces from the North."[1]

It was not until 1969, more than three years after the beginning of the bombing of the north in February 1965, that the anti-Communists could announce real progress in reducing their enemies' presence in the south, claiming control of over three-quarters of the country and a reduction of Communist armed strength from some 300,000 to under 200,000. This had been made possible by the greatest application of military force in a comparable area in history, and perhaps owed almost as much to belated government agrarian and other reforms and to Communist overcommitments as to the brutal applications of American power.

But by the early 1970s, it was too late for South Vietnam. For a Communist core in the south once again had survived all attacks, as for forty years past. Although on the defensive, their very survival both justified the final northern offensives and contributed to the final victory of 1975.

To understand how and why this came about, we must return to the extraordinary events that followed the murders of Presidents Diem and Kennedy in November 1963.

IT WAS NOT UNTIL MID-1965 that a relatively stable anti-Communist government emerged in Saigon—and then only because of the necessity for a semblance of unity among the anti-Communists, together with a parallel need for a government strong enough to appear to guide the application of the ever more enormous quantities of American aid, arms, and personnel.

First, in late 1963, there was a Military Revolutionary Council, headed by General Duong Van Minh ("Big Minh"), who was replaced by General Nguyen Khanh on January 30, 1964. Khanh also assumed the position of premier under the Military Council, and briefly in August, declared himself president of the Republic, but in the autumn was forced to yield to Pham Khac Suu as president and Tran Van Huong as premier. Then following an unsuccessful attempt by Khanh to resume control of the civilian functions of government in January 1965, on February 16 a new government under Premier Phan Huy Quat took office, nine days after the beginning of sustained U.S. bombing of the north. In June 1965, Quat was ousted by Air Force General Nguyen Cao Ky and Army General Nguyen Van Thieu, who became, respectively, premier and head of the Military Council. In September 1967, their positions were reversed, and partly legitimized by the election of Thieu as president and Ky as vice-president of the Republic of South Vietnam.

These were only the surface events in a complex political jungle. In all there were over ten changes of government between November 1, 1963, and the emergence of the Ky government in June 1965, and a Communist source cited Bernard Fall to the effect that since there were "in twenty months, thirteen putsches, nine cabinets and four charters . . . Nguyen Cao Ky made his entrance on the political scene almost unnoticed . . . 'if Mickey Mouse took power in Saigon, no one would have noticed.' "[2] But Ky and especially Thieu soon came to be appreciated by their anti-Communist backers not only as able generals but as surprisingly astute politicians. Nor were there any charges of their flirting with "neutralism" as Big Minh, the Buddhists, and later Khanh, all were charged with doing. Although they were increasingly suspicious rivals, Ky agreed to take second place behind Thieu in the 1967 elections before moving to oppose him in the early 1970s.

Yet it could hardly be claimed that Thieu and Ky guided South Vietnam into a democracy. Although the government proclaimed a new constitution for the second Republic in April 1967, guaranteeing "basic freedoms," historian Joseph Buttinger noted "shocking proofs of election frauds" in September 1967, when Thieu and Ky were elected president and vice-president with about 35 percent of the vote. They had already banned challenges by Big Minh, former economics minister Au Truong Thanh, and others accused of "neutralism." And then, when the runner-up, Truong Dinh Dzu, received 17 percent of the vote on a "peace program," he was promptly jailed as "a pacifist." As rivalry between Thieu and Ky deepened, a third strong man emerged with Thieu's appointment of General Tran Thien Khiem as prime minister in September 1969. And then in the presidential elections of October 3, 1971, Ky was excluded from the race, and Thieu, unopposed, received 91.5 percent of the vote.

By then, not only were advocates of a peaceful solution denied political office, but tens of thousands had been jailed as political prisoners, and many others were apparent victims of political assassinations. In mid-1965, for example, Pham Ngoc Thao, a former Viet Minh leader who had switched sides after 1954 to become, according to Jean Lacouture, "one of the two or three most interesting . . . and capable" potential leaders of the south, was arrested and reportedly tortured to death. His crime? Not only plotting against fellow officers, as in an abortive coup attempt in February 1965, but apparently also, according to French specialists, his advocacy of a "humaine socialist revolution . . . beginning with land reform," and his continuation of Nhu's belated September 1963 attempt to open talks with Hanoi.

Other apparent government-sanctioned or ordered political assassinations, mainly of rivals of Thieu and of advocates of peaceful settlement of the war, continued to occur, sometimes disguised as accidents, or as victims of Viet Cong terror, and sometimes perhaps truly the work of the Communists. Far more opponents or potential opponents of the regime were arrested and, by 1973, Amnesty International and other respected organizations estimated that there were up to 200,000 political prisoners in southern jails, and that they were frequently tortured. The government and the last U.S. ambassador, Graham Martin, claimed this estimate was wildly inflated and that there were rather about 30,000 prisoners, while the Communists claimed the true figure was ten times that. The number of police in the country grew from 19,000 in 1963 to 52,000 in late 1965, to 100,000 in 1971, and over 120,000 by late 1973.

Parallel to the dictatorships that followed that of Diem in the south was one of history's worst examples of large-scale corruption. American sources were cited to the effect that, as of November 1966, up to 40 percent of the then 621 million dollars of economic aid to the south was being raked off by corruption, and considerable portions of the far larger amounts of military aid as well. By 1969, the latter was running at 20 percent of the some 21.5 billion dollars (or more than 4 billion), being allocated by the United States directly to the war. The year before, a U.S. Marine Colonel William Corson, estimated that manipulation of the laundry racket to wash GI clothes at prices far above Vietnamese norms netted corrupt South Vietnamese officers up to 100 million dollars a year. Especially harmful to the war effort was the enrolling of large numbers of "phantom" or "flower" soldiers, whose pay was pocketed by others while they conspicuously roamed the streets of Saigon and other cities. A staff report to the U.S. Senate in May 1974, estimated there were at least 100,000 phantom soldiers and a former Saigon official later documented how such pocketing of money for make-believe recipients was practiced not only in the army, but also for public works, education, and most scandalously for phantom refugees.

Moreover, only one in seven youths ordered to report for military service did so in 1966 and, of those who did, a great number deserted. In 1959, one in five was said to flee the army, and by the late 1960s that figure climbed to about one in three every year. Desertions from the South Vietnamese military forces exceeded 100,000 men each year after 1964, except 1967, and topped 200,000 by 1975. Considering the higher pay, and fewer risks of the government side, perhaps no statistics dramatize more the contrasts of the war. For on the Communist side, defections climbed from about

5,000 in 1964, to over 28,000 in 1969, but then fell to 10,914 in 1971.

Equally shocking was the government's involvement in drugs. By the late 1960s, Saigon and its American backers had become as heavily involved in narcotics rackets as its predecessors. According to an appalling but convincing study of the drug problem by Alfred McCoy published in 1972:

> The U.S. Embassy, as part of its unqualified support of the Thieu-Ky regime, looked the other way when presented with evidence that members of the regime are involved in the GI heroin traffic. While American complicity is certainly much less conscious and overt than that of the French a decade earlier, this time it was not just opium—but morphine and heroin as well—and the consequences were far more serious. After a decade of American military intervention, Southeast Asia has become the source of 70 percent of the world's illicit opium and the major supplier of raw materials for America's booming heroin market.[3]

After about 1957, Diem's brother Nhu and his chief of police, Dr. Tran Kim Tuyen, had taken "steps to revive the illicit opium traffic" and with it "systematic corruption to finance intelligence and counter-insurgency operations."

The CIA soon became at least indirectly involved in these operations in South Vietnam, and directly so in Laos, the primary source of drugs from the Golden Triangle, as the area bordering Thailand and Burma was called. By 1961, the CIA fashioned some 9,000 (later 30,000) Meo tribesmen in Central Laos under a certain Vang Pao into what Fred Branfman called "the President's secret army" to fight the Communists.[4]

To do that, they in effect subsidized and facilitated the marketing of the Meo's traditional crop, adopting the maxim of a French officer ten years before, "To have the Meo, one must buy their opium." According to the McCoy study, the CIA subsidized Vietnam Air Transport, whose pilots, including Nguyen Cao Ky, "took advantage of this situation to fly opium from Laos to Saigon." Then with the takeover after 1965 of South Vietnam's police and intelligence services by Ky protégé General Nguyen Ngoc Loan, Saigon "revived the Binh Xuyen formula [of the late 1940s and early 1950s] for using systematic corruption to combat urban guerilla warfare." Moreover, McCoy reported that another American observer believed "the opium traffic was undeniably the most important source of illicit revenue," far ahead of "sale of government jobs

. . . administrative corruption (graft, kickbacks, bribes, etc.) and . . . military corruption (theft of goods and payroll frauds) . . . ."

By the 1970s, corruption was so bad that Ky could tell a British radio audience in the autumn of 1977, "Most of the money . . . [the United States gave] to us went to the pocket of a minority, corrupted Americans and Vietnamese . . . ." According to Le Phuong, the pseudonym of an official in both the Diem and Thieu governments, only four of some fifty ranking generals of the time could be considered "clean." The rest practiced "squeeze," ranging from the demand for gifts from subject populations to the purchase of positions of all sorts, to the selling of arms and supplies to the Communists, to the smuggling of drugs. Ky denied that he personally had been involved in the latter practice but admitted to the BBC:

> I knew there was a lot of traffic in drugs and everything. I think every [one was] . . . involved in it in Vietnam during the war, the soldiers, the air force, the marines, the navy, the government. I knew that in some cases the Vietnamese Air Force was involved in it. When they flew to Laos and Cambodia for a military operation and when the plane came back the crew brought some drugs, opium . . .[5]

A further striking evidence of the pervasive corruption, and of U.S. involvement in it, was the fact that General Dang Van Quang, alleged at one point to be "the most corrupt of all" as well as "the biggest pusher of drugs" in the south, became not only President Thieu's top "security adviser (his Kissinger if you will)" in the late 1960s, but with supreme irony went on in the early 1970s to control (through a protégé) the "National anti-Narcotics Committee," and to become one of the leading informants of the CIA. According to Frank Snepp, some people in the Agency even concluded that Quang, together with Chief of Police Nguyen Khac Binh, were "perhaps our most important properties in Vietnam."[6]

THE SUCCESSIVE AMERICAN-BACKED GOVERNMENTS and their activities did not go unopposed. In addition to the Communists, the Buddhists above all followed up their struggle against Diem in 1963 with new demands for far-reaching reforms and for new elections, which they hoped to win. In the spring of 1966, they brought the country to the "verge of all-out civil war," as reported by Jerrold Schecter, with protests against Ky's March dismissal of Buddhist favorite, General Nguyen Chanh Thi, commander of the military region around Hue. Despite nine suicides by self-immolation in the single week after May 29, and numerous mass demonstrations, the movement was weakened by internal divisions, and by the vigorous opposition of Catholics and other groups. From May on, the government moved to break up the movement in Da Nang, Hue, Saigon, and other cities, with the arrests of thousands and, according to the Buddhists, the shooting of several hundred others. In contrast to the partial support for the overthrow of Diem in 1963, the United States not only did not help the Buddhists in 1966 but reportedly "relaxed" when the Buddhists were suppressed during the summer. The demonstrations at times demanded to "end foreign domination of our country," and sacked U.S. government buildings in Hue and elsewhere. Washington evidently feared the "possibility that the Buddhists, if they came to power, would negotiate with the National Liberation Front and demand the withdrawal of the U.S. forces." The crisis also showed, in the words of Frances Fitzgerald, "that a good portion of the urban Vietnamese had no confidence in American policies."[7]

Nonetheless, Washington relentlessly continued its escalation. In the year after the beginning of the bombing in February 1965, American troops in Vietnam increased from over 23,000 to over 180,000. Then during the Buddhist crisis of 1966, another 200,000 troops debarked, bringing the total to 385,000, and by mid-1967 to 470,000, with a peak of over 542,000 coming in early 1969.

DURING THESE YEARS, after temporary reversals in 1963, Communist forces began again to expand, especially during the political turmoil of 1964. Their military forces doubled to perhaps 35,000 by February 1965, backed by far larger numbers of supporters and Communist control increased from nearly half of the south in 1960 to perhaps over two-thirds by 1965.

In the face of this expanding Communist power, and anxious to prove his ability to carry out the wishes of his predecessor to protect a non-Communist South, President Lyndon Johnson soon decided to further increase the U.S. commitment to Saigon, although for another year he did so both cautiously and surreptitiously. In December 1963, Washington gave "further consideration to plans for phased operations against North Vietnam" and Laos, and recommendations for what became known as Operation 34A or an "elaborate program of covert military operations against the state of North Vietnam." It included reconnaissance flights, the parachuting of sabotage and psychological warfare teams into the north, commando raids from the sea to blow up rail and highway bridges and the bombardment of North Vietnamese coastal installations by PT boats.

Already by the winter of 1963–1964, some American officials were trying to win approval of both Saigon leaders and President Johnson for the bombing of the north. The hesitation of Duong Van Minh's government to endorse further American escalation and its parallel exploration of talks with at least non-Communist members of the NLF led the United States to become "decisively involved" in Khanh's coup d'état against Big Minh on January 30, 1964. Then, while waiting for authorization for sustained bombing of the north, Washington and Saigon undertook smaller-scale "phased operations" against the Ho Chi Minh Trail in Laos and coastal Vietnam. On March 1, 1964, a memorandum of Assistant Secretary of Defense William Bundy advocated a "blockade of Haiphong" port, and "air attacks at: (a) the key rail lines to Communist China; (b) the key road nets to Laos and South Vietnam; (c) camps . . . used for training cadres for South Vietnam; (d) key industrial complexes . . . ." On March 17, the National Security Council spoke of preparations "to be in a position on seventy-two hours' notice to initiate the full range of Laotian and Cambodian 'border control actions' . . . and the 'retaliatory actions' against North Vietnam, and to be in a position on thirty days' notice to initiate the program of 'graduated overt military pressure' against North Vietnam . . . ."[8]

Therefore, by March 1964 Washington and Saigon had already intensified* "destructive undertakings" against North Vietnam which, in the words of the *Pentagon Papers*, amounted to "a kind of preview of the bombing of the North" that would begin in earnest a year later. And, on March 20, 1964, President Johnson forcefully stated America's intent of "knocking down the idea of neutralization wherever it rears its ugly head . . . by whatever means we can," lest the escalation deemed necessary to "save the south" be prevented. This principle apparently was already at work in the January 30, 1964, coup d'état against Big Minh.

More preparations for the full-scale bombing were deemed necessary, however, both in Vietnam, where President Johnson

---

*Sporadically, small operations against the north had in fact been more or less continuous since Lansdale's operations in the late summer and early autumn of 1954.

duly noted "the immediate and essential task is to strengthen the Southern base," and in America. There a presidential campaign was well under way, in which Johnson's opponent, Republican conservative Senator Barry Goldwater, was calling for an end to "appeasement" and for "victory," but doing so so truculently as to encourage an opposition Democratic campaign for "firmness," with the "prudence" and "restraint" to avoid a wider war in Asia. Where Senator Goldwater, himself a Reserve Air Force general and pilot, at least twice proposed the use of "low-yield atomic weapons" to win the war, President Johnson repeatedly stated we "seek no wider war." On August 29, he went on to declare "I have had advice to load our planes with bombs and to drop them on certain areas that I think would enlarge the war and escalate the war, and result in committing a good many American boys to fighting a war that I think ought to be fought by the boys of Asia . . . And for that reason I haven't chosen to enlarge the war."[9]

This statement, made five months before the massive escalation of February 1965, was a reference to the proposals for "escalation in three stages, from intensification of the current clandestine 34A raids to 'covert U.S. support of . . . serial mining and air strike operations' by Saigon to 'overt joint . . . reconnaissance, naval displays, . . . bombardments and air attacks' by the United States and Vietnam." In May 1964, General Khanh in Saigon called for open U.S. bombing of the north and the introduction of more troops, and in July he propagandized a "march north" campaign, to eliminate the "root of the problem," the Communist government in Hanoi. In June, Washington initiated a debate as to "whether or not the Administration should seek a Congressional resolution giving general authority for action which the President may judge necessary to defend the peace and security of the area . . . ." Simultaneously it offered hints of economic aid to the north (to be conveyed by Canadian representative to the International Control Commission, J. Blair Seaborn), and the pledge that the United States would not try to "overthrow the North Vietnamese regime nor to destroy the country," not least because it feared Chinese intervention to prevent the fall of a Communist state as had happened in Korea in 1950.

At the same time, however, Washington stressed its intention to "maintain the independence and territorial integrity of South Vietnam," and its consideration, as the Department of State put it on June 1, 1964, that "the confrontation with North Vietnamese subversive guerilla action was part of the general Free World confrontation with this type of violent subversion in other lesser developed countries." Meanwhile the 34A raids against the north increased in tempo in the early summer, and on July 25, the U.S. Joint Chiefs of Staff again demanded clandestine U.S. air strikes against the north.

THE OPPORTUNITY TO TEST THE WATERS for such larger-scale military action against the north, and at the same time to procure necessary domestic political support for such action, came with the so-called Tonkin Gulf Incidents of early August 1964. In the wake of escalating South Vietnamese attacks against the north and Communist forces in Laos, including a July 30 raid against two nearby North Vietnamese islands, on August 2 North Vietnamese ships attacked the U.S. destroyer *Maddox*, apparently mistaking it "for a South Vietnamese escort vessel," although it was some twenty-three miles offshore. The destroyer and supporting aircraft fired back, and the next day new South Vietnamese attacks occurred on the north.

On the night of August 4, the *Maddox*, joined by a second destroyer, the *Turner Joy*, sixty-five miles offshore, reported a new North Vietnamese attack, which, however, was later disputed by some evidence that other factors may have caused the radar blips taken for attacking vessels. Nonetheless, on August 5, President Johnson ordered retaliation by U.S. jets from the carriers *Ticonderoga* and *Constellation* against four naval bases on the coast of North Vietnam, destroying some twenty-five patrol boats, and against oil storage depots at Vinh, which were 90 percent destroyed.

Even as new turmoil erupted in Saigon against efforts by Khanh to assume dictatorial powers, on August 10 the U.S. Congress passed overwhelmingly (466 to 0 in the House and 88 to 2 in the Senate) the so-called Gulf of Tonkin Resolution, a different draft of which had already been prepared on June 11, to "support the determination of the President, as Commander in Chief, to take all necessary measures to repel any armed attack against the forces of the United States and to prevent further aggression."[10]

Thus armed politically at home as well as militarily abroad, the president concentrated on his election campaign. In contrast with "war monger" Goldwater, Johnson was "hailed as a man of wisdom, balance and restraint," who would "heal the wounds." In the November 3 election, he compiled a record 61 percent of the vote. Given the dramatic escalation of the war only three months after that, and such future American political events as Nixon's similarly overwhelming defeat of "dove" George McGovern in 1972, the constant remarks by statesmen and journalists that Hanoi should not try to take advantage of U.S. election year politics seemed disingenuous to say the least.

BY THE END OF 1964, Lyndon Johnson decided to embark on the latest version of the "phased escalation" of the war. It was a period of dramatic events throughout the world, including the replacement of Nikita Khrushchev as leader of the Soviet Union by Leonid Brezhnev, Alexei Kosygin, and others, and of the first test of an atomic weapon by the People's Republic of China, both in October.

But Washington was increasingly obsessed with Vietnam, where new naval clashes occurred in the Gulf of Tonkin in September. In the same month, Secretary of Defense McNamara narrowly missed assassination on a visit to Saigon, where a general strike with anti-American overtones, and up to 100,000 participants, was in progress. One writer spoke of Saigon as "an open city" in mid-1964, when Communists forces "encircled the city" and NLF cadres entered Saigon almost at will. Viet Cong terrorist attacks intensified, and four Americans were killed at the Bien Hoa air base near Saigon on November 1. Sidestepping new proposals for negotiations* by United Nations Secretary-General U Thant, among others, on December 1 Washington ordered a new, though still partial, escalation of the war.

Operation Barrel Roll began December 14. Its eight sorties a week aimed primarily at the Ho Chi Minh Trail, newly expanded by Communist gains in Laos, while simultaneously preparations proceeded for new "tit for tat" raids like those of August in response to Communist "aggressions." These would be followed by more sustained bombings of the north which, by September at the latest, Washington had decided would be necessary "at some proximate future date." There was apparent rejection of an intelligence estimate of November 13 that the "primary sources of Communist strength in South Vietnam remain indigenous," and that bombing could not be decisive, since the north would "probably be willing to

*In September discussions, as outlined in *The Pentagon Papers*, Washington officials "stressed that the United States should define its negotiating position 'in a way which makes Communist acceptance unlikely.' "[11]

suffer some damage" to continue its still "substantial" and increasing support of the southern revolutionaries.

Above all, Washington felt "concerned about fragility" of the Saigon government which, as Secretary of State Rusk put it December 4, "makes any dramatic action unwise," but at the same time "does require some additional elements that would tend to lift SVN morale, and would also convey a slightly stronger signal to Hanoi," even though in the president's words, it was also acknowledged that "action against North Vietnamese is contributory, not central." Ambassador Maxwell Taylor, who returned to participate in the Washington planning sessions on November 27, was more specific in recommending the bombing, to "first, establish an adequate government in [Saigon] and only then to "improve the conduct of the counterinsurgency campaign [and] finally persuade or force [Hanoi] to stop its aid to the Viet Cong." No desirable government in Saigon from Washington's point of view would emerge until at least mid-1965, but Washington went ahead with its escalation anyway, as much therefore "to pull the South Vietnamese together" as to try to force the abandonment of lifelong goals of Hanoi's leaders. As Presidential Adviser McGeorge Bundy explained on the very day of the next escalation, February 7, our "immediate and critical targets are in the South—in the minds of the South Vietnamese and in the minds of the Viet Cong cadres."[12]

The American "concern over the fragility" of the government in Saigon reached some kind of peak on December 20, 1964, when the Khanh regime dismissed the High National Council charged with finding a way back to civilian government, and carried out more arrests, including those of twenty-two officials and politicians, in response to new antigovernment Buddhist and student demonstrations. Ambassador Taylor, who had just returned to Saigon to demand pledges of stability as a basis for the initiation of Operation Barrel Roll, reacted with fury. Summoning the so-called Young Turks, including future leaders Nguyen Cao Ky and Nguyen Van Thieu, he proceeded to read them the "riot act," as Ky later put it, "like a school master lecturing a class of errant students." Switching from French to English, Taylor asked, "Do all of you understand English? . . . I told you all clearly . . . we Americans are tired of coups. Apparently, I wasted my words . . . . Now you have made a real mess. We cannot carry you forever if you do things like this." Air Marshall Ky told the BBC in 1977, "I wouldn't let my father talk to me like that."

More importantly, General Khanh now decided Washington was going to mount a coup against him, its "favorite" of the previous year.* He criticized American interference in Vietnamese affairs, and according to another general, Tran Van Don, promptly "switched sides, desperately but deliberately attempting to curry favor with the NLF." Khanh released from prison the wife of NLF leader Huynh Tan Phat, who in response wrote on January 28, 1965, "I heartily approve of your determined declaration against American intervention," and went on to praise Khanh's ardent patriotism, your indomitable spirit in the face of imperialist, colonialist oppression," and to appeal for joint "efforts to accomplish our supreme mission, which is to save our homeland."

The semicoup of December 20, and the disputes between Taylor and Khanh delayed American retaliations against new Communist attacks in late December, notably the bombing of an officer's billet in Saigon, killing two, and a week-long battle won by the Communists for the nearby coastal village of Binh Gia. New Buddhist riots and the sacking of the USIA (United States Information Agency) library in Hue occurred several weeks later, followed by a new coup on January 27, which led to a reshuffling of prime ministers, and for another month to a return to power of General Khanh. Some in Washington still considered Khanh, as Presidential Special Assistant McGeorge Bundy put it on February 7, the "outstanding military man currently in sight." With the continuing confusion in Saigon, however, "key policy makers were coming to the same conclusion that Ambassador Taylor and his colleagues had reached—that it was desirable to bomb the North regardless of what state of government existed in the South," and indeed in order to prevent "key groups starting to negotiate covertly with the Liberation Front or Hanoi." Washington termed that "surrender on the installment plan," and while recognizing "grave difficulties," inasmuch as expanded bombing of the north "commits the U.S. more deeply at a time when the picture of South Vietnamese still is extremely weak . . . [and] would be vigorously attacked by many nations," nonetheless argued, as Assistant Secretary William Bundy put it on January 6, 1965: "On balance, we believe that such action would have

*Earlier in the year, Secretary of Defense McNamara made a political tour of South Vietnam, praising Khanh, and trying to say in Vietnamese "Long Live Vietnam." Unfortunately, because of mistaken pronounciation, his words sounded more like, "Vietnam, go to sleep," or, in a different interpretation, "Southern duck, lie down."

some faint hope of really improving the Vietnamese situation, and above all, would put us in a much stronger position to hold the next line of defense, namely Thailand."[13]

During these final critical evaluations of the escalation policy, one of the only written considerations of Soviet Premier Alexsei Kosygin's announced visit to Hanoi, which began on February 6, 1965, was a CIA memorandum on February 1, citing that visit and other evidence to show increasing Soviet support for North Vietnam, but also the hope that Moscow would use its influence to restrain Hanoi while continuing to "expand U.S.-Soviet contacts." In short, Washington virtually ignored the presence of the Soviet premier when it began the bombing of the north, despite signs that the new Soviet leadership wished to burnish its relations with Hanoi, which had been edging closer to China in both doctrine and actions in the early 1960s. Predictably Kosygin reacted to the bombing on February 7 with assurances that Moscow would supply North Vietnam "all necessary assistance if aggressors dare encroach upon [its] independence and sovereignty."

SUCH WAS THE ASTONISHING BACKGROUND to the greatest bombing campaign in history. It began after an incident judged to be the "ideal opportunity," with large-scale attacks against several northern targets, which already had been cleared with the Saigon government on December 7 and January 25. The incident was a Viet Cong attack the morning of February 7 (February 6, Washington time), 1965, against the U.S. advisory compound and airstrip at Camp Holloway, near Plei Ku in the Central Highlands, killing 9 Americans and wounding more than 100. Later the same day some 49 U.S. jets struck at Dong Hoi forty miles above the Demilitarized Zone, and the next day South Vietnamese aircraft led by Air Marshall Ky hit another 100 miles to the north near Vinh.

The war had escalated with a resounding bang!

According to a telegram from Ambassador Taylor, on the same day, this advance to a "slow squeeze" policy, to be followed by the "fast, full squeeze" advocated by some since at least September, was "a new and encouraging element in the war." For, as Presidential Adviser McGeorge Bundy, just back from a mission to Saigon on February 4 to 7, explained, we now realized "the situation is deteriorating and without new U.S. action, defeat appears inevitable . . . within the next year or so." He argued that if the attacks on the north were continued, and not allowed to lapse as after the Tonkin Gulf Incidents, "we shall be able to speak . . . with growing force and effectiveness . . . there will be a sharp immediate increase in optimism in the South . . . [and] a parallel substantial depressing effect upon the morale of Viet Cong cadres . . . ."

Bundy also admitted "there is plainly a deep and strong yearning among the young and the unprivileged for a new and better social order . . . [which] does not find an adequate response in American policy as Vietnamese see it . . . [and unaccountably, that] we only perceived this problem toward the end of our visit . . . ."[14] Although acknowledging that the problem "needs urgent further attention," it is remarkable, to say the least, that it was "only perceived . . . toward the end . . . " by one of the architects of a massive bombardment of men who for more than a generation had been struggling for their own version of that "new and better social order."

The February 7 air attacks on the north and subsequent admissions that American airmen were flying combat missions against the Viet Cong in the south contrasted ominously with a new White House statement the day the bombing began, "We seek no wider war." Secretary of State Rusk described the raids as "a program of measured and limited air action . . . once or twice a week . . . [against] two or three targets on each day of operation." But even these first raids involved a "few dozen planes at a time," carrying over a ton of bombs each at speeds in excess of the speed of sound, actions that few would call "limited."

Following the first Flaming Dart raids of February 7, Flaming Dart II strikes were carried out February 11 and later, after a Communist attack February 10 at Qui Nhon, which killed twenty-three Americans. A new coup d'état on February 20 finally replaced General Khanh with Nguyen Cao Ky and Nguyen Van Thieu as heads of the Military Council, and installed a new premier, Phan Huy Quat.

Then on March 2 began the first sustained air strikes not described as "reprisals against Viet Cong terror." Already ordered on February 13 and delayed by the new coup, the raids escalated to 4,800 sorties a month in June and 12,000 a month by 1967 against targets that, by April 1966, reached as far north as the outskirts of Hanoi. Termed Rolling Thunder, the raids increased further, though with "pauses" and "limitations," and continued until October 31, 1968. By then, U.S. aircraft had dropped more bombs on

North and South Vietnam, and on Laos, than in all of World War II, even though the American part of the war was only half over.

This launching of the most massive bombing in history was soon followed by the introduction of combat troops, predictably deemed necessary to protect the bases from which the fighter-bombers departed. In this way, one act led to another, and on March 8, the first contingent of 3,500 U.S. Marines arrived near Da Nang. In early April, the president made a significant step further with the decision to "use American ground troops for offensive action," thereby overriding all political and military advice since the Korean War. The first such large-scale ground action occurred northwest of Saigon in the last days of June, not far from where, at Ben Cat Special Zone, on the eighteenth of the month, thirty B-52 bombers had struck enemy positions for the first time.

Each B-52 was capable of unleashing up to 60,000 pounds of bombs, from altitudes so high (up to 55,000 feet) as to prevent any warning sound, making them the most feared of all American weapons. After a relatively slow start, caused by such incidents as the collision of two B-52s on the first strike, by the end of the year the giant aircraft were averaging 300 sorties a month (departing first from Guam, then Thailand), figures that climbed to 1,800 a month in the spring of 1968 and to a peak of 3,150 in June, 1972, followed by the final 729 raids against Hanoi in December 1972. In eight years the B-52s flew 124,532 sorties and dropped 2,949,000 tons, or more than one-third of the total tonnage (7.8) of bombs dropped during the Vietnam War and more than were dropped by all aircraft in all of World War II.

WITH EQUALLY DIZZYING RAPIDITY, the figures of American troops in South Vietnam mounted, especially after the president's decision announced on July 28, 1965, to send an additional 50,000 troops to the country. New requests followed, and the totals reached over 184,000 by the end of that year and a peak of over 542,000 three years later. Although only about one-fifth of these were "combat" troops, the rest serving mostly logistical functions, up to another 64,000 personnel served offshore in the Navy's Seventh Fleet, another 20,000 at three air bases in Thailand, and another 68,900 troops from five allied nations (including up to 49,000 Koreans) assisted an increasing number of South Vietnamese troops in the anti-Communist war effort.

The American commander of this powerful force, General William Westmoreland,* in March 1965 explained the rationale for the increasingly overwhelming military presence since, if the Communists were to be stopped, there was "no solution . . . other than to put our own finger in the dike." Two years later when numerous "search and destroy" missions and the enormous bombings still had not subdued the Communists, Westmoreland told a press conference on Aril 14, 1967, "We'll just go on bleeding them to the point of national disaster for generations. They will have to reassess their position."[15]

The "bleeding" of the Communists was to be measured by the number of dead, euphemistically surveyed by "body counts" in "meat-grinder" operations, which often could be summarized in the hapless phrase "We had to destroy the town to save it."

With mounting fury, the bombing and shelling escalated from over 300,000 tons in 1965 to over one million tons in 1966 and over two million tons each year from 1967 to 1970, (the peak was 2,966,548 tons in 1968) and close to that in 1971 and 1972. By 1973, American and South Vietnamese military forces had unleashed over fourteen million tons of bombs and munitions on Indochina, or over 700 times the force of the atomic bomb dropped on Hiroshima at the dawn of the nuclear age on August 6, 1945. Of these explosives, over seven million tons were dropped from the air, including over four million tons on South Vietnam, over one million tons on North Vietnam, close to one and one-half million tons on Laos, and over a half million tons on Cambodia. It is also estimated that over 400,000 tons of napalm were used by American forces before 1973, as well as 1.7 million tons of defoliants. Although the official purpose of the bombing changed in mid-1965 from an effort "to break the will of North Vietnam" to "cutting the flow of men and supplies from the North to the South" and to support the increasing numbers of ground troops, most thought of the gigantic bombing rather as an American effort to carry out Air Force General Curtis Lemay's advice of November 25, 1965, "We should bomb them into the Stone Age."[16]

*The Military Assistance Advisory Group (MAAG) had given way to the Military Assistance Command, Vietnam (MACV) in February 1962, and Westmoreland replaced General Paul Harkins as its commander in July 1964. General Creighton Abrams replaced Westmoreland in July 1968, and in turn gave way to General Frederick Weyand in June 1972.

YET WHILE BADLY "BLED," the Communists were not about to give up their lifelong goals, either in the north or in the south. On the contrary, in what was described as their boldest action yet, they blew up part of the American Embassy in Saigon on March 29, 1965, killing two, and on May 11 overran for a day Song Be (Phuoc Binh), capital of Phuoc Long province, just one hundred miles to the north.

More importantly, and predictably, the "northern infiltration" so long criticized and feared now greatly increased, although at an understandably slower pace than the American infiltration. The first regular regiment of the People's Army of Vietnam (PAVN) was reported to have moved in April into the Central Highlands, where by the end of the year northerners made up almost 90 percent of Communist forces. But until 1968, for the entire south, southern recruits and returnees remained the predominant portion of Communist forces by far. Northern regulars fighting in the south increased perhaps tenfold to 14,000 by the end of the year, but by then total Communist forces in the south had reached an estimated total of 230,000, and American troop levels already had surpassed 184,000.

Late in May 1965, Viet Cong forces ambushed important government units south of the seventeenth parallel and in June claimed victories northeast of Saigon and in the delta. A terrorist bomb at a Saigon restaurant killed nine Americans on June 25, and then a raid on Da Nang air base on July 1 destroyed several aircraft despite the presence of the Marines sent to prevent that. Together with other setbacks, this led the highest-level dissenter to the escalation policy in Washington, Under Secretary of State George Ball, immediately to conclude "the enemy . . . had obviously gotten advance word" of U.S. operations and that, therefore, Washington faced a "protracted war" unless it could "find a way out" before it was too late.

President Johnson and most American officials, however, "simply could not conceive that a small backward country could stand up against them," and therefore decided, as a recent study by George Herring puts it, to take "the nation into war by . . . indirection and dissimulation . . . [in] a desperate attempt to halt the military and political deterioration in South Vietnam."[17] While General Westmoreland at first argued that his increasing troop levels and more aggressive tactics should enable victory over the Communists in several years, Ho Chi Minh was both more inspirational and, as it turned out, more realistic in stating on June 17, 1966: "The war may last five years, ten years, twenty years or more. Hanoi, Haiphong as well as a certain number of other cities may be destroyed but the Vietnamese people will not be intimidated," and will win ultimate victory.

Just as the Americans and Communists revealed totally different views of the causes of the war, so their perceptions and reporting of the battlefield history of the next years differed profoundly. Frequently both sides claimed victory for the same battle, as was the case with the "first major combat involving American troops." This occurred south of the important American base established at Chu Lai on the central coast on August 18–20, 1965. In a sweep of the Van Tuong Peninsula, south of Da Nang, according to American reports, some 4,000 Marines killed 700 Viet Cong, while losing 50 of their own men. But the Communists, on the contrary, claimed that their 1,000-man force, striking from concealed underground positions, killed 900 of 8,000 attacking Marines, thereby foiling the operation, despite over 1,000 supporting fighter-bomber strikes, which unleashed sixty-four tons of bombs on the area. The Communists maintain they thus again demonstrated their ability to "defeat the U.S. aggressors" directly, as they had already done indirectly at Ap Bac, My Tho province, in January 1963, when they claimed to have "wiped out puppet troops, organized, equipped and commanded by Americans."

Similarly, both sides claimed victory in the biggest battle of 1965, October 19–November 27, at Plei Mei, southwest of Plei Ku, in the Ia Drang Valley of the West Central Highlands. With direct tactical air strikes by fighter-bombers, and for the first time, close support strikes by B-52s,* the United States claimed to inflict over a thousand deaths, or about five times its own losses. Military historian D. R. Palmer, called it "a high point in the history of American arms . . . [to] win one of the war's rare, decisive battles." The Communists, by contrast, claimed to inflict "bloody defeats" and "stunning blows at the U.S. expeditionary corps" of 20,000 men at Plei Mei and elsewhere. On December 4, 1965, Communist sappers blew up the Hotel Metropole in Saigon, claiming to kill 200, includ-

*The B-52s at first were instructed to come no closer than three kilometers of "friendly" troops, at which distance the ground still shook noticeably. To counter a Communist offensive, in May 1972 this distance was reduced to 600 meters. The B-52 strikes between June 18, 1965 and November, bombed "enemy" positions, but at a greater distance from friendly troops.

ing many American officers. And in Hanoi, a Party plenum renewed its pledge "to liberate the South," despite difficulties caused by "the new situation," and despite admitted doubts of some of its own people.

In 1966, the Communists claimed victories along the central coast south of Da Nang, notably in northern Binh Dinh province, despite destruction to the point that "fires were raging day and night, month after month . . . . Bombs and chemicals . . . destroyed all human life, all vegetables, even the grass . . . . In the single district of Bong Son, twenty-five battalions of U.S., South Korean and puppet troops, 500 planes and a large number of armored vehicles combed for a month." These, they claimed, were "large scale terror raids to 'kill all, burn all, destroy all'," as Communists had described Japanese tactics in China after 1937, but which nonetheless failed to pacify the area. American sources acknowledge the use in the province in 1966 of "almost 1.5 million pounds of explosives and 292,500 pounds of napalm," making refugees of up to one-third of Binh Dinh's 875,547 people, which happened also in Quang Ngai province a little latter. Incredibly, new operations in Binh Dinh province in 1967 used more than twice as much firepower again as in the previous year and nonetheless the First Calvary Division, conducting the sweeps, still had to admit that while the province was "free from organized Viet Cong control . . . this is not to mean that . . . [it has] been brought under government control . . . . As far as political control is concerned, [it] . . . is still a power vacuum." As Marine Colonel William Corson explained of similar operations nearby, in 1965 "the Viet Cong had been swept into the sparsely populated hills [near Da Nang] in the face of the Marine advance, but again, like water, they flowed back into the 'liberated' areas as soon as the Marines pushed forward."[18]

Also on the central coast, in Quang Ngai province, the Communists claim up to 40 percent of the population of the countryside went underground into elaborate tunnel systems, to enable the movement to survive U.S. attacks in 1966 and 1967. Nearby, in Quang Nam province near Da Nang, Communist units inflicted heavy casualties in an attack on U.S. Marines on August 17, 1966. And on June 7–8, 1966, near An Loc, about sixty miles north of Saigon, four companies of U.S.-South Vietnamese troops were ambushed.

In the cities, the Buddhist crisis of 1966 temporarily deflected pressure against the Communists, although by late 1966, Saigon's police forces were said to have regained the efficiency they had had under Diem. From October 1966 until January 1968, there were no terrorist incidents in the eighth district of Cholon, for example, where they had been averaging almost forty a month in 1964–1965. Nonetheless, overall Communist strength continued to increase, from over 220,000 (30 percent of whom were believed to be northern troops) in early 1966 to 285,000 by early 1967 (nearly half of whom were thought to be northerners) according to American estimates.

BEGINNING IN 1966, the area twenty to thirty miles northwest of Saigon known as the Iron Triangle also came under extraordinarily heavy attack, as was partly described above in Chapter Seven. In January 1966, Communist sources claim that on about one-half of the area of Cu Chi District, some seventy kilometers square, there fell day and night* an incredible bombardment of 180,000 shells, plus massive bombings by 24 B-52s, 300 fighter bombers, and 500 helicopters; in one area, an average of 27 explosives per square meter! Some 7,000 hectares, or about one-sixth of the area, were ravaged. And yet at one village (An Phu) in this target zone, "thanks to an inextricable labyrinth of tunnels and trenches, a group of nine combattants resisted for eight days in an area of one square kilometer against 6,000 GIs . . . . Communists stated that by about this time, already a network of "about 200 kilometers of tunnels and trenches" had been built throughout the area. Digging on average a meter for every eight hours of labor, the tunnels reached a depth of thirty-six feet, to form the "brass walls" and "steel fortresses" that enabled the Communists to maintain a forward headquarters there throughout the war with "very few losses," despite periodic military sweeps and enormous applications of firepower. GIs referred to the tunnel system as "like the New York subway system." The Communists, for their part, claimed to "completely smash" the January 1966 offensive after some eleven days of combat and to "put out of action" 5,000 GIs in Operation Cedar Falls a year later.

Recalling the French war, Communist writer Pham Cuong in 1968 attributed the revolutionaries' success in Cu Chi to a People's War in which:

> It is not unusual to see people of successive generations fighting side by side. The white-haired grandfathers who had stood up against the

*"At night, the blinding light of flares . . . made night like day, to the point that even a rat hiding in a bush could be seen," according to a Communist report.

> French colonialists at the end of the last century, now cutting stakes for booby traps, the fathers, who fought in the First Resistance and are now taking part in the Second, [while] their children . . . [and] grandchildren run errands for the fighters. . . .

He argued also that "hatred for the U.S. aggressor is a mighty motive power. Every villager has a personal debt to settle with the Yankees," and that building on these traditions and passions, the people of Cu Chi built with their bare hands an impregnable complex of tunnels, underground shelters and communications lines. He explained:

> The Cu Chi tunnels have their history. The first ones, very simple, were dug in grassy or bushy regions and looked like air shelters with bamboo roofs covered with earth. They were easily found out by the enemy . . . The danger of death multiplied initiatives. People set about excavating multistoried tunnels, which were carefully disguised and could shelter whole families . . . [and] joined houses together . . . . To combat smoke and gases, the tunnels were made to zig and zag with air tight rooms . . . . The underground village has combat positions, spike pits and shelters [even for] . . . cattle, poultry and food reserves . . . old folk, children and young mothers . . . ancestral altars . . . underground motion picture and theatrical shows. Songs and dances were punctuated by bomb explosions overhead.

Life went on also above ground as best it could for the 200,000 inhabitants of Cu Chi:

> After each enemy raid, Cu Chi presents a desolate scene with smoking ruins and charred trees . . . . Some fifty buffaloes and oxen are killed on an average. Ricefields strewn with splinters of bombs and shells are no longer cultivable. But . . . in order to "cling to the land and defend the village" production must be carried on . . . at night, covering themselves with straw, cadres and fighters harvested the ricefields bordering enemy lines. In the daytime they dug the soil. The people imitated them. They camouflage themselves by smearing their bodies with mud. When a plane passes overhead, they stay motionless or take shelter in trenches. Anti-aircraft groups are posted . . . . Enemy artillery never ceases firing on the fields . . . . The people avail themselves of every lull to work even at night . . . blood is shed on the ricefield as well as on the battlefield.[19]

In the winter of 1966–1967, the United States launched three new massive offensives against other areas a little further north and west of Saigon. The first, Operation Attleboro, in October and November 1966, focused on Tay Ninh, as did the third and biggest,

Junction City, from February 22 to April 14, 1967. Both were inconclusive, and their primary goal to capture the Communist headquarters (COSVN), thought to be near Tay Ninh, was not attained. Despite some 12,000 tons of bombs thrown against them, the Communists claimed to "put out of combat" 3,200 GIs in Operation Attleboro. Nor did the second operation, Cedar Falls, in January 1967, discover COSVN, although its target area between Ben Cat and Ben Suc lay just to the north of Cu Chi, where at least sections of the Communist headquarters remained.

Perhaps the most graphically and horrifyingly described battle of the war, Cedar Falls aimed "to eliminate the Iron Triangle as a base" for the Communists, and to do that U.S. military historian Charles MacDonald argued in 1979, "the people had to be relocated away from their villages and their houses destroyed . . . [to] make the area a 'free fire zone' at which artillery and air strikes could be directed without concern for civilian casualties. Rome plows subsequently completed the job of leveling the entire region" of sixty square miles.[20]

The operation aimed to displace some 6,000 inhabitants of the Iron Triangle, and according to Commanding General Bernard Rogers, showed the enemy he could not win, and forced headquarters units into Cambodian sanctuaries. What the United States took to be at least a local headquarters was uncovered in a tunnel complex over a kilometer long near the Ho Bo woods, about seven miles north-northeast of Cu Chi. Some five Viet Cong were captured and over forty pounds of documents. Yet, as at Cu Chi a year earlier, the Communist core survived, and a company commander admitted, "We burned the buildings, but we could not do anything to the fortifications: they were just dug too damn deep." Against Junction City further west, from February 22 to April 14, the Communists claimed their greatest victory yet, after reportedly being tipped off by an agent, Sau Doc, who was an "intimate friend" of a Colonel Ngo, a member of Westermoreland's staff. They claimed the killing or wounding of 14,000 allied troops, while the Americans maintained they had killed some 2,728 Communists, and driven others into Cambodia, with a loss of "only" 282 GIs. And Operation Paul Revere supposedly suffered heavy losses near Plei Jirang, thirty miles west of Plei Ku in late November 1966.[21]

In 1967 for the first time, American troops entered the heavily populated MeKong Delta. An estimated 80,000 Viet Cong troops there enabled Communist control of over half of the area's 5,000 hamlets, and Westmoreland argued that GIs near My Tho and elsewhere substantially reduced that Communist presence. Yet in Long An province, for example, where some 3,100 American troops arrived to supplement 14,550 government troops by 1968, Communist forces also increased from 2,180 in 1967 to 3,100 in 1968, and did so in the face of bombardments that were said to reach three tons of bombs per inhabitant in one hamlet (Binh Quang)! Further north, the Communists captured the capital city of Quang Ngai the night of July 31, 1967, long enough to liberate 1,200 prisoners, and then to withdraw again into the hills.

As could have been expected, given the disproportionate arms available to the opposing sides, the Communists suffered enourmously in virtually all of these battles, and the American forces claimed victory accordingly. The kill ratios were supposed to average about ten to one and at times reached forty to one or more in what some called "squirrel shoots," although on average only about one in six corpses were found with their weapons. Therefore, most victims were not "regular" soldiers, although they may indeed have been Communist sympathizers.

Washington should have recalled Ho Chi Minh's statement of September 1946 to the French, "If we have to fight, we will fight. You will kill ten of our men and we will kill one of yours. In the end it will be you who will tire of it." Another Communist writer, Nguyen Xuan Lai, explained in 1968 how they intended to overcome such odds, by linking Party organization, the elaborate tunnel systems and people's war:

> To lead a political or armed struggle, a militant core is needed. For political struggle, it is the "political army," mainly made up of women, the "long haired army," and for armed struggle, the regional, military, and para-military forces, including the regular forces stationed in the region . . . . As long as the cadres hold on [despite all efforts to destroy the "VC infrastructure"], the organizations remain, the popular masses continue to struggle, and all "pacification" plans will end in failure . . . [But] this military core, on which the success of the struggle depends can be preserved only when it is under constant protection by the popular masses. The latter feed the cadres, hide them in their houses, protect them . . . [although] this is a most dangerous task . . . .
>
> [Victory therefore] also depends on a factor of no less importance: the organization of village life . . . in all fields: military, political, economic, cultural, health, educational. By sowing destruction,

> the enemy tries to make life in the countryside impossible. But after each bombing raid, all activities return to normal . . . [as] Protective measures are elaborate. Communication trenches link the houses, hamlets and villages, underground shelters are dug everywhere.
>
> . . . When the bombing or shelling is especially frequent and intense, people live practically underground; men, beasts, hospitals, schools, arms workshops, weaving workshops, and even markets . . . . Everything goes underground . . . . When the enemy comes into a village in the daytime, he finds no sign of life, but at night the place comes to life, people leave their hiding places to do their daily work . . . . The Americans have done everything possible to take the peasants away from their lands, but the latter "stick" to their villages at the risk of their lives . . . [and succeed in] the organization of combat forces . . . . [They also arc ablc] to consolidate the militant core, the mass organizations, guerilla units and the "political army," and to organize the population to make them combat ready, while carrying on all normal activities . . . .[22]

As with the stories of militant fighters like Madame Dinh, and General Vo Nguyen Giap's analysis of the principles of People's War, those quotations go a long way to explain how the Communists survived what they understandably called "a ruthless war to the death."

By 1967, more and more Americans were coming also to the conclusion that the war was at least unwinnable if not totally wrong. The first antiwar demonstrations and "teach-ins" had already taken place in Washington and on many U.S. campuses in April and May 1965, and in October 1967, 35,000 demonstrators descended on Washington. Increasing numbers of government officials as well were beginning to wonder, as reportedly had Assistant Secretary of Defense John McNaughton as early as December 1964, if they were "on the wrong side."

In June 1967, Secretary of Defense McNamara ordered a study by thirty-six analysts of Indochina since World War II, that would become known as *The Pentagon Papers* after its controversial publication exactly four years later. A month earlier, he had wondered about "domestic and world opinion" of possible further escalation, when "the picture of the world's greatest superpower killing or seriously injuring 1,000 noncombatants a week, while trying to pound a tiny, backward nation into submission on an issue whose merits are hotly disputed, is not a pretty one."[23]

Surveys of U.S. public opinion meanwhile showed a drop to 28 percent approval of the president's handling of the war by October 1967, and a still lower rating after the Communist Tet offensive of 1968, although it did not follow that most Americans backed the arguments of the "doves" that the United States should simply fly away. To offset the growing doubts, Washington ordered greater attention to the more optimistic reports of some generals and diplomats, and ordered new American Ambassador Ellsworth Bunker and General Westmoreland to return to Washington in November 1967 for publicity to that effect. Westmoreland told the National Press Club on the twenty-first, "We have reached an important point when the end begins to come into view," and predicted that withdrawals of American troops could begin in two years. As late as January 24, 1968, pacification chief Robert Komer told a Saigon press conference, "We begin '68 in a better position than we have ever been before . . . ."[24]

As so often before, the "hawks," as proponents of expanding the war against the enemy had become known, reckoned without the resourcefulness and dedication of the Communists of Vietnam.

CHAPTER TEN

The End of the Thirty Years' War

BY MID-1967, the Communists decided that the growing contradictions on the side of their enemies, together with their own growing experience in dealing with U.S. power, justified a counterescalation of their own, and initiated planning for the famous Tet offensive of early 1968. It would mark another important divide in the history of the Vietnamese Revolution.

To prepare for the new offensive, Viet Cong and North Vietnamese units tested government-U.S. defenses beginning in the autumn of 1967, at Con Thien near the Demilitarized Zone, then at Loc Ninh and Song Be north of Saigon and at Dak To in the Central Highlands. The Party's Fourteenth Plenum later in the year gave final approval for the strikes, and beginning on January 21, Communist forces initiated an eleven-week siege of the important American base at Khe Sanh in the far northwest. That base lay astride the so-called McNamara Line, which had been undertaken in 1967 with a vast installation of mines and aircraft, operated by electronic sensors programed to stop infiltration southward along the Ho Chi Minh Trail. Because the United States was able to continue to hold Khe Sanh, some observers called that battle, from January 21 to April 14, a "Dien Bien Phu in reverse." However, the McNamara Line proved about as effective as had the De Lattre Line for the French in the early 1950s, and the Communist siege of Khe Sanh at least partly achieved its mission of diverting American attention from the cities of the south that were the primary targets of the Tet offensive.

The directive of November 1, 1967, issued by the Party's southern provincial-level Standing Committee to instruct district and local committees to prepare for "an offensive and uprising . . . in the very near future" is worth quoting at length as an example of a rare inside Party elaboration of how to organize an armed insurrection according to the principles of People's War. Excerpts from the text, as given in Gareth Porter's documentary history follow:

> You are required to formulate a plan to prepare . . . [for] an uprising [which] will take place in the very near future . . . [with] attacks on towns and cities, in coordination with the widespread [uprising] movement in the rural areas . . . to liberate district seats, province capitals and South Vietnam as a whole.
>
> Our victory is close at hand . . . we have long suffered hardships, death and pain. We are looking for an opportunity to avenge evil done to our families, to pay our debt to the fatherland . . . . We cannot afford to miss this rare opportunity. All Party members and cadres must be willing to sacrifice their lives for the survival of the Fatherland . . . .

The directive then asked "How will the uprising be conducted?" and continued,

> There are two fundamental steps: First, annihilate the enemy's political power . . . capture all tyrants . . . and . . . spies. Second, organize our political power . . . .
>
> To conduct an uprising, you must have a roster of all the tyrants and spies and be familiar with the way they live and where they live. Then use suicide cells to annihilate them by any means. The following tasks should also be achieved . . . .
>
> Conduct meetings and give information . . . make use of the populace immediately in sabotage and support activities, and in raid operations against the spies. The masses should be encouraged to go on strike, dig trenches and make spikes all night long . . . All people in each family regardless of their ages should be encouraged to take part.

It continued:

> The cadre, together with the population, will be required to swear that they will stay close to their ricefields, defend their villages and do their utmost to wrest back control . . . . A number of old men, women and children should be made available . . . to report [confusing information] to enemy . . . posts . . . . Young men and healthy farmers will be retained for use in defense wall construction, altering terrain, guard duty and combat . . . .

> Once the task is achieved, make use of a number of agents under legal cover to organize insurrection committees in white (Saigon controlled) hamlets and villages . . . women and children must be recruited immediately to serve in the self-defense corps and guerilla force. A number of loyal farmers, youths and women will be selected for indoctrination . . . instruction on carrying out such policies as that for land will be disseminated in the future . . . .
>
> Each person must directly engage in activities such as altering terrain features, digging tunnels, making spikes, proselytizing the youth, training guerilla fighters, . . . guard duty . . . and waging widespread guerilla actions . . . . Everyone from the commanding officer on down . . . must throughout the period of uprising have in his possession such items as drums and gongs and sabotage equipment, must engage in propaganda actions . . . . We must knock on every inhabitant's door to borrow the maximum possible amount of money and food . . . . In view of the crucial situation, the Standing Committee is convinced that you will master all difficulties and carry out the above . . . .[1]

The date finally chosen for the offensive, in order to achieve maximum surprise, was the most sacred holiday of the Vietnamese year—Tet, or the lunar New Year, which in 1968 fell on January 29 (inaugurating the Year of the Monkey, succeeding the Year of the Goat). In one of its greatest victories over Imperial China, in 1789, the Vietnamese had also surprised their enemy in the midst of the Tet holiday, and in 1968 the Communists publicized a New Year's truce of their own from January 27 to February 3. The U.S. military command, however, was not entirely fooled, and noting the unusual Communist military activities of the previous weeks, prevailed on President Thieu to cancel the government's planned cease-fire in part. It was abolished altogether in the northern provinces because of the attack on Khe Sanh, and limited to a leave of 50 percent of the personnel in the south for twenty-four hours, and that was cancelled immediately on news of the first attack.

On the night of January 29, Communists jumped the gun in at least eight locations, because of faulty communications, a day ahead of the scheduled start of the general offensive. By February 1, however, the full force of the attack by an estimated 84,000 Communist troops was coordinated against thirty-six of forty-four provincial captials and sixty-four district capitals, and many military bases. Among other actions, they temporarily seized large parts of the delta towns of Ben Tre, My Tho, Can Tho, and Soc Trang, and of Phan Thiet, Kon Tum, and other towns to the north.

In Saigon, five battalions of about 1,000 Communist troops succeeded in entering the city, and parts of the Chinese city of Cholon were overrrun for five days. In a particularly spectacular action on January 31, some nineteen sappers stormed the U.S. Embassy, raising the Viet Cong flag, which was photographed and widely reproduced in the world press, as a few days later was an even more infamous picture of Police Chief Nguyen Ngoc Loan summarily shooting a terrorist in the head.* The Embassy was cleared, after six hours of fighting, with the killing of all nineteen in the suicide squad, together with five Americans; but the event seemed to symbolize the overoptimism of Washington's previous claims to see "light at the end of the tunnel."

The fall of the imperial city of Hue to some 7,500 Communist troops on January 31, was a still more dramatic demonstration of the continuing strength of the revolutionaries. The city was retaken on February 25, but only after heavy fighting and bombing which cost the deaths of 119 United States and 363 government soldiers, an estimated 5,000 Communist dead, and another 5,000–6,000 civilians. There is continuing debate as to how many of the latter were killed by Communist terror—up to 4,700 as greatly publicized by Saigon and Washington propaganda—or as others argue, mostly by American firepower. The Communists claim they were supported in Hue by 90 percent of the population, and that three companies of "puppet civil guards" crossed over to their side.[2]

THE AMERICAN MILITARY ARGUES that the Tet offensive of February 1968 resulted in a decisive defeat for the Communists, since in a few weeks they lost 32,000 killed (as against over 2,000 government and about 1,000 Americans), almost half of their guerilla forces, and in addition many thousands of their political cadre. But it is also clear that Tet was a psychological victory for the Communists, at least in the United States. There public doubts about the war rapidly increased with Tet's apparently brutal dashing of all hopes for a rapid end to the conflict. And numerous personnel changes followed almost immediately. Robert McNamara, increasingly doubtful about what had been dubbed his war, gave way as secretary of defense to

*Loan himself was almost killed in another clash with Vietnamese terrorists on May 5, 1968, as were other supporters of Nguyen Cao Ky in June. Some observers infer, however, that they were victims, not of the Viet Cong, but of growing tensions between Ky and Thieu.

Clark Clifford, another "hawk" who soon became a "dove" on Vietnam.

On March 31, 1968, President Johnson produced the biggest shock of all when he declared his intention to withdraw from the coming presidential elections in November. Then on July 1, General Creighton Abrams replaced William Westmoreland as Commander of MACV. As a sure sign of the slow but decisive turning around of opinion in Washington, for the first time in March 1968 Westmoreland's request for another 206,000 troops was turned down, although additional troops were sent to carry the total from 495,000 in February 1968 to a peak of 543,000 a year later, fighting with 626,000 (later 1.2 million) South Vietnamese and close to 70,000 South Korean and other allied forces.

Supporting American arguments that Tet was a military defeat for the Communists was the ending of the siege of Khe Sanh by April 14, thanks in large part to the pulverizing of the surrounding five square miles by over 100,000 tons of bombs (including 60,000 tons of napalm!) which made it "the most heavily bombed target in the history of warfare." (The Hiroshima A-bomb was 20,000 tons.) But then, in the sort of bizarre irony that had become routine, two months later the U.S. command decided to abandon the Khe Sanh base, which in early July was promptly occupied by Communist troops.

And while it was true that the hoped-for "general uprising" of the population did not occur, as was admitted in Party documents, there were some local rebellions in favor of the Communists, as in Hue, and in the Mekong Delta province capital of Tra Vinh (Phu Vinh). More importantly, the populace did not side with the government either. In any case, the Communists had concluded as early as January 31, whatever their hopes before the beginning of the attacks, "we cannot yet . . . achieve total victory in a short period," even though in the words of the Provincial Party Committee directive of November 1, 1968, the attacks had "scored brilliant achievements." In Hanoi, however, Truong Chinh reportedly stressed the need for a readjustment of policies and more moderate approaches in the wake of Tet, indicating some exacerbation of differences among the Communist leadership.

Most important, the key to the war, control of the village, was again temporarily set back, at first to a nearly equal division of control—4,559 hamlets under the government and 4,093 under the Communists, who claimed to have liberated 600 villages in February and March 1968. According to one document, government control of the total population declined from 67.3 percent to 61 percent, while the Communists claimed the liberation of an additional 1.5 million people in all. The government, however, announced it had reattained the pre-Tet figure of 67 percent of the country "pacified" by the late summer of 1968 (and 80 percent four years later). Then a "second wave" offensive against over 100 towns and bases in early May, and a third wave in August were bloodily stopped. Communist troop levels, despite record infiltration, reportedly fell to below 200,000 by 1970, before climbing again to an estimated 252,000 by 1973. Nonetheless, older peasants, who could remember all the fluctuations of earlier decades, could only be skeptical of government claims of progress.[3]

More meaningful to the peasantry than all the bombing and killing were the belated government efforts to enforce a significant land reform. Beginning in 1968, inspired by the shock of Tet, and climaxed by the "land to the tiller" law of March 1970, Saigon finally lowered the maximum land holding from Diem's 100 hectares (250 acres) to fifteen (about thirty-seven acres) with the government buying excess land at up to 100,000 piastres (about $500) per hectare. Largely financed by the United States, the distribution of up to one-half the land of the delta followed, approximately halving the previous tenancy rate of 60 percent. Moreover, powers were restored to the traditional village council, which had been abolished by Diem in 1956. According to the Communists, however, elected village chiefs were again replaced by appointed officials in August 1972, and former government official Le Phuong charged there had been extensive profiteering from the land reform as some government insiders bought land at one-fifth or less the price reimbursed a few months later by the reforms.[4]

In any case, the belated land and other reforms came tragically too late to take root sufficiently to prevent the final Communist victory of 1975.

AGAINST SUCH A BACKGROUND of unprecedented violence, Hanoi and the NLF on one side and the United States and Saigon on the other never stopped talking of "peace," but of peace with an "honor" that each side naturally tied to diametrically opposed positions. Already in April 1965, both sides proposed solutions that only revealed the fundamental gulf between the two sides, a gulf that would take eight more years of full-scale warfare to be partially papered over with the Paris Agreement of January 1973, and only be finally settled with Hanoi's final victory of 1975.

Ironically, both sides appealed to the 1954 Geneva Agreements, but with totally different interpretations of what these meant. Hanoi's basic negotiating position, the "Four Points" of April 8, 1965, argued:

1. . . . According to the Geneva Agreements, the U.S. Government must withdraw from South Vietnam . . . and cancel its military alliance with South Vietnam. It must end its policy of intervention and agression in South Vietnam . . . stop its acts of war against North Vietnam . . . .
2. . . . The 1954 Geneva Agreements on Vietnam must be strictly respected. The two zones must refrain from entering into any military alliance with foreign countries, and there must be no foreign military bases, troops . . .
3. . . . The internal affairs of South Vietnam must be settled by the South Vietnamese people themselves in accordance with the program* of the NLFSV without any foreign intervention.
4. The peaceful reunification of Vietnam is to be settled by the Vietnamese people in both zones without any foreign interference.

The basic U.S. position was given about the same time by President Johnson, who stated on April 7, 1965:

> We are . . . [in Vietnam] because we have a promise to keep. Since 1954 every American President has offered . . . to help South Vietnam defend its independence . . . .
>
> We are also there to strengthen world order. Around the globe, from Berlin to Thailand, are people whose well being rests in part on the belief that they can count on us if they are attacked. To leave Vietnam to its fate would shake the confidence of all these people in the value of an American commitment . . . . The result would be increased unrest and instability and even wider war . . .

---

*The NLF ten-point program of 1960 was frequently repeated in different forms and later resumed in variants of four points; replacement of the American "puppet" governments in Saigon with a "Democratic Government of national coalition," peace, neutrality, and unity.

According to a telegram from Secretary of State Rusk on February 16, 1966, the United States

> fully respects the basic rights of the Vietnamese people to peace, independence and sovereignty, unity and territorial integrity as set forth in the Geneva Accords of 1954. As the US has repeatedly said, it believes that these Accords, together with the 1962 Accords concerning Laos, are an adequate basis for peace in Southeast Asia or for negotiations looking toward a peaceful settlement . . . .

But Washington also insisted, "the U.S. objective is to maintain the independence and territorial integrity of South Vietnam" as the only means of protecting individual freedoms from "Communist tyranny." In its "fourteen points" of January 1966, the Department of State declared, "We have put everything into the basket of peace [for negotiation] except the surrender of South Vietnam," where "we support free elections . . . to give the South Vietnamese a government of their own choice . . . ." The United States and the Saigon government further declared in a joint statement from Honolulu on February 8, 1966:

> The United States seeks no bases. It seeks no colonial presence . . . It seeks only to prevent aggression . . . the principles of the self-determination of peoples, and of government by the consent of the governed. It therefore gives its full support to the purpose of free elections . . . [and] to measures of social revolution including land reform . . . [and] to press the quest for a peaceful settlement in every forum . . . no path to peace shall be unexplored . . . .

The line obviously was tragically and deeply drawn between Washington's commitment to a separate, "free" South Vietnam, protected from "aggression from the north," and the Communist leadership's long-proven dedication to a unified, Communist Vietnam, reinforced by such slogans as "Vietnam is one, the Vietnamese people are one, and no force on earth can deny that reality." Southern rebels, perhaps more than Hanoi's own "hawks," stressed "neutralism" and a slower approach to unification and socialism. As the PRG's minister of justice, Truong Nhu Tang, later stated, "We worked for an autonomous, independent South Vietnam." But like Hanoi statements, the NLF "Five Points" of March 22, 1965, argued: "The U.S. imperialists have continuously interfered in and committed agression against South Vietnam . . . [and therefore] the heroic South Vietnamese people are resolved to drive out the U.S. Imperialists in order to liberate South Vietnam, achieve an independent, democratic, peaceful and neutral South Vietnam, and eventual national reunification . . . ."[5]

The NLF therefore concluded that "all talks with the American Imperialists are impossible" until Washington withdrew from the south and ended its "acts of war." Ky and then Thieu meanwhile ceaselessly proclaimed their refusal even to talk with the NLF, much less accept a "coalition government." And President Johnson, while declaring he would "go anywhere, anytime" to work out a settlement, also asked his troops to "nail the coonskins to the wall." As UN Secretary-General U Thant aptly noted in February 1965, two weeks after the beginning of the bombing of the north, "the prospects for a peaceful settlement . . . will be more and more remote" given the gulf between the two sides and the military actions already under way.

Nonetheless, the expanding violence also raised fears of the war's spread to other areas, which in turn precipitated numerous "peace initiatives" on the part of many nations and groups. While Hanoi and the NLF primarily demanded the withdrawal of U.S. troops and the stopping of the bombing, Secretary of State Rusk claimed that by May 1967 Washington already had advanced twenty-eight different proposals for peace, all of which had been rebuffed or ignored by Hanoi. There were repeated other efforts to end the war by, among others, authorities of the United Nations (from February 1965 on), England and the USSR as cochairmen of the 1954 Geneva Conference (June 1965), India (July 1966), Thailand and other SEATO nations (August 1966), Poland (December 1966), and by England and Russia again, with apparent support from Hanoi (January–February, 1967). But as White House staff member Chester Cooper later stated, "The plain fact of the matter was that by the summer of 1966 the position of both Washington and Hanoi was non-negotiable."

The unbridgeably different positions of the two sides were further hardened by the bombing. While President Johnson claimed five partial and eight total halts to the bombing of the north, culminating in that one ordered on November 1, 1968,* Hanoi predictably countered that such conditional pauses were deceitful attempts of "a thief, crying 'stop, thief' " to confound public opinion as to "who was the aggressor and who the victim." Growing num-

*The bombing, in fact, continued at a level of close to two million tons a year, but until 1972 was largely diverted against the Ho Chi Minh Trail in Laos and Cambodia and Communist areas of the south.

bers of American critics also charged that, on several occasions, Washington escalated its bombing, or hit sensitive targets, precisely in order to torpedo various peace initiatives, as those proceeding in Warsaw in December 1966, and in London, in February 1967, when according to British Prime Minister Harold Wilson, "peace was almost within our grasp."

And where Washington repeatedly stated its willingness "to order a cessation of all bombing of North Vietnam the moment we are assured privately or otherwise that this step will be answered promptly by a corresponding and appropriate de-escalation of the other side," many observers wondered what de-escalation Washington would order if North Vietnam had been bombing the United States and posed similar conditions. China, meanwhile in the throes of its Great Proletarian Cultural Revolution, continued to denounce in the strongest possible terms any talk of peace until a final Communist victory, and in June 1967, Soviet Premier Kosygin, at the Glassboro Conference in New Jersey, again demanded of President Johnson an "immediate withdrawal of the United States and the unconditional cessation of the bombing."

In 1967 there was some slight movement toward more flexible approaches. The NLF broadened its political appeal to the "so-called third force" of Buddhists and others to help them form a "democratic government of national union," and Hanoi began to place more emphasis on a halt to American acts of war rather than on acceptance of the NLF program as a basis of settlement. Then the so-called San Antonio Formula announced by President Johnson on September 29,* similarly stressed a promise to stop the bombing, if that would lead "to productive discussions," more than the previous commitment to "free elections in South Vietnam" and other difficult items of Washington's "Fourteen Points" of January 1966.

But it took the shock of the Tet offensive to finally bring the belligerents to talk face to face. Beginning on May 13, 1968, at the Hotel Majestic, Avenue Kleber, the "Paris Talks on Vietnam"† proceeded, however, almost as tortuously as the war itself. They

*Secretly and privately conveyed to the North Vietnamese diplomats in Paris by then Harvard professor Henry Kissinger.

†Conducted for the United States successively by Averell Harriman (1968), Henry Cabot Lodge (1969), and David Bruce (July 1970 on), for Saigon by Pham Dang Lam, for Hanoi by Xuan Thuy and Ha Van Lau, and for the NLF by Tran Buu Kiem and Madame Nguyen Thi Binh (no relation to Madame Nguyen Thi Dinh).

spread out over four years and eight months, a year longer than all of America's involvement in World War II.

And the Agreement of January 1973 owed more to some nineteen private talks, which began in August 1969, than to the official 174 sessions.[6] As Richard Nixon had narrowly defeated President Johnson's vice-president, Hubert Humphrey, in the November 1968 presidential elections, new National Security Adviser Henry Kissinger (secretary of state after 1973) conducted these talks for the United States, as for Hanoi did Political Bureau member and revolutionary veteran Le Duc Tho.

EVEN AS ALL SIDES CONTINUED to "fight while negotiating," the new American president, Richard Nixon, on June 8, 1969, announced the beginning of the process of scaling down the numbers of American troops, together with a simultaneous strengthening of the South Vietnamese armed forces, under a program that would become known as the Nixon Doctrine for the Vietnamization of the war. The president even spoke at one point, in literally Orwellian words, of a "war for peace," since "the true objective of this war is peace."[7]

Relentlessly, however, the war continued. Although the number of American troops declined from 543,000 in early 1969 to 335,800 by the end of 1970, 133,200 a year later, and none by the spring of 1973, South Vietnamese armed forces climbed from close to 626,000 in early 1968, to 900,000 in late 1969 to more than a million by 1971,* supposedly backed by another four million "people's self-defense forces." And the bombing and shelling of the countries of Indochina continued at staggering, even if slightly reduced, levels. In 1968 the United States had expended a record 2,966,548 million tons of bombs and munitions there, and in following years the totals were as follows: in 1969, 2,823,060 million tons, in 1970, 2,171,980 million tons, in 1971, 1,601,421 million tons, and then 1,905,424 million tons in 1972; in response to a new Communist offensive.[8]

In the face of the continuing high levels of force used against them, of new government military tactics and belated land reform,

*In 1972, there were 429,000 in the South Vietnamese army, 43,000 in the navy, 51,000 in the air force (which had become the fourth largest in the world, with over 1,000 planes), plus 300,000 in the Regional Forces and 250,000 in the Popular (local) Forces. In March 1973, Washington put the number of Communist troops in the south at 252,000.

and their own high losses during the Tet offensives, the Communists faced some partial and temporary reverses after 1968. Documents of October 1969 and early 1971, issued by the Party Headquarters for the South (COSVN), admitted "the enemy has achieved some temporary results" through the Phoenix Program*, and also through the establishment of "an outpost network and espionage and People's Self-Defense Force organizations in many hamlets and villages . . . increased [equipment and] mobility of puppet forces, . . . blocking lines and . . . a new defensive and oppressive system in densely populated rural areas." In the delta, as early as 1967, the Party apparently had to institute a new draft system for males, eighteen to thrity-five, to make up for heavy losses and insufficient volunteers.

They admitted also their own deficiencies in carrying out the "three prongs" of Communist strategy, the military and political struggles, and agitation among enemy troops. The October 1969 document stated "We have not yet promoted a sufficiently widespread armed struggle," or "thoroughly understood the people's war policy." Nonetheless, over a year later, COSVN boasted, correctly as it turned out, "in spite of his oppressive control, the enemy has failed to subdue our people . . . . The revolutionary infrastructure . . . our local and guerilla forces" have held out, and "in some areas were even able to increase."[9] The leadership of COSVN meanwhile had passed to Pham Hung on the death of Nguyen Chi Thanh in July, 1967.† Other members of the southern Communist leadership, as against NLF leaders mentioned earlier, included as before, Nguyen Van Linh (also called Nguyen Van Cuc), Tran Nam Trung, Vo Chi Cong, Tran Van Tra, Madame Nguyen Thi Dinh and others.

Another important development for the southern revolutionaries in the wake of the 1968 offensives was the new broadening of the United Front, as proposed in March 1966. In late April 1968, the Alliance of National, Democratic and Peace Forces grew out of local front organizations created at Tet in Hue, Saigon, and elsewhere. Then on June 8, 1969, a "South Vietnam People's Delegate Congress," of representatives of the NLF, PRP, and other radical groups, formed the Provisional Revolutionary Government of the

*The Phoenix Program "eliminated" up to 40,000 Communist cadres or, according to some sources, even 100,000. See Chapter Seven.

†Apparently a victim of a heart attack, though some believe of bombs.

Republic of South Vietnam. The vice-chairman of the NLF, Saigon architect Huynh Tan Phat, became chairman of the new government, with NLF Chairman Nguyen Huu Tho serving as chairman of the government's Advisory Council. The revolutionary government's foreign minister, Madame Nguyen Thi Binh, promptly went to Paris to represent the southern Communists at the Paris talks. As with the Viet Minh, the National Liberation Front, the People's Revolutionary Party, and other front organizations, the Provisional Revolutionary Government was designed both to appeal to those moderates who objected to a too obvious identification with communism, and to serve as "an effective tool of the Party" which directed it. By mid-1969, an administrative apparatus for the PRG, consisting of People's Revolutionary Councils had been formed in 1,268 townships, 124 districts, and 3 cities.

The Communists also began to become far better armed than ever before. Where lower-level units continued to rely a great deal on their extraordinary arsenal of homemade weapons and defensive complexes, Communist regulars by the mid-1960s were increasingly equipped with the highly reputed AK–47 assault rifle, by the late 1960s with some 130 mm. field guns, and 122 mm. heavy rockets, and then by the 1970s with PT–76 and T–54 tanks, anti-aircraft and other weapons suplied by Russia and China. Until virtually the last campaign of 1975, however, the Communists remained far inferior in arms overall as compared with their enemies, and totally lacked the massive airpower used against them. Although in particular battles they could sometimes exert superior firepower, they relied more often on "close-in" and "hand to hand" fighting, and on their tunnels, to offset these disadvantages. Moreover, American aid to Saigon was far greater than that given by Moscow and Peking to the Vietnamese Communists. Until the January 1973 Accords, Joseph Buttinger estimated the ratio at at least ten times, and Earl Martin cited a congressional report to the effect that the United States spent twenty-five to thirty times the amount spent by Russia and China together for the Communist side. Frank Snepp believed that, in the year before its fall, Saigon still received "roughly twice the amount of military assistance (in dollar terms) that had gone to Hanoi," although U.S. reductions and a three- or fourfold increase in Russian aid enabled Hanoi for the first time to receive more economic aid than Saigon in that year.

Even if later Chinese claims of up to $20 billion worth of aid to Hanoi are accepted, and reckoned with a figure about twice that for Russia, it is clear that the U.S. expenditures of at least $150 billion on the war represent far greater foreign aid for Saigon than for Hanoi, and the disproportion overall was probably far higher. Moreover, the total air superiority of the anti-Communists (over seven million tons worth!), together with such items as China's reported veto of a Russian offer in April 1965 to establish air bases in its southwest to aid Vietnam, and Hanoi's own refusal of a reported offer of 200,000 Chinese troops to fight the United States underline the obvious relative independence of the Communists and dependence of Saigon on American support.[10]

THE GREATEST SYMBOL of that independence, Party founder Ho Chi Minh, did not live to see the completion of his work. He died in Hanoi of a heart attack at the age of seventy-nine on September 3, 1969. But as with other revolutionary leaders before him, Ho's memory served his cause almost as well after his death as his own skills had before it. His heirs in Hanoi, most notably Pham Van Dong, Vo Nguyen Giap, Truong Chinh, Le Duan, and Le Duc Tho, gave the greatest possible publicity to Ho's last testament, already written the previous May 10. It declared in part:

> Our people's struggle against U.S. aggression, for national salvation, may have to undergo even more difficulties and sacrifices, but we are bound to win total victory.
>
> This is a certainty . . . .
>
> Our nation will earn the great honor of being a small country, which through a heroic struggle, has defeated two leading imperialist powers—France and the United States—and made a worthy contribution to the national liberation movement. . . . All my life, I have tried my best to serve the Fatherland, the revolution, and the people. Should I depart from this world now, I will regret nothing, except not being able to serve longer and more. . . .

Ho appealed for "unity and total dedication to the working class, the people, and the Fatherland," for "each Party member, each cadre [to] be deeply imbued with 'revolutionary morality'," and expressed his grief "at the dissensions now dividing the fraternal parties" of the Soviet Union and China.[11]

The reunification of the International Communist Movement and the attainment of its worldwide goals, of course, remained illusory and dependent on other events. But the victory of Vietnamese

Communists over the south was steadily, if still tortuously, approaching.

THE WAR WOULD BE WIDENED FURTHER, however, before the final Communist victories came in Vietnam and, at about the same time, also in Laos and Cambodia. Already in Laos, the 1962 agreement for "neutrality" and the withdrawal of "foreign troops and influence" had long become a dead letter. North Vietnamese troops not only remained but increased to an estimated 70,000, charged mostly with developing and guarding the Ho Chi Minh Trail. The United States, which had intervened in the late 1950s to back Lao rightists, in the 1960s formed its own "private CIA army," of some 30,000 Meo tribesmen under Vang Pao. Then by the late 1960s, the United States was using up to one-quarter, and sometimes one-half, of its yearly total of two million tons of explosives against the parts of Laos harboring the Ho Chi Minh Trail. One part of the Plain of Jars was systematically obliterated by U.S. bombs with the killing or uprooting of its entire population of over 50,000. With bitter eloquence a 1972 study by Frederick Branfman concluded that after five and one-half years of bombing, "by September (1969), the society of fifty thousand people living in and around the area no long existed. History had conferred one last distinction upon it: The Plain of Jars had become the first society to vanish through automated warfare."[12]

Then the 1970 extension of the war into Cambodia provided the greatest shock to world opinion since the Tet offensives two years before. Prior to that, Prince Norodom Sihanouk skillfully worked to maintain the neutrality of his country proclaimed by the Geneva Accords of 1954. On friendly terms with international Communist leaders, he denounced American interference and reaction, renounced U.S. aid in November 1963, and broke relations with Washington between May 1965 and August 1969.

Yet, because of domestic politics, the Communist extension of the Ho Chi Minh Trail through parts of Cambodia, the opening of a Sihanouk Trail from the southern port of Kompong Som (Sihanoukville) into southern Vietnam, and the growing numbers of Viet Cong seeking "sanctuary" from the war in Vietnam, Sihanouk also felt forced to crack down on Cambodian leftists and increasingly to seek control of the Vietnamese Communists using his territory. Earlier, Pol Pot (Saloth Sar) and others had founded the Communist

Party of Kampuchea in September 1960, superseding earlier Vietnamese sponsored organizations and slowly increased antigovernment activities in the countryside. Ieng Sary, Khieu Samphan, and other Khmer Rouge leaders left the capital of Phnom Penh to join the resistance after political crises in 1963 and 1967, respectively. Then elections in the early autumn of 1966 brought in a more conservative government, temporarily under Lon Nol, with Sihanouk as head of state, and in 1967 increasing repressions challenged by peasant rebellions sharpened tensions in the country. As the war in Vietnam gained in violence, Washington chose to interpret Sihanouk statements in 1968 and 1969 as giving permission for "hot pursuit" of Communists into Cambodian sanctuaries, and bombings against them, sardonically titled "menu" strikes, began in March 1969 but were kept secret for another year.

Although Sihanouk managed to keep his country basically at peace and neutral through the 1960s in what must be judged one of the century's great diplomatic juggling acts, the increasing polarization within the country and the continuing violence next door led inexorably to the events of 1970. On March 18 of that year, conservatives under Lon Nol declared Sihanouk, then in Moscow on his way home after a two month "cure" in France, deposed as head of state. Reaching Peking, on the twenty-third, Sihanouk launched a Khmer National United Front with his erstwhile Khmer Rouge enemies against the Lon Nol regime.

While President Nixon and advisor Kissinger later claimed surprise at the ouster of Sihanouk, it must have been a pleasant surprise. For on and after April 29, in response to "a call . . . for assistance" by Lon Nol, American troops and planes joined South Vietnamese forces in invading the "Parrot's beak," "Fish hook," and other border areas of Cambodia, where they claimed some 60,000 Vietnamese Communists and their southern headquarters (COSVN) had taken sanctuary. According to the president, Communist bases "up to twenty miles into Cambodia," "gravely threatened" American and Vietnamese troops with "hit and run attacks," and therefore the time had come to "clean out major enemy sanctuaries [there and to] . . . attack the headquarters of the entire Communist military operation in South Vietnam."[13] That headquarters, believed to be near Mimot, was not found. A later Khmer Rouge document claimed that, protected by up to 10,000 Vietnamese Communists, the headquarters had moved some sixty miles further northwest between Mimot and Kratie. And after the invasion, some

Party Central organs temporarily dispersed as far as the border with Laos, along the Waico River. But an extensive "underground city" was discovered in the "Fish hook" area, near Snoul, with eighteen mess halls, class rooms, a small farm, 300 vehicles, and over 30 tons of supplies and weapons.* Washington also claimed to kill or capture over 15,000 and subsequently to reduce its own casualties in Vietnam.

Whatever marginal military gains were produced by the invasion of Cambodia, however, were more than offset by new antiwar and international protests. These overrode explanations by the president, Kissinger, and others that the Military had long been demanding an end to the Cambodian sanctuaries as the "only way to win the war," that they would in the future respect "the neutrality of the Cambodian people," that all American troops would be withdrawn by the end of June, and that it was not they, but the North Vietnamese, who for years already had been invading Cambodia. The previous November, with great fanfare, antiwar activists had launched a new and wider "moratorium against the war," and now in early May, in response to the Cambodian invasion, over 100,000 protestors gathered in Washington. The atmosphere was further embittered with the killing of four students at Kent State College in Ohio on May 4, and two others at Jackson State College in Mississippi several days later. While the protests calmed somewhat over the summer, it was at this point that the president and Kissinger stepped up their wiretaps and CIA-FBI surveillance of opponents that a year leater would lead to the Watergate break-in, and in August 1974 to the end of the Nixon presidency.

In June 1970, the U.S. Congress reacted to the Cambodian invasion by rescinding the 1964 Tonkin Gulf Resolution, which successive administrations had been using as authorization for the war. The Senate also voted to end all military operations in Cambodia after June 30, including bombing, except for "interdiction" of supply routes into South Vietnam. But the failure of the House of Representatives to ratify, and the president's veto of other restrictions, enabled continued heavy bombing of Cambodia until August 1973. That was six months after its end in Vietnam, and in all the United

*Another footnote of the time, raising parallels with a similar effort in Iran a decade later, was the November 21, 1970, effort to liberate some sixty American prisoners of war believed held at Son Tay prison, twenty miles from Hanoi. The helicopters, however, found the prison deserted, its prisoners having been transferred three months earlier.

States dropped 539,129 tons on the small country or three times the total dropped on Japan in World War II, although only one-eighth that dropped on South Vietnam.

Despite, or because of, the invasion and the bombing, as shown in a 1979 book by William Shawcross, the Khmer Rouge were able to accelerate their growth, from perhaps 4,000 regulars in 1970 to 60,000 three years later, and to move much farther west into the interior of their country. With the help of the exiled Sihanouk, they were able to organize a far broader antigovernment, anti-American Front than ever before, and to recruit with relative ease among the almost one-third of the country's seven million population, said to have been made refugees by the bombing and the war. Their triumphant march into Phnom Penh on April 17, 1975, two weeks before the Communist conquest of Saigon, made a mockery of Nixon's and Kissinger's continuing claims that the invasion of Cambodia in 1970 had served the interests of the anti-Communists.

Even less auspicious was the South Vietnamese attempt to block the Ho Chi Minh Trail by invading southern Laos in February 1971. American intelligence believed that the North Vietnamese had moved to greatly expand the capacity and defenses of the Ho Chi Minh Trail there in late 1970 and, with Saigon, decided on new action. Although the number of American troops had been reduced to about 300,000 and new congressional limits forbade their use in Laos or Cambodia, some 10,000 GIs served as back up for the operation in northwestern Vietnam, and U.S. bombers stepped up their attacks on nearby Communist staging areas, as well as for the first time in over a year on some targets in North Vietnam.

The principal target was Tchepone, believed to be a key position for the Ho Chi Minh Trail, some twenty-two miles (35 kilometers into Laos, northwest of the border. As South Vietnamese units moved toward it after January 30, they met heavy resistance by three divisions of North Vietnamese troops. In two months of heavy fighting up to half of the 17,000 South Vietnamese were killed or wounded while they claimed in turn to kill some 13,636 North Vietnamese. On March 6, the South Vietnamese briefly occupied Tchepone in the "largest . . . helicopter assault of the Vietnam War," but by early April were forced to withdraw completely, often in the kind of disorder, including the storming of departing helicopters, that would disgrace the collapse of 1975. Moreover, the United States reported that within weeks, North Vietnamese traffic was again "moving freely down the trail," and that they and their Pathet Lao allies made substantial gains in central and northern Laos during and after early 1971, even as U.S. air strikes against area targets were "reduced" to 11,750 a month.

A YEAR LATER came the biggest Communist offensive since Tet of 1968. Because of the temporarily greater problems of the southern revolutionaries, depleted by the losses of Tet, by Saigon's new Phoenix, land, and other programs, and encouraged by U.S. withdrawals, Hanoi decided on a more conventional and more direct attack, the kind of "northern invasion" so long decried by Washington. Still, in order to break Vietnamization in the south, Hanoi committed what the U.S. military considered a major error by failing to concentrate all their forces against the northern province of Quang Tri. Diversions against Kon Tum in the Central Highlands and against An Loc, only sixty miles northwest of Saigon, fatally delayed the capture of Quang Tri, and possibly of Hue, according to this view.

Beginning on March 30, 1972, a third of an estimated 120,000 attacking Communist troops using for the first time in force tanks and heavy 130 mm. guns, struck across the DMZ. On April 27 they took the strategic town of Dong Ha and, on May 1, the provincial capital of Quang Tri, as southern troops fled in disorder. In early April, other units attacked in the A Shau Valley toward Hue, and a third Communist force struck toward An Loc and Saigon. Positions near Tay Ninh were overrun, and, by April 7, routes between Saigon and An Loc were cut. Although it had to be resupplied by air until June 25, An Loc held in some of the heaviest fighting of the war, with its defenders coming to be celebrated as the south's greatest anti-Communist heroes by the middle of May. However, as on previous occasions when there were intense military actions further north, other offsetting Communist gains became possible in the southern delta and elsewhere.

The Saigon air force had since February been striking Communist build ups in the north and, after April 6, President Nixon ordered the first heavy strikes against northern targets since the bombing halt of November 1, 1968. Then on May 8, the mining and bombing of Haiphong harbor and other North Vietnamese waters, sought since 1964, by some U.S. leaders, was begun. Despite sharp Russian protests, and damage to some Communist ships, the president was able to carry out his second "summit" of the year, a late May discussion with Breshnev in Moscow, three months after his trip to Peking began the reversal of over two decades of Chinese-American hostility.

Heavy and more accurate uses of American airpower, now equipped with electronically guided "smart bombs," also played a crucial role in breaking the sieges of An Loc by mid-May, of Kon Tum by the end of the month, and in the retaking of most of Quang Tri by the end of the summer. It was estimated that the bombing caused half the 100,000 casualties inflicted on North Vietnamese forces (as against 25,000 South Vietnamese casualties), and that the 1972 counteroffensives "could not have been won without it."[14] In any case, for the moment the Communist spring 1972 offensives had been stopped, first at An Loc, then in the Central Highlands, and finally in Quang Tri.

AS HAD HAPPENED after earlier expansion of the war, the peace talks again accelerated, and, after the horrific "Christmas bombings of Hanoi," finally resulted in the January 1973 Paris Accords for Ending the War and Restoring Peace in Vietnam. In the midst of the 1972 presidential campaign, and further polarized by the aftermath of the previous spring's conclusion of the trial of William Calley for the My Lai massacre, the publication of *The Pentagon Papers*, and the Watergate break-in, the United States was increasingly anxious for "peace with honor" in Vietnam.

The Vietnamese Communists, disappointed by their failure to achieve final victory with the 1972 offensives, also were ready for new approaches. They later expressed anger at China and Russia, whose "narrow national interests" had led them "to help the most reactionary forces" by receiving Nixon in February (China) and May 1972 (Russia), and it appears that Moscow indeed stepped up efforts to bring about a settlement, as did, for the first time, Peking. Furthermore, as Nixon's lead in polls over "dove" George McGovern stretched in the early autumn of 1972, Hanoi may have decided it would get better terms before, rather than after, the election in November.

Concessions came from both sides. By May 1971, Washington had proposed the final withdrawal of all U.S. troops within six months of an agreement, for the first time setting a specific timetable, and had begun to hint that it was not totally bound to Thieu himself, thereby in principle opening the way to a new formula for an administration of "national concord," including both Communist and "third force" elements.

Then following the failure of the spring offensive, the resumption of heavy bombing of the north, and the blockade of Haiphong, on September 11, 1972, three days after Le Duc Tho first mentioned it in Paris, the Provisional Revolutionary Government and Hanoi proposed a new plan. Dropping their previous insistence that Thieu must be eliminated before any agreement could be possible, they proposed to build on the "actual situation . . . [that] exists in South Vietnam, two administrations, two armies, and other political forces." Therefore, they stated the "Vietnam problem" could "be settled in two stages in accordance with the oft-expressed desire of the American side." In the first stage, there would be a cease-fire, an exchange of prisoners, and American withdrawal, and in the second, "the two South Vietnamese parties will settle together the internal matters of South Vietnam" with the creation of a "national council of national reconciliation and Concord of three equal segments." That council, already proposed the previous spring, would oversee the implementation of the agreement and the carrying out of "genuinely free and democratic general elections under international supervision" to decide "the political future of South Vietnam" and to organize the "reunification of Vietnam . . . step by step through peaceful means."[15]

In October, Washington responded with a refinement of its key concession, omitting to demand the withdrawal of northern troops from the south, although it continued to insist on a halt to "infiltration," the "self-determination" of the south, and on its right to continue to supply Saigon's needs. In the autumn of 1972, therefore, Hanoi dropped for the time being its insistence on the replacement of Thieu, while Washington promised to withdraw within sixty days without insisting on the withdrawal of what they estimated were up to 300,000 northern troops in or adjacent to South Vietnam.*

The breakthrough, however, was stalled by the same President Thieu whose presence Hanoi was now accepting for the time being. Kissinger spent five days in Saigon, October 18–23, to try to win Saigon's agreement, but was answered with the demand for up to

*Kissinger claimed that President Nixon first dropped insistence on the withdrawal of northern troops two years earlier, in October 1970, whereas Hanoi revived insistence on Thieu's ouster in the spring of 1975.

sixty-three changes in the proposed text. Two months later, on December 12, 1972, Thieu spelled out his objections to "illogical conditions" which amounted to "a disguised coalition government . . . of three equal segments" and the continued presence of northern troops, in violation of the fact that "South Vietnam and North Vietnam are two separate zones which must be temporarily considered as two separate states . . . ."

Originally scheduled for signing on October 22, Saigon's opposition forced continued delays despite Hanoi's partial publication four days later of the agreement, and Kissinger's remark, also on October 26, that "peace is at hand." President Nixon, however, was unwilling to force Saigon before the election of November 7, nor after it, since he overwhelmed "peace candidate" George McGovern with 60 percent of the vote—about the same margin by which in 1964 Lyndon Johnson had defeated "warmonger" Barry Goldwater.

Predictably, the impase deepened again with continued polemics by both sides, until the catharsis of the final American bombing offensive in late December.

BY DECEMBER 13, it again appeared that the negotiations, which had resumed November 20, were going nowhere, as each side charged obstructions and delays on the part of the other. President Nixon and Kissinger promptly decided on "something new" to bring Hanoi to its knees, with a "brief, but massive use of force" to get our "message through to Hanoi." Where he had already halted the bombing north of the twentieth parallel on October 23, in anticipation of a settlement, the president had simultaneously ordered massive shipments to Saigon of some one billion dollars worth of additional military hardware as a means of appeasing Thieu.

Then the "something new" for Hanoi was what a 1979 military history called the "most concentrated bomber attack in history," known as Linebacker II. Some 2,000 separate strikes between December 18 and December 23 dropped up to 40,000 tons* of bombs on the north, and reduced "to rubble" extensive sections of Hanoi, Haiphong, and other areas. Although according to different counts "only 1,300 to 2,200" civilians were killed—"surprisingly few con-

*Compared with the Hiroshima atomic bomb of 20,000 tons, and the 100,000 tons dropped around Khe Sanh in early 1968.

sidering the tonnage dropped," in part because of Hanoi's previous virtual evacuation of the city—new storms of protest at Washington's "war by tantrum" were all the more bitter, given the hopes that "peace was at hand" and the well-publicized destruction of residential areas and such non-military targets as the Bach Mai Hospital. Hanoi's principal industrial and military targets, factories, and power plants suffered still greater destruction. But the United States also sustained heavy losses, not only diplomatically with the international outcry over the bombings, but militarily, as some thirty-four aircraft, including fifteen B-52s, fell victim to the SAM missiles that rose to meet most of the 729 sorties flown by the giant bombers. Therefore, both sides were anxious to try again, and the president ordered a halt to the bombing on December 29, while Hanoi agreed to resume the talks the next day.

While the real purpose of this last huge outburst of American power may have been aimed, not so much at North Vietnam, as "to persuade South Vietnam to accept a truce," it is also true that the peace talks resumed on January 8, 1973, and reached tentative agreement the next day. January 9 also happened to be the president's sixtieth birthday, and according to Kissinger the new progress came after Hanoi accepted the insertion of a clause stating that "North and South Vietnam will respect the Demilitarized Zone," and agreed that neither Saigon nor the Provisional Revolutionary Government would have to sign the agreement, since Thieu refused to recognize his southern opponents.

In his memoirs, Kissinger wryly noted that this last feature gave the truce "the distinction of being the only document . . . in diplomatic history that does not mention the main parties," Saigon or the Communists. Because the Communists inserted repetition of the July 20, 1954, Geneva language that the seventeenth parallel is "only provisional and in no way constitutes a political or territorial boundary," however, critics soon charged that the only changes made from the September 1972 Communist proposals were "trivial" or "cosmetic." Still more serious were the charges, such as that made by, among others, former Assistant Secretary of Defense Paul Warnke. He stated to the BBC in the autumn of 1977 that Washington "could have ended up with a much better negotiated settlement back in 1968/69 than we finally got in 1973 . . . [as] there would have been the possibility of some sort of a political compromise in the South, but the longer the war went on, the weaker the political situation in the South became. So finally in 1973 there wasn't anything they had to bargain with. . . ."[16]

CRITICS, IN FACT, MIGHT QUESTION not only what the Christmas bombings, or the additional four years of war under the Nixon administration had changed, but indeed what ten years of large-scale warfare and the entire twenty years of American sponsorship of anti-Communist Saigon governments had changed. Kissinger, who moved from national security advisor to become secretary of state in the spring of 1973, argued that he and the president had wanted for Saigon "only a reasonable opportunity to participate in a political structure" that would guarantee the South Vietnamese people "the right to determine their own political future," and further that "but for the collapse of executive authority as a result of Watergate and congressional refusal to provide adequate aid to Saigon, I believe we would have succeeded."[17] However, the January 27 Agreement" differed little from the October 1972 draft, and not very much from the July 20, 1954, text.

The very first article of the 1973 agreement cited the "1954 Geneva Accords on Vietnam," which required that "the United States and all other countries respect the independence, sovereignty, unity and territorial integrity of Vietnam." Subsequent articles called for a cease-fire within twenty-four hours, for the United States to remove its mines from North Vietnamese waters (Article 2), and for the withdrawal of all American troops, including "military advisers . . . and technical . . . personnel," with an exchange of prisoners, within sixty days (Articles 5 and 8).

The 1954 Accords, in fact, were less demanding. Its Final Declaration (Clause 10) specified only that France should withdraw its troops "within periods which shall be fixed by agreement between the two parties . . . ," while like the 1973 Accords banning the introduction of any new foreign military personnel or bases. The three-state International Control Commission of the 1954 Accords (filled by Canada, India, and Poland) was to be superseded by a four-power International Commission of Control and Supervision, filled once more by capitalist Canada and Communist Poland, but with the introduction of another Communist state, Hungary, and with neutral Indonesia replacing India. Four-Power and Two-Power Joint Military Commissions, composed of the belligerents (the fourpower Commission including North Vietnam and the United States as well as Saigon and the Provisional Revolutionary Government) would work with the International Commission "in implementing . . . this Agreement . . . [and] enforcing the ceasefire . . ." (Articles 29–46 [1954] and 16–19 [1973]).

Where the 1954 Accords left vague the nature of the "civil administrations" that were to govern the two zones, thereby enabling Diem with U.S. support to block the 1956 "general elections which will bring about the unification of Vietnam" (Article 14), in the 1973 Accords the Communists tried to specify that the two South Vietnamese parties should consult "to set up a National Council of National Reconciliation and Concord of three equal segments to carry out "free and democratic general elections," and thereby ensure that the "South Vietnamese people shall decide themselves the political future" of the South (Articles 9 and 12).

The previous May 12, Le Duc Tho had explained that the "three segments" were "one belonging to the PRG-SVN, one belonging to the Saigon Government and one segment belonging to patriots . . . people who don't like the U.S., but who also may not support the PRG-SVN." Other articles of the 1973 Accords also recalled those of 1954 in calling for an end to "all hostile acts, terrorism, and reprisals," and to "ensure the democratic liberties" of freedom of speech, press, assembly, movement, politics, belief, etc. (Articles 3 and 11). And Article 20 stated the parties should "respect the 1954 Geneva Accords on Cambodia and the 1962 Geneva Accords on Laos," although Washington, not unnaturally, later explained that that could only come about when the Communists actually brought about a cease-fire in the two countries.

THE MOST OMINOUS PARALLEL between the 1973 and 1954 Accords, however, was their aftermath, which in both cases made a mockery of the promised "cessation of the war."

The Communists had no intention of honoring the provision for "democratic freedoms," at least in any way acceptable to Washington, but neither did the Thieu government have any intention to form a National Council of Reconciliation and Concord including Communists and patriots. And where in 1954 Diem had refused to sign the Accords, in 1973, as intended, only the representatives of Hanoi and Washington did so. The day after the signing, of January 28, Hanoi quoted Thieu as saying, "A ceasefire in place, means to maintain the status quo . . . . If a Communist . . . has no identity card . . . blow his brains out on the spot. . . ." For their part, the southern Communist leadership had already on January 19 interpreted the imminent agreement as "a glorious victory of our people over the most ferocious imperialists of our time," which simply "deprived the puppets of the support of American troops. . . ."[18]

The war, therefore, very much continued. While U.S. aircraft stopped their operations in South Vietnam on January 27, in Laos in April and finally in Cambodia in August, the almost 2,000 planes of the Saigon air force continued to pound away, and the ground war raged on virtually unabated in all three countries of Indochina. Where its death toll of 56,146 had already made the Vietnam war America's third most costly, the far higher Indochinese casualties continued. For the South Vietnamese, indeed, they were higher in 1974 than in the year of the Tet offensive of 1968! And although the last of 24,000 U.S. soldiers left within the agreed sixty days, at least another 8,500 diplomats, military, and CIA "representatives" remained in the country, and strong naval and air forces offshore and in Thailand. Furthermore, such provisions as that (Article 6) requiring the "dismantlement of all military bases in South Vietnam of the United States . . ." was interpreted as not including "installations such as Cam Ranh Bay and Than Son Nhut" since they had already been "transferred to the GVN or to the U.S. Embassy for civilian use prior to the conclusion of the Agreement." The State Department, in February, admitted that "we can expect a dispute on this issue."

Therefore, even for the United States, although increasingly preoccupied with the Watergate scandal (until August, 1974, when President Nixon resigned and was succeeded by his vice-president, Gerald Ford), Vietnam, Laos, and in 1973 especially Cambodia, remained very burning issues. In late June, an increasingly angry Congress voted to end all "military operations in and over Indochina," but presidential vetoes stalled its application for Cambodia until August, while the president declared his intention to "continue to recognize the Government of the Republic of Vietnam as the sole, legitimate government" of the south. The president, on January 5, had already promised to "respond with full force should the settlement be violated by North Vietnam," and in March threatened renewed bombing of the north, as subsequently did Secretary of Defense Schlesinger and other officials.

The Accords (Article 21) also promised the United States would make a "contribution to heal the wounds of war" and the president then wrote Premier Pham Van Dong in Hanoi, on February 1, that in "principle" he would supply some 3.25 billion dollars for "postwar reconstruction," "without any political conditions, . . ." but as "appropriate." That of course was a "carrot" to go with the threatened renewal of the "stick" if deemed necessary, but events would far outpace Washington's reduced powers to influence the outcome of the Vietnamese Revolution.

Predictably the Communists preferred to rely on their own energies and "stick" rather than on diplomatic promises of the type they felt had been repeatedly violated for more than twenty years. In the January 19, 1973, COSVN directive, for "guidance in the initial period of a political settlement and cease fire," the Communist leadership declared their intention

> of pushing back the enemy step by step . . . bringing into play the masses' political violence . . . [and] political movement . . . with the mission of achieving the national democratic revolution in the South . . . [and] socialism in the North as a step toward the unification of our country . . . . [This meant efforts] to disintegrate . . . the puppet army and government, take over control of the rural area, seize power at the base level: simultaneously to build and develop our political and armed forces . . . revolutionary administration . . . and . . . smash all enemy schemes to sabotage the Agreement, prevent large scale conflicts, maintain peace, hold general elections . . . .

It is obvious the Communists had every intention to press their struggle "to bring the South Vietnam Revolution toward the fulfillment of basic objectives," but as in the five years before their escalation of the war against Diem, the Communists at first stressed political struggle over armed struggle, recognizing they would have to remain primarily under cover. The January 19 directive continued: "We must closely combine political struggle with armed struggle and legalistic struggle, using political struggle as the base, armed struggle as support . . . [and] combine the overt form of organization with the semi-overt and clandestine forms of organization, using the clandestine form as a base . . . ."[19] Washington estimated Communist forces in the south in March 1973 at 252,000, of whom 142,000 were believed to be northern troops, and later in the year at about 230,000 including 170,000 northerners and 60,000 Viet Cong regulars and guerillas. Communist control of territory and population supposedly was reduced to 20 and 12 percent respectively, and Communist sources later acknowledged that their front-line troops in the south were reduced to under 100,000 after the January Accords.

GIVEN THE INTRANSIGENCE OF THE TWO SIDES, the key problems after the signing of the January 27 agreements were the political question of the organization and nature of the National Council of "three equal segments" and the military-political question of the desire of both sides to increase their control over contested areas so as to approach the 80 to 90 percent figure both sides had often claimed.

Regarding the political question, Thieu had already in October called the question of "three components . . . an absurd formula" and "a low trick" forced on his government. In attempts to control the "third force," which he obviously feared would side more with the Communists than with him, the government issued a decree requiring all political parties to prove by March 27, 1973, that they had at least 5 percent support in at least one-quarter of the country, thereby, according to Hanoi, eliminating even the venerable VNQDD and Dai Viet, and all but four of the twenty-eight political parties previously in existence. The previous autumn, new requirements, which some Western journalists also charged amounted to censorship, similarly forced the closing of up to half the country's journals and newspapers. The Communists charged further that in August 1972 the government restored Diem's 1956 replacement of elected village and hamlet chiefs with appointed officials, and forcibly displaced another million and a half people from their homes in 1973–1974.

Worse still, instead of the release of imprisoned "Vietnamese civilian personnel . . ." as required by Article 8 of the Accords, the Saigon government was charged by various sources with arresting another 50,000 or 80,000, which more than offset the release of about 5,000 others, to bring the total of political prisoners to some 200,000 or more according to most observers. On January 27, 1973, Thieu was quoted as admitting, "If we allow things to slide, the population may vote Communist as they know how to make propaganda," and on October 12, 1973, as stating "Anyone with enough courage to proclaim himself a neutralist or pro-Communist will not survive five minutes." The number of police increased further from 120,000 to 150,000 (there had been 19,000 in 1963), and South Vietnam became according to leftists "the archetype of neocolonial," sub-Fascist, police state. Up to one in ten members of the population were said to be in the government's bureaucratic, military, or police forces.[20]

Moreover, as direct United States aid to Saigon fell from 2.27 billion dollars in 1973, to 1.01 billion in 1974, and 700 million in 1975, and an estimated 250,000 or 300,000 jobs servicing American troops disappeared, inflation climbed to over 90 percent and unemployment rose far higher than the minimum estimate of 12 percent. As a result, the government was forced to impose new taxes, to again devalue the piastre,* and to undertake other economic measures that naturally further increased popular resentment. There were also important reorganizations of high levels of the government and army, amounting to far-reaching purges of potential Thieu opponents. And in the summer of 1974 the rampant corruption led to a Catholic-sponsored "people's anticorruption movement" under Father Tran Huu Thanh and other formerly progovernment leaders. A few other priests, notably Father Chan Tin, had taken even more radical positions, sometimes in line with those of the NLF since the late 1960s.

The military problems were still less controllable, as both sides charged thousands of "encroachments," and as first the government and then the Communists expanded their large-scale assaults on enemy areas. At the very time of the signing of the Accords, government troops attacked Cua Viet and other areas of the northern province of Quang Tri, lost to the Communists in the 1972 offensives. Then, in subsequent months, the Communists charged large-scale government attacks, most notably in parts of Quang Nam and Quang Ngai provinces on the central coast, in My Tho, Chuong Thien, and other areas of the southern delta, in the Central Highlands, Iron Triangle, and other areas north and west of Saigon. After the January 1973 Accords, they admitted their firm control had been reduced to about one-fifth of the south, and their front-line forces to some 25,000 southern and 50,000 northern troops, far lower than other estimates. But they remained confident of victory and claimed to expect the majority of the population to side with them in the developing showdown.

On October 14, 1973, the Communist leadership, as it had in 1959 against Diem, decided to strike back in self-defense, and spoke

---

*From 35 to the dollar in 1955, the piastre declined to 560 to the dollar in 1974 and higher still on the flourishing black market.

of "thirty-one million violations" by Saigon. Attacks followed on Bien Hoa and Quang Ngai air bases, and elsewhere. At the same time Communist forces went on the offensive in Laos, and the situation continued to deterioriate in Cambodia with Washington demanding that Hanoi stop its attacks throughout the peninsula, but conveniently failing to mention Saigon's own violations and total opposition to the formation of the "national council" and "third force."

The Communists on the contrary decided to go for their final victory. Thieu's manifest failure to abide by the 1973 Accords, the mounting anger and impatience of southern revolutionaries, and the new opportunity afforded by Washington's withdrawal and preoccupation with the Watergate crisis, led Hanoi and COSVN in early 1974 to step up preparations for the offensive that would carry them to final victory a year later, and a full year earlier than expected. These developments, together with the first important Communist victory in the lowlands since the previous January's Accords (at Thuong Duc, west of Da Nang), and the resignation of President Nixon, both in August 1974, led the Party to predict victory through "revolutionary violence," regardless of future events.

It was all over by the end of April 1975, the dramatic climax to the fifty-year Communist struggle for power in Vietnam.

CHAPTER ELEVEN

The Wheels of History

HISTORY, OF COURSE, DID NOT STOP with the Communist conquest of South Vietnam and Cambodia in the spring of 1975, and of Laos by the end of the year.

First of all, the north and the south moved toward the united Vietnam fought for so long and so bitterly. The process was speeded up by northern hardliners, who "drunk with victory, wanted to swallow the South at once," in the words of former PRG Minister of Justice Truong Nhu Tang, who sought refuge in France in the spring of 1980. But it also followed Washington's veto of the applications of both "new Vietnams"—the Democratic Republic of the north and the Provisional Revolutionary Government of the south—to enter the United Nations in the autumn of 1975. Without such external support for the south, the National Assembly, elected in April 1976, was able more easily to reunify the country, and on July 2 of that year renamed it the Socialist Republic of Vietnam (SRV).

At the same time, ancient animosities with neighbors tiny Kampuchea to the southwest and huge China to the northeast resurfaced to replace the struggles against distant France and America as Vietnam's dominant foreign-policy concerns. Still more fundamental questions of poverty, even starvation for the devastated country, and of the conflict between liberty and discipline, if not dictatorship, superseded the new Indochina wars as the country's gravest preoccupations.

IT WAS AS IF THE COMMUNIST VICTORIES in Indochina had brought history full circle. Over five centuries before, the Vietnamese replaced the Khmers as the dominant people of the peninsula (with the Thai to the West) and all lived under the shadow of Imperial China. Only now, China too had a potentially more dangerous neighbor to its north than even the formidable Huns, Turks, Mongols, and Manchus of previous centuries. And in the last half of the twentieth century, tensions between distant America and Russia, not only greatly shaped complex relations with China, but as well, many of the events in Vietnam, Kampuchea, and Laos.

In Indochina itself, ancient memories—Vietnam's expansion southward after the eleventh century at the expense of the Khmer and other peoples—and new problems—differing strategies toward the Sihanouk government in the 1960s, border and refugee disputes, pressures from the Sino-Soviet split, and personal hostilities arising from the extremist policies of the Khmer Rouge leaders—all precipitated mounting hostility between Vietnam and Kampuchea.

Border clashes between the two newly Communist countries—and between Vietnam and China as well—broke out almost immediately after the victories of 1975. Then after a year of relative calm, Cambodian attacks on western Vietnamese provinces from March 1977 onwards produced "a full-scale border war." What the Vietnamese called "the most monstrous genocide ever" also increased in tempo, and led to the deaths apparently of over a million of Kampuchea's population, previously estimated at over seven million. Another half million may have died before 1975.

In 1978, Vietnam decided to use force to back a dissident Khmer Rouge military officer, Heng Samrin, to change this situation. He had participated in a particularly noteworthy revolt against the Pol Pot government in May 1978 and founded the National United Front for the salvation of Cambodia, on December 2. On Christmas Day, over 100,000 Vietnamese troops, nominally supporting Heng Samrin's 10,000 Khmer rebels, invaded Kampuchea, taking the capital of Phnom Penh on January 7, 1979.

Pockets of resistance, mostly along the western border with Thailand, continued into the 1980s, however, and China, the United States, Thailand, and other countries called the invasion an outright "Vietnamese colonialist conquest." They condemned also the twenty-five-year Treaty of Friendship and Cooperation that Hanoi reportedly forced on Laos in July 1977, and demanded the withdrawal of Vietnamese troops from both countries, with the dismantling of such a Hanoi-dominated Indochina Federation. Hanoi, by contrast, maintained that it had acted in good faith and would withdraw its troops from both countries as soon as genuine peace could be established. In Kampuchea, it argued, it had simply supported Heng Samrin, Pen Sovan, and others to end a universally deplored "genocide and war of aggression against Vietnam." It denied "hegemonist" designs over any Indochina Federation and advanced demands rather for a "unity bloc" of the three Indochinese peoples, protected by a demilitarized zone along the Thai border.[1]

It is clear that the Hanoi-Moscow-Peking "great power triangle" greatly shaped both the events in Indochina after 1975, and their interpretation. Despite the death of Mao Zedong in September 1976, hostility between China and Russia continued unabated. And even though China progressively abandoned Maoist policies at home, its anti-Soviet policy dictated its support of the arch-leftist regime of Pol Pot–Ieng Sary against Vietnam, since Vietnam allied ever more closely with the Soviet Union, the only strong country willing to support it. In June 1978, Vietnam joined the Soviet economic bloc, Council for Mutual Economic Assistance (Comecon) and in November 1978 signed its own twenty-five-year Treaty of Friendship and Cooperation with Moscow.

That was too much for China. In retaliation for Vietnam's joining Comecon, in June China had withdrawn its remaining advisers from Vietnam,* and cut off aid estimated the year before at $300 million—again a curious parallel with earlier history, namely, the sudden Russian cut-off of aid to China in August 1960 so bitterly protested by China in ensuing polemics. And Vietnam miscalculated if it hoped that its treaty with Russia would restrain or offset China. On the contrary, almost immediately after Vietnam's invasion of Kampuchea, Peking invaded Vietnam, in turn, speaking of giving a "lesson" to the former vassal state of Imperial China, but seeming rather more to signal a progression of the big fish trying to eat the smaller.

On February 17, 1979, over 100,000 Chinese troops, backed by several times that many (Hanoi says 600,000) attacked the same northern border areas that had seen such heavy fighting between the Viet Minh and the French thirty years previously. Then honor-

---

*In 1980, there remained an estimated 5,000–8,000 Russian soldiers and "advisers" in Vietnam.

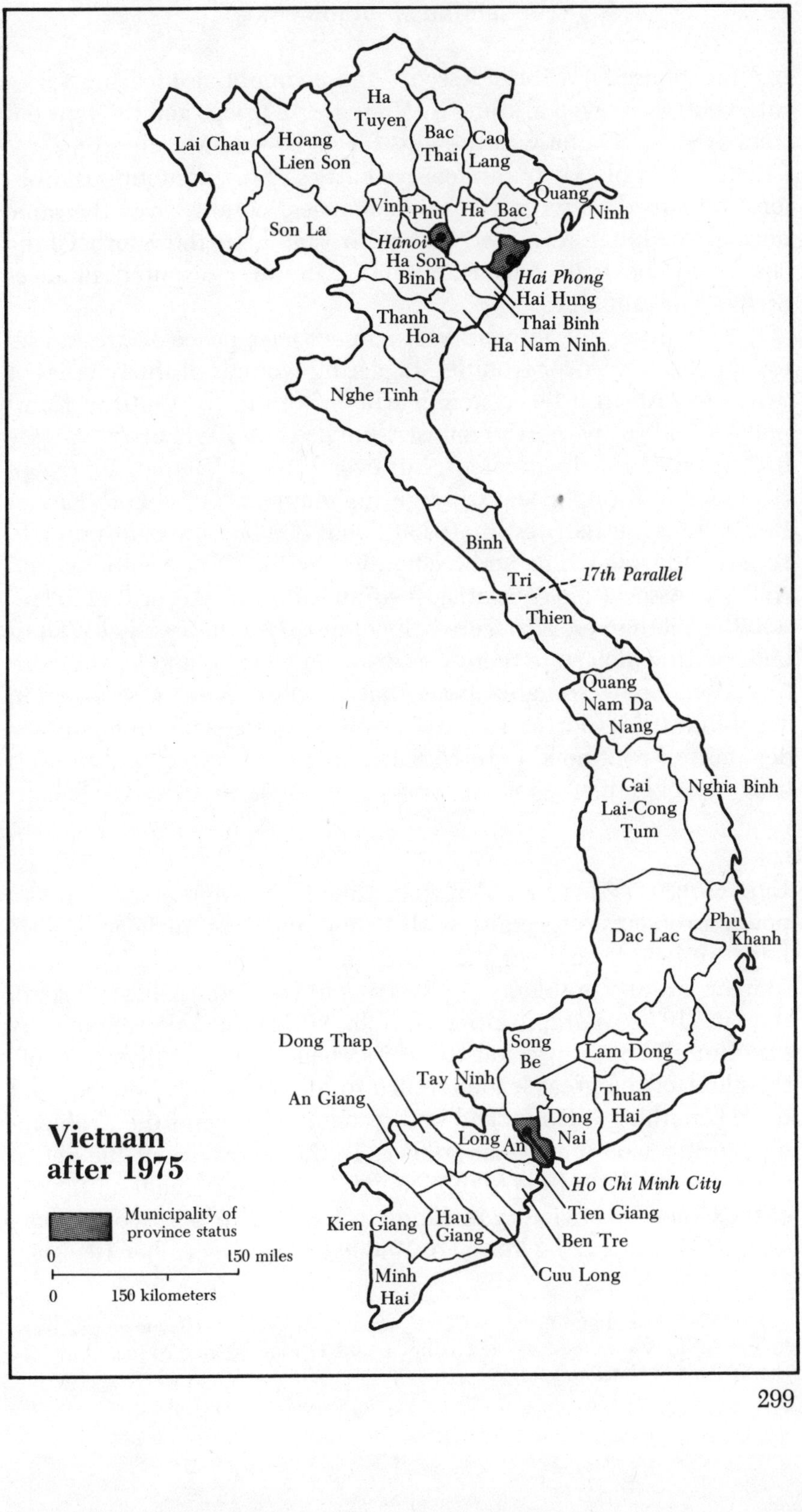
Lai Chau
Hoang Lien Son
Ha Tuyen
Bac Thai
Cao Lang
Quang Ninh
Vinh Phu
Ha Bac
Son La
Hanoi
Ha Son Binh
Hai Phong
Hai Hung
Thai Binh
Thanh Hoa
Ha Nam Ninh
Nghe Tinh
Binh
Tri
17th Parallel
Thien
Quang Nam Da Nang
Gai Lai-Cong Tum
Nghia Binh
Dac Lac
Phu Khanh
Dong Thap
Song Be
Lam Dong
Tay Ninh
An Giang
Thuan Hai
Dong Nai
Long An
Ho Chi Minh City
Tien Giang
Kien Giang
Hau Giang
Ben Tre
Cuu Long
Minh Hai
Vietnam after 1975
Municipality of province status
0
150 miles
0
150 kilometers

ing its promises of a "brief lesson," and no doubt also fearing Soviet intervention, as well as stung by Vietnamese troops and the international outcry, China withdrew its forces by mid-March after close to a month of bloody but indecisive battles.[2] Still, contentious problems remained between the two countries, notably over the same northern frontier, disputed claims to islands in the South China Sea,* and above all, over Kampuchea and over disputed alliances between distant allies.

Therefore, not only did Vietnam not have peace or substantial foreign aid to recover from its staggering wounds of thirty years of war, but instead it faced new warfare, both in the south in Kampuchea and to the north against China. As of 1981, open warfare had subsided for the moment, but over 100,000 Vietnamese troops remained in Kampuchea, still fighting remnants of Pol Pot's Khmer Rouge forces, usually estimated at about 30,000, and continuing to receive aid from China and recognition by the United Nations, and ASEAN (Association of Southeast Asian Nations). According to Hanoi, the Vietnamese also were helped directly or indirectly by Thailand, with which state there was growing tension, and by those international relief organizations that supplied Khmer refugees in Thailand. In the north, a state of hostility, marked by frequent border clashes, continued to force a diversion of resources and showed little sign of ending so long as China and Russia continued to feud.

EVEN MORE DIFFICULT FOR VIETNAM than its severe postwar foreign-policy problems, especially with China and Kampuchea, and related to them because of the diversion of economic and human resources, are the problems of poverty and freedom. A bitter joke of the late 1970s, paraphrasing Ho Chi Minh's famous rallying cry ("Nothing is more precious than independence and liberty") had the ghost of the great leader return to his country to bewail, "but there is nothing." Ho indeed had recognized some of the problems his country would continue to face. In the aftermath of the defeat of France, and recalling Mao Zedong's famous statement on the eve of the Communist victory in China in 1949, "Our past work is only the first step in a Long March of 10,000 Li," on December 19, 1954,

---

*The Paracel and Spratley Islands are east of Hue and Saigon respectively, known to the Vietnamese as the Hoang Sa and Truong Sa, and to the Chinese as the Xi Sha and Nan Sha Islands.

Ho had declared: "We must realize that, like the armed struggle waged during the resistance, the political struggle to be conducted in peacetime will be long and hard, and even more arduous and complex . . . [if we are to have a chance of] achieving national reunification, and bringing independence and democracy to all our country."

Indeed, but it takes considerable imagination to describe a more difficult scenario than that faced after 1975 by Vietnam, a small country, ravaged by thirty years of war, and estimated to have at that time a per capita income of $160.

In the north, the situation was described by a representative of the United Nations High Commission for Refugees, Alexander Casella, who had spent eighteen months in the country in 1976–1977. He wrote in early 1978:

> The North Vietnam that emerged from the war after the signing of Paris agreements was a nation with its morale and social structure intact, but with a shattered economy. There was not a bridge, not a single industry, unrelated as it might have been to the war effort, that had not been destroyed. Agricultural production had been destroyed by cratering, and the widespread destruction of electrical plants had forced the authorities to close down many of the electrical irrigation pumps and resort to manual irrigation. Thus by the spring of 1973, North Vietnam had sunk back to the production level of 1955 [after the French war].[4]

The south in some ways was still worse off. The vast expenditures of the United States left considerable merchandise, transportation, and economic infrastructure, but the destruction of the countryside was appalling. According to the Communists, 9,000 of the 15,000 hamlets of the south had suffered serious damage, while most of the some 10 million hectares of land and 5 million hectares of forest that had been wholly or partially destroyed were located in the south. That region—which had been America's ally!—also absorbed most of the over 1.7 million deaths in the American war (most of the half million deaths of the French war were in the North); and, as well, most of the approximately 26 million bomb craters and an estimated 150 to 300,000 tons of unexploded ordinance left in 1975.[5] In addition to the problems of dealing with the dislocations of some 12 million refugees of the previous decade, Hanoi charges there were over 3 million unemployed in the south after the defeat of the anti-Communists, including over 1 million soldiers and 300,000 civil servants and police, some 600,000 prostitutes, 1 million drug addicts, 1 million victims of tuberculosis, 800,000 orphans, and tens of thousands of gangsters and delinquents. There were also reports of continuing, widespread corruption. Moreover, the country faced severe drought in 1977 and devastating floods in 1978 and 1979, and despite economic and currency reforms, primarily because of lack of production and aid, prices swiftly rose tenfold again after early 1975. If some of these figures are exaggerated, their staggering impact can be imagined if one recalls the the south of Vietnam is one-tenth as populous as the United States and less than one-hundredth as rich!

Soviet bloc aid, climbing from an estimated $900 million in 1977 to $1.5 billion in 1979 could not begin to deal with problems of such magnitude. Nor for that matter would the more than $3.2 billion in reparations Hanoi claimed Washington had promised in 1973, or the $300 million in annual aid that China cut off in 1978. According to an estimate of early 1977, "despite [America's] twenty-three billion in [economic] aid poured into South Vietnam between 1950 and 1974," the country remained "among the twenty-five poorest nations on earth."

Yet astonishingly, and surely one of the most troubling statistics that can be advanced to show the alarming nature of the worldwide population explosion, the Vietnamese population more than doubled, from the 20 million of 1936 to 52,741,766 in 1979, despite the ravages of almost continuous warfare, the loss of over 2 million lives, and continuous grinding poverty. Evidently, the very high natural growth rate of over 3 percent more than offset the horrendous losses of the war, and later of refugees, since at a 2 percent rate of growth, the population doubles every generation. Since 1975 the country's population has been increasing at a million souls a year, and in 1980 was said to be growing at 2.6 percent.[6]

GIVEN THE MENACE AND PARTIAL ACTUALITY of a Third Indochina War in the late 1970s, the lack of substantial foreign aid, the scope and force of the poverty and war damage afflicting the small, poor country, and the nature of the Communist Revolution, it is not surprising that a terrible refugee problem arose after 1975.

Accompanying the U.S. withdrawal and subsequent Communist victory, some 123,000 Vietnamese left the country in 1975, and by late 1980 close to another three-quarters of a million did so. Over 300,000 arrived in other countries by sea (the "Boat People") and another 250,000 fled overland into China. In addition, over several hundred thousand fled both Kampuchea and Laos, mostly into Thailand, while according to Hanoi, another 321,400 (125,600 Khmers, 25,000 ethnic Chinese, and 170,300 Vietnamese) took refuge in Vietnam from the Khmer Rouge terror. An additional quarter of a million may have died at sea. Therefore, in all, over 1.5 million people fled the three new Communist countries of Indochina between 1975 and 1980, among the most tragic groups of an estimated 12.6 million refugees worldwide as of early 1981.[7]

Close to two-thirds of the most publicized of refugees, the Boat People of 1978 and after, and almost all of those who fled overland to China (until the border closing in July 1978), were overseas Chinese (*hua chiao*, called simply Hoa by the Vietnamese), and their plight was an important factor in the deteriorating relations between Vietnam and China. The 300,000 Chinese living in the north (many for generations) had been urged by Peking in 1955 to take Vietnamese citizenship, but in the south, most of the approximately 1.2 million Hoa (especially in the Chinese city of Cholon) resisted the efforts of Diem and subsequent governments to enforce a similar solution.

The developing polemics between Hanoi and Peking once more present a totally different interpretation of what happened next. According to China, a hostile "neo-Fascist" government under Le Duan undertook systematic repressions of the Hoa, expelling them outright from the north overland until July 1978 and then by sea mostly to Hong Kong after the February 1979 Chinese invasion. In the south, according to Peking, blatant discrimination against the Hoa produced the mass exodus, with the relatively richer refugees there forced to pay an average $2,700 in gold (half that for children) for the dangerous privilege of leaving the country by sea, to the profit of both middlemen and the government.

According to Hanoi, Peking deliberately provoked the exodus of the Hoa by false promises of the advantages of coming to China, and especially by urging their kin to flee a country that would regard them as a potential fifth column when caught up in an inevitable war between the two countries. And indeed after the Chinese invasion of February 17, 1979, Hanoi moved from relatively passive acquiescence in the departure of the refugees, to forcing the Hoa to choose between emigration and transfer to difficult "New Economic Zones." In the south, especially critical was an economic control law of March 1978, aiming to break what Hanoi said was the Hoa's monopoly of up to 80 percent of the economy in parts of the south. Already in late 1975, over 30,000 private firms were abolished and a campaign launched against the "compradore bourgeoisie" who had cooperated most with the United States. Another factor was the effort to collectivize southern agriculture, begun in 1977, although only 17.8 percent (up to 85 percent in some central areas) complete overall by 1980.

Whatever the truths of the arguments over the refugees, the upheavals of the Communist "Revolution from Above," the devastating poverty of the country, the virtually universal pattern of hostility between overseas Chinese ("the Jews of Asia") and native populations of Southeast Asia, and the actuality and threats of new wars, all seem more than sufficient explanations for the refugee exodus. But hardly a cure, and the terrible lot of the Indochina refugees has horrified the world. Probably more than 10 percent never survived their flight, especially among those who left by sea, often in rickety boats to face storms, pirates, and hostile receptions over thousands of miles. And for those who survived, there were countless traumas, culminating in desperate searches for homes and jobs.

BEYOND THE FRIGHTFUL ECONOMIC PROBLEMS of the region, the flight of more than one million new refugees from the three countries of Indochina raises the question of "freedom," the sole issue on which France and the United States might have legitimately sought to justify their wars—that is, if they had been able to offer truly "free" alternatives, which they certainly did not.

Ho Chi Minh had also shown his awareness of the problem of human rights, at least in propaganda confrontations. On December 18, 1959, he stated:

> The capitalists often circulate the slander that our socialist regime does not respect the personal interests of the citizen. But in reality only our regime really serves the interests of the people, first and foremost the working people, safeguards all interests of the people and develops democracy to enable the people to take effective part in the management of the State [therefore our draft-amended Constitution gives] . . .
> the right to work
> the right to rest
> the right to study
> the right to personal liberty

freedoms of opinion, of the press, of assembly, of association,
the right to hold demonstrations
freedom of religious belief, to adhere or not to adhere to a religion
the right to elect and stand for election. . . .[8]

Twenty years later, the Party still claimed to advocate "humanitarian policies and respect for the rights of man," stressing that it had not carried out the feared "blood bath," but instead "treated with clemency not only the Vietnamese who collaborated with the enemy, but also military prisoners. . . ." And it claimed with considerable reason that the problem of the refugees was primarily due to the special history and poverty of the country, and that it was eager to work in good faith with the United Nations and other agencies and countries to try to solve the refugee crisis.

The Communists and their enemies, of course, have a radically different understanding of the concepts of "democracy" and "freedom"—to do what one wishes as guaranteed by elected officials, or only what one "should" as defined by the Party, representing the working class. In 1949, in his "On the People's Democratic Dictatorship," Mao Zedong gave a classic Communist statement of the response to the accusation, "You are dictatorial." He replied: "My dear sirs, you are right, that is just what we are. All the experience the Chinese people have accumulated through several decades teaches us to enforce the people's democratic dictatorship, that is, to deprive the reactionaries of the right to speak and let the people alone have that right. . . ."[9]

Non-Communists respond in turn that such thinking leads to the totalitarianism of those who, without constitutional controls, "define the people and their enemies" according to their needs and whims, rather than on principle. They respond that most of the poor as well as the rich want the liberty to decide where they live, what they work at, who governs them, and so forth, and that the many poor refugees prove that. If the majority of those who flee are relatively well off, and with ties direct or indirect with the old regime, many others nonetheless were poor and/or were staunch opponents of the old regime, often with prison records to prove it.

Obviously the suffering, and the arguments as to its causes, will continue. For, as in all great revolutions, the violence and intensity of radical change in Vietnam has hurt many as well as benefitted many others. As Ho Chi Minh and Mao Zedong stated, in the final analysis it depends on who you are, especially on whether you are poor or rich. But the very strengths of the Vietnamese Communist movement, as of the Chinese, above all its high degree of ideological commitment and organization, have exacerbated both extremes—of the benefits and hurt of revolutionary change. And no one, perhaps least of all the Soviet Communist mentors of Vietnam, has been able to solve the problems of bureaucratization for the administration of revolutionary change.

For post-1975 Vietnam, the most concrete aspect of the "freedom" question, for which some documentation is available, is the problem of the "reeducation" of their former enemies, and the postwar "settling of accounts." Hanoi and its defenders claim that, considering what they might have done to the approximately 1.5 million soldiers and civil servants of the Thieu government, they have been remarkably lenient. Athough many of these people, and many others who were not suporters of Diem and Thieu, unquestionably have suffered greatly, Hanoi's arguments on this point seem well taken, at least in comparison with what happened in Kampuchea and also in other comparably intense revolutions and wars, for example, in France after 1789 and 1940, Russia after 1917, and China after 1949.

In December 1979, Hanoi told Amnesty International it retained in detention some 26,000 of about one million people it had subjected to reeducation after 1975, but that as the term implied, reeducation was primarily a mental rather than physical forcing of the recognition of past sins and commitment to the new order. Again there is a huge gap in information and interpretation, and enemies of the Communists charge that the regime maintained through the 1970s up to 700,000 in forced labor and detention as severe or worse than that of previous governments in the south. Arrests included many former anti-Thieu activists, and, among others, Buddhist leader Thich Thien Minh, lawyer Tran Van Tuyen, and intellectual leader Ho Huu Tuong, who all died in Communist-run prisons.

There is also the question of plans to move up to ten million Vietnamese to underdeveloped areas of the country and into some 500 New Economic Zones, mostly in the south, including some in areas still dangerous because of unexploded bombs buried in the fields. The population of Ho Chi Minh Ville (still popularly called Saigon), for example, has been reduced from some four million to about three million people through the refugee outflow and transfers to the countryside. Some have left voluntarily, especially those able to quit the shanty towns for their former villages, but many others understandably are reluctant to trade the city comforts they know for an unknown life in rural areas.

There has, therefore, been considerable reaction to all the poverty, hardship, and demands for continuing sacrifice, and predictably, many Vietnamese have blamed their problems on the Communist dictatorship. Religious groups, including Buddhists, Catholics, and Hoa Hao and Cao Dai, reportedly resumed their opposition to the government almost immediately. A former monk of the An Quang pagoda in Saigon, Thich Tue Quang, who fled the country in June 1979, explained, "Under Thieu, we were only protesting against corruption. Now under Communism, we cannot exist at all." There were said to be new Buddhist immolations by fire in 1976 to protest persecutions, and a Buddhist refugee to France, Thich Tue Minh reported in early 1980, that even Madame Nguyen Thi Dinh's Ben Tre province, which "was one of the most fiercely opposed to the Thieu regime, has become one of the most anti-Communist provinces." There also have been reports of continuing small outbreaks of armed revolts against the Communists, especially in mountainous and minority regions, where some undoubtedly receive active Chinese, if not U.S., encouragement.

Despite much continuing opposition to the Vietnamese Communists, it also seems certain that many others would agree with Saigon journalist Ly Quy Chung who, on July 18, 1979, stated: "In a hundred years, I think [the current] government is the only government that has done a lot for the country of Vietnam. And we have also seen that socialism is something which serves the people the most, and that brings the most equality for the people in general. . . ."[10]

IT WILL TAKE MANY YEARS for the historical perspective to judge the conflicting interpretations of the continuing problems of Vietnam, both at home and abroad.

But this has been a book primarily about the Vietnamese Revolution "from below," climaxed by the Communist conquest of the south in 1975. These further details and observations about the Revolution "from above," and the hostilities with Kampuchea and China, are meant only to mention in passing events that have continued to dominate the world's headlines out of all proportion to the size of the countries of Indochina. By comparison with what Ho Chi Minh, just before his death, called the "great honor of being a small country, which through heroic struggle, has defeated France and the United States,"[11] more recent events must necessarily be left for the future to judge.

Two final sections are in order, however; first, some final commentary about the United States, the war, and postwar Vietnam, and some additional information on the surviving Communist leaders who led the remarkable Vietnamese revolutionary wars.

It seems as difficult at the end of this book as it was in the preface to understand what Bruce Grant's recent study of the refugee problem calls America's "blind spot" about Vietnam. Regarding earlier history, even if one assumes the desirability of Washington's commitment to try to stop the Communist takeover of the south, it was almost as if for twenty years after 1950 the United States proceeded in exactly the wrong way. It failed to enforce necessary reforms with Diem, then used overwhelming military force, and only later instituted reforms that it failed to protect, in exact contrast to the Communists, who for decades used commitment to basic reforms to build their mostly village-level infrastructure, and then based on that, military forces charged with protecting that infrastructure. First a program for reform, then war, clearly made more sense than the reverse.

By the early 1970s, the Saigon government and its U.S. backers had partially halted the growth of Communist power in the south, but then could not protect their gains given predictable trends in American and world politics. One can imagine, if with difficulty, fighting for forty years with almost daily risk of death, as did people like Madame Nguyen Thi Dinh and her fellow revolutionaries, but only if one assumes they were fighting for tangible gains among their own people.

Given the lack of historical legitimacy of their enemies after the 1940s, it took a country as rich and powerful as the United States dealing with a country as small and poor as Vietnam to even consider trying to reverse a comparable situation. And understandably by the 1970s, after a decade of its longest war, America, 12,000 miles distant and increasingly if still only partially aware of Vietnamese realities, decided to scale down its efforts, at the very time that Hanoi decided to use its own growing military force to procure final victory. The northern invasion of the south, simplistically deplored by Washington in the early 1960s, became a self-fulfilling reality in 1972 and 1975.

To argue, as does a 1979 book by Leslie Gelb and Richard Betts, that the Vietnam war was successful from Washington's point of view, in that it stalled the Communist victory in the south for twenty years, until U.S. public opinion and the Congress could accept such an outcome, seems a bizarre justification of a war costing close to two million lives and uprooting ten million refugees.[12] One of Ho Chi Minh's early analogies seems more appropriate. After the escalation of 1965, he likened the United States to a fox who sought to escape from the trap imprisoning his hind feet (South Vietnam), by lunging forward (into North Vietnam) only to have his front paws caught in a new trap. He might equally have cited a Vietnamese fable that recounted how "the rabbit bests the tiger," by tricking it to stick its tail in a bee hive, only to have "the bees . . . rush angrily out and sting the tiger painfully all over his body." All the more so, since the "year of the tiger," according to the traditional Chinese-Vietnamese animal zodiac, ended on February 11, 1975, giving way precisely to the "year of the rabbit," also sometimes called "the year of the cat."[13]

Nor did Washington come to terms with the Communist victory in Vietnam for many years after 1975, even if as before, that was determined more by newly deteriorating relations with Russia than by the Vietnamese revolution itself—and no doubt, as well, by hurt pride at America's first defeat in a foreign war. It is a revealing irony that the "best years of detente" between Washington and Moscow came precisely in the last years of the Vietnam war. After all, in the year when President Richard Nixon opened the way to normal relations with China by a visit to Peking in February 1972 and advanced "detente" with a visit to Moscow in late May, the United States was also exploding 1,905,424 tons of bombs and munitions against the Communists of Vietnam! Hanoi, understandably, later termed their reception of the American leader at such a time, "a betrayal."

In 1977 and 1978, Vietnam and the United States apparently came close to the restoration of normal relations, as newly elected President Jimmy Carter expressed his desire to improve relations, admitting in May 1977, "We fought fire with fire, never thinking that fire is better fought with water."[14] In September, the United States declined to use its veto, as it had in 1975 and 1976, and the united Socialist Republic of Vietnam entered the United Nations. Hanoi for its part, recognizing some realities of American politics, dropped its demands for war reparations and made new efforts to trace the remains of over 1000 Americans still missing from the war.

But the developing refugee and Kampuchean crises, rising tensions with the Soviet Union, and Chinese pressures, all forced not only further delay in Washington's recognition of Hanoi, but new hostile incidents. In November 1978, at the time of Hanoi's Treaty of Friendship with the Soviet Union, Washington suspended its own negotiations with Hanoi, and announced its recognition of China a month later.

Early in 1978, the United States had expelled from New York Vietnam's ambassador to the United Nations, Dinh Ba Thi, on charges of spying. The incident apparently was related to the fifteen-year jail terms decreed the same year, for espionage on behalf of Vietnam, to American Ronald Humphrey and David Truong, son of Truong Dinh Dzu, the "peace candidate," himself imprisoned in Saigon for over four years after finishing second to Thieu in the presidential elections of September 1967.[15] The evidence against these men has been disputed, and no Soviet ambassador was ever expelled, although some certainly had contacts with some of the many Russians expelled from the United States since 1945 for spying. Once again, Vietnam seemed to have had the dubious honor of serving as scapegoat for American frustrations with other, stronger nations.

More importantly, not only did Washington not give aid for the reconstruction of Vietnam, arguing that the Communist offensive of 1975 had ended any such obligation, but it worked to varying degrees against other countries (including Japan and Australia) and organizations (including the World Bank) extending such aid. The United States did receive over 484,000 Indochinese refugees after 1975. Yet, while in accord with the January 1973 Agreement, the United States removed its mines from northern waters, after 1975 it reportedly even refused to give over military maps in its possession telling the positions of some of the over 100,000 tons of unexploded ordinance remaining in the area.

The 2,800,000 American soldiers who served in Vietnam (out of over twenty six million draft-age males in the 1964–1973 period) also continued to face more than the usual problems of returning veterans. They charged scandalous neglect and frequent hostility in the place of honor, all the more poignantly in the case of the mentally and physically scarred.

Washington's purposeful display of ignorance of the Vietnamese revolution also continued at a remarkable level. Where in December 1961 the State Department could speak of the Communists "in 1954 . . . making plans to take over all of Vietnam" without any reference to the first two points of the Party's founding program of 1930 calling for just that, eighteen years later Vice President Mondale went still further in exercising selective memory. Addressing the Geneva Conference on Indochina refugees on July 21, 1979, twenty-five years to the day of the conclusion of the Geneva Conference ending the French Indochina War, he made no reference at all to that conference, so central to the continuing Indochina crisis, but instead stressed the failure of a July 1938 congress, held at nearby Evian "forty-one years ago this very week," to deal with the problem of refugees from Nazi Germany![16]

It was as if Washington decided amnesia offered its best excuse. Even Henry Kissinger, admired for his history of Metternich's early nineteenth-century diplomacy to deal with the aftermath of the French Revolution, often seemed bereft of historical perspective in speaking of Vietnam in his 1979 memoirs. At one point he wrote of his determination "to make Hanoi understand" that Washington would not in 1972 alter a policy "we had refused [to change] for four years," conveniently forgetting to mention that by then the Communists had been fighting for their strategic goals for over forty years! And Kissinger's charge, referring to the Communist use of Cambodian sanctuaries, that "it was they not we, who had decided to fight to the finish on the bleeding body of a people that only wanted to be left alone," also takes on a very different meaning if one starts not in 1969, when Kissinger first took public office, but in 1945, 1955, or 1965.

Some other quotes make equally bad reading, although no doubt they have sometimes been reported out of context. President Carter, for example, when asked on March 24, 1977, if the United States was obliged to bestow reconstruction aid to Vietnam, replied in part, no, because "the destruction was mutual." President-to-be Ronald Reagan, for his part, declared to the Veterans of Foreign Wars in Chicago on August 18, 1980,

> Well, it's time we recognized that ours was in truth, a noble cause. . . . [in Vietnam where the United States sought to defend] a small country newly free from colonial rule . . . against a totalitarian neighbor bent on conquest . . . . We dishonored the memory of

> 50,000 young Americans who died in their cause when we give way to feelings of guilt as if we were doing something shameful . . . .

Like General Westmoreland's dedication to his 1976 memoirs, *A Soldier Reports*, and to the 1979 *The Vietnam War*, stressing the U.S. commitment to uphold "the cause of freedom in South Vietnam," such fine sentiments unfortunately have little connection with the bitter history of Vietnam, where the post-1954 creation of South Vietnam had far more to do with anti-Communism, than with freedom.

General Maxwell Taylor was more direct. In 1965, back from his tour as ambassador to Saigon, he told a graduating class of the International Police Academy in Washington:

> The outstanding lesson [of the Vietnam War] is that we should never let another Vietnam-type situation arise again. We were too late in recognizing the extent of the subversive threat. We appreciate now that every young [sic] emerging country must be constantly on the alert, watching for those symptoms which, if allowed to develop unrestrained, may eventually grow into a disastrous situation such as that in South Vietnam. We have learned the need for a strong police force and a strong police intelligence organization to assist in identifying early the symptoms of an incipient subversive situation . . . .[18]

General Westmoreland repeatedly stated the view of many others that the problem of the U.S. failure in Vietnam was explained largely by the fact of the world press "being saturated with enemy propaganda," so that "the American people were not defeated by bullets but by propaganda." Therefore, "we weren't allowed to win" because of restrictions imposed by Washington. Similarly, President Reagan stated on February 24, 1981, that Americans had been forced to withdraw, "not because they'd been defeated, but because they'd been denied permission to win." Former President Nguyen Van Thieu, on October 6, 1979, was quoted from exile in London, as making the remarkable statement that "without the American presence we could have beaten the Communists." A recent *Rand* Corporation study of other former southern leaders' explanations of what had happened in 1975, however, blamed not only erroneous American policies but Thieu himself more than any other single person, for *The Fall of South Vietnam*, the book's title. One of the twenty-seven officials interviewed stated more accurately, "to sum up, the war was lost from its inception." And Prince Norodom Sihanouk, on the conclusion of an unsuccessful search for

U.S. aid for his proposals for Kampuchea, on April 18, 1980, stated flatly, "the Americans have learned nothing from [their] Vietnam [experience]." New Secretary of Defense Caspar Weinberger, however, declared on January 6, 1981, that Vietnam had not been "vital to American national interests," and that in the future, the United States would fight only if the war was vital to national survival, if the American people supported Washington's policy and fully intended to win."[19]

WHAT OF THE VICTORS after 1975? The remarkable continuity of the leadership of the Vietnamese Revolution largely continued after the death of Ho Chi Minh in 1969, although some cracks appeared with the new tensions, arising from the absorption of the south, the refugee, Kampuchean, and Chinese problems.

Following the unification of the country in July 1976, representatives of the 1,553,500 members of the Party convened the Fourth National Congress on December 14–20, 1976. They elected a new Central Committee of 101 members and 32 alternates, who in turn elected a Political Bureau of 14, with 3 alternates. Most prominently, many of the leaders of the long struggle in the south were promoted. Pham Hung, the leader of COSVN since 1967, was listed fourth in the leadership, after Le Duan, Truong Chinh, and Pham Van Dong. Next was Le Duc Tho, and both ranked ahead of famous military leader Vo Nguyen Giap. In addition, Nguyen Van Linh (Nguyen Van Cuc), and Vo Chi Cong, two other important leaders of COSVN and the PRP in the south, were respectively two of four new full members of the Political Bureau.

Many other southern Party leaders, including Nguyen Thi Dinh, Tran Nam Trung, and General Tran Van Tra, became full members of the Central Committee, but not non-Communist Front leaders Nguyen Huu Tho and Huynh Tan Phat. While the priority of the decision-making Party over the administrative and governmental organizations continued, Front leaders Tho and Phat also were promoted, becoming vice-premiers of the newly united country, and on the death of President and Party veteran Ton Duc Thang in March 1980, Nguyen Huu Tho became the acting president of the Socialist Republic.* Madame Nguyen Thi Binh, the

*In December 1980, the National Assembly proclaimed a new constitution, establishing a Council of State as the executive body of the nation. In July 1981, Truong Chinh was named president of the Council.

Front's foreign minister and representative to the Paris talks, was named minister of education after 1975; Nguyen Van Hieu, minister of culture; and Tran Van Tra, a vice-minister of defense.

The relative prominence of southern leaders in upper echelons of the Party and government was all the more noteworthy in view of the heavy losses suffered by the southern Party during the war. At lower levels of the Party, there may have been some purges for "excessive southern regionalism," but the promotions of southern leaders to numerous top positions must have been in part compensation for the dangerous work and achievements of previous decades. By 1978, there were said to be less than 273,000 members of the Party in the south, representing about 1.3 percent of the population, compared with over one and one-quarter million Party members in the north, and an overall Party representation among the population of 3.13 percent.[20]

The goal of the Party, set by the Fourth National Congress, to lead the revolution "from above" and to construct the "material and technical bases of socialism" within twenty years, is very different, and in its way, no less difficult and complicated than the fifty-year revolution "from below." The strains of the task, especially given the country's situation, have produced the first cracks in the facade of Party unity since the late 1920s and early 1930s.

Perhaps most damaging was the defection to China in July 1979 of party veteran Hoang Van Hoan. Dropped from the Political Bureau and Central Committee in December 1976 but remaining a vice-chairman of the National Assembly, Hoan slipped away from a flight for medical treatment to East Germany, while it was refueling in Karachi. Born in Ho Chi Minh's Nghe An province in 1905, he was a founding member of the Vietnamese Party who had long had close ties with the Chinese Communists. Joining the Revolutionary Youth League in Canton in 1926, he studied at the Whampoa Military Academy, and served in the Chinese as well as the Vietnamese Communist Parties. From 1950–1957 he served as Hanoi's first ambassador to Peking, and in a series of articles following his defection, he charged that "the Le Duan clique" had betrayed Ho Chi Minh's revolution, and that its treatment of the Hoa was "not only worse than Ngo Dinh Diem's, but even worse than Hitler's treatment of the Jews." Ironically, Hoan is ethnically pure Chinese, while Le Duan reportedly is part Hoa.

Then, in the spring of 1980, former southern revolutionary Minister of Justice Truong Nhu Tang defected to France, and promised to work with Hoan and other Vietnamese in exile to prepare a new revolution, to create a "confederation" that would respect the differences betwen the regions of Vietnam, as well as Cambodia and Laos, and end the "unworkable" alliance with the Soviet Union.

Equally disturbing were reports of the confining to house arrest in mid-1979 of some other senior leaders, notably one of the founders of the Communist armed forces in the early 1940s, the Nung, Chu Van Tan, apparently out of fear that, because of their minority and Chinese connections, they might take Peking's side. Southern Party leader Vo Chi Cong was demoted as minister of agriculture in February 1979, although he remained a vice-premier and on the Political Bureau.

In February 1980 came a still larger shake-up of the top Party leadership. Le Duan, Truong Chinh, and Pham Van Dong retained their overall leadership of the Party, National Assembly, and government, respectively, but Van Tien Dung, the architect of both the 1975 victory in the south and of the 1979 invasion of Kampuchea, replaced the illustrious Vo Nguyen Giap as minister of defense. Giap, however, remains a deputy vice-premier, and presumably retains his prestige as one of the principal architects of the Vietnamese Revolution. Among other changes, Pham Hung became minister of the interior, and Nguyen Co Trach minister of foreign affairs.[21]

THE FUTURE OF THE PARTY and government of Vietnam, and even more of its economic, social, and foreign-policy problems, remains cloudy at best. But no one can dispute the victorious struggles of its leaders in the decades before 1975.

To understand those struggles, which has been the aim of this book, it is necessary to start before 1945, when the Communists already took partial power in Vietnam. Only such a larger perspective opens the way to an understanding of the incredible perseverence and resilience of the Vietnamese Communists. It then becomes possible to see that those qualities were a product, perhaps an almost unique product, of a dedication rooted in the country's historical culture, in the religious aspects of the revolutionaries' commitment to nationalism and Marxism, and above all in their organization, which for fifty years mobilized youth, women, and peasant-worker activists to form the "brass citadels" and "steel lands" that withstood some of the greatest odds in history; greater even than those overcome by the Chinese Communists.

These strengths of dedication and organization facilitated the incredible victories of 1954 and 1975, an accomplishment that has every right to go down as a twentieth-century version of the David and Goliath, Hannibal, or Cortez stories. To be sure, there was more in the Vietnamese Revolution that was not admirable than in those legends of biblical, Roman, and early imperialist history, but much of the greater brutality and violence was a product of the twentieth century, and was largely forced on the Vietnamese. They could have avoided it by accepting their situation and French and American promises, but as revolutionaries, the Vietnamese Communists fought back, and fought back again, and again, and again, until finally they indeed "got the better of fire with water," in Ho Chi Minh's phrase.

Of course, the Vietnamese Revolution is too complicated and too recent in time to maintain the simplicity of such myths. Above all, it is too controversial—in the words of Oscar Wilde, "Dying for a cause does not make it just." Yet, aside from the controversies over communism in general and Vietnamese communism in particular, it is remarkable how quickly writers have submerged the historical content of the Vietnamese Revolution into the tragedies of the refugees and Kampuchea, and the disputes of the China-Russia-United States triangle.

What happened in Vietnam, nonetheless, will be recalled as one of history's most remarkable revolutionary wars. It has been the aim of this book to put that revolutionary war, and the subsequent controversies surrounding the Communist victory, into the perspective of the fifty-year Vietnamese Revolution.

NOTES

PREFACE

1. *Time*, April 23, 1979.
2. *Congressional Record*, May 14, 1975, and Le Anh Tu for the American Friends Service Committee, *Vietnam: The Legacy of War*, (Philadelphia, 1979). A Paris-based Vietnamese exile group (Fraternité Vietnam) cited a U.S. Senate Foreign Relations Committee document, giving a year-by-year breakdown of over $239 billion spent on the war, as follows:

Fiscal Year	*Budgetary Costs* (in millions of dollars)	*Supplementary Costs* (in millions of dollars)
1965	100	100
1966	5,800	6,100
1967	20,100	18,000
1968	26,500	23,000
1969	28,800	22,000
1970	23,050	17,000
1971	15,300	12,000
1972	9,261	10,000
1973	6,123	unknown
1974	4,016	unknown
1975	2,603	unknown
Total	141,653	98,000

Combined Total: 239.653 billion

SOURCE: Fraternité Vietnam, eds., *Guerre biochimique et bouleversements écologiques au Vietnam* (Paris, 1975), p. 21.

Other sources give still higher totals, for example, Gabriel Bonnet, *La Guerre revolutionnaire du Vietnam* (Paris, 1969), and *Vietnam: Destruction, War Damage* (Hanoi, 1977), p. 11, which cites "American sources" to state that the costs of the war exceeded $300 billion. See also Wilfred Burchett, *Inside Story of the Guerilla War* (New York, 1965), p. 106; Joseph Buttinger, *Vietnam: The Unforgettable Tragedy* (New York, 1977), pp. 84, 93–94; *New York Times*, September 11, 1977; Guenter Lewy, *America in Vietnam* (New York, 1978), p. 395, George Herring, *America's Longest War: The United States in Vietnam, 1950–1975* (New York, 1979), p. 150; and Paul Isoart, *Le Vietnam* (Paris, 1969), p. 13.

3. There are many scattered references to the bombing totals. See especially R. Littauer and M. Uphoff, eds., *The Air War in Indochina* (Boston, 1972); Fraternité Vietnam, *Destructions de la guerre sur le plan humain et socio-économique* (Paris, 1975); Lewy, op. cit., p. 243.
4. The quotations are taken, in order, from: W. G. Effros, *Quotations Vietnam, 1945–1969* (New York, 1970), p. 33; George McT. Kahin and John Lewis, *The United States in Vietnam: An Analysis in Depth of the History of America's Involvement in Vietnam* (New York, 1967), p. 423; Herring, op. cit., pp. 79, 115; and *The Pentagon Papers*, New York Times, ed., (New York, 1971), p. 255.
5. Secretary of State Dean Acheson, Memorandum to Ambassador-at-Large Philip Jessup, cited by Michael Morrow in *Asia Mail*, January 1977. See also Tang Tsou, *America's Failure in China* (Chicago, 1963), p. 506.
6. John F. Kennedy, "America's Stake in Vietnam," in W. R. Fishel, ed., *Vietnam: Anatomy of a Conflict* (Itasca, Ill., 1968), p. 144.
7. Cited, in order, in Effros, op. cit., p. 49; Buttinger, op. cit., p. 91; and Townsend Hoopes, *The Limits of Intervention* (New York, 1969), p. 93.

Chapter One

1. See Van Tien Dung, *Our Great Spring of Victory* (New York, 1977), pp. 10, 18, 21ff.; Frank Snepp, *Decent Interval* (New York, 1977), p. 30ff., 133–135, 220; and Alan Dawson, *55 Days: The Fall of South Vietnam* (Englewood Cliffs, N.J., 1977), p. 40 passim.
2. Wilfred Burchett, *Catapult to Freedom* (New York, 1978), p. 145ff.
3. *New York Times*, April 22, 1975.
4. T. D. Allman in *Manchester Guardian Weekly*, April 12, 1975, cited in Noam Chomsky and E. S. Herman, *The Political Economy of Human Rights* (Boston, 1979), vol. 2, p. 8.

5. Titziano Terzani, *Giai Phong: The Fall and Liberation of Saigon* (New York, 1976), passim; Dawson, op. cit.; Snepp, op. cit.; Van Tien Dung, op. cit.
6. Van Tien Dung, op. cit., pp. 120, 128, 132, 150, 152, 184, 191, and Denis Warner, *Certain Victory* (Kansas City, 1977), passim.
7. Dawson, op. cit., pp. 13–15, 201–2; Terzani, op. cit., passim; and Vo Nguyen Giap, *Unforgettable Months and Years* (Ithaca, N.Y., 1975), p. 139.
8. Cited, in order, in Georges Chaffard, *Les Deux Guerres du Vietnam: de Valluy à Westmoreland* (Paris, 1969), p. 220; Bernard Fall, *Last Reflections on the War* (New York, 1967), p. 215; Joseph Buttinger, op. cit., pp. 27, 37, 87; Effros, op. cit., p. 76ff.; Vo Nguyen Giap, *The Military Art of People's War* (New York, 1970), p. 83; and James P. Harrison, *The Long March to Power* (New York, 1972), p. 192.
9. See William Duiker, *The Communist Road to Power in Vietnam* (Boulder, Colo., 1981), passim, and Wilfred Burchett, *Grasshoppers and Elephants* (New York, 1977), p. 68ff.
10. *Khoa Hoc Kach Menh* (The Science of Revolution), 1933, no. 1, translated in Annex to Archives de la France d'Outre-Mer, Aix-en-Provence (Document no. 7, F7, F8).
11. Cited in Philippe Devillers, "Viet Nam," in *L'Histoire du XXe siècle; L'Asie du sud-est* (Paris, 1971), vol. 2, p. 772.
12. Nguyen Thi Dinh, *No Other Road to Take* (Ithaca, N.Y., 1976), pp. 59, 65.
13. Ibid., p. 77.
14. Jean and Simone Lacouture, *Vietnam: Voyage à travers une victoire* (Paris, 1976), p. 116. For brief biographies of Dung and other Communist leaders, see Georges Boudarel, *Giap* (Paris, 1977), p. 177; Douglas Pike, *History of Vietnamese Communism, 1925–1976* (Stanford, 1976); and *Le Vietnam en Marche*, Numbers 1–8 (Hanoi, 1962). See also footnote 7, chapter 3, and Truong Nhu Tang, "Comment Hanoi nous à trahi," *L'Express* (June 7–13, 1980).
15. Terzani, op. cit., pp. 160–61; see also Lucien Bodard, *The Quicksand War* (London, 1967), pp. 174, 199ff.
16. Lacouture (1976), op. cit., p. 116.
17. Selig Harrison, *The Widening Gulf* (New York, 1968), p. 114; and Robert Scigliano, *South Vietnam: Nation under Stress* (Boston, 1963), p. 5.
18. Robert F. Turner, *Vietnamese Communism: Its Origin and Development* (Stanford, 1975), p. 204; William Duiker, op. cit., passim; Le Duan, *This Nation and Socialism Are One*, ed. Tran Van Dinh, pp. xvi ff.; and Le Duan, *Ecrits* (Hanoi, 1976).
19. Georges Chaffard, *Les Deux Guerres du Vietnam* (Paris, 1969), p. 241ff.; and Truong Nhu Tang, op. cit.

20. Chaffard, op. cit., pp. 254, 422, 437.

Chapter Two

1. The best general history of traditional Vietnam remains: Le Thanh Khoi, *Le Vietnam: Histoire et civilisation* (Paris, 1955). See also especially Jean Chesneaux, *Contribution à l'histoire de la nation vietnamienne* (Paris, 1955).
2. See Philippe Devillers, *L'Histoire du XXe siècle: L'Asie du sud-est* book 8, *Vietnam* (Paris, 1971), vol. 2, pp. 756, 758, 774; Paul Isoart, *Le Phénomène nationale vietnamien* (Paris, 1961), pp. 193, 200; Pierre-Richard Feray, *Le Vietnam au XXe siècle* (Paris, 1979), pp. 64, 85; John McAlister, *Vietnam: The Origins of Revolution* (New York, 1971), p. 92 passim; see also Joseph Buttinger, *A Dragon Embattled* (New York, 1967), 2 vols; Joseph Buttinger, *Vietnam: A Political History* (New York, 1968); Virginia Thompson, *French Indochina* (New York, 1937); David Marr, *Vietnamese Anti-Colonialism* (Berkeley, 1971); Chesneaux (1955), op. cit., p. 95; and J. W. Foster, *American Diplomacy in the Orient* (Boston, 1903), p. 46ff.
3. Leading biographies of Ho Chi Minh are Jean Lacouture, *Ho Chi Minh* (Paris, 1967, and New York, 1968); N. Khac Huyen, *Vision Accomplished: The Enigma of Ho Chi Minh* (New York, 1971); Christine Rageau, *Ho Chi Minh* (Paris, 1970); Georges Boudarel, "Ho Chi Minh," in *Hommes d'état d'Asie et leur politique*, ed. G. Fischer (Paris, 1980); and Jean Sainteny, *Face à Ho Chi Minh* (Paris, 1970).
4. King Chen, *Vietnam and China, 1938–1954* (Princeton, 1969), pp. 37–38.
5. Ho Chi Minh, *Selected Writings* (Hanoi, 1973), p. 252.
6. Cited in Huyen, op. cit., pp. 12–13.
7. *Thanh Nien* (Youth), no. 69 (November 14, 1926), translated in Archives Nationales de la France: Section Outre-Mer (27 Rue Oudinot, Paris 7): Fonds du Service de Liaison des Originaires des Territoires de la France d'Outre-Mer (hereafter *SLOTFORM*), Serie V, Carton 16.
8. A partial text of Ho's *The Road to Revolution* is given in *Vietnam Courier*, February 9, 1970. See also William Duiker, *The Communist Road to Power in Vietnam* (Boulder, Colo., 1981).
9. See Georges Boudarel, "Les Memoires de Phan Boi Chau," *France-Asie*, no. 194–95 (1968), pp. 196–98, and David Marr, *Vietnamese Anti-Colonialism* (Berkeley, 1971), p. 261.
10. David Hemery, *Revolutionnaires vietnamiennes et le pouvoir colonial en Indochine* (Paris, 1975), p. 64ff., 417, 422; William Duiker, *The Rise of Nationalism in Vietnam, 1900–1941* (Ithaca,

N.Y., 1976), p. 192ff.; see also Alexander Woodside, *Community and Revolution in Vietnam* (Boston, 1976), p. 35ff.; William H. Frederick, "Alexander Varenne and Politics in Indochina, 1925–1926," in *Aspects of Vietnamese History*, ed. Walter Vella (Honolulu, 1973), p. 137ff.; and Milton Sacks, "Marxism in Vietnam," in *Marxism in Southeast Asia*, ed. Frank Trager (Stanford, 1960), p. 119ff.

11. The previous discussion is based on a wide variety of sources, including: William Duiker, *The Comintern and Vietnamese Communism* (Athens, Ohio, 1975), passim; Le Duan, *The Vietnamese Revolution* (New York, 1971), p. 62ff.; Le Duan, *This Nation and Socialism Are One* (Chicago, 1976), p. 55ff.; Ngo Vinh Long, *Before the Revolution: The Vietnamese Peasants under the French* (Cambridge, Mass., 1973), p. 140ff.; Gareth Porter, "Proletariat and Peasantry in Early Vietnamese Communism," in *Asian Thought and Society*, December 1976, p. 333ff.; *Contribution à l'histoire des mouvements politiques de l'Indochine française: Le Parti communiste indochinois, 1925–1933* (Hanoi, 1933); Nguyen Khac Vien, *L'Histoire du Vietnam*, p. 151ff., 164ff.; "Le Parti à huit ans," in *Le Peuple*, January 8, 1938; and *Brève Histoire du parti des travailleurs du Vietnam, 1930–1975* (Hanoi, 1976), p. 10ff.; *Etudes vietnamiennes*, vol. 8 (1966), p. 13.

12. On these political and religious groups, see especially Jayne Werner, "Cao Dai: The Politics of a Vietnamese Syncretic Religious Movement" (Ph.D. diss., Cornell University, 1976); Samuel Popkin, *The Rational Peasant: The Political Economy of Rural Society in Vietnam* (Berkeley, 1979), p. 193ff.; Bernard Fall, "The Political-Religious Sects of Vietnam," *Pacific Affairs*, September 1955; Duiker (1976), op. cit.; articles of William H. Frederick and Milton Osborne, in Walter Vella, ed., *Aspects of Vietnamese History* (Honolulu, 1973); Gerald Hickey, *Village in Vietnam* (New Haven, Conn., 1964), p. 290ff.; Megan Cook, *The Constitutionalist Party in Cochin China* (Clayton, Victoria, Australia, 1977); Alexander B. Woodside, *Community and Revolution in Modern Vietnam* (Boston, 1976); and Jean Chesneaux et al., eds., *Tradition et revolution au Vietnam* (Paris, 1971).

13. On the founding and early history of the Communist Party, besides the official histories and other works cited above, see William Duiker, (1981), op. cit.; Douglas Pike, *History of Vietnamese Communism, 1925–1976* (Stanford, 1978); Robert F. Turner, *Vietnamese Communism: Its Origins and Development* (Stanford, 1975); and I. A. Ognetov, "Komintern i Revolutsionnoe Dvizhenie vo Vietname," (The Comintern and the Revolutionary Movement in Vietnam), in *Komintern i Vostok* (The Comintern and the East) (Moscow, 1969).

14. On the Nghe-Tinh soviet, see especially Ngo Vinh Long, "Peasant Revolutionary Struggle in Vietnam in the 1930s," (Ph.D. diss.,

Harvard University, 1978); Pierre Brocheux, "L'Implantation du mouvement communiste en Indochine française: Le Cas du Nghe-Tinh (1930–1931)," in *Revue d'histoire moderne et contemporaine*, January–March 1977, p. 62ff.; James Scott, *The Moral Economy of the Peasant: Rebellion and Subsistance in Southeast Asia* (New Haven, 1976), p. 124ff., 145ff.; Tran Huu Lien, *Les Soviets du Nghe Tinh* (Hanoi, 1960); and John McAlister, *Vietnam: The Origins of Revolution* (New York, 1971), p. 86ff.

15. Cited in Ngo Vinh Long, "The Indochinese Communist Party and Peasant Rebellion in Central Vietnam, 1930–1931," in *Bulletin of Concerned Asian Scholars* (hereafter *BCAS*), October–December 1978, pp. 23–24.
16. *Ho Chi Minh on Revolution: Selected Writings, 1920–1966*, ed. Bernard Fall (New York, 1967), p. 339. Regarding the arrests, see especially Hemery, op. cit., pp. 141, 181, passim; Duiker (1981), op. cit., passim; and Ngo Vinh Long (1978), op. cit., passim.
17. Dennis J. Duncanson, "Ho Chi Minh in Hong Kong, 1931–1932," *China Quarterly*, vol. 57 (January–March 1974), p. 84ff.; Lacouture (1968), op. cit., p. 62ff.; Huyen, op. cit., p. 38; Sainteny (1970), op. cit., p. 32; and Harrison, op. cit., pp. 154, 220, 563–64.
18. *Breve Histoire* . . . , p. 17; Turner, op. cit., p. 21; Pike, op. cit., pp. 12, 17; and Huyen, op. cit., p. 35.

Chapter Three

1. Most of this material is taken from Hemery, op. cit., p. 34ff., 68–69, 257, 410, 435; Sacks in Trager, op. cit., p. 141ff.; McAlister, op. cit., p. 123ff.; Chaffard, op. cit., p. 114ff., 139; Duiker (1981), op. cit., passim; and Philippe Franchini, *Continental Saigon* (Paris, 1976), p. 86ff.
2. Cited in Hemery, op. cit., p. 413.
3. See especially Sacks in Trager, op. cit., p. 126ff.; Hemery, op. cit., passim; Nguyen Khac Vien, *Histoire du Vietnam* (Paris, 1974), and Duiker (1981), op. cit., p. 170ff.
4. Cited William Duiker, *The Rise of Nationalism in Vietnam, 1900–1941.* (Ithaca, N.Y., 1976), pp. 241–42; see also *Ho Chi Minh on Revolution*, ed. Bernard Fall (New York, 1967), pp. 208–9.
5. Cited (without naming the journalist) in Jean Leroy, *Fils de la rizière* (Paris, 1977), p. 275; see also Philippe Devillers, "Vietnam," in *L'Histoire du XXe siècle: L'Asie du sud-est*, vol. 2 (Paris, 1971), p. 776ff. Also, Duiker, op. cit., pp. 242, 249; and Sacks in Trager, op. cit., p. 141ff.

6. *An Outline History of the Vietnamese Workers' Party* (Hanoi, 1971), p. 15. See also *SLOTFORM*, Series 3, Carton 48, and Annex to Archives de la France, Section Outre-Mer, Aix-en-Provence (1936), nos. 7F8, 7F17, 7F20, 7F26, and 7F30.
7. For biographical information on Pham Van Dong, Truong Chinh and Giap and others, see especially *Le Monde*, April 26, 1977; Bernard Fall introduction to Truong Chinh's *Primer for Revolt: The Communist Takeover in Vietnam* (New York, 1963), p. xi ff.; Georges Boudarel, *Giap* (Paris, 1977); Russell Stetler introduction to Giap's *The Military Art of People's War: Selected Writings of Vo Nguyen Giap* (New York, 1970), p. 13ff.; *Le Vietnam en Marche*, 1962, nos. 3, 8, 9; Archimedes Patti, *Why Vietnam? Prelude to America's Albatross* (Berkeley, Cal., 1980), Appendix II; and David Elliott, "Revolutionary Integration: A Comparison of the Foundations of Post Liberation Political Systems in North Vietnam and China," Ph.D. diss., Cornell University, 1976, Appendix.
8. Devillers (1971), op. cit., p. 785; "Le Parti a huit ans," *Le Peuple*, January 8, 1938, and Duiker (1976), op. cit., p. 269.

Chapter Four

1. The above is based especially on General Chu Van Tan, *Reminiscences on the Army for National Salvation*, trans. and intro. Mai Elliott, p. 18ff.; Duiker (1976), op. cit., p. 262ff.; McAlister (1971), op. cit., p. 109ff.; *History of the August Revolution* (Hanoi, 1972), p. 14ff. and 21; Boudarel (1977), op. cit., p. 174; John McAlister, "Mountain Minorities and the Viet Minh," in Peter Kunstadter, ed., *Southeast Asian Tribes, Minorities and Nations* (Princeton, 1967), pp. 793–94; and Devillers (1971), op. cit., p. 785ff.
2. Cited in *History of the August Revolution* (Hanoi, 1972), p. 23; also ibid., pp. 14ff.; Devillers (1971), op. cit., p. 787; Sacks in Trager, op. cit., p. 145; Duiker (1976), op. cit., pp. 268–69; McAlister, op. cit., pp. 121–23; Popkin, op. cit., p. 216; Gary Porter, *Vietnam: The Definitive Documentation of Human Decisions* (Stanfordville, N.Y., 1979), vol. 2, pp. 33–34; and *Vietnamese Studies* 45 (1976), p. 80ff.
3. McAlister (1967), op. cit., p. 796; see also McAlister (1971), op. cit., p. 134ff.; Chu Van Tan, op. cit., passim; Duiker (1976), op. cit., p. 272ff.; Devillers (1971), op. cit., p. 799; King Chen, op. cit., p. 34ff., 48ff.; Hoang Quoc Viet in Vo Nguyen Giap et al., *Récits de la résistance vietnamienne, 1925–1945* (Paris, 1966), p. 142ff.; and Giap (1970), op. cit., p. 68.
4. Cited in Duiker (1976), op. cit., pp. 275–76.

5. Duiker (1981), op. cit., chapter 4. The Ho Chi Minh quote is in Ho (1973), op. cit., p. 46.
6. See Popkin, op. cit., pp. 218–20, 224, 237–38; Jayne Werner, "Vietnamese Communism and Religious Sectarianism," in William S. Turley, ed., *Vietnamese Communism in Comparative Perspective* (Boulder, Colo., 1980), p. 107ff.; Nguyen Khac Vien, op. cit., p. 180ff.; and Joseph Buttinger, *Vietnam: A Dragon Embattled* (New York, 1967), vol. 2, pp. 150, 258ff., 289.
7. See Truong Buu Lam, "Japan and the Disruption of the Vietnamese Nationalist Movement," in Walter Vella, ed., op. cit., p. 246ff.; Ralph Smith, "The Japanese Period in Indochina and the Coup of March," *Journal of Southeast Asian Studies*, September 1978, p. 268ff.; Franchini, op. cit., pp. 116–29; and *History of the August Revolution*, p. 40ff.
8. Cited in Vo Nguyen Giap (1970), op. cit., pp. 62–63. For the other material in this section, see especially King Chen, op. cit., p. 53ff.; and Giap and Hoang Quoc Viet, in *Récits* . . . (Paris, 1966), p. 81ff., 135ff., 151.
9. Chu Van Tan, op. cit., p. 182.
10. Cited in *History of the August Revolution* (Hanoi, 1972), p. 64; and Vo Nguyen Giap (1970), op. cit., p. 67.
11. *Ho Chi Minh on Revolution*, ed. Bernard Fall (New York, 1967), pp. 139–40.
12. See especially Archimedes Patti, *Why Vietnam: Prelude to America's Albatross* (Berkeley, 1980); *The Pentagon Papers*, New York Times ed. (New York, 1971) (hereafter all references are to this edition, unless otherwise indicated), pp. 4, 8; King Chen, op. cit., p. 90ff.; Robert Shaplen (1965), op. cit., p. 28ff.; and Dean Rusk, in Michael Charlton and Anthony Moncrieff, eds., *Many Reasons Why* (New York, 1978), pp. 15 and 17ff.
13. Philippe Devillers, *Histoire du Vietnam de 1940 à 1952* (Paris, 1952), p. 111. Cited in Lacouture (1968), p. 88.
14. Chu Van Tan, op. cit., p. 185; see also Vo Nguyen Giap (1970), op. cit., p. 70; Vo Nguyen Giap, *Unforgettable Months and Years*, trans. Mai Elliott (Ithaca, N.Y., 1975), p. 47ff.; and Donald Lancaster, *The Emancipation of Indochina* (London, 1961), p. 421.
15. *History of the August Revolution*, pp. 8, 89, 98, 115ff.; see also Turner, op. cit., pp. 37–38; King Chen, op. cit., p. 111ff.; Huyen, op. cit., p. 78ff.; and Sainteny (1970), op. cit., p. 51ff.
16. *History of the August Revolution*, p. 137; also, ibid., p. 124ff.; Ho Chi Minh, (1973), op. cit., pp. 53–56; Huyen, op. cit., pp. 80–83. See also Joseph Buttinger (1967), op. cit., vol. 1, pp. 300, 327–28, 341, 595; Robert Shaplen, *The Lost Revolution* (New York, 1965), p. 6ff., 110; and Peter Poole, *The United States and Indochina From FDR to*

Nixon (Huntington, N.Y., 1973), p. 8ff.; and Duiker (1981), op. cit., chapter 4.

Chapter Five

1. Vo Nguyen Giap (1975), op. cit., p. 39ff.; Nguyen Thi Dinh, op. cit., pp. 4ff., 36ff.; Duiker (1981), op. cit., passim; Lucien Bodard, *The Quicksand War* (London, 1967), p. 103ff.; Pierre Darcourt, *Bay Vien: Le Maitre de Cholon* (Paris, 1977), passim; Devillers (1952), op. cit., p. 142ff.; and McAlister (1971), op. cit., pp. 123, 148, 183ff., 197ff.
2. Joseph Buttinger (1967), op. cit., vol. 1, pp. 335, 413, 416, and passim; see also Nguyen Khac Vien (1974), op. cit., p. 201ff.; Huyen, op. cit., p. 86ff.; Sainteny (1970), op. cit., p. 55ff.; Devillers (1970), op. cit., p. 824ff.; Lacouture (1968), op. cit., p. 148.
3. Cited in Nguyen Khac Vien (1974), op. cit., p. 202; and see Vo Nguyen Giap (1975), op. cit., pp. 4ff., 39ff.; and Nguyen Thi Dinh, op. cit., p. 4ff.
4. Harold Isaacs, *No Peace For Asia* (New York, 1947), p. 173ff.; and Thai Quang Trung, "Staline et les revolutions nationales," *Revue française de science politique*, October 1980, p. 997ff.
5. Truong Chinh, *Primer for Revolt*, ed. Bernard Fall (New York, 1973), p. 40ff.
6. See Jean Raoul Clementin, "Le Comportement politique des institutions catholiques au Vietnam," in Jean Chesneaux, ed., *Tradition et revolution au Vietnam* (Paris, 1971), p. 122; Tran Tam Tinh, *Dieu et Cesar: Les Catholiques dans l'histoire du Vietnam* (Paris, 1978), p. 55ff.; and Pierre Gheddo, *The Cross and the Bo-Tree: Catholics and Buddhists in Vietnam* (New York, 1970).
7. G. Manue, *Le Viet Minh, notre ennemi* (Paris, 1949), p. 3ff.; the Ho Chi Minh quote is given in Huyen, op. cit., p. 134. See also Paul Mus, *Sociologie d'une guerre* (Paris, 1950), p. 88ff.; Harold Isaacs, op. cit., p. 146ff.; and King Chen, op cit., p. 120ff.
8. Devillers (1971), op. cit., p. 815; Jean Sainteny (1970), op. cit., pp. 67, 73, 76, 79ff., 90; and Jean Sainteny, *Histoire d'une paix manquée* (Paris, 1953 and 1967), p. 177ff.
9. King Chen, op. cit., p. 142ff.; Lacouture (1968), op. cit., pp. 119, 123ff., 126, 136; and Vo Nguyen Giap (1975), op. cit., pp. 91, 102.
10. Lacouture (1968), op. cit., pp. 123–24. See also ibid., pp. 137, 144, 147, 150, 154, 187.
11. Vo Nguyen Giap (1970), op. cit., p. 103; see also ibid., p. 91; Buttinger (1967), op. cit., vol. 1, pp. 382, 388, 393, vol. 2, pp. 673ff., 619, 718, 1017; McAlister (1967), op. cit., p. 788ff.; Sainteny (1970),

op. cit., p. 88; and Edward Rice-Maximin, "The French Communists and the First Indo-Chinese War," *Contemporary French Civilization* (Spring 1978).

12. Shaplen (1965), op. cit., pp. 47–48; Feray, op. cit., pp. 204, 213; Chaffard, op. cit., pp. 14, 19, 29ff.; Mus, op. cit., and Popkin, op. cit., p. 188.
13. Cited in Lacouture (1968), op. cit., pp. 162–63. See also Sainteny (1970), op. cit., p. 100ff., 110–11; Huyen, op. cit., p. 160ff.; Bodard, op. cit., p. 15; Buttinger (1967), op. cit., vol. 1, pp. 424ff.; and Duiker (1981), op. cit.
14. Ho Chi Minh (1973), op. cit., p. 68; Huyen, op. cit., p. 169; and Giap (1970), op. cit., p. viii.
15. These quotations come in order from Sainteny (1953), op. cit., p. 231; Lacouture (1968), op. cit., p. 171; Ho Chi Minh (1973), op. cit., pp. 73, 113–14; and Jean Chesneaux, *Le Vietnam* (Paris, 1968), p. 93.
16. Succeeding quotes come in order from Franchini, op. cit., p. 88; Bodard, op. cit., p. 40; Madeleine Riffaud, *Dans le Maquis Viet Cong* (Paris, 1965), p. 240; Jean Lacouture, *Vietnam between Two Truces* (New York, 1966), p. 159; Henri Navarre, *Agonie de l'Indochine* (Paris, 1956), pp. 35, 128; and Georges Boudarel in Chesneaux, ed. (1971), op. cit., pp. 460–61.
17. See Buttinger (1967), op. cit., vol. 1, p. 421ff.; vol. 2, pp. 689–90, 759ff., 771, 782, 1019; Bernard Fall, *The Two Vietnams: A Political and Military Analysis* (New York, 1963), p. 107ff.; Bernard Fall, *Vietnam Witness*, 1953–1966 (New York, 1966), p. 336ff.; McAlister (1971), op. cit., pp. 281, 289; Poole, op. cit., p. 17ff.; Devillers (1970), op. cit., p. 851ff.; Boudarel (1977), op. cit., pp. 54, 63, 70, 73; Isoart (1961), op. cit., p. 390; Pike (1978), op. cit., p. 78; Duiker (1981), op. cit.; and Robert Asprey, *War in the Shadows: The Guerilla in History* (New York, 1975), p. 818; and Lewy, op. cit., p. 4.
18. Bernard Fall, *Street without Joy: Insurgency in Indochina* (Harrisburg, Pa., 1957), p. 30; see also Fall (1963), op. cit., pp. 72, 109ff., 111, 115–16; P. J. Honey, *North Vietnam Today* (New York, 1963); Leroy, op. cit., pp. 163–64, 187, 195; Popkin, op. cit., pp. 240–42; Lancaster, op. cit., p. 420; Devillers (1971), op. cit., pp. 841, 844 and 849; Boudarel, op. cit., p. 73ff.
19. Buttinger (1967), op. cit., pp. 689–90; see also ibid., p. 703ff., 726–27, 778, 836; and Ellen J. Hammer, *The Struggle for Indochina* (Stanford, 1954), p. 203ff.
20. Mus, op. cit., pp. 315–16; see also John McAlister and Paul Mus, *The Vietnamese and Their Revolutions* (New York, 1970), p. 20ff.
21. *An Outline History of the Vietnamese Workers' Party, 1930–1970* (Hanoi, 1971), p. 41. See also Bernard Fall, *The Viet Minh Regime*

(Ithaca, N.Y., 1956), p. 42ff.; and Turner, op. cit., p. 77, and Nguyen Khac Vien (1974), op. cit., p. 229ff.

22. Bernard Fall, "Dien Bien Phu: A Battle to Remember," in M. E. Gettleman, *Vietnam: History, Documents and Opinions on a Major World Crisis* (New York, 1965), p. 113. See also ibid., p. 105ff.; Bernard Fall, *Hell in a Very Small Place: The Siege of Dien Bien Phu* (Philadelphia, 1967); Edgar O'Ballance, *The Indo-China War, 1945–1954: A Study in Guerilla Warfare* (London, 1954); Lancaster, op. cit.; R. Irving, *The First Indochina War: French and American Policy, 1945–1954* (London, 1975); and Jules Roy, *The Battle of Dien Bien Phu* (New York, 1965).
23. Nguyen Khac Vien (1974), op. cit., p. 231; Devillers (1971), op. cit., p. 857ff.; Boudarel, op. cit., p. 78; Huyen, op. cit., p. 230; McAlister (1971), op. cit., p. 279; *The Pentagon Papers*, p. 29; and King Chen, op. cit., p. 291.
24. Robert Scigliano, *South Vietnam: Nation under Stress* (Boston, 1963), p. 132.
25. *La Vérité sur les relations vietnamo-chinois durante les trentes dernières années* (Hanoi, 1979); Francois Joyaux, *La Chine et le reglement de la guerre de l'Indochina: Genève, 1954* (Paris, 1979); Melvin Gurtov, *The First Vietnam Crisis* (New York, 1967), p. 127ff.; Dwight D. Eisenhower, *Mandate for Change* (New York, 1963), p. 372; and Huyen, op. cit., p. 258.
26. Preceding quotations are found respectively in Chesneaux (1968), op. cit., p. 107, and Effros, op. cit., pp. 14, 48. On the conference itself, see especially Robert F. Randle, *Geneva 1954: The Settlement of the Indochina War* (Princeton, 1969); Victor Bator, *Vietnam: A Diplomatic Tragedy* (Dobbs Ferry, N.Y., 1965); and Melvin Gurtov, *The First Vietnam Crisis* (New York, 1967). The text of the 1954 accords is given in numerous places, e.g., Gareth Porter, ed., *Vietnam: The Definitive Documentations of Human Decisions* (Stanfordville, N.Y., 1979), vol. 1, p. 642ff. See also Scigliano, op. cit., p. 131ff.; Buttinger (1967), op. cit., pp. 832ff., 840–44; Charlton and Moncrieff, eds., op. cit., p. 46ff.; Philippe Devillers and Jean Lacouture, *La Fin d'une guerre* (Paris, 1969), p. 158; and Patti, op. cit.

Chapter Six

1. Vo Nguyen Giap, "Armements des masses révolutionnaires, Edification de l'armée du peuple," in *Ecrits*, pp. 411–12.
2. Cited in *Vietnam: A Historical Sketch* (Hanoi, 1974), p. 46. See also Nguyen Khac Vien (1974), op. cit., p. 46; Franchini, op. cit., pp.

117–19; Joseph Buttinger, *A Dragon Defiant: A Short History of Vietnam* (New York, 1972), p. 49; and *Ho Chi Minh on Revolution*, ed. Bernard Fall (New York, 1967), pp. 6–7.

3. Paul Isoart, *Le Phenomène vietnamien* (Paris, 1961), p. 32. The other quotations are from Huynh Dinh Te, "Vietnamese Cultural Patterns," Ph.D. diss., Columbia University, 1962, pp. 53, 71, 148; Ralph Smith, *Vietnam and the West* (Ithaca, 1971), p. 25; and Nguyen Khac Vien, *Tradition and Revolution in Vietnam* (Berkeley, 1974), pp. 27, 31. See also especially Paul Mus, *Vietnam: Sociologie d'une guerre*; John McAlister and Paul Mus, *The Vietnamese and Their Revolution* (New York, 1970); Paul Berman, *Revolutionary Organization* (Lexington, Mass.), 1974; and Frances FitzGerald, *Fire in the Lake* (Boston, 1972).
4. Cited in Helen Lamb, *Vietnam's Will to Live: Resistance to Foreign Aggression from Early Times through the Nineteenth Century* (New York, 1972), p. 100. See also Duiker (1976), op. cit., Marr., op. cit.; and Nguyen Khac Vien, *Histoire . . .*, pp. 113, 119.
5. The above citations from *Thanh Nien* (especially issues dated April 18, November 14, and December 20, 1926; Jauary 23, May 8, July 1, 17, August 1, 14, September 11, 18, 23, 25, and October 10, 1927) are taken from the translations in the Archives de la France, Section Outre-Mer, known as SLOTFORM. Most are contained in Series 5, Carton 16, Rue Oudinot, Paris. Ho Chi Minh's *The Road to Revolution* was partially reprinted in *Vietnam Courier*, February 9, 1970. See also Feray, op. cit., p. 146; Porter, "Proletariat. . . ," p. 335; and Ho Chi Minh (1973), op. cit., p. 195ff.
6. *Tap Chi Cong Son*, December 30, 1933, translated in Archives de la France, Section d'Outre-Mer Annex at Aix-en-Provence (Document no. 7F8). See also Turner, op. cit., p. 320, and Porter, "Proletariat . . . ," passim.
7. Cited in Lacouture (1968), op. cit., p. 45. The other citations above are found in SLOTFORM translations of *Thanh Nien*, April 4, 1926, and February 29, August 7 and 23, and November 8, 1927.
8. A. Neuberg, ed., *L'Insurrection armée* (Paris, 1970 reprint, 1981 ed.). Preface by Erich Wollenberg and Ho Chi Minh in ibid., pp. 257–58 and 267–68.
9. Truong Chinh and Vo Nguyen Giap, *The Peasant Question*, trans. and intro. by Christine Pelzer White (Ithaca, N.Y., 1974), pp. 7–8, 12, 54, 93. Other quotations above are found in "Slotform," Series 3, Cartons 43 and 59; Turner, op. cit., pp. 311, 317, 319–20, 324–25; Hemery, op. cit., pp. 55, 397, 428; and Long (1978), op. cit., pp. x, 13, 34, 243, 247, 304, 347.
10. Archives de la France, Section d'Outre-Mer, Annex at Aix-en-Provence, Document 7F30 (April 1938). See also Hoang Van Chi,

From Colonialism to Communism (New York, 1964), and Popkin, op. cit., pp. 224–29.

11. Ho Chi Minh (1973), op. cit., p. 155ff. See also ibid., p. 169; Hoang Van Chi, op. cit., p. 152; Truong Chinh, *Ecrits*, p. 497ff.; and *Vietnamese Studies*, no. 12 (1966), p. 106.
12. Popkin, op. cit., p. 241.
13. Hoang Van Chi, op. cit., pp. 189–90, passim. See also Fall (1963), op. cit., p. 156ff.; Turner, op. cit., p. 130ff.; Buttinger (1967), op. cit., p. 964ff.; and Feray, op. cit., p. 217.
14. See Gareth Porter, "The Myth of the Bloodbath: North Vietnam's Land Reform Reconsidered," *BCAS*, September 1973; Edward Moise, "Land Reform and Land Reform Errors in North Vietnam," *Pacific Affairs*, Spring 1976; Edwin Moise, "Class-ism in North Vietnam, 1953–1956," in Turley, op. cit., p. 91ff.; and Chomsky and Herman, op. cit., vol. I, pp. 341–45; and Buttinger (1968), op cit., p. 428.
15. Ho Chi Minh (1962), op. cit., vol. 4, p. 34ff.; see also Turner, op. cit., pp. 140, 152ff., 162; Gerard Chaliand, *The Peasants of North Vietnam* (Middlesex, England, 1968), p. 40ff.; Alexander Woodside, "Decolonization and Agricultural Reform in North Vietnam," in *Asian Survey*, August 1970, pp. 705ff., 707; Eric Wolf, *Peasant Wars of the 20th Century* (New York, 1969), p. 159ff.; P.J. Honey, "Ho Chi Minh and the Intellectuals," in Fishel, ed., op. cit., p. 157ff.; and Shaplen (1965), op. cit., p. 194.
16. Vo Nguyen Giap, *Banner of People's War: The Party's Military Line* (New York, 1970), p. 47. See also Vo Nguyen Giap, *The Military Art of People's War* (New York, 1970), p. 104; Le Duan (1976), op. cit., p. 7; Chesneaux (1971), op. cit., pp. 222, 232; and Chesneaux (1968), op. cit., pp. 23, 66, and 115.
17. Georges Boudarel, in Chesneaux (1971), op. cit., pp. 469–70.
18. Vo Nguyen Giap, "People's War, People's Army," in *The Military Art of People's War* (New York, 1970), pp. 104–5. See also ibid, p. 58; William Turley, "The Political Role and Development of the People's Army of Vietnam," in Joseph Zasloff and MacAlister Brown, eds., *Communism in Indochina* (Lexington, Mass., 1974), p. 135ff.
19. Cited in FitzGerald, op. cit., p. 227.
20. Boudarel (1980), op. cit., pp. 118, 125; Ognetov (1969), op. cit., p. 434; Chen, op. cit., pp. 240, 248; Asprey, op. cit., p. 698; and George K. Tanham, *Communist Revolutionary Warfare* (New York, 1967), pp. 15ff., 63.
21. Mao Zedong, "The Present Situation and Our Tasks," *Selected Works*, vol. 4 (December 25, 1947), pp. 161–62.
22. Lin Biao, *The People's War* (Peking, 1965), pp. 20, 32, 57, 66, passim. See also Duiker (1981), op. cit.

23. Vo Nguyen Giap, *Ecrits*, p. 429. See also ibid., pp. 233, 424, 442.
24. Ibid., p. 453ff.; see also ibid., pp. 424, 442ff., 447, 463, 469, 474, 489, 496ff.; and Vo Nguyen Giap, *Banner*. . . , pp. 21, 26, 97.
25. *Ecrits*, pp. 484–85.
26. Vo Nguyen Giap, *People's War against U.S. Aeronaval War* (Hanoi, 1975), p. 27.
27. Vo Nguyen Giap, *Banner* . . . , pp. 23, 26, 42ff., 57, 61, 72, 82.
28. Ibid., pp. 96, 107; see also Vo Nguyen Giap, *Military Art* . . . , pp. 164, 207.
29. Vo Nguyen Giap, *Military Art* . . . , pp. 105, 110, 163, 168–70. See also Vo Nguyen Giap (1973), op. cit., p. 62; Ho Chi Minh (1973), op. cit., p. 255; and Chu Van Tan, op. cit., p. 186.
30. Vo Nguyen Giap and Van Tien Dung, *How We Won the War* (Philadelphia, 1976), pp. 41–42.
31. Cited respectively in Francois Sully, ed., *We, The Vietnamese: Voices from Vietnam* (New York, 1971), p. 201, and Huyen, op. cit., p. 300.
32. Truong Chinh, op. cit., pp. 34, 116–17, 139; see also Chu Van Tan, op. cit., p. 149.
33. The quotes from Le Duan come respectively from Le Duan (1971), op. cit., pp. 47–48, 50, 54, 27, 32–34, and Le Duan (1976), op. cit., pp. 19ff., 74–5, 80ff., 90–91, 94–95. For other references, see Ho Chi Minh (1973), op. cit., p. 205, and Porter, ed. (1979), op. cit., vol. 2, pp. 29, 34, 38–40, 549–50; see also Chen, op. cit., p. 258; Douglas Pike, *Vietcong: The Organizations and Techniques of the National Liberation Front* (Cambridge, Mass., 1966), p. 149; and Turner, op. cit., p. 116ff.
34. Chu Van Tan, op. cit., p. 28. The Le Duan quote of 1958 is in Ngo Vinh Long (1978), op. cit., p. 581.
35. See Ho Chi Minh (1973), op. cit., pp. 60–61, 89; and see also Samuel Popkin, "Pacification: Politics and the Village," *Asian Survey*, August 1970, p. 662ff.; Pike (1966), op. cit., p. 291ff.; Paul Berman, *Revolutionary Organizations* (Lexington, Mass., 1974), p. 68ff.; and Porter, ed. (1979), op. cit., pp. 263–64.
36. Nguyen Khac Vien, *Tradition and Revolution in Vietnam*, trans. Jayne Werner et al., (Berkeley, 1974), pp. 9–13.

Chapter Seven

1. Nguyen Thi Dinh, op. cit., pp. 44–45, 65, 77. The other quotes are taken from Chaliand, (1969), op. cit., p. 73; Vo Nguyen Giap, et al., *Récits* . . . , p. 85; and *La Revue Communiste* (December 1933). See also *Brève Histoire* . . . , p. 12; *Vietnam: A Historical Sketch*, p. 207;

Hemery, op. cit., pp. 35, 55, 397, 437; and Ngo Vinh Long (1978), op. cit., pp. 4, 23, 37, 243, 247, 304ff., 347.

2. Jean Leroy, *Fils de la rizière* (Paris, 1977), pp. 108, 141, 130, 138, 159, 161, 178, 183, 191ff., 196, 203, 245. See also Buttinger (1967), op. cit., vol. 2, p. 782; *Etudes vietnamiennes*, no. 53 (1978), p. 61ff.; and Tran Tam Tinh, op. cit., p. 55ff.; and Nguyen Thi Dinh, op. cit., pp.5ff., 47.
3. Guenter Lewy, *America in Vietnam* (New York, 1978), pp. 127, 142–44, 148; *The Vietnam War: The Illustrated History of the Conflict in Southeast Asia*, ed. Ray Bonds (New York, 1979), p. 152; Shaplen (1965), op. cit., pp. 308–12, 341–44; Chomsky and Herman, op. cit., p. 313ff.; *Vietnam Courier* (August, 1974); and *Newsweek*, June 19, 1972.
4. Douglas Pike, "How Strong Is the NLF," in Fishel, op. cit., p. 421, and Bodard, op. cit., p. 3. See also *Le Monde*, January 4, 1981; Tanham, op. cit., p. 57; Gerard Le Quang, *La Guerre américaine d'Indochine, 1961–1973* (Paris, 1973), p. 119; Pike (1966), op. cit., p. 368ff.; Bernard Fall, *Vietnam Witness, 1953–1966* (New York, 1966), p. 335; and *Etudes vietnamiennes*, no. 54 (1978), p. 103.
5. Nguyen Thi Dinh, op. cit., pp. 64–65, also p. 54; and Lacouture (1976), op. cit., p. 116. See also Chu Van Tan, op. cit., pp. 28; Burchett (1977), op. cit., p. 72; and Riffaud, op. cit., p. 240.
6. Jeffrey Race, *War Comes to Long An* (Berkeley, Calif., 1972), pp. 110, 3ff., 37, 39, 74, 105. See also Race, "How They Won," in *Asian Survey*, August 1970, p. 372, and *Brève Histoire* . . . , p. 95.
7. Nguyen Thi Dinh, op. cit., pp. 62 and 71.
8. *Vietnamese Studies*, no. 20 (1968), p. 212, and Burchett (1965), op. cit., p. 106.
9. The above quotes are found in Race (1972), op. cit., pp. 24ff., 37, 69, 71–72, 75–76, 96, 126ff., 136, 145, 147, 165ff., 171, 175–77, 188, 197, 204, 211–12.
10. David Hunt, *Organizing for Revolution in Vietnam: Study of a Mekong Delta Province*, "Radical America," vol. 8, Cambridge, Mass., January–April 1974, pp. 106–7. See also ibid., pp. 16–19, 122, 129.
11. William R. Andrews, *The Village War: Vietnamese Communist Revolutionary Activities in Dinh Tuong Province, 1960–1964* (Columbia, Mo., 1973), pp. 44, 49, 60, 65, 84ff., 92ff., 104ff., 128-141.
12. Race, op. cit., pp. xv, 24, 26, 96, 126ff., 166–69, 212, 218, 220, 264, 269ff. The other material above is taken from Denis Warner, *The Last Confucian* (New York, 1963), pp. 121ff., 144ff., 151; Andrews, op. cit., pp. 84, 48, 72ff., 92; Hunt, op. cit., pp. 39, 54, 59–60, 90, 101–3; and James Trullinger, *Village at War: An Account of Revolution in Vietnam* (New York, 1980), pp. 1ff., 142ff., 189ff., 192–93.

13. Wolf Ladejinsky, "Agrarian Reform in the Republic of Vietnam," in Fishel, ed., op. cit., p. 517. See also Leroy, op. cit., pp. 179–80, 216.
14. Ladejinsky, in Fishel, ed., op. cit., pp. 537–38; see also ibid., pp. 518–19, 523, 530ff. In Central Vietnam, the average holding of land was 0.36 hectare per person, as against 0.57 in the south and 0.14 in the north. Yves Henri, *Economie agricole de l'Indochine* (Hanoi, 1932), cited by Hoang Van Chi, op. cit., p. 149, and Feray, op. cit., p. 217. See also Le Chau, *La Revolution paysanne du Sud-Vietnam* (Paris, 1966; 1977 reprint), p. 17; Shaplen (1965), op. cit., pp. 143, 157, 171, 178; Gerald C. Hickey, *Village in Vietnam* (New Haven, 1964), pp. 13ff., 44; Jeffrey Paige, *Agrarian Revolution* (New York, 1975), pp. 297, 303–4, 317–18; *Asian Survey*, August 1970, pp. 724ff., 738ff., 751ff.; Fishel, ed., op. cit., pp. 523, 530ff., 533; and Scigliano, op. cit., p. 121ff.
15. R. Sansom, *The Economics of Insurgency in the Mekong Delta of Vietnam* (Cambridge, Mass., 1971), pp. 229, 234, 245; see also Corson, op. cit., p. 67ff.; Lewy, op. cit., pp. 180–87; Buttinger (1967), op. cit., pp. 930–31, 145, 178; Wolf, op. cit., p. 197ff.; and Duiker (1981), op. cit.
16. Charles A. Joiner, "Administrative and Political Warfare in the Highlands," in Fishel, op. cit., p. 344ff.; McAlister in Kundstadter, op. cit., p. 828ff.; Burchett (1965), op. cit., pp. 132, 162; Tran Van Don, op. cit., p. 68ff.; *Etudes vietnamiennes*, no. 8 (1966), p. 135ff.; Buttinger (1967), op. cit., pp. 718, 890–91; 942ff.; 957–58, 1153; Race, op. cit., pp. 18, 22; and Howard Zinn, *Vietnam: The Logic of Withdrawal* (Boston, 1967), p. 41.
17. Race, op. cit., pp. 97 and 126, and Paige, op. cit., p. 331ff.
18. S. Popkin, "Pacification: Politics and the Village," *Asian Survey*, August 1970, p. 663. See also Roy Prosterman, "Land to the Tiller in South Vietnam: The Tables Turn," *Asian Survey*, August 1970, p. 758ff.; MacDonald Salter, "The Broadening Base of Land Reform in South Vietnam," in *Asian Survey*, August 1970, p. 724ff.; Race, op. cit., pp. 219, 269, 271ff.; Hunt, op. cit., p. 103; Lewy, op. cit., p. 187; and Serge Thion in *BCAS*, vol. 10, no. 4 (1978), p. 68.
19. Cited in Pierre Brocheux, "L'Implantation du mouvement communiste en Indochine française: Le Cas du Nghe Tinh (1930–31)," *Revue d'histoire moderne et contemporaine*, January–March 1977; see also Truong Chinh, op. cit., p. 24; and Tran Van Don, op. cit., p. 27.
20. Race, op. cit., p. 166.
21. Pike (1966), op. cit., p. 101; see also Steven Hosmer, *Viet Cong Repression and Its Implications for the Future* (Lexington, Mass., 1970, pp. 6ff., 42; Buttinger (1967), vol. 2, pp. 982, 977, 1170.

22. Race, op. cit., pp. 101, 113–16, 149, 188, 196.
23. Lewy, op. cit., p. 272ff., 451, 453–54. See also Pike (1966), op. cit., p. 249ff.; Hosmer, op. cit., pp. 27ff.; Fishel, ed., op. cit., p. 418; Buttinger (1977), op. cit., pp. 84ff., 93, 95ff.; Gloria Emerson, *Winners and Losers* (New York, 1976), p. 357; Lacouture (1976), op. cit., p. 54; Devillers (1971), op. cit., p. 857; and Gary Porter, "U.S. Political Warfare in Vietnam: The 1968 'Hue Massacre," *Indochina Chronicle*, June 1974.
24. Philip Slater, *The Pursuit of Loneliness* (Boston, 1976), p. 51. See also Fraternité Vietnam, eds., *Destructions . . .* , p. 9ff.; *Vietnam: Destruction, War Damage*, passim; *Vietnamese Studies*, no. 20 (1968), p. 212; Snepp, op. cit., p. 95; Lewy, op. cit., pp. 101, 141, 243; Buttinger (1977), op. cit., pp. 84, 93, 95; *Le Monde diplomatique*, October 1972, p. 13; Herring, op. cit., p. 152; and *Vietnam Newsletter*, July–August 1980, p. 19.
25. Jonathan Schell, *The Military Half: An Account of Destruction in Quang Ngai and Quang Tin* (New York, 1968), pp. 22–23, also p. 20.
26. Jonathan Schell, *The Village of Ben Suc* (New York, 1967), pp. 15–16.
27. Schell (1968), op. cit., pp. 9–10, 27, 88, 198, 200. See also Earl Martin, *Reaching the Other Side* (New York, 1978), pp. 164–65; and Schell (1967), op. cit., pp. 42, 104.
28. Cited in Chesneaux (1968), op. cit., p. 170.
29. Fraternité Vietnam, eds., *Destructions . . .* , p. 25, *The Vietnam War*, p. 180, and Lewy, op. cit., pp. 127, 148, 243, 325–26.
30. Samuel Huntington, "The Bases of Accommodation," *Foreign Affairs*, June 1968.
31. Horst Fass, "Vietnamese Recalls Agonies of Tunnel War," *New York Times*, October 13, 1977; see also Vo Nguyen Giap (1973), op. cit., p. 62; Ho Chi Minh (1973), op. cit., p. 255; Boudarel, op. cit., pp. 73, 97, 123; Pham Cuong and Nguyen Van Ba, *La Revolution au village: Nam Hong, 1945–1975* (Hanoi, 1975), p. 22; and Herring, op. cit., p. 149.
32. Burchett (1965), op. cit., p. 45ff.; Riffaud (1965), op. cit., pp. 36–37, 53–54, 92; *Vietnamese Studies*, no. 20 (1968), pp. 257ff., 277; and *Etudes vietnamiennes*, no. 54 (1978), p. 32ff.
33. Truong Nhu Tang, "Comment Hanoi nous a trahi," *L'Express*, June 7–13, 1980, p. 168; and interview with author, November 7, 1980.
34. Burchett (1977), op. cit., p. 81.
35. Lieutenant General Bernard William Rogers, *Cedar Falls-Junction City: A Turning Point* (Washington, 1974), pp. 54, 67–69; and *Etudes vietnamiennes*, no. 57 (1979), pp. 65ff., 79.
36. Wilfred Burchett, *Catapult to Freedom* (New York, 1978), pp. 188–89. See also ibid., pp. 134–36; Van Tien Dung, op. cit., pp.

188–89; *Le Courrier du Vietnam*, no. 6 (1980), p. 14ff.; Race, op. cit., pp. 34, 105–7; Chaffard, op. cit., pp. 231, 357; and Vo Nguyen Giap (1970), op. cit., p. 73.

37. Lewy, op. cit., pp. 41, 66, 75, 206, 213, 376, 382ff., 391; Warner, op. cit., p. 115; Van Geirt, *La Piste Ho Chi Minh* (Paris, 1971); and Arthur J. Dommen, *Conflict in Laos: The Politics of Neutralization* (New York, 1971), pp. 293ff., 339, 355.
38. Van Tien Dung, op. cit., passim; Dawson, op. cit., pp. 66–67; Chaffard, op. cit., p. 400; and Townsend Hoopes, *The Limits of Intervention: An Inside Account of How the Johnson Policy in Vietnam Was Reversed* (New York, 1969), pp. 77ff., 87.
39. John C. Donnell, "The War, The Gap, and the Cadre," in Fishel, op. cit., p. 366. See also Buttinger (1967), op. cit., pp. 956, 976ff.; and Tran Van Don, op. cit., pp. 52, 159.
40. Riffaud, op. cit., p. 240. See also Nguyen Thi Dinh, op. cit., pp. 54, 63–64; Lewy, op. cit., p. 272ff.; 279ff.; Race, op. cit., p. 237ff.; Palmer, op. cit., p. 225; Chomsky and Herman, op. cit., vol. 1, p. 325, vol. 2, p. 71; Hosmer, op. cit., p. 27; and Robin Moore, *The Green Berets* (New York, 1965).

Chapter Eight

1. Cited in Shaplen (1965), op. cit., pp. 113, 105ff. Biographies of Diem and previous quotes are given in Warner (1963), op. cit., passim, and Fall (1963), op. cit., p. 234ff. See also Buttinger (1967), op. cit., pp. 846ff., 1253ff.; Sully, ed., op. cit., p. 156ff.; Tran Van Don, p. 49ff.; and Leroy, op. cit., p. 139.
2. See Chaffard, op. cit., pp. 192, 309–10, 214ff., 287; Charlton and Moncrieff, eds., op. cit., pp. 43ff., 54ff., 101, 150–51; *The Pentagon Papers*, pp. 16ff., 53–56; George McT. Kahin and John Lewis, *The United States in Vietnam* (New York, 1967), p. 377ff.; Herring, op. cit., p. 44ff.; Selig Harrison, op. cit., pp. 116, 122; Philippe Devillers and Jean Lacouture, *Vietnam: De la guerre française à la guerre américaine* (Paris, 1969), p. 414ff.; Georges Boudarel, "Sciences sociales et contre-insurrection au Vietnam," *Le Mal de voir: 10/18* (Cahiers Jussieu, no. 2), (Paris, 1976), p. 136ff.; *Saigon: Un Régime en question; Les Prisonniers politiques*, ed. Communauté Vietnamienne (Paris, 1974), p. 153ff.; and Edward Lansdale, *In the Midst of Wars* (New York, 1972).
3. Tran Van Don, op. cit., pp. 59–60; see also Fall (1963), op. cit., p. 245ff.; Buttinger (1967), op. cit., p. 859ff., 890–915, 1101; and Scigliano, op. cit., pp. 20ff., 111.

4. Buttinger (1967), op. cit., pp. 957, 1101. See also Scigliano, op. cit., pp. 44, 76, 103, 106, 130; Warner (1977), op. cit., p. 106ff.; Malcolm Brown, *The New Face of War* (New York, 1965), p. 170; Shaplen (1965), op. cit., pp. 130, 157; and Jean Lacouture, *Vietnam between Two Truces* (New York, 1966), p. 20ff. On Diem and the sects, see especially Bernard Fall, "The Politico Religious Sects of Vietnam," *Pacific Affairs*, September 1955; Fall, 1963, op. cit., p. 245ff.; and Werner (1976), op. cit. On Diem and the Catholics, see especially, Tran Tan Tinh, op. cit., p. 101ff., 109, 116; *Études vietnamiennes*, no. 53 (1978), and Scigliano, op. cit., p. 53ff., and Gheddo, op. cit.
5. Buttinger (1967), op. cit., pp. 952, 958–59, 963–64. See also ibid., pp. 731ff., 1146; Tran Van Don, op. cit., pp. 56, 79–80, 128–29; Scigliano, op. cit., pp. 88, 187ff.; Devillers (1971), op. cit., pp. 873–75, 885, 894, Warner, op. cit., p. 119, and Browne, op. cit., p. 170ff.
6. Cited in Charlton and Moncrieff, eds., op. cit., pp. 70–71; and William Manchester, *The Glory and the Dream* (New York, 1975), p. 1122. See also John Mecklin, *Mission in Torment* (New York, 1965), passim.
7. Cited in Porter, ed. (1979), op. cit., pp. 24–29, 119ff.; and Dwight D. Eisenhower, *Mandate for Change* (New York, 1963), pp. 372. See also Huyen, op. cit., pp. 258, 224; Race, op. cit., pp. 29, 75ff., 182ff., 195; Duiker (1981), op. cit., *La Vérité* . . . , p. 37; Hoang Van Hoan in *Beijing Review*, December 10, 1979; Scigliano, op. cit., pp. 98, 133ff.; *The Vietnam War*, pp. 56, 64, 124; Burchett (1978), op. cit., p. 188ff.; Carlyle Thayer, "Southern Revolutionary Organizations and the Vietnam Workers Party: Continuity and Change, 1954–1974," in Zasloff and Brown, eds., op. cit., p. 134ff.; and Bernard Fall, "Viet Cong—The Unseen Enemy in Vietnam," in Raskin and Fall, eds., op. cit., p. 252ff.
8. Cited in Charlton and Moncrieff, eds., op. cit., p. 49, and *The Pentagon Papers*, p. 22. See also Porter (1979), op. cit., pp. 22, 35–36; Nguyen Khac Vien, *Histoire* . . . , p. 258; Devillers (1971), op. cit., pp. 883, 886–87, and Philippe Devillers, "The Struggle for the Unification of Vietnam," *China Quarterly*, January–March, 1962, p. 2ff.
9. Lacouture (1966), op. cit., pp. 20–21, 29–31; see also *The Pentagon Papers*, p. 71ff.; Scigliano, op. cit., pp. 142ff., 178ff.; *Vietnamese Studies*, nos. 18–19 (1968), p. 71ff.; Berman, op. cit., pp. 59, 169–70; Burchett (1965), op. cit., p. 125ff.; Pike (1966), op. cit., pp. 61ff., 116ff.; Lucien Pye, *Guerilla Communism in Malaya*, Princeton, 1956; Lansdale, op. cit.; Milton Osborne, *Strategic Hamlets in South Vietnam* (Ithaca, N.Y., 1965), p. 112; *Black Paper:*

Facts and Evidence of the Acts of Aggression and Annexation of Vietnam against Kampuchea (Pnom Penh, 1978), p. 17; Warner (1963), op. cit., p. 110; and P. J. Honey, "The Problem of Democracy in Vietnam," *World Today*, February 1960, p. 73, cited in Scigliano, op. cit., p. 171.

10. Race, op. cit., p. 110; see also ibid., pp. 13, 121; Turner, op. cit., pp. 127, 130, 237, 382ff.; Duiker (1981), op. cit.; *Black Paper . . .*, pp. 20, 35, 38, 48, 55–58; Thayer, op. cit., in Zasloff and Brown, eds., pp. 34, 36, 43ff., 48; David Halberstam, *The Best and the Brightest* (New York, 1969), p. 186ff.
11. Porter ed. (1979), op. cit., pp. 27, 40, 44ff., 54ff., 121–23, 224–27; Race, op. cit., pp. 29, 195; Burchett (1978), op. cit., p. 188ff.; Dawson, op. cit., pp. 121, 229; and King Chen, "Hanoi's Three Decisions and the Escalations of the Vietnam War," *Political Science Quarterly*, Summer 1975, p. 239ff.; *The Vietnam War*, pp. 120, 126ff.; Hosmer, op. cit., passim; Lewy, op. cit., pp. 23, 272ff.
12. Slater, op. cit., p. 46. On infiltration, see especially Lewy, op. cit., pp. 23–24, 40, 66, 83–84, 391, 453; Theodore Draper, *The Abuse of Power* (New York, 1967), p. 92; Herring, op. cit., pp. 67, 150; Chester Cooper, *The Lost Crusade: America in Vietnam* (New York, 1970), p. 158ff.; Hoopes, op. cit., pp. 77ff., 87; Berman, op. cit., p. 4; Le Quang, op. cit., p. 56; and Charlton and Moncrieff, eds., op. cit., p. 113.
13. Turner, op. cit., pp. 203ff., 224ff., 237ff., 420ff.; Porter (1979), op. cit., pp. 88, 340–41; Chaffard, pp. 238ff., 357; Devillers (1971), op. cit., p. 876ff.; Burchett (1965), op. cit., p. 186ff.; Truong Nhu Tang, op. cit., p. 161ff.; Race, op. cit., p. 122ff.; *Etudes vietnamiennes*, vol. 23 (1970), pp. 31ff.; Pike (1978), op. cit., p. 122ff.; and Turner, op. cit., pp. 224ff.
14. Le Quang, op. cit., pp. 56ff., 173, 193; Boudarel, op. cit., p. 123; Chaffard, op. cit., pp. 357, 400; Herring, op. cit., p. 152; *The Vietnam War*, p. 164; and Burchett (1978), op. cit., pp. 135, 148–49.
15. Charles A. Stevenson, *The End of Nowhere: American Policy toward Laos since 1954* (Boston, 1972), pp. 10ff., 212, 263; Fred Branfman, "The President's Secret Army: A Case Study—the CIA in Laos, 1962–1972," in *The CIA File and the Cult of Intelligence*, ed. J. Marks (New York, 1974); Fred Branfman, ed., *Voices from the Plain of Jars* (New York, 1972), p 12ff.; Dommen, op. cit., pp. 293ff.; Shaplen (1965), op. cit., p. 360ff.; Porter, ed., 1979, op. cit., pp. 95ff., 124, 142; and Paul F. Langer and Joseph J. Zasloff, eds., *North Vietnam and the Pathet Lao: Partners in the Struggle for Laos* (Cambridge, 1970).
16. Cited in *The Vietnam War*, p. 8. Subsequent quotes are found in Herring, op. cit., pp. 79–80, 220; Lewy, op. cit., p. 85ff.; Daniel

Ellsberg, *Papers on the War* (New York, 1972), pp. 42ff., 115; Roger Morris, *An Uncertain Greatness: On Henry Kissinger and American Foreign Policy* (London, 1977), p. 164; Poole, op. cit., p. 75; Devillers (1971), op. cit., p. 894; and Porter (1979), op. cit., pp. 93, 182, 226.

17. Race, op. cit., pp. xv, 264. On the uprisings, see especially Burchett (1965), op. cit., pp. 129ff., 150ff., 185; Chaffard, op. cit., p. 227ff.; *Vietnamese Studies* 18–19 (1968): pp. 125ff., 131ff., 160ff.; Charles A. Joiner, "Administration and Political Warfare in the Highlands," in Fishel, ed., op. cit., p. 344ff.; Frank M. Lebar, Gerald C. Hickey, and John K. Musgrave, *Ethnic Groups of Mainland Southeast Asia* (New Haven, 1964), p. 221ff.; Gerald C. Hickey, "Some Aspects of Hill Tribe Life in Vietnam," and McAlister, op. cit., in Kunstadter, ed., op. cit., pp. 745ff., 771ff.; Georges Condominas, *We Have Eaten the Forest: The Story of a Montagnard Village in the Central Highlands* (New York, 1977); Duiker (1981), op. cit.; Le Quang, op. cit., p. 76ff.; *The Vietnam War*, p. 64ff.; Kahin and Lewis, op. cit., pp. 139, 188; and Shaplen (1965), op. cit., p. 175ff.
18. Halberstam, op. cit., p. 339; Charlton and Moncrieff, eds., op. cit., pp. 88, 95, 135; Tran Van Don, op. cit., p. 69ff., 76, 83ff., 97ff., 110ff.; Porter (1979), op. cit., p. 186ff.; Buttinger (1967), op. cit., pp. 995ff., 1000; and Jerold Schecter, *The New Face of Buddha: Buddhism and Political Power in Southeast Asia* (New York, 1967), p. 173ff.; FitzGerald, op. cit., pp. 174ff. and *Études vietnamiennes*, no. 8 (1966), pp. 115ff. and 138ff.

Chapter Nine

1. Porter, ed. (1979), op. cit., pp. 241, 251, 400; Scigliano, op. cit., pp. 141, 145; *The Pentagon Papers*, op. cit., p. 241; Lewy, op. cit., p. 190ff.; for chronologies of the American war, see Cooper, op. cit., p. 473ff.; and *Vietnamese Studies*, no. 47 (1976); *Front Page Vietnam as Reported by the New York Times* (New York, 1979).
2. *Etudes vietnamiennes*, no. 11 (1966), pp. 127ff., 150–51; see also Sully, ed., op. cit., pp. 178–80; Herring, op. cit., pp. 46, 258; Tran Van Don, op. cit., p. 139ff.; and Lacouture (1966), op. cit., p. 131ff.
3. Alfred W. McCoy, *The Politics of Heroin in Southeast Asia* (New York, 1972), p. 152. See also ibid., pp. 160, 164, 166ff., 173, 181; M. T. Klare, *War without End* (New York, 1972), p. 261ff.; *Saigon . . .*, p. 164ff.; Chaffard, op. cit., p. 340; Hoopes, op. cit., pp. 58–59; Lewy, op. cit., pp. 93, 172, 174, 209; and Le Phuong, *La Corruption au Vietnam* (Montreal, 1978), p. 27ff.

4. Branfman, in Marks, op. cit., pp. 47ff., 61; Stevenson, op. cit., p. 184ff.; Catherine Lamour and Michel R. Lamberti, *The International Connection: Opium from Growers to Pushers* (New York, 1974; Paris, 1972), passim. Contrary views, blaming the Communists for expanding drug use, are given in Richard Deacon, *The Chinese Secret Service* (New York, 1974), pp. 89, 435ff.
5. Nguyen Cao Ky, in Charlton and Moncrieff, eds., op. cit., p. 222; see also McCoy, op. cit., pp. 163, 168–69.
6. Snepp, op. cit., pp. 14–15. In 1966, the United States wanted to have Quang removed as commander of the critical IV Corps in the delta, because of his corruption. See Le Phuong, *La Corruption au Vietnam* (Montreal, 1978), pp. 36–40; McCoy, op. cit., p. 188ff., 194; Corson, op. cit., pp. 99–101; Buttinger (1972), op. cit., p. 102ff.; *Saigon . . .* (Paris, 1974), p. 59ff., 159ff.; Allan E. Goodman, *Politics in War: The Bases of Political Community in South Vietnam* (Cambridge, Mass., 1973), pp. 38ff., 45ff., 55ff.; FitzGerald, op. cit., p. 443ff.; Shaplen (1965), op. cit., p. 308ff., 341ff.; Chaffard, op. cit., p. 339ff.; and *South Vietnam: A Political History, 1954–1970*, Keesing's Research Report (New York, 1970), pp. 89ff., 100ff., 115ff.
7. FitzGerald, op. cit., pp. 323ff., 385, 392; Schecter, op. cit., p. 212ff.; Devillers (1971), op. cit., pp. 900, 905; Shaplen (1965), op. cit., p. 341ff.; Herring, op. cit., pp. 158, 257; *The Vietnam War*, pp. 96, 120, 174; and Lewy, op. cit., pp. 24, 50, 147.
8. Porter, ed. (1979), op. cit., p. 245; see also ibid., p. 227ff.; *The Pentagon Papers*, pp. 235, 238–39, 243, 283; George McT. Kahin, "Political Polarization in South Vietnam: U.S. Policy in the Post Diem Period," *Pacific Affairs*, Winter 1979–1980, pp. 647ff., 664; Tran Van Don, op. cit., pp. 133–34; Herring, op. cit., p. 108ff.; and W. Scott Thompson and D. D. Frizzell, eds., *Lessons of the Vietnam War* (New York, 1977), pp. 8ff., 38ff.
9. Cited in Effros ed., op. cit., pp. 118–19. Other quotes are in ibid., pp. 206–7; Porter, ed., 1979, op. cit., pp. 222ff., 240–59, 275–76, 281; *The Pentagon Papers*, pp. 200, 222, 239, 244–45, 248, 257–59, 285; Cooper, op. cit., p. 245; and Halberstam, op. cit., p. 511ff.
10. Porter, ed., op. cit., pp. 307, 283ff.; Halberstam, op. cit., p. 512ff., 590; *The Vietnam War*, pp. 74–76, 130; Herring, op. cit., p. 119ff.; Kahin and Lewis, op. cit., p. 156ff., 403; Poole, op. cit., p. 114ff.; *The Pentagon Papers*, p. 234ff.; and Eugene Windchy, *Tonkin Gulf* (Garden City, N.Y., 1971), passim.
11. *The Pentagon Papers*, p. 324. See also ibid., pp. 323ff., 329, 331–32, 355; Chesneaux (1968), op. cit., p. 140; and McCoy, op. cit., p. 165.
12. Porter, ed. (1979), op. cit., pp. 326, 332–33, 336ff., 355; *The Pentagon Papers*, p. 337; Halberstam, op. cit., pp. 616–18; and Charlton and Moncrief, eds., op. cit., p. 217ff.

13. Porter, ed., op. cit., pp. 341–43, 345–49, 351–52, 357; Tran Van Don, op. cit., pp. 126, 138ff.; *The Vietnam War*, pp. 82–84, 86–89; *The Pentagon Papers*, pp. 339–41; Leroy, op. cit., p. 125; conversation with Don Luce, December 18, 1979; Poole, op. cit., pp. 138, 140; Duiker (1981), op. cit.; Franz Schurmann et al., *The Politics of Escalation* (New York, 1966); Donald Zagoria, *Vietnam Triangle: Moscow, Peking, and Hanoi* (New York, 1967); Peter Dale Scott, *The War Conspiracy* (New York, 1972); and Marcel Giuglaris, *Le Jour de l'escalade* (Paris, 1966).
14. Porter, ed. (1979), op. cit., pp. 353–56, 348ff.
15. Cited in Leroy, op. cit., p. 73. See also *The Pentagon Papers*, p. 382ff.; Herring, op. cit., pp. 132, 140, 147; and *The Vietnam War*, pp. 96, 120, 130, 174, 198.
16. Halberstam, op. cit., p. 560; *The Pentagon Papers*, p. 468; Lewy, op. cit., p. 243; Bruce Grant, *The Boat People* (New York, 1979), pp. 20–21; Littauer and Liphoff, eds., op. cit. According to a table compiled by Fraternité Vietnam, eds., *Guerre biochimique* . . . , p. 21, citing Washington sources, U.S. air and ground munitions expended in Indochina exceeded 14 million tons, year by year as follows: 1965, 315,000 tons; 1966, 1,107,177 tons; 1967, 2,166,293 tons; 1968, 2,966,548 tons; 1969, 2,823,060 tons; 1970, 2,171,980 tons; 1971, 1,601,421 tons; 1972, 1,905,424 tons; and 1973, 140,823 tons. The actual total of these figures is 15,197,725 tons, although this and most sources give totals of 14.2 or 14.3 million tons. Nguyen Khac Vien in *Le Courrier du Vietnam*, July 1980, p. 14, states that a total of 14,265,000 tons (7,093,000 used by the U.S. air forces, 7,016,000 tons by ground forces, and 0.156,000 tons by the navy) were detonated by anti-Communist forces during the war, giving a total of some 577 kilos (1,269.4 pounds) per inhabitant!
17. Herring, op. cit., pp. 134, 144; *The Pentagon Papers*, pp. 400, 409, 450, 529; Asprey, op. cit., pp. 1100, 1141; Chaffard, op. cit., p. 438; McCoy, op. cit., p. 165ff.; Palmer, op. cit., p. 93ff.; *Outline History* . . . , p. 88; *Études vietnamiennes*, no. 54 (1978), p. 13ff.; Effros, op. cit., p. 192; *The Vietnam War*, pp. 100, 102, 142, 145–46, 200–4.
18. Corson, op. cit., pp. 174–75, 157; Leroy, op. cit., pp. 57ff., 60; Martin, op. cit., pp. 164–65; *Vietnamese Studies*, no. 20 (1966), pp. 208ff., 219; *Études vietnamiennes*, no. 23 (1970), p. 84ff.; *Ten Years of the PLAF* (Hanoi, 1971), and Duiker (1981), op. cit.
19. *Vietnamese Studies*, no. 20 (1968), pp. 271, 275–76, 284–85; see also ibid., pp. 258ff., 268, 273ff., 280; Burchett (1965), op. cit., p. 45ff.; Burchett (1978), op. cit., p. 188ff.; *The Vietnam War*, pp. 52, 168–70, 180; Dawson, op. cit., pp. 114, 302, and Race, op. cit., p. 219.
20. *The Vietnam War*, pp. 142, 146; and Palmer, op. cit., p. 137.
21. Rogers, op. cit., pp. 16ff., 149ff.; *Études vietnamiennes*, no. 57

(1979), pp. 38ff., 67, 95, Lewy, op. cit., p. 324ff., 356–58, and Caputo, op. cit., p. 69.

22. *Vietnamese Studies*, no. 20 (1968), pp. 231–32, 237–40; and Sainteny (1970), op. cit., p. 108.
23. *The Pentagon Papers*, p. 580, and Ellsberg, op. cit., p. 159.
24. FitzGerald, op. cit., p. 518; Herring, op. cit., pp. 173, 176, 181, 199; Halberstam, op. cit., pp. 784–85; and *The Vietnam War*, pp. 144–45.

Chapter Ten

1. Porter, ed. (1979), op. cit., pp. 477–80.
2. *The Vietnam War*, pp. 146ff., 151, 158, 168; FitzGerald, op. cit., p. 518ff.; Dan Oberdorfer, *Tet* (Garden City, N.Y., 1971), passim; Herring, op. cit., p. 183ff.; Palmer, op. cit., p. 148ff.; *Etudes vietnamiennes*, no. 23 (1970), p. 91ff.; *Etudes vietnamiennes*, no. 57 (1979), pp. 107–8; Le Quang, op. cit., p. 115ff.; McCoy, op. cit., p. 178ff.; Hoopes, op. cit., pp. 71–72, 139ff.; Hosmer, op. cit., p. 28; and Gareth Porter, "U.S. Political Warfare in Vietnam—The 1968 'Hue Massacre,' " *Indochina Chronicle*, June 1974.
3. Peter Braestrup, *Big Story: How the American Press and TV Reported and Interpreted the Crisis of Tet in Vietnam and Washington* (Boulder, Colo., 1977), passim; Jack Calhoun, "The Tet Offensive," in *BCAS*, vol. 11, no. 1 (1979), pp. 25ff.; also ibid., no. 3, p. 72; J. Suant, *Vietnam, 1945–1972* (Paris, 1972), p. 299ff.; Porter, ed. (1979), op. cit., pp. 478, 486, 505ff., 525; Lewy, op. cit., p. 274ff.; and Duiker (1981), op. cit.
4. Race, op. cit., pp. 269–76; Lewy, op. cit., pp. 187–89; *Asian Survey*, August 1970, pp. 663ff., 724ff., and 758ff.; Serge Thion, "Current Research on Vietnam," *BCAS*, vol. 10, no. 4 (1978), p. 68; Le Phuong, op. cit., pp. 226–27; *The Thieu Regime Put to the Test, 1973–75* (Hanoi, 1975), p. 20; and Charles Joiner, *The Politics of Massacre* (Philadelphia, 1974).
5. These documents can be found in Kahin and Lewis, op. cit., pp. 218, 390ff., 409, 415ff., 432–33, 436, 444–45; and Porter (1979), op. cit., pp. 276, 413, 433ff., 531. See also Chaffard, op. cit., pp. 417ff., 439; Truong Nhu Tang, op. cit., pp. 165, 169; and Hoopes, op. cit., pp. 93ff., 123ff.
6. See Cooper, op. cit., p. 330ff.; Herring, op. cit., pp. 167ff.; Charlton and Moncrieff, eds., op. cit., pp. 208–9; Poole, op. cit., p. 155ff.; Le Quang, op. cit., pp. 148ff., 152–55; Gareth Porter, *A Peace Denied: The U.S., Vietnam and the Paris Agreements* (Bloomington, Ind., 1976); Allan Goodman, *The Lost Peace: America's Search for a*

Negotiated Settlement of the Vietnamese War (Stanford, 1976); Herbert Schandler, *The Unmaking of a President: Lyndon Johnson and Vietnam* (Princeton, 1977); and Oriana Falaci, *Interview with History* (New York, 1976).

7. Herring, op. cit., p. 219, citing C. S. Sulzberger, *Seven Continents*, p. 507; cf. George Orwell, *1984*, p. 152ff. See also *The Vietnam War*, p. 174ff.; Lewy, op. cit., pp. 147, 167, 455; and Fraternité Vietnam, eds., *Destructions* . . . , p. 3ff.
8. See Chapter Nine, note 16.
9. Porter (1979), op. cit., pp. 549–51; see also Turner, op. cit., pp. 230, 256–60; Pike (1978), op. cit., p. 122ff.; Thayer and Turley in Zasloff and Brown, eds., op. cit., pp. 42ff., 146ff.; *Etudes vietnamiennes*, no. 23 (1970), p. 102ff.; and Duiker (1981), op. cit.
10. Zagoria, op. cit., p. 45ff.; Buttinger (1977), op. cit., p. 94; Martin, op. cit., p. 72; Jon M. Van Dyke, *North Vietnam's Strategy for Survival* (Palo Alto, Calif. 1972), pp. 13, 224ff.; Snepp, op. cit., pp. 65, 137, 161; *The Vietnam War*, pp. 126, 228; Lewy, op. cit., pp. 206, 395; *La Vérité* . . . , pp. 54, 59, 64, 73, 113; *The Thieu Regime* . . . , pp. 13, 28; Deng Xiaoping, in *Le Nouvel Observateur*, September 22, 1980, p. 123; Snepp, op. cit., pp. 65, 137, 161.
11. Ho Chi Minh (1973), op. cit., pp. 359–62; and in Huyen, op. cit., pp. 319ff.
12. Branfman (1972), op. cit., p. 20; see also *The Vietnam War*, p. 62ff.
13. Porter (1979), op. cit., pp. 546–47, 245; *The Vietnam War*, pp. 182ff., 192, 196, 210; Herring, op. cit., p. 233ff.; Poole, op. cit., p. 214ff.; *Black Paper* . . . , pp. 20, 35, 48, 57–58; Norodom Sihanouk and Wilfred Burchett, *My War with the CIA: The Memoires of Premier Norodom Sihanouk* (Baltimore, 1973), pp. 92ff., 279; Norodom Sihanouk, *Chroniques de guerre et de l'espoir* (Paris, 1979); Richard Nixon, *RN: The Memoirs of Richard Nixon* (New York, 1978), p. 733ff.; Henry Kissinger, *White House Years* (New York, 1979), p. 1446ff.; Truong Nhu Tang, op. cit., pp. 163ff., 168; Steven Heder, "Kampuchea's Armed Struggle: The Origins of an Independent Revolution," *BCAS*, vol. 11, no. 1 (1979), p. 2ff.; and William Shawcross, *Sideshow: Kissinger, Nixon and the Destruction of Cambodia* (New York, 1979), pp. 91ff., 213ff., 296, 363ff.
14. Lewy, op. cit., p. 199ff.; *The Vietnam War*, pp. 218ff., 220, 224; Herring, op. cit., p. 240ff.; Le Quang, op. cit., p. 177ff.; Burchett (1977), op. cit., p. 156ff.; and *New York Times*, May 10 and 15, 1972.
15. Porter (1979), op. cit., pp. 576–78, 555, 562–63, 568–70, 585–87; Herring, op. cit., p. 236ff.; Goodman (1978), op. cit.; Porter (1976), op. cit.; *La Vérité* . . . , p. 65ff.
16. Cited in Charlton and Moncrieff, eds., op. cit., pp. 208–9; Kissinger,

op. cit., pp. 1464–5; Porter, ed. (1979), op. cit., pp. 570, 576, 587–91; Cooper, op. cit., pp. 296, 330, 339, 374; *Etudes vietnamiennes*, no. 39 (1974), pp. 238ff., 246; *New York Times*, especially Anthony Lewis and others in issues of December 20, 1976; January 4 and 11, 1978; September 23, and December 27, 1979.

17. Kissinger, op. cit., p. 1470; see also Nixon, op. cit., pp. 733ff.; Herring, op. cit., p. 246ff.; Kahin and Lewis, op. cit., p. 348ff.; Turner, op. cit., pp. 365ff., 456ff.; Porter (1979), op. cit., pp. 569, 588ff., 604.
18. Porter (1949),op. cit., pp. 592, 595, 599–600, 603–4, 639; *The Thieu Regime . . .* , pp. 17, 64–65; *Etudes vietnamiennes*, no. 39 (1974), p. 122ff.; *The Vietnam War*, pp. 208, 225; Lewy, op. cit., pp. 207, 294, 451; Burchett (1977), op cit., p. 182ff.; and Herring, op. cit., p. 253ff.
19. Porter, ed. (1979), op. cit., pp. 596–97, 614–15, 628, 642–43, 653–59, and Duiker (1981), op. cit.
20. *The Thieu Regime . . .* , pp. 8, 19ff., 22, 34ff., 65; *Etudes vietnamiennes*, no. 39 (1974), p. 125ff.; no. 47 (1976), p. 43ff., 47ff.; Duiker (1981), op. cit.; Klare, op. cit., p. 261ff.; Terzani, op. cit., p. 257ff.; Truong Nhu Tung, op. cit., pp. 169–70; Martin, op. cit., p. 151ff.; Chomsky and Herman, op. cit., p. 328ff.; Amnesty International, eds., *Political Prisoners in South Vietnam* (London, 1974); and Holmes Brown and Don Luce, *Hostages of War: Saigon's Political Prisoners* (Washington, 1973).

CHAPTER ELEVEN

1. See Robert Shaplen, *A Turning Wheel: Three Decades of the Asian Revolution* (New York, 1979), p. 39ff.; Shawcross, op. cit., p. 389ff.; David Elliott, ed., *The Third Indochina Conflict* (Boulder, Colo., 1981); Truong Nhu Tang, p. 175; M. Marsal, *Hanoi: Combats pour un empire* (Paris, 1979); *BCAS*, especially vol. 11, nos. 1 and 4 (1979), and vol. 12, no. 4 (1980); *L'Autopsie d'un régime genocide: Le Peuple kampuchean juge Pol Pot et Ieng Sary*, (Paris, 1979), and Truong Chinh, *On Kampuchea* (Hanoi, 1980).
2. Elliott, ed. (1981), op. cit.; Grant, op. cit., p. 86ff.; and *Indochine: Première Guerre entre etats communistes*, ed., La Documentation Française (Paris, 1979); and Alexander Woodside, "Nationalism and Poverty in the Breakdown of Sino-Vietnamese Relations," *Pacific Affairs*, Fall 1979.
3. Ho Chi Minh (1973), op. cit., p. 187.

4. Alexander Casella, "Dateline Vietnam: Managing the Peace," *Foreign Policy*, Spring 1978, p. 174.
5. Bruce Grant, *The Boat People* (New York, 1979), pp. 14, 22; Ngo Vinh Long, "View from the Village," *Indochina Issues*, December 1980, p. 7; *La Vérité* . . . , p. 100; *Ceux qui partent: Le Problème des émigres qui quittent le Vietnam* (Hanoi, 1979), p. 7ff.
6. Pierre Brocheux and Daniel Hemery, "Le Vietnam exsanque," *Le Monde diplomatique*, March 1980; *Time*, February 28, 1977, p. 20; Justus Van Der Kroef, "The Indochina Tangle," *Asian Survey*, May 1980, p. 477ff.; *Le Courrier du Vietnam*, June 1980, p. 13; Nguyen Tien Hung, *Economic Development of Socialist Vietnam, 1955–1980* (New York, 1977); Le Thanh Khoi, *Socialisme et development au Vietnam* (Paris, 1978); and John Donnell, "Vietnam 1979: Year of Calamity," *Asian Survey*, January 1980.
7. Grant, op. cit., pp. 31ff., 80ff., 98, 110, 132ff.; *Time*, November 17, 1980; *Le Monde, Dossiers et Documents*, July 1980; Daniel Montero and Marsha Weber, *Vietnamese Americans* (Boulder, Colo., 1978), Gail Kelly, *From Vietnam to America* (Boulder, Colo., 1977), and *New York Times* (June 7, 1981).
8. Ho Chi Minh (1973), op. cit., p. 225, and *La Vérité* . . . , p. 100.
9. Mao Zedong, *Selected Works*, vol. 4, p. 417.
10. *Vietnam Newsletter*, March–April 1980, p. 14; *Amnesty International Report* (London, 1980), pp. 241–42; *Report of an Amnesty International Mission to the S.R.V.* (London, 1981). *Le Monde*, February 10, 23, April 25, December 28–29, 1980; Grant, op. cit., p. 107; Shaplen (1979), op. cit., pp. 26, 33; Doan Van Toai. *Le Goulag vietnamien.* (Paris, 1979); Holmes Brown and Don Luce, *Hostages of War: Saigon's Political Prisoners* (Washington, 1973).
11. Ho Chi Minh (1973), op. cit., p. 361, and Huyen, op. cit., p. 316.
12. Leslie Gelb and Richard Betts, *The Irony of Vietnam: The System Worked* (Washington, 1979); and Grant, op. cit., p. 200. See also Marilyn Young, "Vietnam Rewrite," *BCAS*, vol. 10, no. 4 (1978), pp. 78–80; William L. Griffen and John Marciano, eds., *Teaching the Vietnam War* (Montclair, N.J., 1979); and Frances FitzGerald, *America Revised: History Schoolbooks in the Twentieth Century* (Boston, 1979), p. 122ff.
13. Chesneaux (1968), op. cit., p. 93; and Ruth Q. Sun, *The Asian Animal Zodiac* (Tokyo, 1974), pp. 23, 60ff.
14. *New York Times*, January 24, 1980; *La Vérité* . . . , p. 62ff.; Grant, op. cit., p. 136ff.
15. Fred J. Solowey, "The Vietnam Spy Case," *Rights*, July 1980; and Jack Colhoun, "Spy Trial Verdict: Grim News for Activists," *Win*, November 1, 1980.

16. *Department of State Bulletin*, October 1979, pp. 1–4; Grant, op. cit., pp. 142–43; conversation with Don Luce, December 18, 1979; and John Pilger, "America's Second War in Indochina," *New Statesman*, August 1, 1980.
17. *Washington Post*, August 19, 1980; Kissinger, op. cit., cited in *Time*, October 8, 1979, pp. 37, 45; *New York Times*, March 25, 1977; Chomsky and Herman, op. cit., vol. 2, pp. 57, 320; *Le Monde*, August 20, 1980, and Lawrence Baskir and William Strauss, *Chance and Circumstance: The Draft, the War and the Vietnam Generation* (New York, 1978).
18. U.S. State Department Press Release, December 17, 1965, cited in Jan Knippers Black, *The U.S. Penetration of Brazil* (Philadelphia, 1977), p. 143.
19. *New York Times*, September 25, 27, 1977, October 17, 1979, January 7, 1981, February 25, 1981; *Far Eastern Economic Review*, December 26, 1980, p. 27; *South East Asia Chronicle*, no. 76 (December 1980), p. 7; *Honolulu Advertiser*, August 28, 1978; *Time*, January 15, 1979; William Westmoreland, *A Soldier Reports* (New York, 1976); Lawton Collins, *The Development and Training of the South Vietnamese Army, 1950–1977* (Washington, 1975); Douglas Kinnard, *The War Managers* (Hanover, N.H., 1977); and *Le Monde*, April 18, 1980.
20. William S. Turley, "Vietnam since Unification," *Problems of Communism*, March 1977, p. 38ff.; Woodside (1979), op. cit., pp. 403; Duiker (1981), op. cit.; Joseph Zasloff and M. Brown, *Communism in Indochina and U.S. Foreign Policy* (Boulder, Colo., 1978), p. 29ff.; Grant, op. cit., p. 47; and Wilfred Burchett in *Vietnam Newsletter*, July–August 1980, p. 11.
21. *Le Monde*, February 9, 1980; Nayan Chanda in *FEER*, August 10, 1979, and January 23, 1981; Tai Sung-an, "Vietnam: The Defection of Hoang Van Hoan," *Asian Affairs: An American Review*, May–June 1980, p. 288ff.; and *Beijing Review*, August 17, November 23 and 30, December 7, 1979, and February 18, 1980.

BIBLIOGRAPHY

I. Bibliographies and Research Aids

Chen, J. H. M. *Vietnam: A Comprehensive Bibliography*. Metuchen, N.J., 1973.

Colter, Michael. *Vietnam: A Guide to Reference Sources*. Boston, 1977.

Griffin, William L., and Marciano, John, eds. *Teaching the Vietnam War*. Montclair, N.J., 1979.

Hall, D. G. E., ed. *Atlas of Southeast Asia*. New York, 1964.

Indochina Curriculum Group, eds. *The Vietnam Era*. Cambridge, Mass., 1978.

Phan, Thien Chau. *Vietnamese Communism: A Research Bibliography*. Westport, Conn., 1975.

Whitfield, D. *Vietnam*. Metuchen, N.J., 1976.

II. Journals and Documentary Services

Asian Survey (Berkeley, Calif.)

Asian Thought and Society (Oneonta, N.Y.)

Beijing Review (Peking)

Bulletin of Concerned Asian Scholars (*BCAS*, Charlemont, Mass.)

Far Eastern Economic Review (*FEER*, Hong Kong)

Indochina Chronicle (Berkeley, Calif.)

Indochina Issues (Washington)

Joint Publications Research Service (*JPRS*, Washington)

Journal of Asian Studies (*JAS*, Ann Arbor, Mich.)

Journal of Southeast Asia Studies (Singapore)

Pacific Affairs (*PA*, Vancouver)

Problems of Communism (Washington)

Service de Liason des Originaires des Territoires de la France d'Outre Mer: Archives Nationales de la France: Section d'Outre Mer, Paris and Aix en Provence. (SLOTFORM)

Southeast Asia Chronicle (Berkeley, Calif.)
Sud-est Asie (Paris)
Vietnam (Hanoi)
Vietnamese Studies (Etudes vietnamiennes, Hanoi) Published in Hanoi and then translated into a number of languages. As serial numbers for the original and the translations do not always correspond, I have cited in my notes the actual source I consulted.
Vietnam Courrier (Le Courrier du Vietnam, Hanoi) The same situation as with *Vietnamese Studies* exists here.
Vietnam Info (Paris)
Le Vietnam en marche (Hanoi)
Vietnam Newsletter (Montreal)
Vietnam Quarterly (Cambridge, Mass.)
Vietnam: Revue d'Information (Paris)

III. Recommended Reading

Adams, Nina, and McCoy, Alfred, eds. *Laos: War and Revolution*. New York, 1970.
Amnesty International, *Report of a Mission to the S.R.V.* London, 1981.
Andrews, W. *The Village War: Vietnamese Communist Revolutionary Activities in Dinh Tuong Province, 1960–1964*. Columbia, Mo. 1973.
Arnaud, Jean-Louis. *Saigon: D'un Vietnam à l'autre*. Paris, 1977.
Asprey, Robert. *War in the Shadows: The Guerilla in History*. New York, 1975.
L'Autopsie d'un régime genocide: Le Peuple kampuchean juge Pol Pot et Ieng Sary. Paris, 1979.
Bain, Chester A. *The Roots of Conflict*. Englewood Cliffs, N.J., 1967.
Bain, David H. *Aftershocks: A Tale of the Vietcong*. New York, 1980.
Baker, Mark. *Nam*. New York, 1981.
Bao Dai. *Le Dragon d'Annam*. Paris, 1960.
Barron, John, and Paul, Anthony. *Murder of a Gentle Land: The Untold Story of Communist Genocide in Cambodia*. New York, 1977.
Baskir, Lawrence, and Strauss, William. *Chance and Circumstance: The Draft, the War and the Vietnam Generation*. New York, 1978.
Bator, Victor. *Vietnam: A Diplomatic Tragedy*. Dobbs Ferry, N.Y., 1965.
Bernard, Paul. *Le Problème economique indochinois*. Hanoi, 1934.
Bergot, Erwan. *Les 170 Jours de Dien Bien Phu*. Paris, 1979.
Berman, Paul. *Revolutionary Organization*. Lexington, Mass., 1974.
Black Paper: Facts and Evidence of the Acts of Aggression and Annexation of Vietnam against Kampuchea. Phnom Penh, 1978.

BLAUFARB, DOUGLAS S. *The Counterinsurgency Era: U.S. Doctrines and Performance*. New York, 1977.

BLOOMFIELD, L. P. *The United Nations and Vietnam*. New York, 1968.

BODARD, LUCIEN. *The Quicksand War*. Vol. 1 of *La Guerre d'Indochine* (5 vols., Paris, 1963, et seq.). London, 1963.

BOETTIGER, JOHN, ed. *Vietnam and American Foreign Policy*. Boston, 1968.

BONDS, RAY, ed. *The Vietnam War: The Illustrated History of the Conflict in Southeast Asia*. New York, 1979.

BONNET, GABRIEL. *La Guerre revolutionnaire du Vietnam*. Paris, 1969.

BOUDAREL, GEORGES. *Giap*. Paris, 1977.

______. "Ho Chi Minh." In *Hommes d'état d'Asie et leur politique*. Edited by G. Fischer. Paris, 1980.

______. "Les Memoirs de Phan Boi Chau." *France-Asie*, nos. 194–195 (1968).

______. "Sciences sociales et contre-insurrection au Vietnam." In *Le Mal de voir 10/18* (Cahiers Jussieu, no. 2). Paris, 1976.

BRAESTRUP, PETER. *Big Story: How the American Press and TV Reported and Interpreted the Crisis of Tet 1968 in Vietnam and Washington*. Boulder, Colo., 1977.

BRANFMAN, FRED. "The President's Secret Army: A Case Study—The CIA in Laos, 1962–1972." In *The CIA File and The Cult of Intelligence*. Edited by J. Marks. New York, 1974.

BRANFMAN, FRED, ed. *Voices from the Plain of Jars*. New York, 1972.

Brève Historie du parti des travailleurs du Vietnam, 1930–1975. Hanoi, 1976.

BROCHEUX, PIERRE. "Grands proprietaire et fermiers dans l'ouest de la Cochinchine pendant la periode coloniale." *Revue historique*, July 1971.

______. "L'Implantation du mouvement communiste en Indochine française: Le Cas du Nghe Tinh (1930–1931). In *Revue d'histoire moderne et contemporaine*, Janvier–Mars, 1977.

BROCHEUX, PIERRE, and HEMERY, DANIEL. "Le Vietnam exsangue." In *Le Monde Diplomatique*, March 1980.

BRODINE, VIRGINIA, and SELDEN, MARK, eds., *Open Secret*. New York, 1972.

BROWN, HOLMES, and LUCE, DON. *Hostages of War: Saigon's Political Prisoners*. Washington, 1973.

BROWN, WELDON A. *Prelude to Disaster*. Port Washington, N.Y., 1975.

______. *The Last Chopper*. Port Washington, N.Y., 1976.

BROWNE, MALCOLM. *The New Face of War*. New York, 1965.

BROWNING, FRANK, and FORMAN, DOROTHY, eds. *The Wasted Nations: Report of the International Commission of Enquiry into United States Crimes in Indochina*. New York, 1972.

BRYAN, C. D. B. *Friendly Fire*. New York, 1976.

BUNTING, JOSIAH. *The Lionheads*. New York, 1972.

BURCHETT, WILFRED. *Catapult to Freedom*. London, 1978.

______. *Vietnam: Inside Story of the Guerilla War*. New York, 1965.

______. *Vietnam Will Win*. New York, 1969.

______. *Grasshoppers and Elephants*. New York, 1977.

______. *The Second Indochina War*. New York, 1970.

BUTTINGER, JOSEPH. *A Dragon Defiant: A Short History of Vietnam*, New York, 1972.

______. *The Unforgettable Tragedy*. New York, 1977.

______. *Vietnam: A Dragon Embattled*. 2 vols. New York, 1967.

______. *Vietnam: A Political History*. New York, 1968.

CAPUTO, PHILIP. *A Rumor of War*. New York, 1977.

CARNEY, TIMOTHY MICHAEL, ed. *Communist Party Power in Kampuchea* [Cambodia]. Ithaca, N.Y., 1977.

CASELLA, ALEXANDER. "Dateline Vietnam: Managing the Peace." *Foreign Policy*, Spring 1978.

Ceux qui partent: Le problème des émigrés qui quittent le Vietnam. Hanoi, 1979.

CHAFFARD, GEORGES. *Les Deux Guerres du Vietnam: De Valluy à Westmoreland*. Paris, 1969.

CHALIAND, GERARD. *The Peasants of North Vietnam*. Baltimore, 1969.

______. *Revolution in the Third World*. New York, 1977.

CHARBONNEAU, RENE, and MAIGRE, JOSÉ. *Les Parias de la victoire*. Paris, 1980.

CHARLTON, MICHAEL, and MONCRIEFF, ANTHONY, eds. *Many Reasons Why*. New York, 1978.

CHEN, KING. "Hanoi's Three Decisions and the Escalation of the Vietnam War." *Political Science Quarterly*, Summer 1975.

______. *Vietnam and China, 1938–1954*. Princeton, 1969.

CHESNEAUX, JEAN. *Contribution à l'histoire de la nation vietnamienne*. Paris, 1955.

______. *Le Vietnam*. Paris, 1968.

CHESNEAUX, JEAN, et al., eds. *Tradition et revolution au Vietnam*. Paris, 1971.

CHAING YUNG-CHING *Hu Chih Ming Tsai Chung Kuo* (Ho Chi Minh in China). Taipei, 1971.

CHOMSKY, NOAM. *At War with Asia*. New York, 1970.

CHOMSKY, NOAM, and HERMAN, E. S. *The Political Economy of Human Rights*. 2 vols. Boston, 1979.

CHU VAN TAN. *Reminiscences on the Army for National Salvation*. Translated by Mai Elliott. Ithaca, N.Y., 1974.

CINCINNATUS (pseudonym of Currey, Cecil B.). *Self Destruction: The Dis-*

integration and Decay of the United States Army during the Vietnam Era. New York, 1981.

COLLINS, LAWTON. *The Development and Training of the South Vietnamese Army, 1950–1972*. Washington, 1975.

COMMITTEE OF CONCERNED ASIAN SCHOLARS, eds. *The Indochina Story*. New York, 1970.

CONDOMINAS, GEORGES. *We Have Eaten the Forest: The Story of a Montagnard Village in the Central Highlands*. New York, 1977 (Paris, 1957).

Contribution à l'histoire des mouvements politiques de l'Indochine française: Le Parti communiste indochinois, 1925–1933. Hanoi, 1933.

COOK, MEGAN. *The Constitutionalist Party in Cochin China*. Clayton, Victoria, Australia, 1977.

COOPER, CHESTER. *The Lost Crusade: America in Vietnam*. New York, 1970.

CORSON, WILLIAM R. *The Betrayal*. New York, 1968.

CRAWFORD, ANNE. *Customs and Culture of Vietnam*. Rutland, Vt., 1966.

DANNAUD, J. P. *Guerre morte*. Paris, 1956.

DARCOURT, PIERRE. *Bay Vien: Le maître de Cholon*. Paris, 1977.

______. *Vietnam: qu'as-tu fait de tes fils?* Paris, 1975.

DAWSON, ALLAN. *55 Days: The Fall of South Vietnam*. Englewood Cliffs, N.J., 1977.

Days with Ho Chi Minh. Hanoi, 1962.

DEACON, RICHARD. *The Chinese Secret Service*. New York, 1974.

DEBRIS, JEAN-PIERRE, and MENRAS, A. *We Accuse*. Washington, 1973.

DE FRANCIS, JOHN. *Colonialism and Language Policy in Vietnam*. The Hague, Netherlands, 1977.

Democratic Republic of Vietnam: Thirty Years of Struggle of the Party. Hanoi, 1960.

DEVILLERS, PHILIPPE. *Histoire du Vietnam de 1940 à 1952*. Paris, 1952.

______. "Vietnam." In *L'Histoire du XXe siècle: L'Asie du sud-est*. Vol. 2. Paris, 1971.

______. "Vietnam in Battle." *Current History*, December 1979.

DEVILLERS, PHILIPPE, and LACOUTURE, JEAN. *La Fin d'une guerre: Indochine, 1954*. Paris, 1968.

______. *Vietnam de la guerre française à la guerre américaine*. Paris, 1969.

DICKSON, PAUL. *The Electronic Battlefield*. Bloomington, Ind., 1976.

DOAN VAN TOAI. *Le Goulag Vietnamien*. Paris, 1979.

DOMMEN, ARTHUR J. *Conflict in Laos: The Politics of Neutralization*. New York, 1971.

DONNELL, JOHN. "Vietnam 1979: Year of Calamities." *Asian Survey*, 1980.

DOYON, JACQUES. *Les Soldats blancs de Ho Chi Minh*. Paris, 1973.

______. *Les Vietcongs*. Paris, 1968.

DRAPER, THEODORE. *The Abuse of Power*. New York, 1967.

DUFFETT, JOHN, ed. *Against the Crime of Silence: Proceedings of the International War Crimes Tribunal: Stockholm, Copenhagen*. New York, 1968.

DUIKER, WILLIAM. *The Comintern and Vietnamese Communism*. Athens, Ohio, 1975.

______. *The Communist Road to Power in Vietnam*. Boulder, Colo., 1981.

______. *The Rise of Nationalism in Vietnam, 1900–1941*. Ithaca, N.Y., 1976.

______. *Vietnam since the Fall of Saigon*. Colombus, Ohio, 1980.

DUNCANSON, DENNIS. *Government and Revolution in Vietnam*. New York, 1968.

______. "Ho Chi Minh in Hong Kong." *China Quarterly*, no. 57 (January–March 1974).

EFFROS, WILLIAM G. *Quotations Vietnam: 1945–1970*. New York, 1970.

EISEN-BERGMAN, ARLENE. *Women of Vietnam*. San Francisco, 1975.

EISENHOWER, DWIGHT D. *Mandate for Change*. New York, 1963.

ELLIOTT, DAVID. "Revolutionary Reintegration: A Comparison of the Foundations of Post-Liberation Political Systems in North Vietnam and China." Ph.D. dissertation, Cornell University, 1976.

ELLIOTT, DAVID W. P., ed. *The Third Indochina Conflict*. Boulder, Colo., 1980.

ELLSBERG, DANIEL. *Papers on the War*. New York, 1972.

EMERSON, GLORIA. *Winners and Losers*. New York, 1976.

EUDIN, XENIA J. and NORTH, ROBERT C. *Soviet Russia and the East: 1920–1927: A Documentary Survey*. Stanford, 1957.

FALK, RICHARD, ed. *The Vietnam War and International Law*. 4 vols. Princeton, 1967–1976.

FALK, RICHARD, et. al., eds. *Crimes of War*. New York, 1971.

FALL, BERNARD. *Hell in a Very Small Place: The Siege of Dien Bien Phu*. Philadelphia, 1967.

______. *Last Reflections on the War*. New York, 1967.

______. *Street without Joy: Insurgency in Indochina*. Harrisburg, Pa., 1957.

______. "The Political Religious Sects of Vietnam." *Pacific Affairs*, September 1955.

______. *The Two Vietnams: A Political and Military Analysis*. New York, 1963.

______. *The Viet Minh Regime*. Ithaca, N.Y., 1956.

______. *Vietnam Witness, 1953–1966*. New York, 1966.

FALLACI, ORIANA. *Interview with History*. New York, 1976.

FASS, HORST. "Vietnamese Recalls Agonies of Tunnel War." *New York Times*, October 13, 1977.

FERAY, PIERRE-RICHARD. *Le Vietnam au XXe siècle*. Paris, 1979.

FIFIELD, RUSSELL H. *Americans in Southeast Asia: The Roots of Commitment*. New York, 1973.

FISHEL, W., ed. *Vietnam: Anatomy of a Conflict*. Itasca, Ill., 1968.

FITZGERALD, FRANCES. *Fire in the Lake: The Vietnamese and the Americans in Vietnam*. Boston, 1972.

FLEMING, D. F. *America's Role in Asia*. New York, 1969.

FOREST, ALAIN. *Le Cambodge et la colonization française*. Paris, 1979.

FRANCHESCHI, P. *L'Exode vietnamien*. Paris, 1980.

FRANCHINI, PHILIPPE. *Continental Saigon*. Paris, 1976.

FRATERNITÉ VIETNAM, eds. *Destructions de la guerre sur le plan humain et socio-économique*. Paris, 1975.

______. *Guerre biochimique et bouleversements écologiques au Vietnam*. Paris, 1975.

FRIANG, BRIGITTE. *La Mousson de la liberté: Vietnam du colonialisme au stalinisme*. Paris, 1976.

Front Page Vietnam: As Reported by the New York Times. Edited by Arlene Keylin and Suri Boiangiu. New York, 1979.

GANIAGE, JEAN, ed. *L'Expansion coloniale de la France sous la Troisieme République, 1871–1914*. Paris, 1968.

GARRETT, STEPHEN A. *Ideals and Reality: An Analysis of the Debate over Vietnam*. Washington, 1978.

GELB, LESLIE, and BETTS. RICHARD. *The Irony of Vietnam: The System Worked*. Washington, 1979.

GETTLEMAN, M. E., ed. *Vietnam: History, Documents and Opinions on a Major World Crisis*. New York, 1965.

GHEDDO, PIERRE. *The Cross and the Bo-Tree: Catholics and Buddhists in Vietnam*. New York, 1970.

______. *Vietnam: Christiani e Communisti*. Torino, 1976.

GIRLING, JOHN. *America and the Third World: Revolution and Intervention*. London, 1980.

GIUGLARIS, MARCEL. *Vietnam: Le Jour de l'escalade*. Paris, 1966.

Glorious Daughters of Vietnam. Hanoi, n.d.

GOLDSTEIN, JOSEPH, et al. *The My Lai Massacre and Its Cover Up: Beyond the Reach of Law?* New York, 1976.

GOLDSTON, ROBERT. *The Vietnamese Revolution*. New York, 1972.

GOODMAN, ALLAN E. *The Lost Peace: America's Search for a Negotiated Settlement of the Vietnamese War*. Stanford, 1978.

______. *Politics in War: The Bases of Political Community in South Vietnam*. Cambridge, Mass., 1973.

GOUGH, KATHLEEN. *Ten Times More Beautiful: The Rebuilding of Vietnam*. New York, 1978.

GOUROU, PIERRE. *Les Paysans du delta tonkinois: Etude de géographie humaine*. Paris, 1936.

GRANT, BRUCE. *The Boat People*. New York, 1979.

GRAS, YVES. *L'Histoire de la guerre d'Indochine*. Paris, 1979.

GREENE, GRAHAM. *The Quiet American*. New York, 1955.

GRIMAL, HENRI. *Decolonization: The British, French, Dutch and Belgian Empires, 1919–1963*. Boulder, Colo., 1978.

Guide touristique générale de l'Indochine. Hanoi, 1937.

GURTOV, MELVIN. *The First Vietnam Crisis*. New York, 1967.

HALBERSTAM, DAVID. *The Best and the Brightest*. New York, 1969.

______. *The Making of a Quagmire*. New York, 1964.

HAMMER, ELLEN. *The Struggle for Indochina*. New York, 1954.

HARRISON, JAMES P. *The Communists and Chinese Peasant Rebellions*. New York, 1969.

______. *The Long March to Power: A History of the Chinese Communist Party, 1921–1972*. New York, 1972.

HARRISON, SELIG. *The Widening Gulf*. New York, 1978.

HEMERY, D. *Revolutionaires vietnamiennes et pouvoir coloniale en Indochine*. Paris, 1975.

HENDRY, JAMES. *The Small World of Khanh Hau*. Chicago, 1964.

HENRY, YVES. *Economie agricole de l'Indochine*. Hanoi, 1932.

HERMAN, E. S. *Atrocities in Vietnam: Myths and Realities*. Phillipsburg, N.J., 1970.

HEROD, BILL and PEGGY. *The Sino-Vietnamese Conflict and U.S. Policy*. Washington, 1979.

HERR, MICHAEL. *Dispatches*. New York, 1977.

HERRING, GEORGE. *America's Longest War: The United States and Vietnam, 1950–1975*. New York, 1979.

HERSH, SEYMOUR. *My Lai 4*. New York, 1971.

HICKEY, GERALD C. *Village in Vietnam*. New Haven, 1964.

HIGGINS, HUGH. *Vietnam*. London, 1975.

HILDEBRAND, G., and PORTER, G. *Cambodia: Starvation and Revolution*. New York, 1976.

HILSMAN, ROGER. *To Move a Nation*. New York, 1969.

L'Histoire militaire de l'Indochine française. Paris, 1931.

History of the August Revolution. Hanoi, 1972.

Ho Chi Minh on Revolution: Selected Writings, 1920–1966. Edited by Bernard Fall. New York, 1967.

HO CHI MINH. *Selected Works*. 4 vols. Hanoi, 1961–1962.

HO CHI MINH. *Selected Writings, 1920–1969*. Hanoi, 1973.

HOANG VAN CHI. *From Colonialism to Communism*. New York, 1964.

HOANG VAN HOAN. "Distortion of Facts about Militant Friendship between Vietnam and China Is Impermissible." *Beijing Review*, December 7, 1979 (also August 17, November 23 and 30, and February 18, 1980).

HOLLAND, WILLIAM. *Asian Nationalism and the West*. New York, 1953.

HONDA, KATSUICHI. *Vietnam War: A Report through Asian Eyes*. Tokyo, 1972.

HONEY, P. J. *North Vietnam Today*. New York, 1963.

HOOPES, TOWNSEND. *The Limits of Intervention: An Inside Account of How the Johnson Policy in Vietnam Was Reversed*. New York, 1969.

HOSMER, STEVEN. *Viet Cong Repression and Its Implications for the Future*. Lexington, Mass., 1970.

HOSMER, STEVEN, et. al., eds. *The Fall of South Vietnam: Statements of Vietnamese Civilian Military and Civilian Leaders*. Washington, 1979.

HUNT, DAVID. *Organizing for Revolution in Vietnam: Study of a Mekong Delta Province*, "Radical America," vol. 8, Cambridge, Mass., January-April, 1974.

HUYEN, N. KHAC. *Vision Accomplished: The Enigma of Ho Chi Minh*. New York, 1971.

HUYNH DINH. "Vietnamese Cultural Patterns." Ph.D. dissertation, Columbia University, 1962.

"Indochine: Première guerre entre états communistes," *La Documentation française*, no. 373 (October 1979).

IRVING, R. *The First Indochina War: French and American Policy, 1945–1954*. London, 1975.

ISAACS, HAROLD. *No Peace for Asia*. New York, 1947.

ISOART, PAUL. *Le Phénomène national vietnamien*. Paris, 1961.

ISOART, PAUL, ed. *Le Vietnam*. Paris, 1969.

JOHNSON, LYNDON B. *The Vantage Point*. New York, 1971.

JOINER, CHARLES A. "Administration and Political Warfare in the Highlands." In Fishel, W., ed. *Vietnam: Anatomy of a Conflict*. Itasca, Ill., 1968.

______. *The Politics of Massacre*. Philadelphia, 1974.

JOYAUX, FRANCOIS. *La Chine et le reglement de la guerre de l'Indochine: Genève, 1954*. Paris, 1979.

KAHIN, GEORGE MCT. "Political Polarization in South Vietnam: U.S. Policy and the Post-Diem Revolution." *Pacific Affairs*, Winter, 1979–1980.

KAHIN, GEORGE MCT. and LEWIS, JOHN. *The United States in Vietnam*. New York, 1967.

KELLY, GAIL. *From Vietnam to America*. Boulder, Colo., 1977.

KINNARD, DOUGLAS. *The War Managers*. Hanover, N.H., 1977.

KISSINGER, HENRY. *The White House Years*. New York, 1979.

KLARE, MICHAEL T. *War without End*. New York, 1972.

KNOEBL, KUNO. *Victor Charlie: The Face of War in Vietnam*. New York, 1967.

KNOLL, E., and MCFADDEN, V., eds. *War Crimes and the American Conscience*. New York, 1970.

KOLKO, GABRIEL. *The Politics of War.* New York, 1970.
KOVIC, RON. *Born on the Fourth of July.* New York, 1976.
Kratkaia Istoria Partii Trudiaschikhsi (A Short History of the Workers Party). Moscow, 1971.
LACOUTURE, JEAN. *Ho Chi Minh.* Paris, 1967 (New York, 1968).
______. *Vietnam between Two Truces.* New York, 1966.
LACOUTURE, JEAN and SIMONE. *Vietnam: Voyage à travers une victoire.* Paris, 1976.
LAKE, A., ed. *The Legacy of Vietnam.* New York, 1976.
LAMB, HELEN. *Vietnam's Will to Live: Resistance to Foreign Aggression from Early Times through the Nineteenth Century.* New York, 1972.
LAMOUR, CATHERINE. *Enquete sur un armée secrete.* Paris, 1975.
LAMOUR, CATHERINE, and LAMBERTI, MICHEL R. *The International Connection: Opium from Growers to Pushers.* New York, 1974 (Paris, 1972).
LANCASTER, DONALD. *The Emancipation of French Indochina.* London, 1961.
LANGER, PAUL, and ZASLOFF, JOSEPH. *North Vietnam and the Pathet Lao: Partners in the Struggle for Laos.* Cambridge, Mass., 1970.
LANSDALE, EDWARD. *In the Midst of Wars.* New York, 1972.
LARTEGUY, JEAN. *L'Adieu à Saigon.* Paris, 1975.
______. *The Bronze Drums.* New York, 1967.
______. *Un million de dollars le Viet.* Paris, 1965.
LEBAR, F. M., HICKEY, G. C., and MUSGRAVE, J., eds. *Ethnic Groups of Mainland Southeast Asia.* New Haven, 1964.
LE CHAU. *La Revolution paysanne du Sud Vietnam.* Paris, 1966.
LE DUAN. *Ecrits.* Hanoi, 1976.
______. *The Vietnamese Revolution.* New York, 1971.
______. *This Nation and Socialism Are One.* Chicago, 1976.
LE PHUONG. *La Corruption au Vietnam.* Montreal, 1978.
LE QUANG, GERARD. *La Guerre américaine d'Indochine, 1961–1973.* Paris, 1973.
LEROY, JEAN. *Fils de la rizière.* Paris, 1977.
LE THANH KHOI. *Socialisme et développment au Vietnam.* Paris, 1978.
______. *Le Vietnam: Histoire et civilisation.* Paris, 1955.
LEWALLEN, JOHN. *Ecology of Devastation: Indochina.* Baltimore, 1971.
LEWY, GUENTER. *America in Vietnam.* New York, 1978.
LIN BIAO. *The People's War.* Peking, 1965.
LITTAUER, R., and UPHOFF, W. N., eds. *The Air War in Indochina.* Boston, 1972.
LUCE, DONALD, and SOMMER, JOHN. *Vietnam: The Unheard Voices.* Ithaca, N.Y., 1969.
LUGUERN, JOEL. *Vietnam: Des Poussières par millions.* Paris, 1975.
______. *Quel Age as-tu Giao?* Paris, 1977.
LY QUI CHUNG. *Between Two Fires: The Unheard Voices of Vietnam.* New York, 1970.

McAlister, John. *Vietnam: The Origins of Revolution*. New York, 1971.

______. "Mountain Minorities and the Viet Minh: A Key to the Indochina War." In Kunstadter, Peter, ed. *Southeast Asian Tribes, Minorities and Nations*. Vol. 2. Princeton, 1967.

McAlister, John, and Mus, Paul. *The Vietnamese and Their Revolution*. New York, 1970.

McCarthy, Mary. *The Seventh Degree*. New York, 1967.

McClane, Charles. *Soviet Strategies in Southeast Asia*. Princeton, 1966.

McCoy, Alfred. *The Politics of Heroin in Southeast Asia*. New York, 1972.

McGarvey, Patrick, ed. *Visions of Victory: Selected Vietnamese Communist Military Writings, 1964–1968*. Stanford, 1969.

Manchester, William. *The Glory and the Dream*. New York, 1975.

Maneli, M. *War of the Vanquished*. New York, 1971.

Manning, Robert, ed. *The Vietnam Experience*. Boston, 1981 et seq.

Manue, G. *Le Vietminh, Notre ennemi*. Paris, 1949.

Mao Zedong. *Selected Works*. Peking and New York, 1954 et seq.

Marr, David. *Vietnamese Anti-Colonialism*. Berkeley, 1971.

Marsal, M. *Hanoi: Combats pour un empire*. Paris, 1979.

Martin, Earl. *Reaching the Other Side*. New York, 1978.

Masson, André. *Histoire du Vietnam*. Paris, 1960.

Massu, Jacques. *L'Aventure Viet Minh*. Paris, 1980.

Mecklin, John. *Mission in Torment*. New York, 1965.

Melman, Seymour, ed. *In the Name of America*. New York, 1968.

Mkhitarian, Suren A. *Rabochii Klass i Natsionalismo Dvizhenie vo Vietnam, 1885–1930* (The working class and the national movement in Vietnam). Moscow, 1967.

Montero, Daniel, and Weber, Marsha. *Vietnamese Americans*. Boulder, Colo., 1978.

Moore, Robin. *The Green Berets*. New York, 1965.

Morris, Roger. *An Uncertain Greatness: Henry Kissinger and American Foreign Policy*. London, 1977.

Mulligan, Hugh. *No Place to Die: The Agony of Vietnam*. New York, 1967.

Mus, Paul. *Ho Chi Minh, Le Vietnam, L'Asie*. Paris, 1971.

______. *Vietnam: Sociologie d'une guerre*. Paris, 1950.

Navarre, Henri. *L'Agonie de L'Indochine*. Paris, 1956.

Neilands, J. B., et al. eds. *Harvest of Death: Chemical Warfare in Vietnam and Cambodia*. New York, 1972.

Neuberg, A., ed. *L'insurrection armée*. Paris, 1970 (republication of 1931 edition).

Ngo Vinh Long. *Before the Revolution: The Vietnamese Peasants under the French*. Cambridge, Mass., 1973.

______. "The Indochinese Communist Party and Peasant Rebellion in Central Vietnam, 1930–1931." (*BCAS*), October–December 1978.

______. "Peasant Revolutionary Struggles in Vietnam in the 1930s." Ph.D. dissertation, Harvard University, 1978.

NGUYEN CAO KY. *Twenty Years and Twenty Days*. New York, 1976.

NGUYEN KHAC VIEN. *Histoire du Vietnam*. Paris, 1974.

______. *Tradition and Revolution in Vietnam*. Translated by Jayne Werner et al. Berkeley, 1974.

NGUYEN TIEN HUNG. *Economic Development of Socialist Vietnam, 1955–1977*. New York, 1977.

NGUYEN THI DINH. *No Other Road to Take*. Translated by Mai Elliot. Ithaca, N.Y., 1976.

NGUYEN VAN PHONG. *La Société vietnamienne de 1882–1902*. Paris, 1971.

NIXON, RICHARD. *RN: The Memoirs of Richard Nixon*. New York, 1978.

NONNEMANN, H. C. *Médecin au Vietnam*. Paris, 1970.

O'BALLANCE, EDGAR. *The Indo-China War, 1945–1954: A Study in Guerilla Warfare*. London, 1964.

O'BALLANCE, EDGAR. *The Wars in Vietnam, 1954–1973*. New York, 1975.

OBERDORFER, D. *Tet*. Garden City, N.Y., 1971.

O'BRIEN, TIM. *Going after Caciato*. New York, 1978.

OGNETOV, I. A. "Komintern i Revolutsionnoe Dvizhenie vo Vietname" ("The Comintern and the Revolutionary Movement in Vietnam"). In *Komintern i Vostok* (The Comintern and the East). Moscow, 1969.

O'NEILL, ROBERT. *General Giap: Politician and Strategist*. New York, 1969.

L'Oncle Ho. Hanoi, 1979.

OSBORNE, M. *The French Presence in Cochin China and Cambodia: Rule and Response*. Ithaca, N.Y., 1969.

OSBORNE, MILTON. *Strategic Hamlets in South Vietnam*. Ithaca, N.Y., 1965.

OSBORNE, MILTON. *Before Kampuchea*. London, 1979.

An Outline History of the Vietnamese Workers Party, 1930–1970. Hanoi, 1971.

PAIGE, JEFFREY. *Agrarian Revolution: Social Movements and Export Agriculture in the Underdeveloped World*. New York, 1975.

PALMER, D. R. *Summons of the Trumpet: U.S.-Vietnam in Perspective*. San Rafael, Calif., 1978.

PARRISH, JOHN A. *12, 20 and 5: A Doctor's Year in Vietnam*. New York, 1972.

"Le Parti à cinq ans." *La Revue Bolchevik*, December 1934.

"Le Parti à huit ans." *Le Peuple*. January 8, 1938.

PATTI, ARCHIMEDES. *Why Vietnam: Prelude to America's Albatross*. Berkeley, 1980.

The Pentagon Papers. New York Times ed, 1 vol. New York, 1971.

The Pentagon Papers. Senator Gravel ed., 5 vols., Boston, 1971.

PETTIT, CLYDE. *The Experts*. Secaucus, N.J., 1975.

PHAM CUONG and NGUYEN VAN BA. *Le Revolution au village: Nam Hong, 1945–1975*. Hanoi, 1975.

PHAM VAN DONG. *Ecrits*. Hanoi, 1977.

PIC, ROGER. *Au coeur du Vietnam*. Paris, 1968.

______. *Le Vietnam d'Ho Chi Minh*. Paris, 1976.

PIKE, DOUGLAS. *History of Vietnamese Communism, 1925–1976*. Stanford, 1978.

______. *The Vietcong: The Organization and Techniques of the National Liberation Front*. Cambridge, Mass., 1966.

PIN, YAHTAY. *L'Utopie meurtrière*. Paris, 1980.

POMONTI, J. C. *La Rage d'étre Vietnamien: portraits du sud*. Paris, 1974.

PONCHAUD, FRANÇOIS. *Cambodge, Année zero*. Paris, 1977.

POOLE, PETER. *The United States and Indochina from FDR to Nixon*. New York, 1973.

POPKIN, SAMUEL. *The Rational Peasant: The Political Economy of Rural Society in Vietnam*. Berkeley, 1979.

PORTER, GARETH. *A Peace Denied: The U.S., Vietnam, and the Paris Agreements*. Bloomington, Ind., 1976.

______. "Proletariat and Peasantry in Early Vietnamese Communism." *Asian Thought and Society*, December 1976.

______. "U.S. Political Warfare in Vietnam—The 1968 'Hue Massacre'."*Indochina Chronicle*, June 1974.

PORTER, GARETH, ed. *Vietnam: The Definitive Documentation of Human Decisions*. 2 vols. Stanfordville, N.Y., 1979.

PYE, LUCIAN. *Guerilla Communism in Malaya*. Princeton, 1956.

RACE, JEFFREY. *War Comes to Long An: Revolutionary Conflict in A Vietnamese Province*. Berkeley, 1972.

RADVANYI, JANOS. *Delusion and Reality: Gambits, Hoaxes and Diplomatic One Upmanship in Vietnam*. South Bend, Ind., 1978.

RANDLE, ROBERT B. *Geneva, 1954: The Settlement of the Indochinese War*. Princeton, 1969.

RASKIN, MARCUS G., and FALL, BERNARD B., eds. *The Vietnam Reader*. New York, 1965.

RIFFAUD, MADELEINE. *Dans les Maquis Vietcong*. Paris, 1965.

ROGERS, BERNARD W. *Cedar Falls, Junction City: A Turning Point*. Washington, 1974.

ROUSSET, PIERRE. *Le Parti communiste vietnamien: Contribution a l'étude du mouvement communiste au Vietnam*. Paris, 1973.

ROY, JULES. *The Battle of Dien Bien Phu*. New York, 1965.

RUBIN, JONATHAN. *The Barking Deer*. New York, 1974.

RUSSELL, BERTRAND. *War Crimes in Vietnam*. London and New York, 1967.

SACKS, I. MILTON. "Marxism in Vietnam." In *Marxism in Southeast Asia*, edited by F. Trager. Stanford, 1960.

Saigon: Un régime en question: Les Prisonniers politiques. Edited by Communauté Vietnamienne. Paris, 1974.
SAINTENY, JEAN. *Fàce à Ho Chi Minh.* Paris, 1970.
______. *Histoire d'une paix manquée.* Paris, 1953.
SAMPHAN, KHIEU. *Cambodia's Economy and Industrial Development.* Translated by Laura Summers. Ithaca, N.Y., 1981.
SANSOM, ROBERT. *The Economics of Insurgency in the Mekong Delta of Vietnam.* Cambridge, Mass., 1970.
SANTOLI, AL, ed. *Everything We Had: An Oral History of the Vietnam War As Told by Thirty Three American Soldiers Who Fought It.* New York, 1981.
SCHANDLER, HERBERT Y. *The Unmaking of a President: Lyndon Johnson and Vietnam.* Princeton, 1977.
SCHECTER, JEROLD. *The New Face of Buddha: Buddhism and Political Power in Southeast Asia.* New York, 1967.
SCHELL, JONATHAN. *The Military Half: An Account of Destruction in Quang Ngai and Quang Tin.* New York, 1968.
______. *The Village of Ben Suc.* New York, 1967.
SCHLESINGER, ARTHUR M., Jr. *The Bitter Heritage: Vietnam and American Democracy, 1941–1966.* Boston, 1966.
SCHURMANN, FRANZ, SCOTT, PETER DALE and ZELNIK, REGINALD. *The Politics of Escalation.* New York, 1966.
SCIGLIANO, ROBERT. *South Vietnam: Nation under Stress.* Boston, 1963.
SCOTT, JAMES C. *The Moral Economy of the Peasant.* New Haven, 1976.
SCOTT, PETER DALE. *The War Conspiracy.* New York, 1972.
SEITZ, PAUL. *Le Temps des chiens muets.* Paris, 1977.
SHAPLEN, ROBERT. *The Lost Revolution.* New York, 1965.
______. *The Road from War: Vietnam, 1965–1970.* New York, 1970.
______. *A Turning Wheel: Three Decades of the Asian Revolution.* New York, 1979.
SHAWCROSS, WILLIAM. *Sideshow: Kissinger, Nixon and the Destruction of Cambodia.* New York, 1978.
SIHANOUK, NORODOM. *Chroniques de guerre et de l'espoir.* Paris, 1979.
SIHANOUK, NORODOM, and BURCHETT, WILFRED. *My War with the CIA: The Memoirs of Premier Norodom Sihanouk.* Baltimore, 1973.
SLATER, PHILIP. *The Pursuit of Loneliness.* Boston, 1976.
SMITH, RALPH. *Vietnam and the West.* Ithaca, N.Y., 1971.
SNEPP, FRANK. *Decent Interval.* New York, 1977.
SONTAG, SUSAN. *Trip to Hanoi.* New York, 1968.
South Vietnam: A Political History, 1954–1970. Keesing's Research Report. New York, 1970.
SPAGGIARI, ALBERT. *Faut Pas rire avec les barbares.* Paris, 1977.
STAROBIN, JOSEPH. *Eyewitness in Indochina.* New York, 1954.

STEVENSON, CHARLES. *The End of Nowhere: American Policy Toward Laos since 1954*. Boston, 1972.

SUANT, J. *Vietnam: 1945–1972*. Paris, 1972.

SULLY, FRANCOIS, ed. *We, The Vietnamese: Voices from Vietnam*. New York, 1971.

SULZBERBER, C. L. *Seven Continents and Forty Years*. New York, 1977.

SUN, RUTH. *The Asian Animal Zodiac*. Tokyo, 1974.

TABOULET, G. *La Geste française en Indochine*. 2 vols. Paris, 1955.

TANHAM, GEORGE K. *Communist Revolutionary Warfare*. New York, 1967.

TAO KIM HAI. *L'Indochine française depuis Pigneau de Behaine*. Tours, 1939.

TAYLOR, TELFORD. *Nuremberg and Vietnam: An American Tragedy*. New York, 1970.

Ten Years of the PLAF. Hanoi, 1971.

TERZANI, TITZIANO. *Giai Phong: The Fall and Liberation of Saigon*. New York, 1976.

TEULIERES, A. *La Guerre du Vietnam, 1945–1975*. Paris, 1978.

THAI QUANG TRUNG. "Stalin et les Revolutions Nationales." *Revue Française de Science Politique*. October 1980.

Thanh Nien (Youth). Canton, 1925–1929. (translated in "Slotform").

THICH NHAT HANH. *Vietnam: Lotus in a Sea of Fire*. New York, 1967.

THOMPSON, ROBERT G. K. *Defeating Communist Insurgency: The Lessons of Malaya and Vietnam*. New York, 1966.

THOMPSON, VIRGINA. *French Indochina*. New York, 1937.

THOMPSON, W. SCOTT, and FRIZZELL, D., eds. *The Lessons of the Vietnam War*. New York, 1977.

TRAN HUU LIEU. *Les Soviets du Nghe Tinh*. Hanoi, 1960.

TRAN TAM TINH. *Dieu et Cesar: Les Catholiques dans l'histoire du Vietnam*. Paris, 1978.

TRAN VAN DON. *Our Endless War*. San Rafael, Calif., 1978.

TRINQUIER, ROGER. *Modern Warfare: A French View of Counterinsurgency*. New York, 1964.

TRUONG BUU LAM. *Patterns of Vietnamese Response to Foreign Interventions, 1858–1900*. New Haven, 1967.

TRUONG CHINH. *Primer for Revolt* (*The August Revolution* and *The Resistance Will Win*). Edited by Bernard Fall. New York, 1973.

______. *On Kampuchea*. Hanoi, 1980.

TRUONG NHU TANG. "Comment Hanoi nous a trahi." *L'Express*, June 7–13, 1980.

TRULLINGER, JAMES WALKER. *Village at War*. New York, 1980.

TURLEY, WILLIAM. "Vietnam since Reunification," *Problems of Communism*, March 1977.

TURLEY, WILLIAM, ed. *Vietnamese Communism in Comparative Perspective*. Boulder, Colo., 1980.

TURNER, ROBERT. *Vietnamese Communism: Its Origins and Development*. Stanford, 1975.

U.S. STATE DEPARTMENT. *A Threat to the Peace: North Vietnam's Effort to Conquer South Vietnam*. Washington, 1961.

———. *Aggression from the North: The Record of North Vietnam's Campaign to Conquer South Vietnam*. Washington, 1965.

VAN, GEIRT. *La Piste Ho Chi Minh*. Paris, 1971.

VAN DER KROEF, JUSTUS. "The Indochina Tangle." *Asian Survey*, May 1980.

VAN DYKE, JON M. *North Vietnam's Strategy for Survival*. Palo Alto, 1972.

VAN TIEN DUNG. *Our Great Spring of Victory*. Translated by Don Luce. New York, 1977.

La Vérité sur les relations vietnamo-chinois durante les trentes dernières années. Hanoi, 1979.

VELLA, RALPH, ed. *Aspects of Vietnamese History*. Honolulu, 1973.

VIET TRAN. *Vietnam: J'ai choisi l'exile*. Paris, 1979.

Vietnam: Destruction and War Damage. Hanoi, 1977.

Vietnam: Documents and Research Notes. Edited and translated by U.S. Embassy, Saigon, 1967–1972.

Vietnam: A Historical Sketch. Hanoi, 1974.

Vietnam and Human Rights. Edited by U.S./Vietnam Friendship Association of California, 1979.

Vietnam as a Tourist Center. Saigon, 1973.

Vietnam Veterans against the War: The Winter Soldier Investigation. An Enquiry into American War Crimes. Boston, 1972.

The Vietnam War: The Illustrated History of the Conflict in Southeast Asia. Edited by Ray Bonds. New York, 1979.

Vietnamese Women in Society and Revolution. n.p., 1974.

VO NGUYEN GIAP. *Armement des masses revolutionnaires: Edification de l'armée du peuple*. Hanoi, 1974.

———. *Ecrits*. Hanoi, 1977.

———. *Banner of People's War: The Party's Military Line*. New York, 1970.

———. *Big Victory, Great Task*. New York, 1968.

———. *Dien Bien Phu*. Hanoi, 1974.

———. *The Military Art of People's War*. New York, 1970.

———. *National Liberation War in Vietnam*. Hanoi, 1971.

———. *Nhiem Vu Quan Su Truoc Mat Chuyen Sang Tong Phan Cong* (The Military Responsibility for Preparing the Counteroffensive). Hanoi, 1950.

———. *Once Again We Will Win*. Hanoi, 1966.

———. *People's War, People's Army*. New York, 1962 (Hanoi, 1959).

______. *People's War against the U.S. Aero-Naval War*. Hanoi, 1973.

______. *Unforgettable Months and Years*. Translated by Mai Elliott. Ithaca, N.Y., 1975.

VO NGUYEN GIAP, et. al. *Récits de la resistance vietnamienne, 1925–1945* (Reminiscences of the Vietnamese Resistance). Paris, 1966.

VO NGUYEN GIAP and TRUONG CHINH. *The Peasant Question*. Translated by Christine White. Ithaca, N.Y., 1974.

VO NGUYEN GIAP and VAN TIEN DUNG. *How We Won the War*. Philadelphia, 1976.

WARNER, DENIS. *Certain Victory*. Kansas City, 1977.

______. *The Last Confucian*. New York, 1963.

WASMES, ALAIN. *Vietnam: La Peau de pachyderme*. Paris, 1976.

WEBB, JAMES. *Fields of Fire*. Englewood Cliffs, N.J., 1978.

WERNER, JAYNE. "Cao Dai: The Politics of A Vietnamese Syncretic Religious Movement." Ph.D. diss., Cornell University, 1976.

WESTMORELAND, WILLIAM. *A Soldier Reports*. New York, 1976.

WHITE, CHRISTINE. "Revolution and Its Adherents: The Development of the Revolutionary Movement in Vietnam." Unpublished Manuscript, 1973.

WILLEM, JEAN PIERRE. *Médecin au Vietnam en feu*. Paris, 1979.

WINDCHY, EUGENE. *Tonkin Gulf*. Garden City, N.Y., 1971.

WOLF, ERIC. *Peasant Wars of the Twentieth Century*. New York, 1969.

WOODSIDE, ALEXANDER. *Community and Revolution in Modern Vietnam*. Boston, 1976.

______. "Nationalism and Poverty in the Breakdown of Sino-Vietnamese Relations." *Pacific Affairs*, Fall 1979.

______. "Problems of Education in the Chinese and Vietnamese Revolutions." *Public Affairs*, Winter 1976–1977.

______. *Vietnam and the Chinese Model: A Comparative Study of Vietnamese and Chinese Government in the First Half of the Nineteenth Century*. Cambridge, Mass., 1971.

ZAGORIA, DONALD. *The Vietnam Triangle: Moscow, Peking, Hanoi*. New York, 1967.

ZASLOFF, JOSEPH. *The Pathet Lao*. Lexington, Mass., 1973.

ZASLOFF, J., and BROWN, M., eds. *Communism in Indochina*. Boston, 1975.

______. *Communism in Indochina and U.S. Foreign Policy*. Boulder, Colo., 1978.

ZINN, HOWARD. *Vietnam: The Logic of Withdrawal*. Boston, 1967.

INDEX